Encyclopedia of Women's Health Issues

Kathlyn Gay

Oryx Press

Westport, Connecticut • London

The rare Arabian Oryx is believed to have inspired the myth of the unicorn.
This desert antelope became virtually extinct in the early 1960s. At that time
several groups of international conservationists arranged to have nine
animals sent to the Phoenix Zoo to be the nucleus of a captive breeding
herd. Today the Oryx population is nearly 1,000, and over 500 have
been returned to reserves in the Middle East.

Library of Congress Cataloging-in-Publication Data

Gay, Kathlyn.
    Encyclopedia of women's health issues / Kathlyn Gay.
       p. cm.
    Includes bibliographical references and index.
    ISBN 1–57356–303–X (alk. paper)
      1. Women—Health and hygiene—Encyclopedias.   2. Women—Diseases—Encyclopedias.
I. Title.
    RA778.G39 2002
    613'.04244'03—dc21   2001037342

British Library Cataloguing in Publication Data is available.

Library of Congress Catalog Card Number: 2001037342
ISBN: 1–57356–303–X

First published in 2002

Oryx Press, 88 Post Road West, Westport, CT 06881
An imprint of Greenwood Publishing Group, Inc.
www.oryxpress.com

Printed in the United States of America

The paper used in this book complies with the Permanent
Paper Standard issued by the National Information
Standards Organization (Z39.48–1984).

10 9 8 7 6 5 4 3 2 1

Contents

Preface

Health topics are the focus of hundreds of books and countless magazine and newspaper articles and television features. Attention usually centers on diagnosis, prevention, treatment, and control of various diseases or health conditions. Recently, however, health discussions in the United States and Canada have included much more than strictly medical aspects. The social, economic, and political issues that affect health decisions are increasingly scrutinized. Often these issues have a collective effect on women's health. As the Office on Women's Health of the U.S. Department of Health and Human Services notes: "A woman's health reflects both her individual biology and her sociocultural, economic, and physical environment."[1] These issues are the main emphasis of this *Encyclopedia*.

Until the last few decades of the twentieth century, the subject of women's health centered for the most part on reproductive functions. Little attention was paid to health concerns before or after the childbearing years. A primary factor in this narrow approach to women's health "has been the general discrimination against women that pervaded society" until well into the twentieth century. Seldom were women's concerns voiced in public.

> Victorian morality . . . often prevented women from discussing their most intimate health problems with their (usually male) physicians and, simultaneously, restrained physicians in the extent of their examinations. . . . Only recently have scientists, clinicians, and women felt liberated enough to discuss such concerns as breast cancer, sexually transmitted diseases, and menopause openly and to acknowledge them as personal and public health concerns.[2]

During the 1960s and 1970s, the women's health movement stressed the need for women to be informed health-care consumers, and an increasing number of women began to call for comprehensive health care—a holistic approach

---

1 Office on Women's Health, "Women's Health Issues: An Overview," background paper, May 2, 2000.
2 Judith H. LaRosa, and Vivian W. Pinn, "Gender Bias in Biomedical Research," *Journal of the American Medical Women's Association* (September/October 1993), p. 145.

to their health. Prominent women also began to publicly discuss diseases, such as breast cancer and depression, which previously were taboo subjects.

However, in the early 1990s, widespread public attention focused on women's health with publication of the U.S. General Accounting Office report criticizing the National Institutes of Health and its exclusion of women in research and clinical trials. Spurred by the efforts of the Congressional Women's Caucus and other activists in the U.S. Congress, congressional hearings were held on these exclusionary practices, which were labeled discriminatory and paternalistic. Congresswomen Patricia Schroeder and Olympia Snowe expressed "outrage" and declared that women "paid their fair share of tax dollars...[but] derived little benefit" from studies funded by the federal government.[3]

Gender inequity in medical research became a significant public health concern, and it is just one of the issues addressed in the *Encyclopedia of Women's Health Issues*. The *Encyclopedia* focuses on social, economic, political, and ethical issues that affect policy decisions regarding women's health as well as women's physical and mental well-being. Although many of these issues have long histories, some have emerged with advances in medical technology, such as the ethical questions surrounding egg donors, surrogate mothers, and assisted reproductive technology.

In the United States and Canada, the vast majority of women make health-care decisions for themselves and their families. Within some minority groups, women traditionally seek advice on health care from family members and close friends. But overall American women are major consumers of health care. They consult medical practitioners or other health-care providers, such as those who offer complementary or alternative treatments. Millions of women also get information about diseases and health conditions from health-care magazines, books, and Internet World Wide Web sites. Many of these resources describe symptoms, explain causes, and advise treatment.

While this book discusses health and medical problems, it does not include medical advice. Discussions about remedies here usually focus on current or past debates about treatment, which sometimes have social, economic, or political implications.

In more than 200 entries, terms are defined, and the health problems and issues surrounding them are explained. Where appropriate, an entry includes historical perspective on a specific issue. For example, sexually transmitted diseases (STDs) are defined and explained, but the emphasis is on social, economic, and political ramifications of STDs, not on symptoms and treatment. Another example is an entry on health issues of particular concern to working women today; some historical perspective is provided to contrast the issues of the past with those of the present.

Many federal, state, and local laws cover health concerns of interest to women, but most legislation applies to general or specific health problems that affect both genders. Included in the *Encyclopedia* are descriptions of some representative laws and court decisions that are directly related to women's health

3 Quoted in Karen L. Baird, "The New NIH and FDA Medical Research Policies: Targeting Gender, Promoting Justice," *Journal of Health Politics, Policy and Law* (June 1, 1999), p. 531.

issues. Programs and events targeted specifically at women's health needs and programs designed for the specific health needs of ethnic and racial minority women are included. In addition, organizations addressing women's health are described. Some entries cover Canadian groups, although most are focused on U.S. efforts.

Hundreds of women have made medical, scientific, legal, and social service contributions that have enhanced the quality of American health care, and thus improved women's health. But only a small number of women, representing a cross-section of backgrounds, were selected to highlight individuals who have brought women's health *concerns* to public attention, from Margaret Sanger to Maggie Kuhn to Antonia Novello. Some biographical information also is included in such entries as Women in Medicine, Women in Science, and Women's Health-Care Advocates.

A lengthy bibliography and a selected list of Internet sites point the reader to reference materials and other resources on women's health and issues affecting their well-being. Most resources are readily available in public libraries or can be easily accessed by computer users. The addresses and telephone numbers of organizations described in entries are listed. Many of these organizations provide free materials on women's health.

Acknowledgment

A special thank you to Karen Hamilton for her help with research.—K.G.

Introduction

Since the beginning of recorded history, there have been accounts of women who have been health-care providers and advocates for themselves, their families, and others in their communities. In ancient times women frequently were the healers. They prepared herbs and other natural ingredients to treat a great variety of ailments. They cared for the arthritic, the wounded, the disabled, and for pregnant women and their newborns.

Over the centuries in ancient Egypt, Greece, and Rome a number of women became well known for their medical skills and herbal lore. In Egypt,

> women had a significant role as physicians, notably in the medical schools at Heliopolis and Sais.... Some women in classical Greece were known for their medical skill. Philista (318–372 BC) lectured so well that pupils flocked to her, and was so attractive that she had to lecture behind a curtain. About the same time, Agnodice was a pupil of the more famous Alexandrian Herophilus. Women physicians were numerous during Roman times, though few of their writings have survived; but there are a significant number of tombstones like that to "Primilla, my sainted goddess, a medical woman...." In the same period women physicians were common among the Germanic "barbarians."[4]

On the North American continent, for hundreds of years, Native American women have gathered herbal plants for medicinal purposes. To learn secrets of healing with herbs, they assisted the medicine man, or their mothers and grandmothers taught them the art of herbal medicine. If a woman became a medicine woman,

> her powers still had to be validated by a dream in which a spirit, in the form of a human, an animal, or perhaps just a voice, gave her personal knowledge. Women who had the gift for curing spent considerable time wandering around the areas surrounding their encampment, gathering herbs and other natural ingredients to pre-

---

4 Ian Carr, University of Manitoba Department of Obstetrics, Gynecology, "Women in Healing and the Medical Professions," <http://www.umanitoba.ca/outreach/manitoba_womens _health/wominmed.htm>

pare their medicines. In most Plains tribes, a medicine woman was not allowed to practice by herself until she reached middle age and older. The power to heal usually remained with a woman until her death. [5]

Suppression

Between about 1400 and 1800, European women known for their ability to heal with herbal medicines were labeled witches and persecuted by Inquisitors of the Catholic Church, who questioned and judged people thought to be heretics. Both men and women were accused of heresy and witchcraft, but by far many more women than men were condemned as witches. Thousands were burned alive.

As the medical profession became established during the 1700s, "a more formal and rigid set of institutions and a hierarchical structure" developed in Europe.

> Guilds of physicians were in many though not all times and places largely male, and did not admit women to their apprenticeship. Progressively over the centuries they built up and jealously guarded their exclusive status, which was not based on the effectiveness of their treatment. Such male dominance was emphasized by the male dominated Christian religions. Women could not obtain access to Universities, and partly as a result of this were barred from a medical training.
>
> There were few women in the formal medical profession as opposed to the practice of healing until around 1900; it is therefore not surprising that most of the treatment and investigation in traditional physician dominated medicine until that date was carried out by men, who controlled entry into the profession.[6]

In spite of opposition, many notable women of the nineteenth and twentieth centuries addressed social problems that had an impact on women's health. One notable example was Dorothea Dix (1802–1887), who visited prisons and insane asylums and wrote about the horrible conditions that existed in these facilities. Because of her efforts, the mentally ill were treated more humanely. Clara Barton (1821–1912) was a volunteer nurse during the Civil War and became the president of the American Red Cross, initiating disaster relief for Americans as well as people in other countries. Jane Addams (1860–1935) founded Hull House in Chicago and began the Settlement Movement. Settlement houses were set up in city slums to help poor women, primarily immigrants, and their children achieve healthier and safer lives.

By the late 1980s women began to gain key leadership positions in the U.S. Congress, health-care facilities, medical schools, and other institutions. They were poised to unite their efforts after a General Accounting Office (GAO) investigation criticized the National Institutes of Health (NIH) for failing to implement its policy of including women in research studies. The report, *National Institutes of Health: Problems in Implementing Policy on Women in Study Populations,* was published in mid-1990 and was a catalyst for pressuring Congress and the NIH to take action.

---

5 American Indian Culture Research Center, "Medicine Women," <http://www.bluecloud.org/medicine.html>

6 Carr.

The 1990s and 2000s

By the end of 1990, various laws or amendments to existing legislation addressing women's health issues were passed, and the NIH established the Office of Research on Women's Health (ORWH). One of the office's earliest efforts included the development of a research agenda to identify and address gaps in the biomedical community's knowledge of women's health. The ORWH also began strengthening and revitalizing already-existing NIH guidelines and policies for the inclusion of women and minorities in clinical studies. In 1991, the NIH undertook the Women's Health Initiative, a fifteen-year study of women and their health. The U.S. Congress passed the National Institutes of Health Revitalization Act of 1993, which requires that NIH include women and members of minority groups in clinical research and studies.

> The amount of legislative and programmatic activity to promote gender equity in health access and biomedical research of this period was unprecedented. The nation also witnessed a hitherto unseen level of support for reform of medical education to take advantage of the new information base in women's health. Women's health groups became increasingly professionalized, including some of the first generation groups from the 1960s–1970s, as well as newer organizations....there was a surge of new women's health centers—largely sponsored by hospitals and mainstream organizations that recognized the important market force that women's health represents.[7]

Throughout the federal government, particularly the U.S. Department of Health and Human Services, programs on women's health issues and offices of women's health were established. These included the Office of Women's Health at the Centers for Disease Control and Prevention, which created "The Changing Face of Women's Health," the first major national exhibition devoted exclusively to women's health. The exhibit illustrates many critical issues facing women today and underscores the fact that knowledge about women's bodies and minds is changing the understanding of what affects health: a blending of biology, culture, and the choices people make. Risk, prevention, detection, and control—four major factors that intersect again and again over a person's lifetime—are explored in the exhibit, which can be seen on the Internet and in person. The exhibit tours the United States through 2003.

Offices of Women's Health also were set up in other federal agencies such as the Food and Drug Administration and the Health Resources and Services Administration (HRSA). One of HRSA's commitments is to ensure that the nation's health-care system appropriately addresses the needs of women, which includes reducing barriers to health care and improving the health status of underserved and vulnerable populations. The Department of Justice established the Violence Against Women Office, which awards grants and funds efforts to prevent domestic violence, combat violence against women on college campuses, and raise

---

7 Carol S. Weisman, "Two Centuries of Women's Health Activism," address during "The History and Future of Women's Health," Seminar sponsored by the Public Health Service's Office on Women's Health and PHS Coordinating Committee on Women's Health (June 11, 1998) <http://www.4woman.gov/owh/pub/history/2century.htm>.

awareness of violence against women as a major public health issue. Among the many issues that the Women's Bureau of the Department of Labor addresses are child care and elder care, which traditionally are the responsibility of female workers.

Along with federal agencies, the scientific community, professional organizations, and consumer groups are attempting to advance a women's health agenda. The Public Health Service's (PHS) Office of Women's Health (OWH) coordinates efforts of government and private sector groups such as these:

- Collaborative Group on Women and HIV/AIDS
- Federal Coordinating Committee on Breast Cancer Federal Interagency Working Group on Women's Health and the Environment
- Healthy People 2010 Women's Health Working Group
- Multi-Agency Consortium on Imaging Technology to Improve Women's Health
- National Advisory Committee on Violence Against Women
- OWH Organ and Tissue Donation Initiative
- PHS Coordinating Committee on Women's Health
- OWH Minority Women's Health Panel of Experts
- OWH Nursing Task Force on Violence Against Women
- PHS/NCI (National Cancer Institute) Working Group on Methodological Issues in Clinical Trials for Technology Assessment
- President's Interagency Council on Women
- Violence Against Women Act (VAWA) Steering Committee
- Working Group on HIV/AIDS and Women

In addition, the U.S. Public Health Service's Coordinating Committee on Women's Health is focusing on women's health over the lifespan, which is a departure from the long-held view that women's health centered on their reproductive functions. The committee created a framework to articulate, develop, and implement women's health research, services, and education throughout the U.S. Department of Health and Human Services (DHHS). The theme of this framework is "Women Living Long, Living Well" (WLLLW), and it was presented for public comment in January 1999. WLLLW emphasizes that U.S. women currently have a life expectancy of about eighty years, and "the totality of the female life span and factors that affect health for women at each stage of life must be considered." As a woman progresses through each stage, her health may be affected by her social and economic circumstances, family patterns, and individual behavior. "Strong evidence suggests that critical elements of a healthy lifestyle are physical activity, adequate nutrition, personal safety, mental health, and the avoidance of tobacco use," WLLLW points out. In addition, as knowledge about genetic risks becomes clearer, women will need this information to better understand what these risks mean for their own health and for that of their families, and what can be done to treat or lessen genetic health risks. Notes WLLLW:

As women live longer, they should be able to delay if not entirely avoid the onset of chronic conditions once thought to be the inevitable consequences of aging. These conditions include osteoporosis, arthritis, urinary incontinence, heart failure, hypertension, and diabetes. These conditions significantly affect individuals' ability to participate in activities of daily living. Among women ages 65 to 85, at least 27 percent suffer from two chronic diseases, and 24 percent suffer from three or more. Persons at any age with more than one chronic condition report the highest number of days of activity limitation, suggesting potential economic consequences as assistance is required to accomplish household or personal tasks, and time is diverted from either employment or leisure activities.

Limitations in daily activity may also challenge personal safety. Limited mobility may make a woman vulnerable to crime, or to injuries in day-to-day activities. Lifting or carrying a bag of groceries may be difficult; just getting to a market where fresh, wholesome, affordable food is available may be a struggle. In the home, poor lighting and failing eyesight combine to raise the risk of fall hazards, which can be life-threatening for women with osteoporosis, diabetes, or heart conditions. Finally, women with mobility and developmental impairments may be more vulnerable to physical abuse or violence from family members, care givers, or strangers.[8]

Current Women's Health Issues

At the beginning of the twenty-first century, a major factor influencing women's health is the growing disparity in wealth and access to health insurance among women. Gender equity and social justice are crucial elements in bringing about adequate health care for all women.

Another issue is the aging of the baby boom generation. By the year 2030, one in four American women will be over the age of 65, and the number of women living over age 85 is expected to triple. Unless these women reach their elder years healthier than women of the past, the United States "could be facing a 21st century catastrophe," according to Wanda Jones, deputy assistant secretary of the U.S. Public Health Service's Office of Women's Health. In a keynote address before a Portland, Oregon, conference on women's health in 1999, Jones said:

> Our ever increasing rates of obesity and sedentary lifestyle are of particular concern. Another major concern is how our society will meet the health and social needs of our aging population. Today, most of the informal caregiving burden falls on women. Of the estimated 15 percent of Americans who currently provide informal care for someone, approximately 72 percent are women—often sandwiched between caring for an ailing relative and caring for their own children.
>
> We also have an increasing proportion of older women taking on the parenting responsibilities for their grandchildren or other children—and this is a phenomenon that we are not keeping up with in terms of our health and social policies, or daily practices.
>
> On the other hand, there has also been good news recently...with decreasing rates of disability among the elderly, and studies finding that even with some limi-

---

8 "Women Living Long, Living Well" (WLLLW), draft for public comment (January 1999), <http://www.4woman.gov/owh/pub/WLLLW/>

		Leading Causes of Death for American Women by Racial/Ethnic Group (2000)				
Rank	All American Women	African American	Asian/Pacific Islanders	Caucasian	Hispanic/Latina	Native Americans/ Alaskans
1st	Heart Disease	Heart Disease	Cancer	Heart Disease	Heart Disease	Heart Disease
2nd	Cancer	Cancer	Heart Disease	Cancer	Cancer	Cancer
3rd	Cerebrovascular Diseases (includes stroke)	Cerebrovascular Diseases (includes stroke)	Cerebrovascular Diseases (includes stroke)	Cerebrovascular Diseases (includes stroke)	Cerebrovascular Diseases (includes stroke)	Unintentional injuries
4th	Chronic Obstructive Pulmonary Diseases	Diabetes Mellitus	Pneumonia and Influenza	Chronic Obstructive Pulmonary Diseases	Diabetes Mellitus	Diabetes Mellitus
5th	Pneumonia and Influenza	Pneumonia and Influenza	Unintentional Injuries	Pneumonia and Influenza	Unintentional Injuries	Cerebrovascular Diseases (includes stroke)
6th	Diabetes Mellitus	Unintentional Injuries	Diabetes Mellitus	Unintentional Injuries	Pneumonia and Influenza	Pneumonia and Influenza
7th	Unintentional Injuries	Chronic Obstructive Pulmonary Diseases	Chronic Obstructive Pulmonary Diseases	Diabetes Mellitus	Chronic Obstructive Pulmonary Diseases	Chronic Liver Disease and Cirrhosis
8th	Alzheimer's Disease	Septicemia	Suicide	Alzheimer's Disease	Conditions Originating in the Perinatal Period	Chronic Obstructive Pulmonary Diseases
9th	Nephritis, Nephrotic Syndrome, and Nephrosis	Nephritis, Nephrotic Syndrome, and Nephrosis	Nephritis, Nephrotic Syndrome, and Nephrosis	Nephritis, Nephrotic Syndrome, and Nephrosis	Chronic Liver Disease and Cirrhosis	Nephritis, Nephrotic Syndrome, and Nephrosis
10th	Septicemia	HIV/AIDS	Conditions Originating in the Perinatal Period	Septicemia	Congential Anomalies	Septicemia

Source: National Women's Health Information Center. <http://www.4woman.gov>

tations in activity, many elderly still pursue happy and satisfying lives. As American women attain greater education and economic independence there is hope for a healthier future for our aging population, but only if women actively engage in healthy behaviors today.

Against that backdrop we are seeing another, major demographic shift as the mostly white landscape grows into a myriad of shades: by the year 2030, one in five American women will be of Hispanic heritage, one in eleven will be Asian, one in eight will be African American, and one in 100 women will be American Indian or Native American. In fact, by the year 2050, non-Hispanic white women will represent barely half of the adult female population in America.... we must start today to address issues of diversity and racial and ethnic gaps in health, if we want to be prepared for the changing faces of our nation tomorrow.[9]

---

9 Wanda Jones, "Keynote Address," Fourth Annual Women's Health Conference, Portland, Oregon (April 17, 1999).

Guide to Selected Topics

This list includes names of entries in the book, arranged by topic. Included are cross-references to help you find some topics that are either important subtopics within entries or that are alternative names for entries.

Agencies, Groups, Organizations, Programs

Alan Guttmacher Institute
American College of Obstetricians and Gynecologists
American Medical Women's Association
American Osteopathic Association Women's Health Initiative
American Society for Reproductive Medicine
Association of Women's Health, Obstetric & Neonatal Nurses
Boston Women's Health Book Collective
Bureau of Primary Health Care
Canadian Women's Health Network
Center for Reproductive Law and Policy
The Commonwealth Fund's Commission on Women's Health
Healthy People 2000 and *Healthy People 2010*
Jacob's Institute of Women's Health
La Leche League
Maternal and Child Health Bureau
Mothers' Voices United to End AIDS
National Abortion and Reproductive Rights Action League
National Abortion Federation
National Asian Women's Health Organization (UNDER Asian American Women's Health)
National Center on Women and Aging

National Centers of Excellence on Women's Health
National Cervical Cancer Coalition
National Council on Women's Health
National Family Caregivers Association
National Institute's Health Office of Research on Women's Health
National Women's Health Information Center
National Women's Health Network
National Women's Health Organization
National Women's Health Resource Center
Occupational Safety and Health Administration
Older Women's League
Planned Parenthood Federation of America
Public Health Service's Office on Women's Health
RESOLVE
Silent Spring Institute
Society for Women's Health Research
United States Department of Health and Human Services
United States Health Resources and Services Administration
Women for Sobriety
Women in Prison
Women Living Long, Living Well
Women's Health Initiative
Women's Health Interactive

Biographical Sketches

Calderone, Mary S.
Dennett, Mary Ware
Hamilton, Alice
Healy, Bernadine
Kübler-Ross, Elisabeth
Kuhn, Margaret
Libov, Charlotte (UNDER Women's Health-Care Advocates)
Love, Susan, M.D. (UNDER Breast Cancer)
Novello, Antonia
Roulet, Sister Elaine (UNDER Women in Prison)
Sanger, Margaret
Wald, Florence (UNDER Hospice Care)
Women's Health-Care Advocates
Women in Medicine
Women in Science

Events

Annual Congress on Women's Health (UNDER Women's Health Conferences)
Canada-U.S.A. Women's Health Forum
"The Changing Face of Women's Health"
Hospital Mergers
National Women's Heart Health Day
Scientific Advisory Meeting
Women's Health Conferences

Health Issues

Abortion
Abortion Providers
Acquired Immune Deficiency Syndrome (UNDER AIDS)
Adolescent Girls' Health
African-American Women's Health
Aging
Agoraphobia
AIDS
Alcohol Abuse and Alcoholism
Alternative Medicine (UNDER Complementary and Alternative Medicine)
Alzheimer's Disease
Artificial Insemination
Asian American Women's Health
Assisted Reproductive Technologies
Autoimmune Diseases
Battered Women (UNDER Domestic Violence)
Birth Control
Body Image (UNDER Dieting and Diet Drugs; Weight Discrimination)
Breast Cancer

Breast Implants
Breastfeeding
Caffeine
Cardiovascular Diseases
Caregiving (UNDER Family Caregiving)
Carpal Tunnel Syndrome
Cervical Cancer
Cesarean Section
Child Sexual Abuse
Childbirth Practices
Child-Free (by choice)
Chronic Fatigue Syndrome
Clinic Violence (UNDER Abortion Providers)
Clinical Studies (UNDER Gender-Biased Research and Treatment)
Complementary and Alternative Medicine
Contraceptives (UNDER Birth Control)
Cosmetic Surgery (UNDER Plastic Surgery)
Death (UNDER Life Expectancy)
Depression
DES
Diethylstilbestrol (UNDER DES)
Dieting and Diet Drugs
Domestic Elderly Abuse
Domestic Violence
Doula
Drug Abuse and Addiction
Drug-Dependent Mothers
Eating Disorders
Egg Donors
Elder Care (UNDER Aging)
Emergency Contraception (UNDER Birth Control)
Endometriosis
Environmental Health Hazards
Environmental Illness (UNDER Multiple Chemical Sensitivity)
Epilepsy
Estrogen Replacement (UNDER Hormone Replacement Therapy)
Factitious Disorders
Family Caregiving
Female Genital Mutilation
Female Migrant/Seasonal Workers
Fertility Drugs (UNDER Infertility)
Fetal Alcohol Syndrome
Gender Based Biology
Gender-Biased Research and Treatment
Genetic Testing
Hair Loss in Women
Health Care Access
Health Insurance

A

Abortion

Most people define an abortion as a deliberate termination of a pregnancy by medical or surgical means. However, when a woman's body rejects a fetus because of biological reasons, disease, or injury, she technically has what is called a spontaneous abortion, commonly known as a miscarriage. The latter seldom stirs debate. But deliberate or elective abortion has prompted controversy and has been a major health, social, moral, and legal issue in the United States for decades. It has affected millions of American women.

Within limits, an elective abortion during the first trimester of pregnancy is legal in the United States; every year, two out of every 100 women between the ages of 15-44 have abortions. According to statistics published by the Alan Guttmacher Institute, more than 50 percent of U.S. women who have abortions are under the age of 25. Women choose abortion for various reasons: They do not want to be single parents; a baby would disrupt school or work responsibilities; the family cannot afford a child; they are having problems with their intimate partners or within their marriages.

In colonial America elective abortion was governed by common law, patterned af-ter English law; social custom generally allowed a pregnant woman to choose an abortion before quickening, the time when the fetus first moves in the womb—about the fourth month. However, some Americans during the early 1800s strongly opposed abortion. In particular, because of their own falling birth rates, white Anglo-Saxon Protestants feared becoming outnumbered by immigrant groups of other religious, national, and racial backgrounds, and their leaders promoted state laws restricting abortion. They were joined by members of the American Medical Association who were concerned about the increasing number of abortion-related injuries and deaths due to the unavailability of antiseptics and other medications and the use by women of toxic herbal medicines to abort. In addition, unlicensed practitioners performed abortions that frequently maimed or killed pregnant women.

Connecticut was the first state to pass legislation (1821) making abortion illegal after quickening. New York followed with a similar law in 1828. From the 1830s through the 1850s, other states also enacted statutes making post-quickening abortion a felony.

Most of the state laws banned abortions except to save the life of the mother.

Number, ratio* and rate† of legal abortions performed, by year—United States, 1970–1997

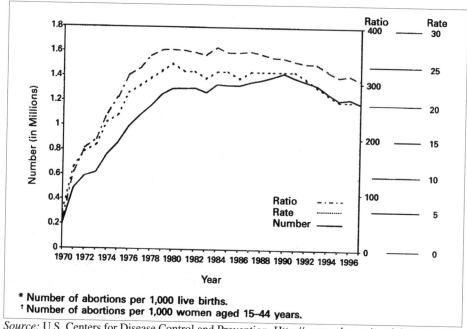

Year

* Number of abortions per 1,000 live births.
† Number of abortions per 1,000 women aged 15–44 years.

Source: U.S. Centers for Disease Control and Prevention. Http://www.cdc.gov/nccdphp/drh/pdf/mmwr_ww/Ss4911_fig1.pdf

New York state law, for example, punished a woman with a prison sentence if she used any means to bring about her own miscarriage, unless it was necessary to preserve her life. But that did not prevent some pregnant women from having illegal abortions or performing life-threatening abortions on themselves, using drugs or inserting clothes hangers or other sharp instruments. Much later, during the 1980s and 1990s, such acts were described in numerous magazine articles and books, among them *The Choices We Made*, in which now-famous Whoopi Goldberg and others recount their ordeals before and after abortions.

Each year before abortion procedures were legalized in the 1970s, illegal abortions killed between 1,000 and 5,000 pregnant women. After legalization the mortality rate steadily dropped. The U.S. Centers for Disease Control and Prevention, which has compiled abortion data since 1969, in-

dicated in 1999 that deaths related to legal induced abortions occurred rarely—approximately one death per 100,000 legal induced abortions.

Movements to reform highly restrictive abortion laws began in the 1960s, particularly after thousands of American women contracted German measles during an epidemic from 1962 to 1965. An estimated "fifteen thousand deformed babies were born as a result. In that decade, doctors came to be prosecuted more often for performing abortions under existing laws, a fact that drew some medical professionals into reform efforts." (Harrison, 233)

It was the women's movement of the 1960s and 1970s that helped propel revisions of state laws to allow abortion for health reasons or in cases of rape and incest. In 1967 Colorado became the first state to liberalize its abortion laws. During the 1970s some states, beginning with New York, changed their laws to allow licensed physicians to perform elective abortions during the first 24 weeks of a pregnancy. Other states maintained more restrictive laws.

In 1973, state restrictions were struck down by a United States Supreme Court decision in *Roe v. Wade*. The Court ruled that a woman's right to privacy extends to her decision, in consultation with her doctor, to terminate her pregnancy. In its decision, the High Court declared that no state could regulate abortion during the first trimester of pregnancy or restrict abortion after *viability* (when the fetus is likely to survive on its own—approximately 20 to 28 weeks from conception) if the mother's mental health and physical health were in jeopardy.

Since the Roe decision, states have attempted to pass new abortion laws, but these have been subject to Court review. In general, the High Court has allowed states some restrictions on elective abortions. For instance, at least 30 states require a minor to obtain parental consent or notify a parent before having an abortion (unless a judge determines that this would endanger the minor). Some states also require a pregnant woman to wait 24 to 48 hours and/or be subject to counseling before she can obtain an abortion. In most instances, state abortion laws have been determined by the political climate of the individual state.

In 1977, a federal law called the Hyde Amendment banned the use of federal funds for abortions, except when a woman's life was in danger. The number of federally funded abortions dropped dramatically from 294,600 in 1977 to 165 in 1990, according to Planned Parenthood.

After the Roe decision, opposition groups (usually called prolife) formed to campaign, often violently, to restrict or altogether ban abortion; other groups (prochoice) organized to adamantly defend a woman's right to make her own reproductive choices. Today the prolife movement includes activists involved in such organizations as national and state Right to Life groups; Operation Rescue; National Students for Life; University Faculty for Life; American Life League; and Human Life International. Prochoice activists are members of such groups as the Alan Guttmacher Institute; Planned Parenthood; National Organization for Women; National Abortion Federation; National Abortion and Reproductive Rights Action League; and the Feminist Majority Foundation.

According to a study released in 1999, states with the strongest antiabortion laws generally spend less on needy children in foster care, welfare programs, adoption of children with physical and mental handicaps, and education. The study, by Jean Schroedel, an associate professor of political science at the Claremont Graduate University in California, shows that antiabortion states make it difficult for women to end pregnancies, while also seldom helping these women provide for the children once born.

Many abortion arguments today originate because of conflicting ideas about "personhood"—when life begins and a fetus becomes a person. In general there are two sides. According to one view, life begins at conception—the moment the female egg is fertilized by the male sperm to form a single-celled organism. On the other side are those who contend that personhood is not achieved until the fetus is viable or able to live outside the womb. Concepts of personhood stem from religious doctrines and medical and scientific findings as well as legal decisions. Some religious doctrines (Roman Catholic and evangelical Protestant, for example) base their claim that life begins at conception on biblical pronouncements and declare that any harm to the fetus is immoral and should be illegal. Yet other religions (Judaism, Unitarianism, and some Protestant groups among them) insist that biblical codes on reproductive matters are not clear-cut and are open to personal interpretations.

A major public controversy began in mid-1990 over a procedure known medically as dilation and extraction (D&X) and called "partial-birth abortion" by antiabortionists. D&X is a vaginal abortion in the second or third trimester of a pregnancy; the person performing the abortion partially delivers a fetus, then destroys the fetus in order to complete the delivery. It is usually performed to protect or save the life of the mother.

In recent years, states have attempted to ban this type of late-term abortion, proposing or passing laws patterned after a congressional bill known as the Partial-Birth Abortion Ban Act of 1995. That Act would have made it illegal for a physician or other practitioner to perform a partial-birth abortion. It included provisions that could have been used to prevent almost any type of abortion. Advocates for reproductive choice and such medical groups as the American College of Obstetricians and Gynecologists called the bill "inappropriate, ill advised and dangerous." President Bill Clinton vetoed the Act twice.

Although 31 states have enacted legislation similar to the proposed federal bill, courts have blocked these laws as unconstitutional in more than a dozen states because they are vague and overly broad. A Nebraska law not only banned "partial-birth abortion" but also made it a criminal offense and provided for a sentence of up to 20 years for any doctor who performed such an abortion, unless a woman's life was in danger. No exception was made for the health of a pregnant woman. A federal district court found the law unconstitutional, and supporters appealed to the High Court. In June 2000, the U.S. Supreme Court upheld the district court's ruling in a 5-4 decision. Recognizing the "controver-

sial nature" of abortion, Justice Stephen G. Breyer wrote for the majority:

Millions of Americans believe that life begins at conception and consequently that an abortion is akin to causing the death of an innocent child; they recoil at the thought of a law that would permit it.

Other millions fear that a law that forbids abortion would condemn many American women to lives that lack dignity, depriving them of equal liberty and leading those with least resources to undergo illegal abortions with the attendant risks of death and suffering. Taking account of these virtually irreconcilable points of view, aware that constitutional law must govern a society whose different members sincerely hold directly opposing views, and considering the matter in light of the Constitution's guarantees of fundamental individual liberty, this Court, in the course of a generation, has determined and then redetermined that the Constitution offers basic protection to the woman's right to choose.

Antiabortionists angrily denounced the High Court ruling and vowed to continue their efforts to overturn *Roe v. Wade*. Because of the narrowly split Court, prochoice supporters expressed concern that a woman's right to choose will constantly be in jeopardy. *See also* Abortion Providers; Alan Guttmacher Institute; American College of Obstetricians and Gynecologists; Prolife Movement; *Roe v. Wade*.

Further Reading
Alan Guttmacher Institute. "Induced Abortion" Fact Sheet. New York and Washington, DC: Alan Guttmacher Institute, 1998.
Bender, David L., and Bruno Leone, eds. *Abortion: Opposing Viewpoints.* San Diego, CA: Greenhaven Press, 1991.
Bonavoglia, Angela, ed. *The Choices We Made: Twenty-Five Women and Men Speak Out about Abortion.* New York: Random House, 1991.
Boston Women's Health Book Collective. *The New Our Bodies, Ourselves.* New York: Simon & Schuster, 1992.

Claiborne, William. "Study Links Abortion Laws, Aid to Children." *Washington Post* (October 9, 1999).

Gay, Kathlyn. *Pregnancy: Private Decisions, Public Debates.* New York: Franklin Watts, 1994.

Greenhouse, Linda. "Court Rules That Governments Can't Outlaw Type of Abortion." *New York Times* (June 29, 2000).

Harrison, Beverly Wildung. *Our Right to Choose: Toward a New Ethic of Abortion.* Boston: Beacon Press, 1983.

Koonin, Lisa M., et al. *Abortion Politics.* New York: The Free Press, 1992.

Montalbano, Linda A. Bartlett, and Jack C. Smith, Division of Reproductive Health, National Center for Chronic Disease Prevention and Health Promotion, CDC. *Abortion Surveillance—United States, 1996* (July 30, 1999). <http://www.CDC.gov/epo/mmwr/preview/mmwrhtml/ss4804a1.htm>.

Planned Parenthood Federation of America. *The Planned Parenthood Women's Health Encyclopedia.* New York: Crown Trade Paperbacks, 1996.

Reagan, Leslie J. *When Abortion Was a Crime, Medicine and Law in the United States, 1867–1973.* Berkeley: University of California Press, 1998.

Schroedel, Jean. *Is the Fetus a Person: A Comparison of Fetal Policies across the 50 States.* Ithaca, NY: Cornell University Press, 2000.

Wymelenberg, Suzanne for the Institute of Medicine. *Science and Babies Private Decisions, Public Dilemmas.* Washington, DC: National Academy Press, 1990.

Abortion Clinics

See Freedom of Access to Clinic Entrances Act of 1994

Abortion Providers

Abortion providers are clinics, hospitals, surgical centers, and doctors who perform legal abortions in the United States. For years, controversial political and moral issues have surrounded the activities of abortion providers as well as the antiabortionists who demonstrate against them. On one side are the medical practitioners who say that providing an abortion is necessary to protect the health of some women, and the freedom of choice for all women. On the other side are antiabortionists, who believe that providers are murderers; some insist that any means, including violence, should be used to stop them from providing abortions.

About 1,000 abortion clinics exist in the United States, according to Abortion Clinics OnLine, an Internet Web site founded in 1995 in Atlanta, Georgia, which maintains an up-to-date list of abortion facilities by state. But many clinics have been bombed, set afire, or vandalized, and individual physicians and clinic staff have been harassed, stalked, injured, and sometimes killed by antiabortion activists. The National Abortion Federation, which collects statistics on violence and disruption against abortion providers, reported

In 1997 the number of arsons doubled and the number of bombings tripled over levels in 1996.... The sophistication of arsons and bombings has also increased. The amount of monetary damages suffered by clinics in 1997 amounts to approximately $1,015,500. Two clinics each suffered damages of over $400,000 and had to reduce services while they rebuilt the clinics. Since 1990, abortion clinics have suffered over $8.5 million in damages due to arsons and bombings. In addition, it is impossible to quantify the emotional toll this reign of terror has taken on clinic personnel, their families, and the women who rely on these clinics for vital health care services.

Another problem confronting women who opt for abortions is the increasing difficulty in finding doctors trained to perform safe abortions. Before abortion was decriminalized in the 1970s, many doctors were well aware of the bloody injuries, infections, and other impairments women suffered from self-induced abortions or abortions performed by unlicensed practitioners. Younger physicians, however, seldom see these impairments. Thus, they are not as mindful as older doctors of the public health benefits that safe abortions ensure.

Even those young doctors who are committed to providing safe abortions to their patients may have trouble getting the training they need. In surveys conducted during the 1990s, researchers found that medical training for first-trimester abortion techniques was routine in only 12 percent of America's obstetric/gynecology residency programs. About 56 percent offered this training only as an elective, and 27 percent provided no opportunity at all for young doctors to learn to do safe abortions. The National Abortion Federation launched an Access Initiative Project specifically to address this escalating problem. Through the project, the federation works with "medical residency programs, educational institutions, health care associations, legal experts, public policy organizations, and interested individuals to ensure that qualified clinicians are able to get the training they need to provide safe abortions and that women can continue to have access to the quality health care they deserve."

In 1995, the Accreditation Council for Graduate Medical Education (ACGME), the agency responsible for accrediting medical residency programs, issued new regulations regarding abortion training. The ACGME now requires obstetric/gynecology residency programs to provide training in abortion, birth control, and sterilization to any residents who choose to study these procedures. If hospitals refuse to perform abortions, they must allow their residents to take elective studies at facilities that do practice these procedures.

Numerous antiabortion advocates have protested the ACGME's regulations. They say abortion training should not be part of a medical education.

The continuing controversy surrounding abortion has taken a toll on abortion providers. In recent years numerous abortion doctors have been forced to wear bullet-proof vests and to find ways to safeguard their families because of threats on their lives. Some doctors have declined to perform abortions because of fears for their safety, and some staff at abortion clinics have quit—which is what antiabortion activists have hoped to achieve.

By the end of 1999, a group of antiabortionists who had turned to domestic terrorism to achieve their goals had killed four abortion doctors and three staff at abortion clinics. Following the October 1998 murder of Dr. Barnett Slepian, an abortion provider in Buffalo, New York, four members of the clinic where he worked resigned. Some said "their families could no longer endure the threat of violence and others [explained] they were simply too overwrought." (Berger) To intensify the intimidation, a small group of violent antiabortionists added the names of the clinic director and assistant director to an Internet Web site called "The Nuremberg Files." The Web site posted a list of abortion providers labeled "baby killers," including Dr. Slepian, and asked readers to send in details about their lives—where they lived, their license plate numbers, and their children's names. A day after Dr. Slepian was murdered, his name was crossed through.

In 1999, Planned Parenthood and a group of doctors brought a lawsuit in a Portland, Oregon, federal court against the antiabortionists who maintained the Web site. The plaintiffs charged violation of federal racketeering statutes and the 1994 Freedom of Access to Clinic Entrances Act (FACE), which makes it illegal to incite violence against abortion doctors and their patients. Although the defendants argued that they were not advocating violence and were exercising free-speech rights by disseminating their views on the Internet, a federal jury found otherwise; the jury ordered creators of the Web site to pay more than $107 million to the plaintiffs. However, antiabortionists transferred their funds to others and declared they had no means to pay, a tactic used by antiabortionists in similar trials in other states. (Verhovek)

Along with federal laws such as FACE designed to protect abortion providers and women exercising their legal right to an abortion, the United States Supreme Court has ruled against antiabortion protesters who prevent or impede doctors, staff, and patients from entering abortion clinics. For example, in a 1994 Florida case, *Madsen v. Women's Health Center*, the High Court ruled that antiabortionists cannot cross a fixed buffer zone around abortion clinics to stage protests. This decision was upheld in 1997. *See also* Abortion; Freedom of Access to Clinic Entrances Act of 1994

Further Reading

Berger, Joseph. "Doctor's Slaying Leaves Buffalo Clinic Struggling." *New York Times* (January 24, 1999).

Greenhouse, Linda. "Justices Uphold Abortion Clinic Buffer Zone." *New York Times* (February 20, 1997).

National Abortion Federation. "Antiabortion Violence and Harassment, 1997: An Analysis of Trends." <http://www.prochoice.org/violence/vdanaly97.htm>.

Verhovek, Sam Howe. "Creators of Antiabortion Web Site Told to Pay Millions." *New York Times* (February 3, 1999).

Acquired Immunodeficiency Syndrome

See AIDS

Adolescent Girls' Health

The term "adolescent girls" usually refers to females 12 to 18 years of age. Today, adolescent girls' health is at risk because of personal and social choices that can have lifelong consequences. Many of these choices have created widespread public controversies over how to prevent such problems as alcohol and substance abuse, smoking, eating disorders, and teenage pregnancy and childbearing. These issues have been addressed by government and private programs, including those sponsored by religious groups, to alert adolescent girls to behavior choices that threaten their health.

For example, motor vehicle accidents are a leading killer of adolescent girls. More than 40 percent of all motor vehicle deaths involve alcohol—riding with a drunk driver or driving while drunk. Among girls aged 12 to 17, 41 percent report that they have tried alcohol, 23 percent have tried some type of illicit drug, and 7 percent are binge drinkers.

Initiation of sexual activity at a young age is a primary risk factor for unintended pregnancy as well as sexually transmitted diseases. Peer pressure is the main reason teenagers do not wait until they are older to engage in sexual intercourse. Adolescents and young adults also are inclined to experiment with new behaviors during this period in their lives. In addition, they have a strong need to assert their independence and even to rebel. Meanwhile, the media often glamorize sex but rarely show the negative consequences of risky sexual behaviors.

A two-year study released in late 1999 by the National Center on Addiction and Substance Abuse (CASA) at Columbia University found that teenagers "who drink or use drugs are much more likely to have sex, initiate it at younger ages—as early as middle school—and have multiple partners, placing them at higher risk for sexually-transmitted diseases (STDs), AIDS and unplanned pregnancies." Titled *Dangerous Liaisons: Substance Abuse and Sex*, the 170-page CASA report includes these findings:

Prevalence of Damaging Behaviors

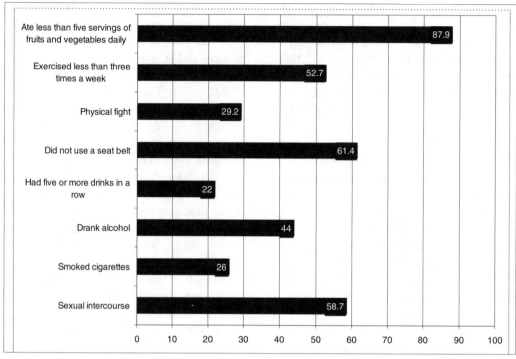

Ages 14–21 years and never married

Source: U.S. National Women's Health Information Center.

Teens 14 and younger who use alcohol are twice as likely to have sex than those who don't.

Teens 14 and younger who use drugs are four times likelier to have sex than those who don't.

Teens 15 and older who drink are seven times likelier to have sexual intercourse and twice as likely to have it with four or more partners than non-drinking teens.

Teens 15 and older who use drugs are five times likelier to have sexual intercourse and three times likelier to have it with four or more partners than those who don't. (CASA Press Release)

Physical or sexual abuse is also a risk factor for teenage girls. One in five teen girls has been physically or sexually abused—usually at home and by someone she knows. Over half of women who report being raped at some time in their lives were under 17 years of age at the time of the rape, according to the Office of Women's Health in the Department of Health and Human Services (DHHS).

Body image is a social issue that affects the health of many adolescent girls. One-third of all girls in grades 9–12 think that they are overweight, and many diet or develop eating disorders and do not get the nutrients they need, risking health problems in later life.

Another factor affecting adolescent health is their low rate of contact with health-care providers.

Adolescents have among the lowest rates of physician contact among all age groups in the United States, and many adolescents of color have even lower rates of contact. Although white youths ages 12 to 17 in 1988 reported 3.6 contacts with a physician during the past year, black, Hispanic, and Asian and Pacific Islander youth reported fewer (2.4, 2.4, and 1.0, respectively). American Indian/Alaska Native adolescents reported 7.0 physician contacts during the past year. (*Women of Color Health Data Book*, 154)

Because of little contact with health-care providers, signs of depression among adolescent girls may not be recognized. Girls are twice as likely as boys to attempt suicide, although boys more often succeed in taking their own lives.

To combat some of the risks to adolescent girls' health, the DHHS sponsors Girl Power, a national public education campaign to help encourage and motivate 9- to 14-year-old girls to make the most of their lives. Girl Power focuses on the specific needs, interests, and challenges of adolescent girls, and presents these messages on a colorful Internet Web site as well as in public service announcements for the print and broadcast media. Girl Power also offers numerous research reports on adolescent girls' health.

Another effort to target adolescent girls with health information is a manual, "Our Health, Our Futures: A Project By and For Adolescent Girls," jointly produced by the Metropolitan Life Foundation and Smith College's Summer Science program. The resource manual published in 2000 covers teen health and wellness issues and is designed for teachers, health educators, community leaders, and girls themselves. The content of the resource manual developed "from adolescent girls' concerns and questions, as reported in focus groups and interviews," Smith College reported. The manual includes chapters on such topics as relationships, domestic violence, nutrition, and sexual health, written in a way that is relevant and accessible to girls. The manual reportedly is the first of its kind to focus holistically on issues af-

fecting adolescent girls. *See also* AIDS; Alcohol Abuse and Alcoholism; Eating Disorders; Office of Women's Health; Rape; Sexually Transmitted Diseases; Smoking; Teenage Pregnancy and Child-bearing; U.S. Department of Health and Human Services.

Further Reading

Elders, M. Joycelyn. "Adolescent Pregnancy and Sexual Abuse." *The Journal of the American Medical Association* (August 19, 1998).

National Center on Addiction and Substance Abuse at Columbia University. "CASA Study Reveals Dangerous Connection Between Teen Substance Use and Sex." Press Release (December 7, 1999).

National Women's Health Information Center. "Adolescent Health Issues, Critical Health Issues Reproductive Health Issues." <http://www.4woman.gov/owh/pub/adolescent/adcritical.htm>.

National Women's Health Information Center. *Women of Color Health Data Book*. "Factors Affecting the Health of Women of Color, Adolescent Females of Color." <http://www.4woman.gov/owh/pub/woc/adolesc.htm>.

Office on Women's Health, Department of Health and Human Services. "The Health of Adolescent Girls." Information Sheet (January 1998).

African-American Women's Health

While the issues that affect the health of all American women have come to the forefront in recent years, the economic, social, cultural, and political issues that have an impact on African-American women's health are not widely publicized. Frequently problems are underscored by the disparities between blacks and whites. In 1999, the U.S. Centers for Disease Control and Prevention (CDC) reported that in every age group African-American women's risk of dying is higher than whites for every specific cause of death. For example, the maternal mortality ratio (MMR)—the number of deaths per 100,000 live-born infants—is 19.6 for African-American women compared with 5.3 for white women, nearly four times greater. Other causes of death that carry more risks for blacks than whites include heart disease and hypertension (stroke), cancer, pneumonia, chronic obstructive pulmonary disease, accidents, diabetes, and AIDS. Heart disease and cancer are the major killers among all American women.

Except for inherited diseases such as sickle cell anemia (which contrary to popular opinion is not restricted to African-Americans), most major health risks for black women are not related to race. Instead they are linked to social and economic inequities, lack of health-care access and quality of health care, cultural patterns, and other interrelated factors. In the case of higher death risks for black women from heart disease and stroke, for example, lower income and education levels and inadequate health care are contributing factors, experts say.

Hypertension, or high blood pressure, is a chronic disease that affects African-American women far more than other groups. It is often called the silent disease because it goes undetected among those who cannot afford regular health care and medication and who frequently suffer from a great deal of stress. One medical practitioner in Washington, DC, noted that a doctor

cannot adequately treat a black woman with hypertension without obtaining a complete social and work history. There is no doubt that job stress is a major contributing factor to the development of hypertension.... In addition to the workplace, many women of color face another battleground when they return home. It is a sad and sobering fact that many women return to a home where they are the head of the household. They serve as the sole provider for themselves, their children, their grandchildren, and other extended family members as needs arise.

With all these responsibilities and the low earnings of many African-American women, "it is not at all unusual for pa-

tients to bypass the purchase of their medicine in order to pay for other necessities, such as food, shelter, and transportation." (Cynthia Crawford-Green in Collins, 65–66)

Obesity also plays a role in hypertension as well as other diseases. Fifty percent of African-American women are obese, a health problem related to the so-called poverty diet—foods high in fat and sugar and low in fruits and vegetables. Poor diet and obesity are also tied to diabetes and its complications, which kill many more black women than white women. Weight loss through diet and exercise is important in the treatment of diabetes, but women who work or who are single with children have difficulty finding reasonable and affordable ways to exercise, including walking, jogging, community sports, or in-home exercise videos.

Another health risk faced by more African-American women than Caucasian women is breast cancer. The National Cancer Institute found in a recent study that African-American women are more than twice as likely as Caucasian women to die from breast cancer, but no studies have determined why this is so. Although research indicates there are no basic differences in the disease between populations, more African-American women than other populations are diagnosed with larger tumors. When breast cancer is found at more advanced stages, it is more difficult to treat, and survival rates are lower.

As with health care in general, there may be economic and other barriers to treatment for breast cancer among many low-income African-American women. Breast cancer treatment can be expensive, even if insurance covers the actual costs of treatment. Additional costs may include travel to and from the medical center for treatment, childcare, care for elderly parents, or care to manage a home while the woman is recovering. Women may lose wages because they are unable to work or they must reduce their work hours during treatment. Some women may be unable to complete all recommended treatment for these and other reasons, leading to poorer chances for survival.

Elderly African-American women are among the estimated 1.5 million Americans who suffer from severe dementia, and their vascular dementia is primarily related to obesity and hypertension. Health issues surrounding these elderly also include heart disease, cancer, cerebrovascular disease, unintentional injuries, homicide, and elder abuse. Reduction in smoking, alcohol intake, drug abuse, and an increase in exercise could diminish the mortality rates among older African-Americans, according to the Office of Minority Health Resource Center (OMHRC) of the U.S. Department of Health and Human Services. The OMHRC also points out that older African-American women tend to adhere to many cultural beliefs in determining how sick they are and what forms of medicine they should take. They rely on emergency rooms for health-care services and seek this service as a last resort, factors that can jeopardize their health and lives.

Improving the health of African-American women in all age groups has been the mission of the National Black Women's Health Project (NBWHP), which was founded in 1981 by health activist Byllye Y. Avery. An internationally known grassroots organization headquartered in Washington, DC, NBWHP is "committed to improving the health status and lives of 17.8 million Black women." The organization's vision, according to its Web site, "includes maximizing opportunities to address the health and lifestyle issues confronting Black women through wellness promotion messages and programs, increasing coalition building with national Black institutions...partnering with other national organizations to ensure voices of Black women

are woven throughout their work, and re-establishing international partnerships with women of color organizations who seek empowerment through leadership development and collective advocacy."

The OMHRC also has set goals to eliminate the health disparities experienced by racial and ethnic minority populations in the United States. In 1998, President Bill Clinton announced a major national commitment to identify and address the underlying causes of higher levels of disease and disability in racial and ethnic minority communities. According to the OMHRC

> Compelling evidence that race and ethnicity correlate with persistent, and often increasing, health disparities among U.S. populations demands national attention. Indeed, despite notable progress in the overall health of the Nation, there are continuing disparities in the burden of illness and death experienced by blacks, Hispanics, American Indians and Alaska Natives, and Pacific Islanders, compared to the U.S. population as a whole.... Groups currently experiencing poorer health status are expected to grow as a proportion of the total U.S. population; therefore, the future health of America as a whole will be influenced substantially by our success in improving the health of these racial and ethnic minorities.

The OMHRC and the Department of Health and Human Services will focus on infant mortality, cancer screening and management, cardiovascular disease, diabetes, HIV infection/AIDS, and immunizations. *See also* AIDS; Asian-American and Pacific Islander Women's Health; Breast Cancer; Cardiovascular Diseases; Latina Women's Health; Native American Women's Health

Further Reading
Associated Press. "Blacks More Likely to Die During Pregnancy." *USA Today* (June 18, 1999).

Collins, Catherine Fisher, ed. *African-American Women's Health and Social Issues.* Westport, CT: Auburn House, 1996.

National Black Women's Health Project. <http://www.nationalblackwomenshealthproject.org/>.

Noble, Holcomb B. "New York Is Ranked High for Deadly Heart Attacks." *New York Times* (February 16, 2000).

Office of Minority Health Resource Center. "Eliminating Racial and Ethnic Disparities in Health" on the Internet <http://www.omhrc.gov/>.

Office of Minority and Women's Health, Bureau of Primary Health Care. "Health Status of Racial/Ethnic Older Women." <http://bphc.hrsa.gov/omwh/OMWH_9.htm>.

"State-Specific Maternal Mortality among Black and White Women—United States, 1987–1996." Newsline. *Journal of the American Medical Association Women's Health Information Center.* <http://www.ama-assn.org/special/womh/newsline/special/mmwr99/mm4823.htm>.

Stolberg, Sheryl Gay. "Black Mothers' Mortality Rate Is Under Scrutiny." *New York Times* (August 8, 1999).

White, Evelyn C., ed. *The Black Women's Health Book: Speaking for Ourselves.* Seattle, WA: Seal Press, 1990.

Aging

Within the past few decades, aging—growing old—in the United States has become a women's issue with widespread economic and political ramifications. American women are likely to enjoy an average life span of 79 years, as compared to 72 years for men. Today, 34 million Americans, or one in eight, are age 65 or older, and three out of five are women, according to the U.S. Administration on Aging (AoA). The challenges of aging are often more pronounced among older women. As AoA reports, "Compared with men, elderly women are three times more likely to be widowed or living alone, spend more years and a larger percentage of their lifetime disabled, are nearly twice as likely to reside in a nursing home, and are more than twice as likely to live in poverty."

One of every six older women is a member of a minority group—African-American, Hispanic, Native American or Asian-American/Pacific Islander—and many live at the poverty level (less than $8,000 per year income). In fact, poverty is especially predominant among older women of color and older women who live alone. Among all U.S. women poverty increases with age, but more than half of elderly widows were not poor before the deaths of their husbands. Being poor means that women are extremely limited in what they can pay for health care.

Older women, particularly widows and single women, often depend on the federal Medicare program or other government-funded programs to help pay their medical expenses. More than half the Medicare beneficiaries are women between the ages of 65 and 74, and women between ages 75 and 84 account for 61 percent. Women over the age of 85 make up 71 percent of those receiving Medicare. However, older women spend up to 25 percent of their disposable income for out-of-pocket health-care expenses and often cannot afford the costs of nursing home care, home care, or private long-term care insurance. Thus health-care costs can push aging women into poverty.

As the elderly population increases, women's economic concerns regarding health care will increase as well. Americans ages 60 and older are expected to total 85 million by 2030; those ages 85 and older will number an estimated 8 million. The majority of the elderly will be women. Because they have a longer average life expectancy than men and tend to marry men older than themselves, seven out of ten are expected to outlive their husbands and be widowed for 15 to 20 years. More than 50 percent of American women who reach age 65 are likely to spend part of their remaining years in assisted living, adult day care, home care, or a nursing home, the *New England Journal of Medicine* reported in 1999. Preparing for long-term care is, therefore, one of the most important health and economic issues confronting aging women.

Physical and mental impairments are other major issues that aging women face. They are at risk for chronic illnesses such as Alzheimer's, cancer, and heart disease and disabling conditions caused by arthritis and osteoporosis, which can eventually require long-term care. Thus prevention, screening, and early testing are critical to women's health care. But the majority of older women cannot afford the costs of preventive services or they believe that such services are not needed. In addition, their physicians may fail to advise them about preventive measures, such as exercising, not smoking, and eating nutritious food. More than half of the doctors treating older women also fail to ask them about their mental and emotional well-being, according to a 1998 study by Brandeis University's National Center on Women and Aging. "Even more alarming," the study found, "is the fact that even women who have suffered clinical depression are not asked about their mental health by their providers. Two out of five such women reported that their doctors had not raised these questions." (National Center on Women and Aging)

Numerous agencies and organizations, however, work to inform aging women about preventive health care and also to provide needed services. Among them are the Asian Pacific Women's Network, American Society on Aging, Gay and Lesbian Medical Association, National Alliance for Caregiving, National Center on Women and Aging at Brandeis University, National Hispanic Council on Aging, National Latina Health Organization, National Resource Center for Rural Elderly, and the Women's Initiative of AARP. The Older Americans Act (OAA) of 1965, which has been amended over the years, established the Administration on Aging and state units on aging, which are located in every state and territory. All individuals 60 years of age and older are eligible for services under the OAA, although priority attention is given to those who are in greatest need. At the federal and state levels, OAA-mandated programs include elderly support services such as home-delivered meals, homemaker aid, transportation, daycare community centers, fitness programs, employment counseling, education on elder abuse and consumer fraud, and other assistance to help prevent the unnecessary institutionalization of aging citizens. The AoA of the U.S. Department of Human Services maintains a Web site that provides extensive information on programs and resources for the elderly, with special emphasis on older women. *See also* Alzheimer's Disease; Depression; Health Insurance; Life Expectancy; Older Women's League; Poor Women's Health Care; United States Department of Health and Human Services; Widowhood

Further Reading

Administration on Aging. "Older Women: A Diverse and Growing Population." <http://www.aoa.dhhs.gov/factsheets/ow.html>.

National Center on Women and Aging. "National Study Shows Doctors Neglecting Emotional Health of Older Women." Press Release (October 8, 1998). <http://www.brandeis.edu/heller/national/ind.html>.

Butler, Robert N., Karen Scott Collins, Diane E. Meier, Charlotte F. Muller, and Vivian W. Pinn. "Older Women's Health: 'Taking the Pulse' Reveals Gender Gap in Medical Care." *Geriatrics* (May 1995).

New York Times News Service. "Health Care for Aged Is Now Women's Issue." *St. Petersburg Times* (September 13, 1999).

Agoraphobia

Agoraphobia is a Greek word that literally means "fear of the marketplace." This mental disorder, which affects twice as many women as men, is the irrational fear of leaving the familiar setting of one's home because of previous experiences with anxiety or panic attacks in various settings. There is no proven cause for agoraphobia, but one study found that inherited factors may account for the disproportionate number of women with the disorder. (Jang, et al.) The condition, which is often misunderstood by the general public, creates social and economic problems for the sufferers.

Agoraphobia can occur with or without a panic attack, but a person suffering from the disorder is afraid to be in a setting or situation where escape is difficult if an attack occurs, such as in stores or on expressways. A person suffering a panic attack may have chest pains; experience heart palpitations; feel dizzy, nauseous, lightheaded, or flushed; have difficulty breathing; or even be convinced death is at hand.

Usually agoraphobia strikes during adolescence or young adulthood and affects people from all walks of life. Because the disorder is more prevalent in women, it was once called the housewives' disease. A woman suffering from untreated agoraphobia feels she cannot leave her home and is almost entirely dependent for daily needs on her husband or other family members. This leads to stereotypes, and a woman with agoraphobia is frequently viewed as an irrational or "hysterical" person.

Agoraphobia becomes a social and economic problem when the disorder causes a person to avoid situations where panic might occur. This creates increasing isolation, thus limiting social activities and relationships and employment opportunities. Although many female agoraphobics hesitate to seek medical help for fear of being stereotyped, some are learning about the disorder and treatment options (which include medication, psychotherapy, and self-help practices such as exercise) on Internet Web sites and print materials available from various medical centers. *See also* Mental Illness

Further Reading

Jang, Kerry L., Murray B. Stein, Steven Taylor, and W. John Livesley. "Gender Differences in the Etiology of Anxiety Sensitivity: A Twin Study." *Journal of Gender-Specific Medicine* (April 1999).

"New Treatments for Panic Disorder: An Interview with Mark H. Pollack, MD." *Therapeutic Spotlight: Psychiatric Illness in Primary Care*, supplement to *Clinician Reviews* (March 1999).

New York Online Access to Health (NOAH), New York Hospital Cornell Medical Center. "Fact Sheet: Panic Disorder (and Agoraphobia)." <http://www.noah.cuny.edu/illness/mentalhealth/cornell/conditions/panicago.html>.

AIDS

AIDS, which stands for acquired immunodeficiency syndrome, is a fatal disease caused by the human immunodeficiency virus (HIV). A sexually transmitted disease, AIDS was once thought to affect only homosexual men, but today it is well known to strike heterosexuals, both men and women, from all walks of life. Between 650,000 and 900,000 people living in the United States are infected with HIV, according to the U.S. Centers for Disease Control and Prevention (CDC). Approximately 40,000 new cases of HIV occur in the United States each year. Seventy percent of the new infections occur among men and 30 percent among women. Although AIDS cases and deaths from the disease declined between 1996 and 1998, as of mid-1999, reported AIDS cases totaled 711,344 with 592,552 cases reported among men and 118,789 cases among women. Deaths from AIDS have also declined from 37,221 in 1996 to 17,771 in 1998. (CDC Update, December 1999)

After the disease was first diagnosed in the United States during the early 1980s, the number of cases among homosexual men continued to rise. But the disease received little attention because of the stigma of homosexuality and widespread homophobia in the United States. By the end of the decade, the public began to understand that AIDS was spread primarily by intravenous drug use and unprotected sex, but also often by transfusions of blood from individuals with HIV. Even as increasing numbers of heterosexual men, particularly intravenous drug users, have become infected with HIV, they have not been routinely cautioned to take responsibility for protecting their female partners, and until recently few women have been educated about the risk factors for AIDS.

During the 1990s, "the HIV infection increased significantly among U.S. women, especially among women of color," the CDC reports. In 1992, nearly 14 percent of Americans with AIDS were women; two years later, the proportion grew to just over 19 percent. By mid-1999 the AIDS epidemic had increased most dramatically among women of color. African-American and Hispanic women together represent less than one-fourth of all U.S. women, yet they account for more than three-fourths (77%) of AIDS cases reported.

> While AIDS-related deaths among women are now decreasing, largely as a result of recent advances in HIV treatment, HIV/AIDS remains among the leading causes of death for U.S. women aged 25–44. And among African-American women in this same age group, AIDS still results in more deaths than from any other cause. (CDC, 1999)

Pregnant women and teenage girls with AIDS present not only a public health problem but also ethical dilemmas. The HIV infection can be passed from the pregnant woman to the fetus or to the infant during delivery or through breastfeeding, which raises questions about abortion and/or mandatory birth control for women at risk for HIV. The option of abortion is in itself controversial, but as one feminist writer put it:

> Contrary to what many right-to-life advocates might argue, there are quite compelling moral grounds for advocating that an infected women is justified in aborting a fetus she might be carrying: a prospective mother might be said to have an obligation to any potential child to spare it a certain and gruesome death...to ensure and protect her own health for as long as she can...to have an obligation to society not to bear children for whom society may have to provide. (Bell, 57)

Mandatory testing is another controversial issue associated with AIDS. Some argue that if a woman tests positive for HIV she may be forced to have an abortion or to abstain from sex, or be punished with legal sanctions, all of which could infringe on her reproductive rights. Others contend that testing should be voluntary and that a woman who learns that she is HIV-positive should seek treatment as soon as possible, and perhaps choose not to continue a pregnancy in which she risks infecting her fetus with a deadly disease.

One of the most difficult issues regarding HIV and AIDS is how to educate at-risk populations about preventive measures, such as safe-sex practices. Until about the 1980s, there were long-standing taboos against educational programs and advertising for contraceptives. However, as AIDS became an increasing public health threat, health and social service information programs began to advertise the use of condoms as protection against HIV. In spite of protests from various religious groups, public school systems in some major cities also began to offer programs in which condoms were distributed among teenagers to help prevent the spread of AIDS (as well as to lower teenage pregnancy rates).

The CDC is the leading federal agency providing information on prevention pro-

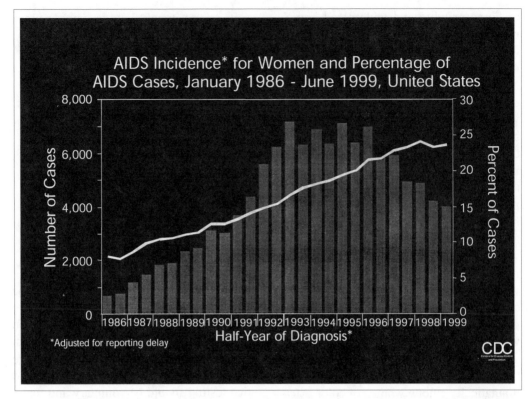

AIDS Incidence* for Women and Percentage of AIDS Cases, January 1986 - June 1999, United States

*Adjusted for reporting delay

Half-Year of Diagnosis*

Source: U.S. Centers for Disease Control and Prevention. <http://www.cdc.gov/hiv/graphics/images/1264/1264-1.ppt>

grams that have worked in communities. Its Prevention Research Synthesis (PRS) database includes evaluations of HIV-prevention programs, from school-based education to street outreach for injection drug users. CDC also tracks the course of HIV and AIDS so that communities will have timely information about trends for the disease and what behaviors place people at risk. In addition, CDC researchers use a variety of techniques to prevent HIV transmission, noting that

> as AIDS increasingly affects women, it is critical that prevention methods be developed that are easily within women's control. CDC researchers are working with scientists worldwide to evaluate the effectiveness of female condoms and to develop effective microbicides that can kill HIV and the pathogens that cause other STDs. As with any new tool for preven-

tion, scientists must also determine what influences people's willingness and ability to use these methods. CDC behavioral scientists are simultaneously working to evaluate the factors that will contribute to women's use of these products and how these new prevention methods can and should be balanced with existing prevention options. (Centers for Disease Control and Prevention, 1998)

Other groups advocating for women with AIDS include the Center for Women Policy Studies, the Latina Roundtable on Health and Reproductive Rights, the Lesbian AIDS Project, the National Black Women's Health Project, the Native American Women's Health Education Resource Center, and a great variety of regional, state, and local organizations. *See also* Abortion; Birth Control; Lesbian Health

Concerns; Pregnancy; Sexually Transmitted Diseases

Further Reading

Bell, Nora Kizer. "Women and AIDS: Too Little, Too Late?" In Holmes, Helen Bequaert, and Laura M. Purdy, eds. *Feminist Perspectives in Medical Ethics.* Bloomington and Indianapolis, IN: Indiana University Press, 1992.

Centers for Disease Control and Prevention, National Center for HIV, STD, and TB Prevention, Divisions of HIV/AIDS Prevention. "CDC's Role in HIV and AIDS Prevention." Fact Sheet, July 28, 1998. <http://www.CDC.gov/nchstp/hiv_aids/pubs/facts/cdrole.htm>.

Centers for Disease Control and Prevention, National Center for HIV, STD, and TB Prevention, Divisions of HIV/AIDS Prevention. "CDC Update: A Glance at the HIV Epidemic." (December 1999).

Healy, Bernadine. *A New Prescription for Women's Health.* New York: Viking, 1995.

Hoffman, Eileen, M.D. *Our Health, Our Lives: A Revolutionary Approach to Total Health Care for Women.* New York: Simon & Schuster, 1995.

Alan Guttmacher Institute

The Alan Guttmacher Institute (AGI), named for Alan F. Guttmacher, an eminent obstetrician-gynecologist, teacher, and writer, has been involved in women's health—specifically reproductive health—for more than three decades. During that time AGI has sometimes been the focus of controversy, in part because of its support for government-funded family planning services and the use of contraceptives, which are opposed by some religious groups. Because of its prochoice stance, the organization has also been falsely accused by antiabortion activists of promoting abortion.

Founded in 1968 as the Center for Family Planning Program Development, the organization, following the lead of federal administrations from Presidents John F. Kennedy to Richard Nixon, called attention to the problem of unplanned and unwanted childbearing and its consequences for the nation, communities, and individual women, men, and children. "By integrating nonpartisan social science research, policy analysis and public education, the Center hoped to provide a factual basis for the development of sound governmental policies and for the public consideration of the sensitive issues involved in the promotion of reproductive health and rights. This purpose and commitment continue today."

Originally, the Center was a division of Planned Parenthood Federation of America (PPFA). After Guttmacher's death in 1974, it was renamed in his memory. In 1977, AGI became an independent, not-for-profit corporation, but it is still affiliated with PPFA and maintains offices in New York and Washington, DC.

Most of the funds for AGI come from private contributions, which are supplemented by occasional grants for specific projects from the National Institutes of Health and other government agencies. Among AGI publications are two peer-reviewed journals, *Family Planning Perspectives* and International *Family Planning Perspectives*, plus *The Guttmacher Report on Public Policy.* (AGI) *See also* Planned Parenthood Federation of America

Further Reading

Alan Guttmacher Institute Web site <http://www.agi-usa.org/home.html>.

Alcohol Abuse and Alcoholism

Alcohol abuse—heavy drinking of alcoholic beverages—and alcoholism, a chronic disease that is characterized by an addiction to the drug alcohol and the inability to control periodic drinking of alcoholic beverages, are major problems in the United States. In 1998, the National Institutes of Health (NIH) estimated that their combined economic cost of alcohol abuse and alcoholism was $148 billion in 1992 alone, the most recent year for such data.

Alcohol abuse and addiction have more impact on women than men, and more alcoholic women than men die from alcohol-related accidents, violence, and suicide. Throughout their lives women in general have less tolerance to alcohol—usually one alcoholic drink has the same effect on a woman as two drinks have on a man. In addition to a higher sensitivity to alcohol and health risks to herself, a heavy drinker during pregnancy is likely to give birth to a child with fetal alcohol syndrome, a condition related to mental retardation, slow physical growth, and other defects. Women have even less tolerance to alcohol as they grow older because of physical and mental changes related to aging.

Most of what is known about alcohol abuse comes from studies of men who are heavy drinkers; they outnumber women in that category two to one, although among teenagers, male and female alcohol abusers are almost evenly divided. In fact, alcohol is the drug most often abused by teenagers, whether female or male, and alcohol-related traffic accidents are the second leading cause of teenage death. Moreover, reports U.S. Surgeon General David Satcher, alcohol use is frequently

linked with teen deaths by drowning, fires, suicide and homicide and is a leading cause of teen injuries. Teens who use alcohol are more likely to become sexually active at earlier ages, to have sex more often and to have unsafe sex...to be victims of violent crime, including rape, aggravated assault and robbery...[and] much more likely to have serious school-related problems.

Equally troubling is the latest research showing that children who begin drinking before the age of 15 are four times more likely to become alcoholics sometime during their lives than those who begin drinking at or after the legal age of 21.

Binge drinking (consuming five or more alcoholic beverages during one sitting) and heavy drinking are highest among women 18 to 25 years of age, reports the National Institute on Alcohol Abuse and Alcoholism (NIAAA). The highest rates of heavy drinking and drinking-related problems occur among single women—never married, divorced, and separated.

Alcohol abuse has been well publicized by such prominent persons as Betty Ford, former first lady and founder of the National Center on Addiction and Substance Abuse (known as CASA) at Columbia University. In its 1996 report on substance abuse among women, CASA noted that heavy drinking is much more prevalent among working women than among homemakers and unemployed women "are more than 400 percent likelier to drink heavily than women who are working full or part-time." (CASA Releases Report)

Some older women also are heavy drinkers. An estimated 1.8 million American women 60 years and older abuse alcohol but only about 11,000 receive treatment for the disease, according to CASA, which focused on this issue in a 1998 report, *Under the Rug: Substance Abuse and the Mature Woman*. The first comprehensive analysis of this kind, the report notes that alcohol abuse is hidden among older women because those with drinking problems usually drink alone and seldom discuss the possibility of alcoholism with family, friends, or health-care providers. The problem is also unrecognized by primary physicians. Doctors as a rule do not consider alcohol or substance abuse in mature women. Instead they frequently diagnose early symptoms of alcohol or drug abuse as depression, and indeed some women do try to treat their symptoms of depression with alcohol abuse.

Increasing public awareness of alcohol-related problems and helping those who abuse alcohol are functions of a variety of organizations such as CASA, Alcoholics Anonymous (AA), Al-Anon and Alateen (support groups for family and friends of alcoholics), the National Council on Alcoholism and Drug Dependence (NCADD), and the NIAA. All of the groups issue published materials and maintain Internet Web sites to inform the public about alcohol abuse and alcoholism. The NCADD also sponsors an Alcohol Awareness Week each year. *See also* Betty Ford Center; Depression; Fetal Alcohol Syndrome; Substance Abuse; Working Women.

Further Reading

National Center on Addiction and Substance Abuse. "CASA Releases Report, Substance Abuse and the American Woman." Press Release. New York: National Center on Addiction and Substance Abuse at Columbia, June 5, 1996.

National Center on Addiction and Substance Abuse. *Under the Rug: Substance Abuse and the Mature Woman*. New York: National Center on Addiction and Substance Abuse at Columbia, 1998.

National Institute on Alcohol Abuse and Alcoholism. "Alcohol What You Don't Know Can Harm You." Pamphlet. Bethesda, MD: NIAAA, National Institutes of Health, 1999.

National Institute on Alcohol Abuse and Alcoholism. "Use of Alcohol and Other Drugs Among Women." Bethesda, MD: NIAAA, National Institutes of Health, January 1998.

National Institutes of Health. "Economic Costs of Alcohol and Drug Abuse Estimated at $246 Billion in the United States." Bethesda, MD: National Institutes of Health. Press Release (May 13, 1998).

Satcher, David. Letter to colleagues as part of Alcohol Awareness Month kit. New York, NY: National Council on Alcoholism and Drug Dependence, 1999.

Wren, Christopher S. "Many Women 60 and Older Abuse Alcohol and Prescribed Drugs, Study Says." *New York Times* (June 5, 1998).

Alternative Medicine

See **Complementary and Alternative Medicine**

Alzheimer's Disease

Alzheimer's disease (AD) is the most common cause of dementia, or disruption of brain function, in older people. However, as many health experts point out, it is not a normal process of aging. Because women live longer than men and the risk of AD increases with age, AD is a concern of many aging women. In addition, a major social concern is the fact that women are disproportionately caregivers of AD patients.

AD is a progressive, degenerative disease affecting the parts of the brain that control thought, memory, and language. Although there is no known cure for AD, some research suggests that it may be prevented or delayed with hormone replacement therapy for post-menopausal women. Evidence also suggests that non-steroidal anti-inflammatory drugs may prevent, delay, or help treat the disease.

An estimated 4 million people in the United States suffer from AD, including about 3 percent of the population between the ages of 65 and 74; 19 percent of the group between age 75 and 84; and nearly one-half of the population ages 85 and older are afflicted by AD. A disproportionate number of them are women. Currently women make up 72 percent of Americans ages 85 and older; nearly one-half of this group have AD. With the aging population increasing, 14 to 20 million Americans are projected to have AD by 2040 unless preventive measures are found.

Eighty percent of AD caregivers are women, usually the wife, daughter, or daughter-in-law of the individual with the disease. Patients with AD frequently live from eight to twenty years, with increasingly deteriorating health; eventually they die from pneumonia or other diseases. Those involved in family caregiving suffer from stress and exhaustion that can lead to poor physical and mental health. In recent years, Alzheimer's support groups have focused on ways to help caregivers recognize the stress of family caregiving and to alleviate some of it with respite services, day care for AD patients, or if necessary nursing home care.

The costs of care for AD patients are another aspect of the disease that impacts significantly on aging women. Paid care to augment family caregiving in the home averages $12,500 per year and nursing home care can range from $42,000 to $70,000 annually. Because Medicare and most private health insurance policies do not cover the type of long-term care that most people with AD need, women who are caregivers can quickly become strapped for funds.

The increasing economic and social impacts along with the deteriorating health problems of AD have prompted numerous studies on the disease. In 1999, the federal government spent approximately $400 million on AD research. The National Institute on Aging (NIA), part of the National Institutes of Health (NIH), is the lead federal agency researching AD, and study of this disease is one of its major priorities. Several other NIH institutes conduct and sponsor studies on Alzheimer's disease, including the National Institute of Neurological Disorders and Stroke, the National Institute of Mental Health, and the National Institute of Nursing Research. In the private sector, the Alzheimer's Association based in Chicago, Illinois, is the only voluntary national organization dedicated to research on Alzheimer's and education about the disease. The Association also provides support services for people with Alzheimer's disease and their families. See also Aging; Family Caregiving; Hormone Replacement Therapy

Further Reading

Alzheimer's Association. "Alzheimer's Disease: A Major Health Issue for Women" (September 24, 1999). <http://www.alz.org/news/right.htm>.

"The Elder Care Report. (Caring for someone with Alzheimer's Disease)." *Discover* (June 1999).

Healy, Bernadine. *A New Prescription for Women's Health*. New York: Viking, 1995.

Mace, Nancy L., and Peter V. Rabins. *The 36-Hour Day*, rev. ed. Baltimore: The Johns Hopkins University Press, 1991.

McNeil, Caroline. Public Information Office, National Institute on Aging. *Alzheimer's Disease: Unraveling the Mystery*. Washington, DC: U.S. Department of Health and Human Services, Public Health Service, National Institutes of Health, National Institute on Aging, October 1995.

U.S. Department of Health and Human Services, Public Health Service, National Institutes of Health, National Institute on Aging. "Alzheimer's Disease Fact Sheet" (August 1995).

American College of Obstetricians and Gynecologists

Founded in Chicago in 1951, the American College of Obstetricians and Gynecologists (ACOG) is a private, nonprofit organization of physicians providing health care for women. An obstetrician/gynecologist is the primary care physician for many American women. The ACOG, which has a membership today of more than 39,000 physicians specializing in obstetric-gynecological care, not only advocates for quality health care for women but also promotes awareness of economic and social issues that affect women in their reproductive years. One issue is multiple embryo pregnancy during fertility treatments. The ACOG's ethical guidelines advise physicians to

Limit the number of embryos transferred to the uterus or elect not to artificially trigger ovulation when ultrasound indicates multiple follicles. ACOG also stressed the importance of counseling patients about the potential risks of multiple gestation. While acknowledging the pressure to maximize the chances of conception, physicians must, as in any medical situation, place the best interests of the patient and the future child or children at the center of the risk-benefit equation. (ACOG Press Release)

In another advocacy effort, the ACOG and the American Medical Association, American Academy of Family Physicians, American Academy of Pediatrics, American College of Physicians-American Society of Internal Medicine and American College of Surgeons have launched a campaign for universal health-care coverage. These organizations want to put health care for the uninsured at the forefront of public debate. Currently, more than 43 million Americans lack health insurance, and the number is expected to grow to more than 47 million by 2005.

Another advocacy effort is ACOG's national calcium education campaign to help prevent osteoporosis, which the organization calls "an urgent women's health issue that has reached epidemic proportions." (ACOG News Release, 1998) Other efforts include opposition to unnecessary regulations that limit or delay access to reproductive health care, such as laws and regulations that require parental involvement when adolescent girls seek abortion services. ACOG takes the position that health risks to the adolescents are so impelling that legal barriers and deference to parental involvement should not stand in the way of needed health care.

When a member of the ACOG, Dr. Barnett Slepian of New York, was murdered in 1998 in his home by an antiabortion activist, the organization released a statement strongly condemning the violence and pointing out that

Dr. Slepian's death is a tragedy for the women of New York. He courageously provided reproductive health care to women who otherwise might not receive it. An obstetrician-gynecologist with a private practice in Amherst, Dr. Slepian offered a range of gynecologic and obstetric services to women in his community. He also provided abortion services at the Buffalo GYN Women's Services clinic, because he believed strongly that

women who want abortions deserve access to such care.

Dr. Slepian's death was the second murder of an ACOG Fellow who provided abortion services; Dr. David Gunn of Pensacola, Florida, was murdered in 1993. Another ACOG Fellow, Dr. Garson Romalis of Vancouver, Canada, was seriously injured by a sniper in his home in 1994, and four other abortion providers and clinic employees have died due to antiabortion violence since 1993. "As the level of violence has escalated, the time has come to do more than express our horror. Only by standing together can the entire community ensure that acts of brutality end," the ACOG stated. *See also* Abortion; Abortion Providers; Adolescent Girls' Health; Health Insurance; Infertility; Osteoporosis; Pregnancy

Further Reading

American College of Obstetricians and Gynecologists. "Adolescent Health Care." <http://www.acog.org/from_home/departments/dept_web.cfm?recno=7>.
———. "American College of Obstetricians and Gynecologists Release Ethical Guidelines on Nonselective Embryo Reduction." News Release, April 5, 1999.
American College of Obstetricians and Gynecologists. "Statement on the Death of Dr. Barnett Slepian." News Release, October 26, 1998.
American College of Obstetricians and Gynecologists. "The American College of Obstetricians and Gynecologists Launch National Calcium Campaign." News Release, May 11, 1998.

American Medical Women's Association

Like many other medical and scientific organizations, the American Medical Women's Association (AMWA) has launched programs that highlight social, economic, and political issues affecting women's health. The organization was founded in 1915 when women physicians were a decided minority. Today women make up more than 21 percent of all practicing physicians, and more than 10,000 women physicians and medical students are members of the AMWA. Operating at the local, national, and international levels, the AMWA encourages the advancement of women in medicine and helps to raise awareness of women's health needs. As a voice for women's health, the AMWA keeps abreast of legislative issues that affect the health of women and also conducts educational projects on smoking and heart disease in women, reproductive health, breast and cervical cancer screening, and other topics.

The AMWA publishes the peer-reviewed *Journal of the American Medical Women's Association,* established in 1946. Special issues have focused on Women and Cardiovascular Disease, Abortion and Medicine, Women and HIV/AIDS, Managed Care, and the Health of the Oldest Women. AWMA also has published several books on women's health, including the *Women's Complete Wellness Book* and the *Women's Complete Healthbook.* Excerpts from selected chapters of the latter book are available on AMWA's Web site. The organization has published numerous position papers on topics that include Abortion, Breast Cancer Screening and Treatment, Coronary Artery Disease, Care of the Dependent Elderly, Domestic Violence, Lesbian Health Issues, Maternity Leave, Reproductive Health, and Tobacco Control and Prevention. *See also* Abortion; Breast Cancer; Cervical Cancer; Lesbians; Smoking

Further Reading
American Medical Women's Association. AWMA Web site <http://www. amwa-doc.org/>.

American Osteopathic Association Women's Health Initiative

In 1998, the American Osteopathic Association (AOA) launched the Women's Health Initiative, a three-year effort de-

signed to promote health care for women and women's health. The AOA also has established an Office on Women's Health that advocates for women's health beyond the initial promotional program.

The AOA represents about 45,000 doctors of osteopathy (DOs) who are licensed to prescribe medication and perform surgery but pay special attention to the whole person and the interconnection of the body's systems. DOs integrate osteopathic manipulative treatment (OMT) into their medical practice, which is not chiropractic manipulation but instead uses the hands to diagnose and treat illness or injury. OMT may also be used to augment or replace medication or surgery.

During AOA's national symposiums on women's health, the first of which was held in 1998, practitioners have delivered lectures on a variety of women-oriented topics, including arthritis, breast cancer, complementary medicine, hormone-replacement therapy, osteoporosis, and OMT for pregnant women. The AOA also maintains an Internet Web site and posts press releases, fact sheets, legislation, and other information on women's health issues. *See also* Breast Cancer; Complementary and Alternative Medicine; Hormone-Replacement Therapy; Osteoporosis; Pregnancy

Further Reading
"About the Women's Health Initiative" <http://www.aoa-net.org/Consumers/WomensHealth/whi.htm>.
Kaczmarczyk, Joseph M. "Alternate Care Appeals to Women." *DO Magazine* (June 1999).
Tettambel, Melicien A. "OMT Benefits Mothers, Babies." *DO Magazine* (June 1999); also <http://www.aoa-net.org/Consumers/WomensHealth/omtpreg.htm>.

American Society for Reproductive Medicine

The American Society for Reproductive Medicine (ASRM) is a voluntary, nonprofit organization that is of particular interest to women and men who are concerned about fertility, a reproductive issue with interpersonal, social, and economic factors. ASRM, formerly the American Fertility Society, was established in 1944, to advance the knowledge and expertise in reproductive medicine and biology. With headquarters in Birmingham, Alabama, the ASRM also has an office in Washington, DC. Its affiliates include the Society for Reproductive Surgeons, the Society of Reproductive Endocrinology and Infertility, the Society for Male Reproduction and Urology, and the Society for Assisted Reproductive Technology.

Although ASRM supports reasonable compensation for women who donate eggs for artificial insemination, or assisted reproductive technology procedures, the organization is opposed to auctions and similar methods to provide eggs to the highest bidder, calling such commercialization unethical and offensive. ASRM's efforts include the publication of guidelines for women and their partners considering fertility treatments. For example, the organization has issued guidelines on the number of embryo transfers (which can result in multiple births); guidelines on advertising by assisted reproductive technology programs; and guidelines for in vitro fertilization, gamete intrafallopian transfer, and related procedures. These and other publications are available on ASRM's Internet Web site.

The ASRM also supports RESOLVE, the national infertility association that calls attention to infertility issues and the latest advances in treatment for infertility during National Infertility Awareness Week each year. As ASRM points out, "Great medical advances have been made in the treatment of infertile couples. For the majority of couples, simple treatment methods that don't involve surgery have been increasingly successful." (ASRM Web site) *See*

also Assisted Reproductive Technology; Infertility; RESOLVE

Further Reading

American Society for Reproductive Medicine <http://www.asrm.org>.

Carson, Sandra, and Peter Casson, eds. *Complete Guide to Fertility.* Chicago, IL: Contemporary Books, 1999.

Annual Congress on Women's Health

See **Women's Health Conferences**

Artificial Insemination

Artificial insemination dates back about 200 years when researchers were first able to artificially impregnate animals. That practice led to procedures that physicians could use to treat infertility—a disease of the reproductive system that prevents humans from reproducing by sexual intercourse. According to the American Society for Reproductive Medicine an estimated 6.1 million women and men have infertility problems, which in turn sometimes create relationship difficulties and social concerns. Treating infertility with artificial insemination techniques has raised diverse issues, such as whether or not it is ethical for a couple to accept donor sperm to create a pregnancy. Debates over the legal rights of parents and donors have also occurred. Other controversies have developed over financial costs of some artificial insemination techniques and the use of artificial insemination by unmarried women.

The most basic type of artificial insemination is known today as intrauterine insemination (IUI), which can be relatively simple. A doctor may place semen from a donor (usually a woman' husband) in a small cap that fits over the woman's cervix, or the physician puts semen in a syringe and deposits sperm directly into the vagina. A person without medical expertise can perform this type of artificial insemination, but most states require a physician to perform the procedure with donated sperm. Laws regarding artificial insemination are designed to ensure appropriate screening to prevent the spread of venereal disease and genetic disorders from donated sperm.

Although married couples who have difficulty conceiving are the primary users of artificial insemination, single women and women in nontraditional relationships (lesbian couples for example) also have artificially conceived. However, because of social customs and religious beliefs, many Americans condemn conception by lesbian women and any unmarried women. In fact, doctors can deny the procedure to single women. Nevertheless, some women have artificially inseminated themselves, using a simple kitchen utensil like a turkey baster, or a syringe with semen purchased from a sperm bank—a laboratory where sperm is preserved.

Some forms of artificial insemination require more complex medical intervention known as Assisted Reproductive Technologies (ART), which include in vitro (glass) fertilization (IVF). Developed during the late 1970s, IVF is a method of placing the female ovum, or egg, and male sperm in a glass petri dish so that the ovum can be fertilized and then placed in a woman's body to develop as in a normal pregnancy. Within the past few decades, various ART techniques have been used by thousands of couple to conceive. *See also* American Society for Reproductive Medicine; Assisted Reproductive Technology; Egg Donors; Infertility; Surrogate Mother; RESOLVE

Further Reading
American Society for Reproductive Medicine. "Fact Sheet: Infertility." <http://www.asrm.org/fact/infertility.htm>.

Gay, Kathlyn. *Pregnancy: Private Decisions, Public Debates*. New York: Franklin Watts, 1994.

Wymelenberg, Suzanne for the Institute of Medicine. *Science and Babies Private Decisions, Public Dilemmas*. Washington, DC: National Academy Press, 1990.

Asian-American and Pacific Islander Women's Health

Asian-American and Pacific Islander (AAPI) women face health concerns similar to those of all American women. But the health of AAPI women is greatly affected by cultural, economic, and language barriers.

AAPI women are part of the fastest-growing population group in the United States. There are 28 Asian and 19 Pacific Islander groups with a vast array of languages and cultures. Some are indigenous groups such as Native Hawaiians and American Samoans; others are fourth- and fifth-generation Asian-Americans, while 75 percent are recent immigrants and refugees.

Some of the social factors impacting on the health of immigrant AAPI women in the United States stem from preferences for traditional health-care practices, which include what is generally known as alternative medicine in the United States; acupuncture, the use of herbs, and spiritual healing practices are examples. Some women in AAPI groups may hesitate to seek care from western practitioners, believing that illness or discomfort is one's fate or a "natural" part of life or because of language problems or poverty. Among Asian-American groups, some women, especially recent immigrants, do not seek preventive care such as pap smears and breast examinations because of their culture's emphasis on modesty or insistence that no male other than her husband examine her body.

Another problem for AAPI women is the increased risk for abusive situations. Many women come from cultures where they are subservient to men, and domestic

Early Detection in Asian American Women

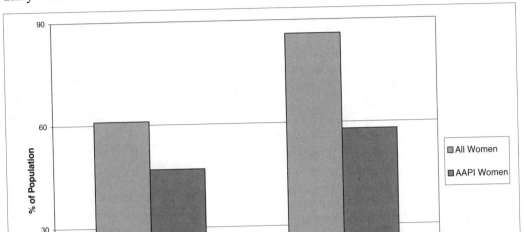

Source: Behavioral Risk Factor Surveillance System (CDC, 1999).

violence may be accepted as a condition of life. Violence may be hidden

because the victim is often isolated from the general community and may not know how or where to ask for help. Some refugee groups may be small and may lack the support of their fellow compatriots in times of difficulty. Women's shelters may not be an option since some shelters may not be able to provide services because of language and cultural barriers. Additionally, women with children may be reluctant to go to shelters, because they are in an unfamiliar setting. (Kang, et al.)

While the incidence of HIV/AIDS is low among AAPI women, the disease has not been well documented in this population group. Data on HIV/AIDS have been difficult to compile because of

a conspiracy of silence and cultural beliefs. Denial, shame, and privacy con-

cerns associated with AIDS prevent those with the disease from revealing their status to friends and family. Misconceptions that Asians are not at risk for HIV and that homosexuality is not common also inhibit discussion and information sharing. Moreover, language difficulties impede effective communication. (Zhan, 82–83)

Other health issues of particular concern to Asian and Pacific Islander women include

- Limited access to health care due to cultural and language differences, as well as economic and other barriers.
- Rates of breast and cervical cancer screening rates that are much lower than the national average.
- Tuberculosis cases, which are 13 times more common among Asian populations, especially those from Cambodia, China, Laos, Korea, India, Vietnam, and the Philippines.

- Cancer as the leading cause of death among Asian-American and Pacific Islanders.

- High rates of hepatitis B, which is 25 to 75 times more common among Samoans and immigrants from Cambodia, Laos, Vietnam and China than the U.S. average.

- Cervical cancer rates among Vietnamese women, which are nearly five times those of white women.

- Breast cancer mortality rates among Native Hawaiians, which are the highest for any racial/ethnic group in the United States: 37.2 per 100,000. Chinese and Japanese-American women have higher rates than in China and Japan.

- High suicide rates among Asian-Americans ages 15 to 24 and those over age 65.

- Special risk for osteoporosis among Asian-American women due to their relatively lower bone mass and density, smaller frames, and lower intake of calcium compared to other population groups. (The National Women's Health Information Center)

In 1999, President Bill Clinton signed an executive order establishing the White House Asian and Pacific Islander Initiative. The initiative is designed to improve the quality of life of Asian-Americans and Pacific Islanders by increasing overall participation in federal government programs, such as those providing health care and economic and community development.

Private organizations are also active in efforts to bring better health information to AAPIs. The Association of Asian Pacific Community Health Organizations (AAPCHO), formed in 1987, is a national association representing community health organizations dedicated to improving the health status of AAPIs in the United States and its territories, especially the medically underserved. The association advocates for policies and programs that will improve community health-care services so that they are affordable, linguistically accessible, and culturally appropriate.

The National Asian Women's Health Organization (NAWHO) was founded in 1993 to improve the health status of Asian-American women and families through research, education, and public policy advocacy. The organization helps Asian-Americans provide leadership for their communities, and build coalitions that address the broader social justice issues impacting all under-served groups in the United States.

Another organization, Asian and Pacific Islander American Health Forum, is dedicated to promoting policy, program, and research efforts to improve the health and well-being of Asian-American and Pacific Islander communities. Founded in 1986, the Health Forum advocates on health issues of significance to AAPI communities and conducts community-based technical assistance and training. The organization also holds regional and national conferences on AAPI health. *See also* AIDS; Complementary and Alternative Medicine; Domestic Violence

Further Reading

Beller, Tanya, Michelle Pinker, Sheila Snapka, and Denise Van Dusen. "Korean-American Health Care Beliefs and Practices." <http://www.baylor.edu/~Charles_Kemp/korean_health.htm>.

Jenkins, Christopher, Stephen J. McPhee, Joyce Adair Bird, Giao Qui Pham, Bang H. Nguyen, Thoa Nguyen, Ky Quoc Lai, Ching Wong, and Thomas B. Davis. "Effect of a Media-Led Educational Campaign on Breast and Cervical Cancer Screening among Vietnamese-American Women." *Preventive Medicine* (April 28, 1999).

Kang, David S., Lucinda R. Kahler, and Catherine M. Tesar, "Medicine and Society: Cultural Aspects of Caring for Refugees." *American Academy of Family Physicians* (March 15, 1998).

"Loatian Health Care Beliefs and Practices: A Summary." <http://www.baylor.edu/~Charles_Kemp/laotian_summary.html>.

The National Women's Health Information Center. "Asian-American & Pacific Islander Women's Health." <http:// www.4woman.org/faq/Asian_Pacific.htm>.

Zhan, Lin, ed. *Asian Voices Asian and Asian-American Health Educators Speak Out*. Sudbury, MA: Jones and Bartlett Publishers, 1999.

Assisted Reproductive Technology

Assisted reproductive technology (ART) is a form of artificial insemination that requires medical intervention and includes a variety of techniques, many of which raise ethical, social, and economic questions and debates. One of the most well-known ART techniques is in vitro (glass) fertilization (IVF), which was developed in Great Britain during the late 1970s. IVF is a method of placing the female ovum, or egg, and male sperm in a glass petri dish so that the ovum can be fertilized. Once a zygote is formed, it is placed in a woman's body to develop as in a normal pregnancy. At first ethical questions were raised about producing an infant in this manner because little was known about the safety of the procedure and whether a deformed child would be born. Since its inception in the United States, however, IVF has safely produced at least 45,000 babies.

Since the late 1970s, scientists have developed various types of ART, which along with IVF has resulted in a total of 70,000 babies. The beginning procedure is to use hormones to stimulate the production of more than one egg during a woman's ovulation cycle. This method provides a better chance to produce a healthy embryo for implantation. Once a woman ovulates, her partner produces a sperm sample, which is then "washed," in a process that concentrates the hardiest sperm into a small dense pellet. Using a catheter, a doctor puts the pellet directly into a woman's uterus near a fallopian tube, or the doctor may place the sperm directly into one or both fallopian tubes, a technique known as gamete intra-fallopian transfer (GIFT), which may produce fertilization.

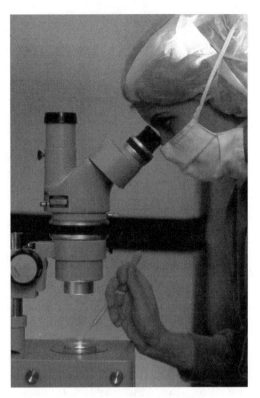

In vitro fertilization. ©Hank Morgan/Photo Researchers, Inc.

A variation of GIFT is ZIFT, in which the egg is fertilized in a petri dish and the resulting zygote is placed in the fallopian tube. A microinjection is one more variation: using a thin needle, the sperm is injected into the egg. Still one more technique is zona drilling, in which a hole is drilled into the egg's protective shell to allow the sperm to penetrate. "There are more than 70,000 babies born in the United States as a result of all assisted reproductive technologies, including 45,000 as a result of IVF," states the American Society for Reproductive Medicine (ASRM). ART procedures resulted in 20,659 babies born in 1996, the latest year for a report issued by the Centers for Disease Control and Prevention (CDC). CDC's report is a requirement of the Fertility Clinic Success Rate and Certification Act of 1992 and is co-authored by the CDC, ASRM, the Society for Assisted Reproductive Technology (SART), an affiliate society of ASRM, and RESOLVE, the national infertility patient advocacy group. The report summarizes all outcomes and success rates from 300 centers in the United States offering assisted reproductive technologies.

Many couples who have been unable to conceive praise ART procedures, but questions have been raised about costs. The costs for ART are well beyond what low-income and most middle-income patients can afford, and medical insurance policies vary in ART coverage. Laws in only a dozen states require insurers that cover maternity benefits to pay for ART, although the laws do not usually require insurance companies to offer the benefit or employers to include such a benefit in insurance plans.

Legal, moral, and political implications of "high tech" reproduction methods are issues also. During the 1980s, "the major question for the technology was whether it was morally right to create life in a dish." Currently as scientists are "increasingly able to analyze (and perhaps alter) the DNA of an embryo, ethical questions...focus on what, if any, limits should be set for embryo manipulation." (Wymelenberg, 148)

Embryo cryopreservation, or embryos frozen or preserved in liquid nitrogen, is one other issue. Critics of embryo freezing say the practice downgrades women and raises the status of the embryo. Advocates point out that, if an embryo implant fails, a frozen embryo can be thawed and used without subjecting a woman to a complete IVF cycle.

Mistakes have occurred, however. One case in point involved Donna Fasano and Deborah Perry-Rogers, who both were implanted with frozen embryos on the same day in 1998 at the same Manhattan fertility clinic. Fasano became pregnant but Perry-Rogers did not. Not long after the proce-

dure, the two women learned that their doctor, Lillian Nash, had implanted Fasano with not only her eggs fertilized by her husband but also others from Rogers and her husband. After Fasano gave birth to two boys, one white and the other black, the mixup was confirmed. DNA tests showed that Perry-Rogers and her husband were parents of the black boy. Although the Fasanos considered both boys their own, they agreed to give up custody of the black boy to his genetic parents with the condition that the Fasanos would have visitation rights so that the two boys would know they were brothers.

Other problems arise regarding frozen embryos if a couple divorces or dies. Legal decisions must be made about ownership and how, when, and whether to dispose of embryos. In mid-1999, a judge in Illinois refused to allow Margaret Hale, who was undergoing divorce proceedings, to have two of her frozen embryos implanted. The embryos were created by Hale and her estranged husband, who does not want Hale to have his child. The state of Illinois has yet to decide the legal issues involved in such cases.

Only a few similar cases have been determined in other state courts. In a Tennessee divorce proceeding, Mary Sue and Junior Davis argued over the "custody" of seven frozen embryos. Junior Davis did not want them implanted in his divorced wife. But a judge awarded them to Mary Sue, claiming that the embryos

were "human beings" from the moment of conception and that their "best interests" lay in being born. But that ruling was reversed on appeal. In the first such judicial opinion in the nation, the Tennessee Supreme Court found in 1992 that Junior Davis had a constitutionally protected right to avoid procreation. (Peres)

Besides the issue of personhood and whether an embryo deserves government protection, commercialization is also a concern. Reproductive clinics frequently recruit and pay women to be egg donors to help create embryos in the laboratory or to use their uteruses to develop embryos for implantation in other women. Ethicists question whether women are being exploited to perform this service, which usually pays several thousand dollars. Offers have ranged up to $50,000 for egg donations from women with specific characteristics. *See also* Artificial Insemination; American Society for Reproductive Medicine; Egg Donors; Infertility

Further Reading

American Society for Reproductive Medicine. "Fact Sheet: Infertility." <http://www.asrm.org/fact/infertility.htm>.

American Society for Reproductive Medicine. "Results of Joint SART/ASRM, CDC and RESOLVE 1996 Assisted Reproductive Technology Success Rate Report." Press Release (February 2, 1999).

Benderly, Beryl Lieff for the Institute of Medicine. *In Her Own Right: The Institute of Medicine's Guide to Women's Health Issues.* Washington, DC: National Academy Press, 1997.

Center for Reproductive Health. "Assisted Reproductive Technologies." <http://www.fertilitext/org/art.htm>.

Kolata, Gina. "$50,000 Offered to Tall, Smart Egg Donor." *New York Times* (March 3, 1999).

Peres, Judy. "Couple's Divorce Entangles Frozen Embryos." *Chicago Tribune* (August 7, 1990).

Yardley, Jim. "After Embryo Mix-Up, Couple Say They Will Give Up a Baby." *New York Times* (March 30, 1999).

Association of Women's Health, Obstetric and Neonatal Nurses

A nonprofit organization founded in Chicago, Illinois, in 1969 and now based in Washington, DC, the Association of Women's Health, Obstetric and Neonatal Nurses (AWHONN) has a membership of 22,000 health-care professionals in the United States, Canada, and Europe. Members are staff nurses, nurse midwives, nurse practitioners, professors, nurse scientists, administrators, managers, and entrepreneurs. Their work has a significant impact on the care of women and newborns and such issues as a woman's choice regarding who will attend a birth and other reproductive matters. AWHONN members practice in a variety of settings such as hospitals, home health agencies, physician's offices, universities, and public health agencies.

AWHONN provides nurses with resources that enhance their practice, such as research-based practice projects. One such project was a clinical study of women with urinary incontinence, a problem for women from all walks of life. As a result of the study, AWHONN found that women could retrain their bodies with an exercise program and other techniques to improve continence. (AWHONN press release, April 1999) Other resources AWHONN provides are clinical publications and continuing education programs.

A key component of AWHONN's program is reproductive health. AWHONN publications and programs address such issues as limited ultrasound, perinatal education, critical care intrapartum nursing, perinatal home care, postpartum depression, and management of preterm labor. AWHONN's renowned Fetal Heart Monitoring Principles and Practices program provides thousands of nurses with the critical skills necessary to correctly perform fetal assessment, and also offers members the opportunity to become instructors, enhancing their skills and their marketability. (AWHONN Web site)

AWHONN programs include advocacy for longer hospital stays for new mothers and their babies, recognizing that "newborns and families need care, assistance, education and training in the days following a birth." The association also supports legislation mandating that health-care plans include contraceptive (birth control) services, which would help families space pregnancies and protect women's heath. In the view of AWHONN, "Mandated coverage for contraceptives will inevitably result in cost savings to the health care system by decreasing unwanted pregnancies and providing women the health benefit from oral contraceptives e.g. protection from benign breast changes, cancer of the uterus, cancer of the ovary, pelvic infection and anemia." (AWHONN Web site)

AWHONN strongly advocates voluntary but not mandatory testing for human immunodeficiency virus (HIV), which leads to the deadly disease AIDS. If HIV is identified, treatment can decrease the risk of transmitting the virus to newborns.

At its thirtieth anniversary convention in 1999, AWHONN's president pointed out that nurses "are the glue that holds the health care system together" and that they need the best and most current information to care for their patients. To that end, the conference covered such important issues affecting women's health as domestic violence, hereditary reproductive cancers, infertility treatments, incontinence treatments, and alternative therapies for menopause. *See also* AIDS; Birth Control; HIV Positive Women; Incontinence; Infertility; Nurses; Menopause; Postpartum Hospital Stays

Further Reading

Association of Women's Health, Obstetrics and Neonatal Nurses Web site. <http://www.awhonn.org>.

Association of Women's Health, Obstetrics and Neonatal Nurses. "AWHONN Research Improves Quality of Life for Women." Press Release (April 27, 1999).

Association of Women's Health, Obstetrics and Neonatal Nurses. "Breakthroughs and Advances in Women's Health Research and Clinical Practice Top Agenda at National Nurses' Convention." Press Release (June 13, 1999).

Autoimmune Disease

Autoimmune disease is an "umbrella term" used to categorize 80 chronic and progressively disabling illnesses that disproportionately affect women. Autoimmune disease has not been adequately researched, creating a women's issue because the disease is often misunderstood and misdiagnosed. One of the most common autoimmune diseases is multiple sclerosis; others include lupus, Sjogren's disease, and rheumatoid arthritis. "In autoimmune disease...the immune system becomes the body's own worst enemy, functioning in an overactive and confused way. Instead of recognizing and attacking foreign substances in the body, it attacks a person's own cells and organs." (Blumenthal)

Approximately 75 percent of the disorders that are labeled autoimmune disease occur in women. Multiple sclerosis, for example, strikes more women than men in ratios greater than 2:1. Women with rheumatoid arthritis outnumber men by a ratio of 4:1. Lupus and Sjogren's disease affect nine times more women than men.

Because of the lack of research about autoimmune disease, the National Women's Health Information Center of the Office of Women's Health in the U.S. Department of Health and Human Services held one of its series of *Healthy Women 2000* educational programs on the topic. Called "Unlocking the Mysteries: Autoimmune Disease and Women," the 1996 conference addressed this previously neglected women's health issue, which costs the nation an estimated $86 billion annually. The conference focused on gender differences in autoimmune disorders (which include hormone-related events, such as menses, pregnancy, and menopause, that can alleviate or aggravate a disorder), research and treatment, and the psychosocial and economic impacts of autoimmune disease.

Other government agencies such as the National Institutes of Health, the Centers for Disease Control and Prevention, and the Food and Drug Administration, as well as numerous private organizations also sponsor research on specific autoimmune diseases and provide educational materials, many of which are posted on Internet Web sites. These include the Arthritis Foundation, the National Multiple Sclerosis Foundation, the Lupus Foundation of America, the Scleroderma Research Foundation, and the Sjogren's Syndrome Foundation. *See also* Gender-Biased Research and Treatment

Further Reading

Blumenthal, Susan J., U.S. Department of Health and Human Services. "Introduction and Opening Remarks." *Healthy Women 2000* conference (June 1996). <http://www.4women.gov/owh/autoimm/opening.htm>.

Brewerton, Derrick. *All About Arthritis*. Cambridge, MA: Harvard University Press, 1992.

Grelsamer, Ronald P. *The Columbia Presbyterian Osteoarthritis Handbook*. New York: Simon & Schuster, 1996.

McIlwain, Harris D., and Debra Fulghum Bruce. *The Fibromyalgia Handbook*. New York: Henry Holt, 1996.

B

Battered Women

See **Domestic Violence**

Betty Ford Center

The Betty Ford Center at the Eisenhower Medical Center in Rancho Mirage, California, is a facility devoted exclusively to the treatment of alcohol and other forms of drug dependency—major health problems in the United States. The center serves both males and females, but it came about because of Betty Ford's efforts to call attention to the issue of alcohol and drug addiction among millions of American women. The center was named for the former first lady, who was also its co-founder.

Greatly admired for her honesty and forthrightness when her husband, President Gerald R. Ford was in office (1974 to 1997), as well as in the years after, Betty Ford also helped raise awareness of breast cancer by publicly discussing her mastectomy in the 1970s, when few women were willing to openly acknowledge this kind of surgery. A few years later she risked public censure to reveal her dependency on alcohol and prescription drugs. After leaving Washington, DC, she was determined to help others overcome their addictions through the center, which consists of a campus of seven buildings located on 14 acres with the San Jacinto Mountains in the background. According to the center's description on its Web site, the setting

provides the serenity and spirituality that add a special quality to the recovery program.... More than a decade of experience has proved that the location and

Betty Ford. Photo provided by the Betty Ford Center.

uniquely designed facility of the Betty Ford Center provide an environment that can and does make a difference in treatment. (Betty Ford home page)

See also Alcohol Abuse and Alcoholism; Drug Abuse and Addiction

Further Reading

Betty Ford Center Web site. <http://www.bettyfordcenter.org>.

Ford, Betty. *A Glad Awakening*. Garden City, NY: Doubleday, 1987.

Ford, Betty with Chris Chase. *The Times of My Life*. New York: Harper & Row, 1978.

Gay, Kathlyn, and Martin K. Gay. *Heroes of Conscience: A Biographical Dictionary*. Santa Barbara, CA: ABC-CLIO, 1996.

Birth Control

For thousands of years women have tried to prevent or control their pregnancies through practices that are now known as birth control. Birth control today creates religious, social, and economic issues and debates as well as health concerns.

The long history of birth control includes the ancient Egyptian practice of using a type of tampon (wads of cloth) soaked in a mixture of honey and fermented tips of the acacia bush. This prescription, which was found on a scrap of papyrus dating to 1850 B.C., though crude was probably effective. "Stewed acacia leaves produce lactic acid, an effective spermicidal ingredient also used in contraceptive ointments in the 1940s and 1950s." (Wymelenberg) Tampons were also soaked in lemon juice or vinegar in the belief that, when inserted into the vagina, the acidity would kill sperm. Sponges were used to block the cervix, the entrance to the uterus.

Today methods of birth control (a term coined in 1914) include the use of barrier devices and spermicides, injections, implants, pills, complete abstinence from sexual intercourse, and sterilization. While birth control is widely accepted in the United States, it has a long history of religious and political controversy. In 1873 the federal Comstock law was passed banning the dissemination of contraceptive information. Various states passed similar laws. In Connecticut, for example, a law barred married couples from using contraceptives and made it illegal for anyone to distribute information about birth control. The U.S. Supreme Court struck down the law in 1965 with its decision in *Griswold v. Connecticut.*

Opponents of mechanical means to prevent pregnancies contend that such practices are morally wrong and that the primary reason for sexual intercourse is to procreate. Thus the only acceptable forms of birth control include abstinence, withdrawal (the man completely removes his penis from the woman's vagina before he ejaculates), and the so-called natural or rhythm method. A couple using the rhythm method must know when the woman ovulates and avoid sexual intercourse during ovulation. Knowing when ovulation takes place requires a woman to carefully monitor her temperature and watch for changes in the mucus produced by the vagina. The temperature change is usually only about half of a degree Fahrenheit. According to clinical trials, this method of birth control can be effective but its success depends on whether a woman's menstrual cycles are predictable and on how conscientious she is in monitoring.

Margaret Sanger, who was a nurse in New York City slums, was one of the leading forces in the early 1900s to establish birth control clinics that offered family planning services and contraceptives to American women. After witnessing the death of many poor women from botched or self-induced abortions, Sanger became convinced of the need to distribute contraceptive information. She has often been erroneously credited with founding the National Birth Control League in 1914, but the organization was actually started by Mary Ware Dennett, who was considered Sanger's rival in the birth control movement. When Sanger opened a birth control clinic in Brooklyn in 1916, she was arrested.

Although the right to provide birth control information was eventually established, there was not widespread access to birth control in the United States until about the 1960s. By that time, a synthetic female hormone in pill form was available. Known as "the Pill," the medication suppresses ovulation so conception cannot take place. It became one of the most popular and effective means of birth control for women.

A contraceptive called Norplant uses medication similar to that used in the pill. The hormone is placed in capsules about the size of matchsticks that are implanted in a woman's upper arm above the elbow where they can be felt but not seen. The implants release low doses of synthetic hormone that inhibit ovulation and make it difficult for sperm to reach the egg.

Other popular methods of birth control are barrier devices that prevent or make it very difficult for sperm to reach the ovum. They usually are used with or contain a backup spermicide. The diaphragm and cervical cap are types of barrier birth control devices. A diaphragm fits over the cervix and is usually filled with contraceptive jelly; a cervical cap is similar but smaller in diameter. Another barrier/spermicidal device, the contraceptive sponge, was approved by the Food and Drug Administration in April 1983 and produced until 1995, when it was withdrawn from the market because of manufacturing problems. Production of the device began again in late 1999. The sponge is made of polyurethane and a spermicide. It is popular with many women because it is convenient and easy to use, and the risk of adverse side effects is low.

For centuries men have used contraceptive condoms made of various materials to wear over the erect penis during intercourse. Condoms today are usually made of polyurethane or latex and are relatively effective in preventing sperm from entering the vagina. A latex condom for women became available in the early 1990s. Like a diaphragm it fits around the cervix as a barrier device.

The intrauterine device (IUD) is a type of birth control that has been used since ancient time. Most IUDs today are small plastic or copper devices in T-shape form or straight rods that measure about 3 cm. When inserted directly into the woman's uterus through the vagina, the IUD prevents the fertilized egg from attaching to the uterine walls.

Among married couples in the United States, a surgical procedure known as sterilization is the leading birth control method. A vasectomy is performed on men; a portion of each sperm tube is removed and the tubes are tied. For women, tubal ligation is similar except that the fallopian tubes are cut or cauterized and tied.

Emergency contraceptive (ECP) methods are among the most recent types of birth control for unintended pregnancies, although emergency procedures have been used since the 1960s for rape victims. One of the most well-known is the "Yuzpe Regimen," named for A. Albert Yuzpe, a Canadian professor who published the first studies on this topic in 1974. Using this regimen, a woman takes two doses of oral contraceptive pills that combine the hormones estrogen and progestin. The first dose is taken within 72 hours of unprotected intercourse with the second dose following 12 hours later. According to the Planned Parenthood Federation of America,

Before September 1998, because no dedicated ECP product had been approved, labeled and marketed in this country, emergency hormonal contraception had been available in the U.S. only as an "off-label" use of oral contraceptive pills. Off-label use of approved medications is a common and legal practice, and some hospital emergency rooms, family planning clinics, and university health centers have been providing women with emergency contraception in this manner. Despite decades of safe and effective use of ECPs around the world, the off-label status of ECPs made some providers in the U.S. fearful of legal liability. Physicians were reticent to educate women about ECPs, and with no commercial advertising for it, most women knew nothing about it. In reproductive health circles, emergency contraception became known as "America's best-kept secret."

In spite of the various contraceptive methods available, nearly half of the six million annual pregnancies in the United States are accidental. These unintended pregnancies result in 1.4 million abortions each year "as well as 1.1 million births that women either did not want to have until later or did not want at all. Eighty percent of teen pregnancies are unintended, and each year, one in nine young women aged 15-19 become pregnant; more than half become mothers." (Planned Parenthood)

Reproductive health professionals nationwide contend that information about birth control and family planning must be more widespread in the United States in order to prevent unintended pregnancies and abortions. Yet political pressure to prevent dissemination of such information still comes into play as opposition groups argue that birth control information encourages and condones sexual intercourse outside of marriage. Such political opposition has eased somewhat, however, as many groups have tried in recent years to inform the public about the use of condoms to protect against the threat of the human immune deficiency virus (HIV) that causes AIDS and to prevent other sexually transmitted diseases (STDs).

One of the most controversial birth control methods is the drug mifepristone, sometimes called RU-486, which technically is an abortifacient. During the first seven weeks after conception, the use of mifepristone combined with another drug causes an abortion, much like a spontaneous miscarriage. The drug was recently approved for manufacture in the United States, but in mid-2000, the Food and Drug Administration (FDA) suggested placing restrictions on who can prescribe RU-486. The FDA wants only doctors who perform surgical abortions to prescribe the drug, which "would effectively eliminate what advocates of abortion rights see as mifepristone's main advantage, moving the procedure out of potentially high-profile clinics and into the private offices of gynecologists, family practitioners and other doctors," the *New York Times* reported. If these rigid restrictions are applied, access to RU-486 will be denied to many women who would like to use it, advocates say. (Stolberg) *See also* Comstock Law; Dennett, Mary Ware; Mifepristone; Planned Parenthood Federation of America; Sanger, Margaret; Sexually Transmitted Diseases; Teenage Pregnancy

Further Reading

Leary, Warren E. "Contraceptive Sponge Returns to Market." *New York Times* (March 30, 1999).

Planned Parenthood Federation of America. "Fact Sheet—A Short History of Emergency Hormonal Contraception." (September 1998). <http://www.plannedparenthood.org/library/BIRTHCONTROL/EmergContra.htm>

Chen, Constance M. *"The Sex Side of Life": Mary Ware Dennett's Pioneering Battle for Birth Control and Sex Education.* New York: The New Press, 1996.

Chesler, Ellen. *Woman of Valor: Margaret Sanger and the Birth Control Movement in America.* New York: Simon & Schuster, 1992.

Stolberg, Sheryl Gay. "F.D.A. Adds Hurdles in Approval of Abortion Pill." *New York Times* (June 8, 2000).

Wymelenberg, Suzanne for the Institute of Medicine. *Science and Babies Private Decisions, Public Dilemmas.* Washington, DC: National Academy Press, 1990.

Body Image

See **Dieting and Diet Drugs; Eating Disorders; Weight Discrimination**

Boston Women's Health Book Collective

Founded in 1969 and incorporated in 1972, the Boston Women's Health Book Collective (BWHBC) in Somerville, Massachusetts, is a nonprofit organization devoted to women's health education and the many social, economic, ethical, and political issues that impinge on women's health. BWHBC is known primarily for its revolutionary and highly acclaimed book *Our Bodies, Ourselves*, first published commercially in 1973. The book not only contained frank information about reproduction but also explicit drawings (uncommon at the time) of female genitalia. *Our Bodies, Ourselves* has been updated several times and translated into fifteen different languages. In 1998, a new edition entitled *Our Bodies, Ourselves for the New Century* was published. During Spring 2000, a new Spanish-language edition was published, titled *Nuestros Cuerpos, Nuestras Vidas (Our Bodies, Our Lives).* The Spanish version is aimed at a growing Hispanic population and emphasizes mutual help and caring for others. Interdependence is an important aspect of Latin culture, and this is reflected in the book's revisions, which may also be incorporated into the next edition published in English. (Berger)

The Boston Women's Health Book Collective organized in 1969, after a group of twelve women attended a women's liberation conference in Boston and took part in a workshop on women's health topics. There the women, who were frustrated with the kind of health care they received, decided to search for accurate information about women's bodies and reproductive health, which was not readily available at the time. Calling themselves the Doctors Group, they eventually developed and compiled a series of papers on women's health topics in a booklet entitled *Women and Their Bodies,* which was used to teach an informal course at the Massachusetts Institute of Technology. The booklet was expanded and published as *Our Bodies, Ourselves* by Simon & Schuster.

Although the BWHBC book presents a great deal of factual information, its major purpose is empowering women by providing them with knowledge about their bodies, health, and sexuality. That is still the primary mission of the Collective. As BWHBC states on its Web site:

Through publications, coalition-building, media work, and other forms of outreach, the BWHBC provides quality information on women and health, often with a feminist critique of health and medical care. As part of national and global Women's Health Movements, the BWHBC believes that women's health issues must be addressed in an economic, social and political context, and that women should have a much greater role in health policy decisions. The BWHBC highlights the role of poverty and societal oppression as major determinants of health and encourages women to organize for social change. American women today are much better informed about health issues than were their counterparts of the 1950s and 1960s. However, because many women face obstacles to woman-centered health care, the Collective continues to challenge the institutions and systems that devalue women and prevent women from gaining full control over their bodies.

See also Sexuality

Further Reading

Berger, Leslie. "Adapting a Feminist Icon to a New Audience." *New York Times* (June 13, 2000).

Boston Women's Health Book Collective. *Our Bodies, Ourselves for the New Century.* New York: Touchstone/Simon & Schuster, 1998.

Boston Women's Health Book Collective. "Our Mission." <www.ourbodiesourselves.org>.

Feinberg, Madaline. "The Boston Women's Health Book Collective Celebrates Its 25th Anniversary!" *The Network News* (May–June 1996).

Breast Cancer

Breast cancer is one of the most terrifying and dreaded diseases among American women. According to the National Cancer Institute (NCI), an estimated 180,000 women are diagnosed with breast cancer each year. Breast cancer is expected to kill more than 41,000 people in 2000. It is the second leading cause of cancer death in women, after lung cancer. But because there is less public awareness of lung cancer's leading role in cancer deaths among women, it creates less terror than does breast cancer.

One reason there is more awareness of breast cancer may be the long-time success of advocacy groups in making breast cancer a political issue, prompting the federal government to spend much more on breast cancer research than on lung cancer research. Another reason is that many women fear disfigurement if they must have a mastectomy, a view that some social critics say is tied to the "beauty myth" and the cultural notion that women's breasts enhance their sexuality. Breast cancer patients also believe they will die from the disease. As one oncology expert noted:

Fear of breast cancer is virtually universal among American women. Stimulated by media reports emphasizing rising incidence and pointing—with or without data—to a growing variety of risk factors, an increasing number of women are bringing their concerns to their primary care physicians. (Schnabel, 2083)

Whether or not women are justified in this anxiety, some women who have family histories of breast cancer opt for preventive mastectomy, often having both breasts removed to decrease their risks of contracting the disease. While such radical surgery may save lives in some instances, it is an issue only recently being addressed by physicians and other medical practitioners.

Until about the 1990s, the main concern for organizations such as the American Cancer Institute (ACS), the National Cancer Institute, and the National Breast Cancer Coalition (co-founded by breast cancer surgeon Susan M. Love) was raising public awareness of breast cancer as a major health problem and lobbying for increased federal appropriations for breast cancer research. Their warnings that one in eight women is at risk for developing the disease, encouraged many women to have breast examinations and mammograms, which in turn has led to early detection and

Dr. Susan Love, MD. Courtesy susanlove.com Photo by Jerry Bauer.

treatment of cancer and higher survival rates. But the high risk rate is misleading because it represents the entire population and does not reflect the fact that risk factors vary and increase with age. One out of 250 women is at risk during her thirties, for example, but during their eighties the risk for women is one out of 45.

Medical experts are attempting to present clearer data on risk factors in order to lessen apprehension. Cancer researchers advise physicians and their patients to look at probabilities on an age-specific basis, and to focus on known risks. For instance, although the majority of breast cancer cases occur in women older than age 50, misconceptions prevail among older women, underscoring the need for broader dissemination of information. The NCI found in a telephone survey during Spring 1999 that more than one-third of women ages 65 and older were not as concerned about getting breast cancer as they were when they were younger. They also were not aware of the medical benefits of having a screening mammogram every one or two years.

Lifetime Probability of Breast Cancer in American Women

by age 30...	1 out of 2,000
by age 40...	1 out of 233
by age 50...	1 out of 53
by age 60...	1 out of 22
by age 70...	1 out of 13
by age 80...	1 out of 9
Ever...	1 out of 8

Source: National Cancer Institute Surveillance, Epidemiology, and End Results Program, 1995–1997.

The NCI developed a Breast Cancer Risk Assessment Tool to help identify the characteristics that can put a woman at risk of getting the disease. But the NCI points out that many women who "develop breast cancer have no known risk factors other than growing older, and many women with known risk factors do not get breast cancer." To assess risks, the NCI identifies such factors as "personal history of breast abnormalities, current age, age at first menstrual period, age at first live birth, breast cancer history of close relatives, whether a woman has had a breast biopsy, and race." (NCI, October 1998)

Other factors include the use of birth control pills or hormone replacement therapy, a high-fat diet, alcohol consumption, and environmental pollutants. However, researchers do not know to what extent these factors play a role or what are their possible risks.

Treatment for breast cancer patients is another area of concern, one that sometimes creates controversy. The National Comprehensive Cancer Network (NCCN) and the American Cancer Society (ACS) developed a patient guide to explain in lay terms various types of breast cancer and treatment. Based on the NCCN Oncology Practice Guidelines for medical personnel, the patient guide can be ordered from ACS or NCCN or accessed on Internet Web sites at ACS (http://www.cancer.org) and NCCN (http://www.nccn.org).

Another major issue in conjunction with breast cancer is finding ways to prevent the disease. More than 13,000 premenopausal and postmenopausal women at high risk of breast cancer are part of a clinical study sponsored by NCI to determine whether the osteoporosis prevention drug raloxifene is as effective in reducing the chance of developing breast cancer as tamoxifen has proven to be. Tamoxifen has been available for more than two decades. Results of a study known as the Breast Cancer Prevention Trial (BCPT), which were published in the *Journal of the National Cancer Institute* in 1998, showed that tamoxifen reduced the chance of developing breast cancer by about half. "However, the drug increased the women's chances of developing four potentially life-threatening health problems: endometrial cancer (cancer of the lining of the uterus), deep vein thrombosis (blood clots in large veins), pulmonary embolism (blood clot in the lung), and possibly stroke." (NCI, May 1999)

In the view of surgeon Susan M. Love, who is well known for her book on breast cancer and as director of the Santa Barbara (California) Breast Cancer Institute, research funds should be used to develop preventive measures rather than new drugs for breast cancer treatment. She contends that all cancer is genetic and that techniques must be developed to access and investigate the inner part of the breast for malignant cells. She received a $500,000 grant from the Department of Defense to develop an intraductal approach to breast cancer. In her research, she concentrates on the anatomy of the breast and mapping its network of ductal systems. She hopes her efforts will lead to methods for "cleaning out" ducts and transporting new genes into areas where cells malfunction. *See also* Aging; Lung Cancer; Mastectomy

Further Reading

Brody, Jane. "Coping with Fear: Keeping Breast Cancer in Perspective." *New York Times* (October 12, 1999).

Grady, Denise. "Breast Cancer Data, Hope, Fear and Confusion." *New York Times* (January 26, 1999).

Love, Susan M. *Dr. Susan Love's Breast Book.* 2d rev. ed. Reading, MA: Addison-Wesley, 1995.

National Cancer Institute. "Estimating Breast Cancer Risk." Press Release (October 6, 1998).

National Cancer Institute. "Misconceptions Persist among Older Women in Spite of Rising Mammography Rates." Press Release (October 20, 1999).

National Cancer Institute. "Breast Cancer Prevention Study Seeks Volunteers: Study of Tamoxifen and Raloxifene (STAR) Under Way Across North America." Press Release (May 25, 1999).

Oster, Nancy. "Susan Love Interview." <http://www.silcom.com/~quality/slove.html>

Ratner, Elaine. *The Feisty Woman's Breast Cancer Book.* New York: Hunter House, 1999.

Schnabel, Freya R. "Breast Cancer: What the History Can Tell You about Risk—and What You Can Tell Your Patient." *Consultant* (September 1998).

Sternberg, Steve. "Toxins Not Linked to Breast Cancer." *USA Today* (February 2, 1999).

Breast Implants

Breast implants are artificial devices made with a rubbery outer sac, or shell, that is filled with either a silicone gel or saline solution; they are designed to be surgically implanted in women's breasts. Breast implants were developed in the early 1960s as a way to restore a woman's body and her self-esteem after having a breast removed for medical reasons—usually cancer or the high risk of cancer, a misshapen breast, or other physical impairment. The use of breast implants for reconstructive surgery procedures totaled 183,000 in 1999, the latest year for such statistics, which have been tracked since 1992 by the American Society of Plastic Surgeons (ASPS).

When healthy women also began to have implants solely to augment their breast sizes, to create body shapes considered more appealing to men, cosmetic breast implant surgery became big business. ASPS statistics show that breast augmentation is one of the top three cosmetic surgery procedures (along with liposuction and eyelid surgery), increasing from 32,607 breast-augmentation procedures in 1992 to 167,318 in 1999.

But breast implants have created controversy. One issue was whether women were being unduly manipulated by society's concept of a so-called perfect body and thus led to believe they were "deformed" or unattractive if they had small breasts. Some social critics accused cosmetic surgeons of exploiting the "cleavage craze." The American Society of Plastic Surgeons aggressively touted their role as "self-image enhancers" and even declared in one press release that small breasts were "deformities...really a disease." (Faludi, 217)

Implant safety has been another concern. By 1989, increasing numbers of women with breast implants were reporting problems such as implant ruptures, leakage, scarring, hardening of tissues, nerve damage, and autoimmune diseases, often called connective tissues diseases, such as lupus, rheumatoid arthritis, and scleroderma. Between 1985 and 1992, the U.S. Food and Drug Administration (FDA), which regulates medical devices, received about 3,400 complaints linked to silicone gel implants and about 3,000 reports of problems with saline-filled implants. (Wolfe) After a *Connie Chung Show* in late 1990 focused on alleged injuries from breast implants, thousands more women began airing their complaints. Autoimmune diseases are the most controversial injuries related to breast implants. Some medical experts and researchers link leaking silicone from breast implants to autoimmune diseases; others, including experts at Harvard Medical School, the University of Michigan, and Mayo Clinic, disagree. Nevertheless, in January 1992 the FDA ordered a moratorium on the use of silicone implants. Several months later the FDA allowed silicone gel–filled implants on the market under controlled clinical studies for reconstruction after mastectomy, correction of congenital deformities, or replacement for ruptured silicone gel–filled implants for augmentation. The FDA denied the use of silicone breast implants for cosmetic purposes except for about 2,000 women enrolled in clinical studies to test the safety of the devices.

Even before the FDA restrictions, women with injuries linked to breast implants were filing lawsuits against manufacturers—Dow Corning Corporation being the most notable—which added another dimension to the health issue. As litigations grew, Dow Corning declared bankruptcy. After reorganization the company agreed to a $3.2 billion settlement, in spite of Dow's contention that no evidence showed Dow to be liable for injuries, but that continuing the legal process would have cost even more. In late 1998, Federal Court Judge Sam Pointer of Alabama convened a panel of medical experts to determine whether there were links between silicone breast implants and disease, but the panel found no such links. Then in 1999, the prestigious Institute of Medicine (IOM) issued a report from a panel of 13 independent scientists, who at the request of Congress in 1997 began an investigation of breast implant safety. The IOM panel interviewed researchers and women with implants and studied scientific literature on breast implants. In a 400-page report, the panel concluded that there was no scientific evidence to support claims that breast implants caused autoimmune diseases, breast cancer, or chronic fatigue syndrome, or that they contaminated breast milk. Activists claimed the panel's conclusions were flawed because they were based on reviews of research conducted by breast implant manufacturers. Some medical practitioners believe there is still a need for more research and that toxic materials in breast implants can cause health problems.

For years concerns have also been raised about saline-filled breast implants, although they have been considered safer than the silicone variety and have been marketed without FDA approval since 1976, when the agency was legally authorized to regulate medical devices. Risks include infections, hardening of breast tissue, and the need for repeated surgeries, several studies have shown. Nevertheless in Spring 2000, the FDA approved the use of saline-filled breast implants, stipulating that manufacturing companies would have to inform women of the relatively high health risks involved and that women and their doctors could then make their own decisions about the implants. *See also* Chronic Fatigue Syndrome

Further Reading

American Society of Plastic Surgeons, Plastic Surgery Information Service. "Most Popular Cosmetic Surgery Procedures Just Became More Popular." Press Release (July 20, 2000). <http://www.plasticsurgery.org/mediactr/stats.htm>.

Faludi, Susan. *Backlash: The Undeclared War against American Women.* New York: Dial/Doubleday Press, 1991.

Gay, Kathlyn. *Breast Implants: Making Safe Choices.* New York: New Discovery Books/Macmillan, 1993.

Hazelton, Richard A. "The Breast Implant Controversy." *Vital Speeches* (December 1, 1998).

Kolata, Gina. "Panel Confirms No Major Illness Tied to Breast Implants." *New York Times* (June 21, 1999).

Sissell, Kara. "Panel Finds No Link to Disease." *Chemical Week* (December 9, 1998).

Stolberg, Sheryl Gay. "Saline Breast Implants Win U.S. Approval After Studies." *New York Times* (May 10, 2000).

Wolf, Naomi. *The Beauty Myth: How Images of Beauty Are Used against Women.* New York: Morrow, 1991.

Wolfe, Sidney M., M.D. Testimony before the FDA Advisory Committee on General and Plastic Surgery Devices (November 22, 1988).

Breastfeeding

Breastfeeding—nursing or feeding a baby with milk from a mother's breast—was once the most common (and sometimes the only) way to nourish an infant. In the United States, according to an Institute of Medicine report, 75 percent of the babies born in the late 1930s were breastfed. By the 1970s, however, only 25 percent were nursed. Mothers were choosing instead to bottle feed their babies with formula milk, which at the time was considered the most "scientific" way to nourish an infant. Research since then has consistently shown that mother's milk is the most nutritious food for infants and that children who have been breastfed are healthier than those who have not. The practice of breastfeeding

also is beneficial for the mother and is being encouraged worldwide. As the American Academy of Pediatrics declared in a December 1997 report, breastfeeding has health, nutritional, immunologic, developmental, psychological, social, economic, and environmental advantages unmatched by other feeding options.

Aggressive advertising by formula manufacturers, however, influences mothers to opt for human-milk substitutes even though formula costs more than breastfeeding and its use endangers infants' health. For decades, activist groups have attempted to encourage breastfeeding, particularly in the developing world where infants were dying. In 1977, Infant Formula Action Coalition (INFACT) began an international boycott of Nestlé products, alleging that the company's advertising did not recognize breastfeeding as the best

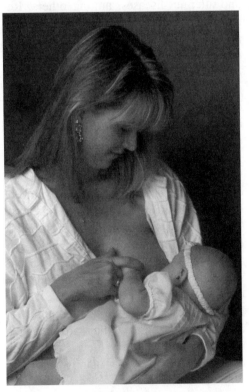

Mother breastfeeding infant. ©Scott Liles/Unicorn Stock Photos.

form of infant nutrition. Activists argued that in poor countries women often mixed the formula with contaminated water, causing diarrhea and malnutrition in infants, and sometimes death. In 1984, Nestlé agreed to abide by marketing codes for infant formula established by the World Health Organization (WHO), and the boycott was called off. But in 1988, the boycott was reinstated when monitoring by the United Nations Children's Fund (UNICEF) and other groups showed that Nestlé was violating WHO codes in some countries.

Studies conducted in the United States and other developed countries have provided evidence that breastfeeding can decrease the incidence or severity of conditions such as diarrhea, ear infections, and bacterial meningitis, and that it may offer protection against sudden infant death syndrome (SIDS), insulin-dependent diabetes, and allergic diseases, among others. Research also indicates that breastfeeding can reduce a mother's risk of several medical conditions, including ovarian and premenopausal breast cancer; save a family more than $400 on the cost of infant formula during the first year of life; and reduce parental absence from work due to child illness. Despite these extensive findings, in 1995 only 59.4 percent of women in the United States were breastfeeding either exclusively or in combination with formula at the time of hospital discharge, and only 21.6 percent were nursing at 6 months. (AAP press release)

To encourage breastfeeding, various support groups have been organized. One of the most well known is La Leche League International, with headquarters in Schaumburg, Illinois. Others are statewide or local groups that provide breastfeeding counselors for mothers having difficulty with nursing.

Support groups, medical experts, and health insurance companies have been em-phasizing the economic benefits of breastfeeding. Various estimates indicate that in the United States between $2 and $4 billion could be saved on health care each year if all women breastfed their infants for just three months. Companies can also save money by providing working mothers with unpaid time from the job and a place to breastfeed their babies at the job or to use a breast pump to extract milk. In March 1999, a bill was introduced in the 106th Congress to "amend the Internal Revenue Code of 1986 to allow employers a credit against income tax for expenses for providing an appropriate environment on the business premises for employed mothers to breastfeed or express milk for their children." Called the Breastfeeding Promotion and Employees' Tax Incentive Act, HR 1163 is supported by health groups as well as lactating mothers.

One contentious issue in regard to breastfeeding is the right of mothers to nurse their babies in public. Some Americans believe that uncovering a breast to nurse a child is obscene, indecent exposure, harmful to small children who observe the practice, or at the least a public nuisance. Because of that view nursing mothers have been harassed or discriminated against when they have attempted to feed their babies in public places such as stores, restaurants, and transportation facilities. During the 1990s some states passed laws or proposed legislation to protect mothers who breastfeed in public. A Florida law, for example, states that "The breastfeeding of a baby is an important and basic act of nurture which must be encouraged in the interests of maternal and child health and family values." The Florida statute makes clear that "A mother may breastfeed her baby in any location, public or private, where the mother is otherwise authorized to be, irrespective of whether the nipple of the mother's breast is uncovered during or incidental to breastfeeding."

The law also states that nursing is "not under any circumstances harmful to minors." Nor is breastfeeding in public obscene and it does not "under any circumstance constitute nudity...[or] sexual conduct." Laws in more than a dozen other states provide similar protections. *See also* Birth Control; La Leche League International; Menstruation

Further Reading

American Academy of Pediatrics News Release. "AAP Releases New Breastfeeding Recommendations." (December 1, 1997).

Lewis, Paul. "Increased Breast Feeding Could Save Lives, Study Finds." *New York Times* (March 4, 1999).

Boston Women's Health Book Collective. *The New Our Bodies, Ourselves.* New York: Simon & Schuster, 1992.

Planned Parenthood Federation of America. *The Planned Parenthood Women's Health Encyclopedia.* New York: Crown Trade Paperbacks, 1996.

Bureau of Primary Health Care

The Bureau of Primary Health Care (BPHC) is one of four bureaus of the Health Resources and Services Administration, an agency in the Department of Health and Human Services (DHHS). Its mission is to increase access to comprehensive primary and preventive health care for underserved and vulnerable populations, which include millions of American women. A great variety of health problems confront women who are poor, homeless, victims of domestic violence, at high risk for complications from pregnancy, migrant workers, uninsured, and have little or no access to health care providers. To address these social and economic issues, the BPHC helps build community-based primary care infrastructures and helps provide family-oriented, culturally competent primary care that is linked to social services. The Bureau also sponsors the National Health Service Corps, which offers service opportunities for primary care providers in exchange for educational assistance, and recruits health-care providers to serve in rural and urban areas where there is a shortage of health professionals. In addition, the Bureau identifies creative and effective programs that serve as nationwide models for health care in underserved communities. Information about bureau activities is available on its Internet Web site <http://www.bphc.hrsa.dhhs.gov/>. *See also* Domestic Violence; Homeless Women; Poor Women's Health Care; United States Department of Health and Human Services

C

Caffeine

Controversy has long surrounded the question of whether a person's health is endangered by the consumption of foods or beverages that contain caffeine, a naturally occurring stimulant found in dozens of different species of beans, leaves, and plants. Some of the most common products with caffeine are coffee, tea, cola drinks, and chocolate, all of which have been consumed for hundreds of years. The debate over caffeine's health effects has had economic ramifications as numerous caffeine-free products have been developed to meet the demands of consumers concerned about their well-being.

At various times, researchers have warned women that consuming a beverage or food with caffeine could be harmful. One small study in 1988, for example, concluded that caffeine had an adverse effect on fertility. However, larger studies, particularly one conducted in 1990 by researchers at the Centers for Disease Control and Prevention and Harvard University, showed that caffeine consumption did not increase the risk of infertility. Other studies concluded that caffeine does not cause birth defects or adversely affect reproduction.

During the 1970s, medical practitioners often advised women with fibrocystic disease to abstain from caffeine to eliminate their breast tenderness and other symptoms, although no scientific study confirmed that caffeine was an aggravating factor. In 1986 the National Cancer Institute undertook a study of 3,000 women and found no evidence of a link between caffeine and fibrocystic disease. Studies have also shown that caffeine is not associated with risks of breast cancer, osteoporosis, and heart disease.

One of the most debated issues is whether caffeine is addictive. Some researchers argue that people can become dependent on caffeine; and most coffee drinkers (and many cola drinkers) contend that they need their caffeine intake to get going in the morning and coffee breaks for further stimulation during the day. Some people report having headaches if they abstain from coffee. Nevertheless, during a national meeting of the American Chemical Society in 1999, the research director at the French National Health and Medical Research Institute presented data indicating that caffeine increases energy but "At doses of one to three cups of coffee a day, a fairly typical consumption for Americans, caffeine has no affect on the area of the brain involved with addiction, dependence, and reward." (American Chemical Society) *See also* Breast Cancer; Drug Abuse and Addiction; Osteoporosis

Further Reading

American Chemical Society. "Debate Brews over Caffeine Addiction—Study Also Confirms Caffeine Improves Alertness and Energy." Press Release (March 22, 1999).

Associated Press. "Study: Caffeine Not Addictive for Most." (March 23, 1999).

IFIC Info and Association of Women's Health, Obstetric and Neonatal Nurses. *Caffeine and Women's Health* (brochure)(July 1998).

Calderone, Mary Steichen (1904–1998)

A physician and author, Mary Steichen Calderone was a pioneer in the field of human sexuality and the leading advocate of early and honest sex education in the United States. Her work has been especially important to women who were taught to avoid discussions about sex and seldom had access to information about or understanding of their own sexuality. Through Calderone's efforts uncounted numbers of women have been able to free themselves of inhibitions regarding sexual matters. In addition, she has helped educate women about frigidity and birth control methods.

The daughter of famous photographer Edward Steichen, Mary went to France at the age of 10 to live with her father after her parents divorced. Although she attempted acting for a few years and then helped to produce several photography books with her father, she gave up both as career paths. She married an actor, and the couple had two daughters; one died of pneumonia at the age of eight.

After divorcing her husband in 1933, Calderone decided to become a doctor, earning her degree at the University of Rochester Medical School and doing her graduate work in public health at Colum-

Mary Calderone, President and founder of Sexuality Information and Education Council of the United States. Courtesy of the Sexuality Information and Education Council of the United States, 130 W. 42nd St., New York, NY 10036-7802.

bia University. She worked in public health for several years and during that time met Dr. Frank Calderone, who eventually became administrative head of the World Health Organization. In 1941, Frank and Mary Calderone married; they had two daughters.

In 1953, Calderone took the position of medical director of Planned Parenthood Federation of America. During her 11 years as director of Planned Parenthood, she became "aware of how ignorant so many people were about questions regarding sex, masturbation, frigidity, and contraception. This inspired her determination to help people of all ages understand and appreciate how and why sex is such an integral part of life." (Epstein, 39)

In 1964, Calderone co-founded the Sex Information and Education Council of the United States (SIECUS), whose primary issue was liberating people from unhealthy and repressive attitudes about human sexuality. Calderone served as president of the organization from 1975 to 1982. As spokesperson for SIECUS, she was frequently accused of encouraging sexual promiscuity and blamed for increases in sexually transmitted diseases (STDs), abortions, and teenage pregnancies. As one writer noted, she was a "favorite target of religious extremists, fringe groups, and other conservative elements in the country." Members of the Ku Klux Klan burned crosses on her lawn, and right-wing groups "spent an estimated $40 million on a virulent campaign" in 1969 to denounce her. (Epstein, 39)

Mary Calderone's numerous writings include *Questions and Answers about Sex and Love; Sexuality and Human Values; Manual of Family Planning and Contraceptive Practices; The Family Book about Sexuality;* and *Talking With Your Child About Sex.* She was awarded many honors, among them the Margaret Sanger Award from Planned Parenthood; the Lifetime Achievement Award from the Schlesinger Library, Radcliffe/Harvard; the Browning Award for Prevention of Diseases from the American Public Health Association; and the Elizabeth Blackwell Award for Distinguished Services to Humanity. Before and after her death at the age of 94, Calderone's admirers have praised her efforts in providing honest and straightforward sex education for thousands, if not millions, of people. *See also* Planned Parenthood Federation of America; Sexuality

Further Reading
Epstein, Harriet. "The Grande Dame of Sex Education." *The Humanist* (January 1999).

Canada–U.S.A. Women's Health Forum

Women's health and the many social and environmental factors that play a role in their well-being or lack of well-being were the main thrust of the Canada-U.S.A. Women's Health Forum in 1996. Canadian Minister of Health, the Honourable David C. Dingwall, and U.S. Secretary of Health and Human Services, Dr. Donna Shalala, co-sponsored the forum, which was held in Ottawa, Canada. Three hundred delegates exchanged information about their respective country's programs and policies, identified shared interests and activities, examined health challenges for women, and highlighted future opportunities for the mutual advancement of women's health. Among the topics experts discussed were the "Changing Concepts of Women's Health—Advocating for Change" and "Future and Emerging Issues for Women's Health in the 21st Century."

During the three-day event, workshops focused on key women's health issues, and on how the health system and its infrastructure impact on women's health. These issues included

- Health conditions and disease: gender differences and gender-specific approaches
- Environmental health impacts
- Occupational health impacts
- Health aspects of violence against women
- Reproductive and sexual health
- Health issues relevant to indigenous women

Health-system issues were also discussed, such as preventive strategies, research, health-care delivery, and legal, ethical, and legislative issues. An informative Web site at <http://www.hc-sc.gc.ca/canusa/info.htm> includes full-length papers on some of the presentations at the forum and explanations about joint Canadian-U.S. efforts to address women's health-care issues. *See also* Environmental Health Hazards; Health-Care Access; United States Department of Health and Human Services

Canadian Women's Health Network

Launched in 1993, the Canadian Women's Health Network (CWHN) focuses on women's health issues and represents more than 70 organizations from every province and territory in Canada. Health-care workers, educators, advocates, consumers, and other Canadians committed to sharing information, resources, and strategies to better women's health are part of the network. Like many counterpart organizations in the United States, the CWHN is committed to building regional and national links among organizations and individuals who care about improving women's health and health-care options. According to its Internet Web site, the CWHN strives to

- Provide easier access to health information, resources, and research

- Produce user-friendly materials and resources

- Promote and develop links to information and action networks

- Provide forums for critical debate

- Act as a "watchdog" on emerging issues and trends that may affect women's health

- Work to change inequitable health policies and practices

- Encourage community-based participatory research models

- Promote women's involvement in health research

Building and strengthening the women's health movement worldwide is one of the network's missions. In addition, the network states

> Health is a human right that, because of poverty, politics and dwindling resources for health and social services, eludes many women. Guided by a woman-centered, holistic vision of women's health, the CWHN recognizes and respects the diverse realities of women's lives and takes an active stance in ending discrimination based on gender, region, race, age, language, religion, sexual orientation, or ability. (About CWHN)

Another purpose of the network is to provide Internet resources on women's health, such as information on illness, prevention, chronic pain, disabilities, and other health topics. The network posts new research information from Canada's Centres of Excellence for Women's Health, which was set up in 1996 to fund five-year studies on such women's health issues as the effects of poverty on health, violence against women, and the media's influence on women's health. The network also posts articles, press releases, and information sheets from health organizations that may not have their own Web Site, but that are actively involved in women's health. The Canadian Health Network, funded by the federal government, is another site with trustworthy information. *See also* Women's Health Movement

Further Reading
"About the Canadian Women's Health Network." <http://www.cwhn.ca/about.html>.

Marron, Kevin, "Net Boon and Bane to Patients: Site Prescriptions." *Globe and Mail* (July 30, 1999).

Nichols, Mark. "Women's Health: New Attitudes and Solutions." *Maclean's* (January 12, 1998).

Cardiovascular Diseases

The greatest life-threatening diseases affecting American women are cardiovascular diseases, disorders of the heart and blood vessels. Women are 20 percent more likely than men to die in the hospital following a heart attack, notes the Agency for Health Care Policy and Research. According to the American Heart Association (AHA), all types of cardiovascular diseases kill more than half a million women each year, "more lives than the next 16 causes of death combined." Yet less than 10 percent of American women believe cardiovascular diseases are major threats to their health; instead, the majority cites breast cancer, which kills more than 40,000 women annually, as the leading health threat. Only in the past five to ten years have health-care practitioners and advocacy groups begun to give strong warnings about the risks of cardiovascular diseases among women.

One form of the disease is coronary heart disease (or coronary artery disease), which is a buildup of plaque on the artery walls causing a condition known as arteriosclerosis. Coronary heart disease can damage the heart and result in a heart attack (myocardial infarction) or sudden death; it kills nearly twice the number of females as all forms of cancer.

Until recent years, heart disease was considered primarily a man's problem, and much of the public still links heart disease to men rather than women. Health-care practitioners have often misdiagnosed women with serious heart problems. In addition, doctors have not followed up as often on women who have had stress electrocardiogram tests showing problems as they have on men with similar test results.

Some women with stress-test irregularities or symptoms of heart disease (such as indigestion, fatigue, and chest pain) have been told that their problems were

Comparable Death Rates Stroke & Heart Disease Black & White Females (1997 data age adjusted 2000)

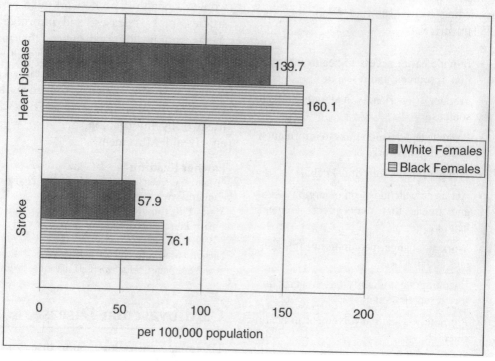

Source of Data: U.S. Centers for Disease Control and Prevention and American Heart Association, 2000.

due to menopause, stress, or even the "empty-nest syndrome."

Most research on cardiovascular diseases has been conducted on men with coronary artery disease. Although women are not as likely as men to have cardiovascular problems during their reproductive years, both genders are at the same risk of heart disease after age 60. Older women, though, generally have not been included in studies because they frequently have other chronic illnesses that could affect the research results.

Some risk factors for cardiovascular disease are similar for women and men: heredity, smoking, high blood pressure, high cholesterol levels, lack of exercise, obesity, diabetes, and stress. Yet American women generally are more afraid of cancer than cardiovascular diseases, which has prompted organizations such as the American Heart Association and federal agencies under the U.S. Department of Health and Human Services to stress the seriousness of cardiovascular diseases among women—now a prime health issue in the United States.

During the 1990s scientists began to recognize the gender gap in cardiovascular research as well as the fact that women have different and often more subtle symptoms of heart disease. One difference is blood levels of fats called triglycerides in the bloodstream, which indicate "increased risk of heart disease in women but not in men." Research also shows that

treatments that work well in men may not work equally well in women. More women than men die while undergoing coronary bypass surgery to restore blood flow to the heart muscle. Women also fare worse than men with less-invasive procedures for the treatment of artery-narrowing plaques, such as balloon angioplasty...and surgical removal of a plaque from an artery.... Women also suffer more complications from the procedures than do men. No one knows yet whether women fare more poorly than

men because of their smaller size, their more advanced age, the existence of other illnesses...or because women receive less than adequate or delayed medical care. Whatever the reasons...the standard practice of basing advice to women on studies of men may be useless, and sometimes even dangerous. (Notelovitz, 7–8)

In early 2000, the Centers for Disease Control and Prevention and West Virginia University released a study of death rates among women with heart disease by race and ethnic origin and also by region. Researchers found that "social and economic factors, including the style of living," contributed to the highest death rates, which were in the states of New York, Mississippi, and West Virginia. The lowest death rates "were in the Pacific Northwest, the Rocky Mountain region of Colorado and New Mexico and in parts of Wisconsin and North and South Dakota." (Noble)

Another leading cardiovascular cause of disability and death among women is stroke, a disruption of the blood supply to the brain. A stroke can occur when a blood clot blocks the flow of blood to the brain or when an artery in the brain bursts. Although women are less likely than men to suffer a stroke, black women are more at risk than white women. The death rate from stroke in 1996 was 59 per 100,000 population for whites compared to 78.9 for blacks, according to the AHA.

While no outright cures for cardiovascular diseases exist, they can be prevented; organizations such as the AHA and the National Heart, Lung and Blood Institute have a wealth of materials on prevention measures to ward off heart disease and stroke. The AHA, medical groups, and federal agencies publish numerous fact sheets, including statistical data, to alert women about the risks of cardiovascular diseases. Campaigns to help prevent heart disease are also common, such as efforts to encourage women to exercise. According to a 1999 survey of women who are part of the long-term Nurses' Health Study at Brigham and Women's Hospital in Boston, women who walked briskly or exercised vigorously reduced their risk of heart disease by between 30 and 50 percent. *See also* African-American Women's Health; Smoking

Further Reading

American Heart Association. "Women and Cardio-vascular Diseases." Biostatistical Fact Sheet <http://www.amhrt.org/statistics/biostats/biowo.htm>. (1999).

Benderly, Beryl Lieff for the Institute of Medicine. *In Her Own Right: The Institute of Medicine's Guide to Women's Health Issues*. Washington, DC: National Academy Press, 1997.

Editors of the Johns Hopkins Medical Letter, Health After 50. *The Johns Hopkins Medical Handbook: The 100 Major Medical Disorders of People over the Age of 50*. New York: Rebus, 1992.

"Facts about Heart Disease and Women: Are You at Risk?" <http://www.nhlbi.nih.gov/health/public/heart/other/wmn_risk.htm> NIH Publication No. 98-3654.

Noble, Holcomb B. "New York Is Ranked High for Deadly Heart Attacks" *New York Times* (February 16, 2000).

Notelovitz, Morris, M.D., and Diana Tonnessen. *The Essential Heart Book for Women*. New York: St. Martin's Griffin, 1996.

Planned Parenthood Federation of America. *The Planned Parenthood Women's Health Encyclopedia*. New York: Crown Trade Paperbacks, 1996.

Caregiving

See Family Caregiving

Carpal Tunnel Syndrome

Women are the primary victims of carpal tunnel syndrome (CTS), a painful and disabling injury to the wrist, hand, and arm usually due to repetitive tasks on the job. But some employers hesitate or refuse to recognize CTS and accuse female employees of faking the injury in order to avoid work. CTS leads to lost work time, creating economic problems for employees as well as employers.

The carpal tunnel is formed by the eight bones in the wrist, called carpals. The structure is filled with flexor tendons which control finger movement, and also provides a pathway for the median nerve to reach sensory cells in the hand. Repetitive flexing and extension of the wrist may cause a thickening of the protective sheaths which surround each of the tendons. The swollen tendon sheaths apply increased pressure on the median nerve and produce CTS. Women are prone to carpal tunnel syndrome because they have smaller, square-shaped wrists and thus have a narrower carpal tunnel passage, which predisposes them to developing injuries. In addition women have traditionally been employed in jobs that require repetitive motion—secretaries, computer operators, cashiers, assembly-line workers, sewing machine operators, and meat packers. One report by the National Institute of Occupational Safety and Health revealed that more than half of all cashiers in food markets, who are predominately female, suffer to some degree from CTS and other repetitive stress injuries as a result of scanning products at high speed.

The Union of Needle and Industrial Textile Employees (UNITE), whose membership is 75 percent women, reports that nearly one-fourth of its members suffer from CTS and similar injuries. An unknown number of women who are not UNITE members but work in the sweatshops of the textile and garment industries also suffer from CTS.

Some poultry processing workers, who seldom earn enough in wages to meet the government-defined poverty line, have been forced out of jobs because they have complained about or been diagnosed with CTS. In 1999, the nonprofit organization Public Justice Center (PJC) published a study, funded by the United Food and Commercial Workers International Union, which found that

> repetitive motions and speed of the production line in poultry processing has led to high incidences of occupational injuries and illnesses. Many poultry workers have had to undergo corrective surgery or live with daily pain and suffering, unable to perform simple tasks such as raising their hands over their heads or lifting their own children. The latest statistics from the Bureau of Labor Statistics indicate that the poultry industry recorded the fifth highest rate of cumulative trauma disorders—535 per 10,000 workers (the average rate for the private sector was 33.5 cases per 10,000 workers).

The study also includes work-related problems described by poultry workers, the majority of whom are women. According to PJC,

> The primary issues identified in the study were work-related health risks, the inability of the workers to use the bathroom as needed, and the general treatment of all workers as a "disposable workforce." The report will be used as an advocacy tool and as a springboard for future litigation.

In Spring 2000, public hearings began on ergonomic rules for the workplace proposed by the U.S. Occupational Safety and Health Administration (OSHA). The rules "would require about 1.9 million work sites to adopt ergonomics programs that include employee training, analysis of job hazards, and medical management of injuries. All manufacturing jobs would be covered, along with those that involve manual handling or lifting—from auto assembly to zoo maintenance. Also included would be workplaces that are not covered but report injuries." (Spake)

Many female employees are unaware that they are eligible for workers' compensation (insurance benefits) if they are forced to take time off from the job because of the disability. An emerging issue is whether the increasing number of telecommuters (employees who work in their home offices for a company) are covered by an employer's insurance for carpal tunnel syndrome and other injuries due to work-related repetitive tasks at the computer.

Information on CTS is posted on numerous Internet Web sites, but many of these sites are sponsored by companies selling products to ease the pain of CTS. Several sites are strictly informative and include WebMd.com, healthpages.com, and CDC.gov/niosh/. *See also* Occupational Safety and Health Administration; Sweatshops; *Women: Work and Health*

Further Reading

Centers for Disease Control and Prevention, National Institute of Occupational Safety and Health. "Carpal Tunnel Syndrome." Fact Sheet (June 1997).

Public Justice Center. *Disposable Workforce: A Worker's Perspective: A Documentation Study Conducted by the Public Justice Center of Working Conditions in Delmarva Poultry Processing Plants.* (January 1998).

Spake, Amanda. "A Pain in the Neck, and Then Some." *U.S. News & World Report* (March 20, 2000).

Unsworth, Edwin. "Telecommuting Brings Ergonomics Risks." *Business Insurance* (May 11, 1998).

Center for Reproductive Law and Policy

The Center for Reproductive Law and Policy (CRLP) promotes women's reproductive rights through litigation, policy analysis, legal research, and public education. CRLP's programs attempt to achieve women's equality in society and ensure that all women in the United States and internationally have access to appropriate and freely chosen reproductive health services.

The organization has litigated for numerous reproductive health issues, particularly those that violate *Roe v. Wade*, the 1973 U.S. Supreme Court case that struck down state laws severely restricting abortion. One of CRLP's most recent causes has been its petition to the High Court to overturn state bans on so-called partial-birth abortion, a nonmedical term used by antiabortionists to describe a late-term abortion procedure. The procedure is used primarily to protect the life of the pregnant woman. In 2000, the High Court struck down Nebraska's ban on "partial-birth abortion." Before the Court's decision, CRLP noted:

"Partial-birth abortion" laws—whether on the federal or state levels—are designed to overturn *Roe v. Wade*. On September 24, 1999, in the first ruling by a Federal appellate court, the U.S. Court of Appeals for the Eighth Circuit found in three separate but unanimous decisions that "partial-birth abortion" laws passed in Arkansas, Iowa, and Nebraska are unconstitutional.

The Eighth Circuit Court ruling declares that these laws...place an undue burden on a woman's right to choose and describe a procedure that is not recognized in medical journals... "Partial-birth abortion" bans—pending in Congress and blocked or limited in 20 states—encompass virtually all abortions. These laws don't merely target one procedure; they potentially restrict the safest and most commonly used abortion methods....

"Partial-birth abortion" bans are extreme measures that make no exceptions for serious harm to a woman's health. These bans criminalize most abortion procedures. The American College of Obstetricians and Gynecologists, representing over 90 percent of all ob-gyn specialists, rejects this law as "inappropriate, ill advised and dangerous."

Other issues of concern to the CRLP are congressional efforts to pass federal legislation that would treat the "unborn child" as a separate and distinct victim of crime, and if passed would, for the first time, consider a fetus—and even a fertilized egg—an independent victim for purposes of federal law. Such legislation, if enacted, would also consider the fetus a "person" with the same legal protections as a pregnant woman; thus a woman would be unable to obtain an abortion without violating the rights of the fetus. *See also* Abortion; American College of Obstetricians and Gynecologists; *Roe v. Wade*

Further Reading
Center for Reproductive Law and Policy. " 'Partial-Birth Abortion' Bans Unconstitutional, Deceptive, Extreme." <http://www.crlp.org/decetpextreme.html>.

Cervical Cancer

Cervical cancer, or cancer of the cervix, affects the narrow portion of the uterus that opens into a woman's vagina. Cervical cancer is a preventable disease, but it must be detected before it can be treated. The American Cancer Society (ACS) estimated that, in the year 2000, about 12,800 new cases of invasive cervical cancer would occur, and about 4,600 women would die from this disease. "Cervical cancer used to be one of the most common causes of cancer death for American women," ACS notes. "But between 1955 and 1992 the number of deaths from cervical cancer declined by 74%. The main reason for this change is the use of the Pap test to find cervical cancer early."

The Papanicolaou test, or Pap smear, is a proven screening method for cervical cancer in which a health professional takes a sample of loose cells from the cervix and examines it under a microscope to determine if abnormal cells are present. The Pap test can detect precancerous changes in the cervix, which allows for early treatment and prevention of nearly all deaths from cervical cancer, according to the National Centers for Disease Control and Prevention (CDC).

In early 2000, two studies published in the *Journal of the American Medical Association* showed that a newer test may be more effective than the Pap smear. A woman can perform the new procedure herself, using a cotton swab to collect a sample of vaginal cells. The sample is then sent to a laboratory for analysis. "The findings are unlikely to lead to immediate changes in medical practice in the United States, the researchers said, but the newer test might eventually replace the Pap test for older women or be used along with it to increase the accuracy of detection." (Grady)

Cervical cancer screening is more common than breast cancer screening (with mammograms). More than 80 percent of women ages 18 years or older have regular Pap smears, but rates of recent Pap screening among women ages 60 and older are substantially lower than for younger women. Rates of screening are also lower among some economically disadvantaged groups, uninsured women, and members of some racial and ethnic minority groups, the CDC reports. The lower rates of screening are frequently attributed to lack of a regular medical provider, lack of health insurance, and lack of information about the importance of early cancer detection. Health-care advocates nationwide urge that programs be established to educate women, particularly those who do not get regular examinations by a health-care provider, about screening tests for the disease.

Because early detection of breast and cervical cancer is important in lowering the risk of death from these diseases, the U.S. Congress passed the Breast and Cervical Cancer Mortality Prevention Act in 1990. This legislation authorized the CDC to establish the National Breast and Cervical Cancer Early Detection Program. As part of the program, the CDC publicizes factors that increase the risk of cervical cancer. These include first intercourse at an early age; multiple sex partners; smoking; and genital infection with human papilloma virus (HPV). HPVs are sexually transmitted diseases, viruses that can cause wart-like growths on the genitals. The National Cancer Institute notes "Scientists have identified more than 70 types of HPV; 30 types infect the cervix, and about 15 types are associated with cervical cancer." HPV is a major risk factor for cervical cancer. In fact, nearly all cervical cancers show evidence of HPV. However, not all cases of HPV develop into cervical cancer.

The prevalence of HPV is a health issue for adolescent girls, because the virus is found in 15 to 38 percent of sexually active adolescent girls, increasing their risk of cervical cancer. Daughters of mothers who were given the drug diethylstilbestrol (DES) to prevent miscarriage and other reproductive problems also are at increased risk. DES was commonly prescribed for this purpose from about 1940 to 1970, but the practice has since been discontinued. *See also* Adolescent Girls' Health; Breast Cancer; Diethylstilbestrol; Mammogram; Sexually Transmitted Diseases

Further Reading

American Cancer Society. The Cervical Cancer Resource Center. "Cervical Cancer Overview" (March 16, 2000). <http://www.CDC.gov/od/owh/whbc.htm>.

Centers for Disease Control and Prevention, Office of Women's Health, "Breast and Cervical Cancer." <http://www.CDC.gov/od/owh/whbc.htm>.

Grady, Denise. "New Test for Cancer Surpasses the Pap One, Studies Show." *New York Times* (January 5, 2000).

Healy, Bernadine. *A New Prescription for Women's Health*. New York: Viking, 1995.

Hoffman, Eileen, M.D. *Our Health, Our Lives: A Revolutionary Approach to Total Health Care for Women*. New York: Simon & Schuster, 1995.

National Cancer Institute. "Questions and Answers about the Pap Test." Fact Sheet (1997).

National Cancer Institute. "What You Need to Know about Cancer of the Cervix." Booklet (1998).

Cesarean Section

Cesarean section, often referred to as c-section, is the delivery of a baby by surgical means—through an incision in the abdomen. A c-section may be necessary or urgent when certain problems arise before or during labor, such as fetal distress, the baby being too large for the birth canal, a breech baby, complication that results from the hemorrhage and accumulation of blood between the placenta and the wall of the uterus, active genital herpes, HIV infection, and excessive scarring from previous surgeries. However, the number of cesarean sections in the United States has increased dramatically since the 1970s from a little more than 5 percent of all births each year to between 21 and 25 percent of the four million babies born annually, raising questions about the necessity of the surgery.

Numerous factors contribute to the high c-section rate. Obstetricians and gynecologists may advise cesarean birth because they fear litigation if complications arise during vaginal delivery. Convenience is another factor; a c-section can be scheduled and performed more quickly than a difficult labor and a vaginal delivery. Women who have had difficult deliveries may request cesareans to avoid previous problems.

Cesarean section has been performed since ancient times, when they were performed primarily on pregnant women who died. The term is commonly believed to be derived from Julius Caesar's decree that an operation should be performed on a dying or dead pregnant woman to save the life of her child. Over the centuries, there have been reports from many parts of the world that cesarean sections also were successful in saving the lives of both the child and the mother. Successful operations usually took place in remote rural areas, where farmers had knowledge of animal husbandry and some understanding of anatomy.

This meant that cesareans could be undertaken at an earlier stage in failing labor when the mother was not near death and the fetus was less distressed. Under these circumstances the chances of one or both surviving were greater. These operations were performed on kitchen tables and beds, without access to hospital facilities, and this was probably an advantage until the late nineteenth century. Surgery in hospitals was bedeviled by infections passed between patients, often by the unclean hands of medical attendants. (National Library of Medicine)

During the nineteenth century, as western medical practices advanced, anesthetics were developed, allowing surgeons time to operate with more precision and with less agony for the mother. A woman undergoing the surgery was also less likely to suffer shock, a leading cause of death.

With the increase in c-sections over the past few decades in the United States, the cost of surgical delivery has become an issue. Other concerns include the longer recovery time required after a c-section than after a vaginal delivery and the higher risk of maternal death from c-sections compared to vaginal deliveries. Cesarean birth may pose still other types of problems. Some women who undergo the surgery feel they have "failed" in some way and are disappointed or angry. Their partners may share those feelings.

The U.S. Department of Health and Human Services in its *Healthy People 2000* project set a goal of reducing the c-section rate to 15 percent. But some medical practitioners contend that the advantages of vaginal delivery (lower cost and lower morbidity rates) "apply only to safe vaginal deliveries and that reducing the rate of cesarean delivery may lead to higher costs and more complications for mothers and their babies." (Sachs, et al.) Many doctors have long believed that when a woman is having a difficult labor, a cesarean section would be best for the baby. But a recent study in the *New England Journal of Medicine* indicates that, if a woman is already in labor, a baby can be delivered just as safely with the use of forceps or a vacuum tool. *See also* Childbirth Practices

Further Reading

Deutchman, Mark. "Cesarean Section in Family Medicine." Position paper prepared for the American Association of Family Physicians' Commission on Quality and Scope of Practice (1997).

Grady, Denise. "In Birth Study, No Less a Risk in a Cesarean." *New York Times* (December 2, 1999).

National Library of Medicine. "Cesarean Section— A Brief History." <http://www.nlm.nih.gov/exhibition/cesarean_2.html>.

Sachs, Benjamin P., Cindy Kobelin, Mary Ames Castro, and Fredric Frigoletto. "The Risks of Lowering the Cesarean-Delivery Rate." *The New England Journal of Medicine* (January 7, 1999).

Wertz, Sidney M., and Dorothy C. Wertz. *Lying-In: A History of Childbirth in America.* New Haven: Yale University Press, 1989.

Wolfe, Sidney M. *Women's Health Alert.* Reading, MA: Addison-Wesley, 1991.

"The Changing Face of Women's Health"

"The Changing Face of Women's Health" is the title of an exhibit launched in the spring of 1999 at the Maryland Science Center in Baltimore. The $3.4 million exhibit is the first of its kind devoted exclusively to women's health issues, but it appeals to both genders and to age groups ranging from 10 on up. Designed for a five-year tour to 10 major U.S. science centers, the exhibit was initiated by the Women's Health Project of the National Health Sciences Consortium (NHSC), a group of top science institutions across the country. The consortium developed an educational exhibit that includes "public programming and instructional materials with the goal of making science and research related to women accessible and engaging for the public." In addition to the exhibit itself, information about its contents is available on a Women's Health Project Internet site. The Web site also includes teacher materials and instructions for planning student field trips to the exhibit.

Funded by the National Institutes of Health, U.S. Centers for Disease Control and Prevention, Metropolitan Life Foundation, and Pfizer Women's Health, the exhibit

> is based on the concepts that women's health issues are created and shaped by society, biology, and personal behavior; that women have a high level of interest in taking charge of their own health; and that this active approach is changing the way health studies are conducted, the way physicians and patients relate, and the way research is undertaken and interpreted. (*Public Health Reports*)

Going well beyond reproductive issues, the exhibition focuses on women's health from menarche to old age and highlights illnesses that occur more often in women than men. The exhibit is divided into four health areas: risks, prevention, detection, and control. Multimedia displays provide opportunities to learn about such health issues as the effects of smoking on the lungs, how genetics determines various human characteristics, the weakening effect of osteoporosis on bones, and how to do a self-examination for cysts or lumps in the breast.

The exhibit's Resource Center provides information about women's health topics and includes books, videos, and access to the women's health exhibit Web site and other health-related sites on the Internet. Brochures from health organizations are also available. *See also* Online Medicine

Further Reading
Lamberg, Lynne. "Putting a New Face on Women's Health." *The Journal of the American Medical Association.* (April 14, 1999).
Reif, Wanda J. "Women's Health: From Puberty to the Grave." *The Lancet* (May 1, 1999).
"What Is the Women's Health Project?" <http://www.whealth.org>.
"Women's Health Exhibit to Tour US." *Public Health Reports* (May 1999).

Child Sexual Abuse

Millions of American women as well as men are survivors of child sexual abuse, a significant social, moral, and health issue in the United States. The American Medical Association defines child sexual abuse as "any sexual act or sexual contact with a child performed by an adult or an older child. It also includes showing an adult's genitalia to a child, showing the child pornographic pictures or videotapes, or using the child as a model for pornographic purposes." According to data published in 1998 for the Children's Bureau of the U.S. Department of Health and Human Services (DHHS), there were about one million substantiated victims of child abuse or neglect in 1996. Among those cases, 12 percent were sexually abused; 77 percent of the victims were girls. Substance abuse is responsible for one-third of all child abuse and neglect cases, according to the HHS.

Sexually abused children frequently suffer emotional and physical health problems during their adult years and sometimes throughout their lives. For young women, "sexual abuse is a common antecedent of adolescent pregnancy, with up to 66% of pregnant teens reporting histories of abuse.... A history of sexual abuse has been linked to high-risk behaviors" such as abusing alcohol and other drugs and engaging in prostitution. (Elders, 648)

Child sexual abuse occurs among all socioeconomic groups, with studies showing "no significant differences between the prevalence and circumstances of African-American and White women's child sexual abuse." However, research on child sexual abuse among Latina women is scant, according to a 1999 report in the *Hispanic Journal of Behavioral Sciences.* (Romero, 351)

Many health experts believe there is a "conspiracy of silence" regarding child sexual abuse in the United States. Families, child caregivers, and sexually abused children tend to keep this form of maltreatment a secret, and abused children who talk about being molested or raped are frequently not believed. Thus many cases are not reported.

Because of the under-reporting of child sexual abuse, psychiatrists and other adults have conducted various types of interviews, which frequently have included the use of anatomical dolls and leading questions, to try to obtain facts from children thought to have been sexually abused. During the 1980s and early 1990s, such interviews were used to help convict directors of daycare centers in various parts of the country of sexually abusing children. In recent years these convictions have been overturned; debates about the interview methods and the accuracy of children's reports have been ongoing.

Since the 1980s at least "500 studies have been conducted on children's 'suggestibility'—the extent to which suggestions implanted by adult interviewers can influence children's recollections and accounts." Psychologists generally agree that "most children display a tremendous capacity to be accurate; but under certain conditions, if they are pushed and prodded in the wrong ways, children may say false things. And preschoolers of 3 and 4 tend to be more suggestible than older children." (Goldberg)

Even though accusations of child sexual abuse against some adult caregivers are false, there is little doubt that every year tens of thousands of children are sexually abused. Some surveys of women on welfare have shown that more than 40 percent were victims of child sexual abuse. According to a report in the *New York Times*, "many people who interview welfare families at length, from ethnographers to psychological counselors, say they hear stories of childhood sexual abuse with unsettling regularity." (De Parle)

Some organizations and groups working to prevent child sexual abuse include the National Clearinghouse on Child Abuse and Neglect Information in Washington, DC; the Administration of Children and Families of the Department of Health and Human Services; the American Medical Association; Mothers Against Sexual Abuse; and numerous local groups. The U.S. Congress enacted legislation known as the Protection of Children from Sexual Predators Act of 1998, which includes provisions to increase penalties for transportation of minors or assumed minors for illegal sexual activity and related crimes and for child pornography offenses; and death or life in prison for certain offenses whose victims are children. *See also* Teenage Pregnancy and Childbearing

Further Reading

Califano, Joseph A. "The Least among Us." *America* (April 24, 1999).

De Parle, Jason. "Life after Welfare: Early Sex Abuse Common among Welfare's Women." *New York Times* (November 28, 1999).

deYoung, Mary. "Another Look at Moral Panics: The Case of Satanic Day Care Centers." *Deviant Behavior: An Interdisciplinary Journal* (July–September, 1998).

Elders, M. Joycelyn. "Adolescent Pregnancy and Sexual Abuse." *Journal of the American Medical Association* (August 19, 1998).

Goldberg, Carey. "Getting to the Truth in Child Abuse Cases: New Methods." *New York Times* (September 8, 1998).

"Protecting Our Children: Sexual Abuse of Children Is Common, and Too Often Undetected." *The Journal of the American Medical Association* (December 2, 1998).

Rogan, Mary. "Judgment Call." *Chatelaine* (October 1998).

Romero, Gloria J., Gaile E. Wyatt, Tamra Burns Loeb, Jennifer Vargas Carmona, and Beatriz M. Solis. "The Prevalence and Circumstances of Child Sexual Abuse among Latina Women." *Hispanic Journal of Behavioral Sciences* (August 1, 1999).

U.S. Department of Health and Human Services, Children's Bureau. *Child Maltreatment 1996: Reports from the States to the National Child Abuse and Neglect Data System.* Washington, DC: U.S. Government Printing Office, 1998.

Childbirth Practices

Childbirth practices in the United States were fairly routine until the late 1930s. Babies were delivered at home, usually by the local midwife who often received help from female friends, neighbors, and/or relatives of the pregnant woman. Male physicians, however, "gradually gained control of child birth among the upper and middle classes, a control that represented political and economic triumph rather than scientific necessity." Fearing that pregnant women would prefer professionals of their own gender in the medical profession, male doctors "deliberately, systematically excluded women from medical training." (Boston Women's Health Collective, 437)

As male obstetricians and gynecologists increased their influence over and control of women's health, childbirth became so "medicalized" that American women now use more drugs and technological interventions while giving birth than do women in any other part of the world. One example is the high number of cesarean sections performed. A cesarean section is a surgical procedure for giving birth, which can be life-saving for women with serious problems during pregnancy. But, critics say, the procedure is too fre-

Lamaze birthing class. Lawrence Migdale/Photo Researchers, Inc.

quently scheduled for the doctor's convenience.

Throughout the latter part of the twentieth century, women began to rely more and more on doctors and medical technology to bring babies into the world. For decades this trend has been a controversial issue among some women's health-care advocates, who contend that childbirth should not be treated as an illness but rather as a natural, healthy event.

In 1999, the *New York Times* reported on a study conducted by Joy L. Hawkins, director of obstetric anesthesia at the University of Colorado School of Medicine, which

> showed that the number of women in labor who received regional anesthesia—spinal or epidural injections to numb the pelvic region—soared from 1981 to 1997. The surge, documented by a survey of 750 hospitals, was particularly evident in large hospitals, where the percentage of mothers receiving such injections tripled, to 66 percent. Dr. Hawkins attributed the increase to the ability of anesthesiologists to ease labor pain with smaller doses of medicine and fewer side effects than in years past. (Chivers)

Natural childbirth advocates are highly critical of the increasing number of women using anesthesia, primarily because of the possibility that the baby could be "drugged." Advocates also argue that anesthetized women are not as alert as those who practice natural delivery methods, and that "young women who pass up the opportunity to overcome labor pain on their own are missing out on one of life's great transforming experiences." (Grady)

Although 90 percent of pregnant women deliver their babies in hospitals, a minority continue to seek alternative childbearing procedures that reduce or eliminate medical intervention. Women make choices early in their pregnancies about who will assist in delivery—a family physician, women-centered obstetrician, or midwife, for example. A fairly recent innovation is the use of a doula, a childbirth educator who is trained to provide continued support for a woman during labor. Women can also make decisions on where delivery will take place—in a hospital setting, an alternative childbirth center, or at home with or without professional assistance. Nurse-midwives usually attend birthings at home, but most doctors do not advise home delivery

> because they're concerned about unexpected complications, which can include sudden detachment of the placenta, fetal distress (usually caused by lack of oxygen to the fetus during labor), an unexpected multiple pregnancy such as twins, and complications after delivery such as excessive bleeding (postpartum hemorrhage). Home delivery should be considered only by women who have already had at least one uneventful pregnancy and delivery. A doctor or certified nurse midwife, preferably the same person who provided prenatal care, should attend. If possible, a home near a hospital should be used; if a woman's home is too far away, the home of a relative or friend could be considered. A plan for rapid transport from the home to the hospital should be made in case it's needed. (*Merck Manual,* Chapter 248)

During the process of selecting a doctor, a woman can learn what a physician's attitude is regarding the use of drugs and birthing positions other than the hospital position of lying on the back with the feet up in stirrups, which women-centered health-care professionals consider the worst and most dangerous position for labor. Women can also make decisions about what labor and delivery methods will be used.

One method popular in the late 1950s and early 1960s, for example, was developed in the 1930s by Grantley Dick-Read, a British physician who advocated that men join in the birthing process by being in the delivery room to encourage their partners. Following this so-called Dick-Read method, women learn to use breathing and visualization techniques to help them relax and reduce tension and deliver without distress and anesthesia. The Lamaze and Bradley methods use similar techniques and the support of a partner who learns how to encourage and coach a woman during delivery.

As women have taken more active roles in their own childbirth experiences, they have prompted changes in hospital procedures. Today an increasing number of hospitals have birthing centers that are family-oriented. Pregnant women and their partners usually attend childbirth education classes at the centers, and classes cover proper nutrition, exercise, preparation for labor and birth, care for newborns, and breastfeeding. A woman can choose to have an obstetrician or a midwife attend her delivery.

Centers strive for a homelike atmosphere. The birthing center at St. Luke's-Roosevelt Hospital Center in New York City, for example, advertises as a "home away from home" where a woman and her "partner can feel comfortable and secure, knowing that advanced medical care and technology are minutes away, if they are needed." *See also* Breastfeeding; Cesarean Section; Doula; Midwifery; Pregnancy

Further Reading
Berkow, Robert, Editor-in-Chief. *Merck Manual of Medical Information—Home Edition*, Chapter 248. Whitehouse Station, NJ: Merck & Co., 1997. <http://www.merck.com/pubs/mmanual_home>.
Boston Women's Health Book Collective. *The New Our Bodies, Ourselves.* New York: Simon & Schuster, 1992.
Chivers, C.J. "The Great Childbirth Debate: Drug-Assisted, or Natural?" *New York Times* (October 18, 1999).
Grady, Denise. "Something's Often Missing in Childbirth Today: The Pain." *New York Times* (October 13, 1999).
Hoffman, Eileen, M.D. *Our Health, Our Lives: A Revolutionary Approach to Total Health Care for Women.* New York: Simon & Schuster, 1995.
Planned Parenthood Federation of America. *The Planned Parenthood Women's Health Encyclopedia.* New York: Crown Trade Paperbacks, 1996.
Treichler, Paula, "Feminism, Medicine, and the Meaning of Childbirth." In *Body/Politics: Women and the Discourses of Science.* Mary Jacobus, Evelyn Fox Keller, and Sally Shuttleworth, Eds. New York: Routledge, 1990.

Child-Free

Child-free is a term used to describe women who choose to be childless, as opposed to those who have infertility problems. Child-free women may be able to conceive but make the choice not to have children. That choice, however, often results in social censure.

Child-free women are frequently accused of hating children or being selfish, emotionally cold, or irresponsible. In some cases, they incur emotional and physical health problems brought on by relatives, friends, coworkers, and others who object to their decision to remain childless and frequently equate reproduction with fulfilling adult responsibilities. It is common for relatives (particularly parents) to try to pressure childless married women to produce children.

In the workplace, childless women (as well as men) are frequently asked to take over tasks of workers with children who must be absent or leave the job early because of family concerns. This sometimes makes child-free workers feel exploited. Many employers do not offer equal health-care coverage or deduct premiums equal to that of workers with children.

In spite of the stress sometimes caused by the social stigma of being child-free, an increasing number of women are refusing to be manipulated into pregnancy and are determining for themselves if or when they will procreate. During the 20 year period from 1976 to 1996, the number of childless women doubled. Some decide not to have children because their choice allows them greater freedom and more opportunities to pursue career choices. In some cases, couples choose to be child-free because they believe they benefit by having the time and energy to devote to their relationship. *See also* Infertility; Pregnancy

Further Reading

Casey, Terri. *Pride and Joy: The Lives and Passions of Women Without Children.* Hillsboro, OR: Beyond Words, 1998.

Heaton, Tim B., Cardell K. Jacobson, and Kimberlee Holland. "Persistence and Change in Decisions to Remain Childless." *Journal of Marriage and the Family* (May 1999).

Ireland, Mardy S. *Reconceiving Women: Separating Motherhood from Female Identity.* New York: Guilford Publications, 1993.

Kling, Cynthia. "Childless by Choice." *Harper's Bazaar* (June 1996).

Lisle, Laurie. *Without Child: Challenging the Stigma of Childlessness.* New York: Ballantine, 1995.

Murray, Kathleen. "The Childless Feel Left Out When Parents Get a Lift." *New York Times* (December 1, 1996).

Chronic Fatigue Syndrome

A debilitating condition, Chronic Fatigue Syndrome, or CFS, is characterized by unexplained and profound exhaustion that lasts six months or more, interferes with daily activities, and includes a set of symptoms (a syndrome), usually muscle and joint pains and inability to concentrate. CFS is diagnosed in two to four times as many American women as men, "which may be the result of biological, psychological, and social influences," states the National Institute of Allergy and Infectious Diseases (NIAID), a component of the National Institutes of Health.

Debates over the definition of CFS have been ongoing since the disease was first named in 1988 by Stephen Straus, M.D., head of the Laboratory of Clinical Investigation at the NIAID. During the 1990s researchers conducted numerous studies in attempts to identify causes of CFS and its multiple symptoms, which often mimic the flu or accompany diseases such as Alzheimer's disease and multiple sclerosis. CFS as an illness has been difficult to diagnose, and some health-care professionals dismiss it as a psychological problem. Thus, many women are reluctant to talk to their physicians about CFS because they fear their chronic ailments will not be taken seriously or will be misdiagnosed.

In 1993, the U.S. Centers for Disease Control and Prevention (CDC) called a conference of researchers and clinicians treating CFS and developed a criterion for identifying the illness. A case definition and guidelines for the evaluation and study of CFS were published in December 1994. According to the guidelines, every patient should have a clinical evaluation that includes a medical history, physical examination, mental status examination, and laboratory tests to determine that the patient's fatigue is not the result of other illnesses or exertion unrelieved by rest and sleep.

The guidelines also state that four or more of the following symptoms must be present to diagnose CFS: substantial impairment in short-term memory or concentration; sore throat; tender lymph nodes; muscle pain; multi-joint pain without swelling or redness; headaches of a new type, pattern, or severity; unrefreshing sleep; and post-exertional malaise lasting more than 24 hours. These symptoms must have persisted or recurred during six or more consecutive months of illness and must not have predated the fatigue.

Although researchers have found no specific proven treatment for CFS, health-care providers may prescribe anti-viral, anti-depressant, or anti-inflammatory drugs; they may also try to help patients manage the illness by learning to pace themselves in order to avoid physical, emotional, and mental stress, which can intensify symptoms.

Support groups may also be helpful, and some maintain Internet Web sites that provide information on CFS and offer coping strategies. The NIAID and the CDC also provide copious information and recent research findings on CFS. *The Journal of Chronic Fatigue Syndrome: Multidisciplinary Innovations in Research, Theory & Clinical Practice* publishes ongoing debates and discussions on issues related to CFS as well as multidisciplinary original research and CFS case reports. *See also* Alzheimer's Disease

Further Reading
National Institute of Allergy and Infectious Diseases, National Institutes of Health. "Chronic Fatigue Syndrome." Fact Sheet (1995).
National Institute of Allergy and Infectious Diseases, National Institutes of Health. "Overview of the NIAID Chronic Fatigue Syndrome Research Program." Fact Sheet (1999).
Planned Parenthood Federation of America. *The Planned Parenthood Women's Health Encyclopedia.* New York: Crown Trade Paperbacks, 1996.

Clinical Studies

See **Gender-Biased Research and Treatment**

The Commonwealth Fund's Commission on Women's Health

In 1993, The Commonwealth Fund (TCF), based in New York City, established a $4 million, three-year program to address serious and neglected problems in women's health. To guide the program, the Fund formed a Commission on Women's Health, charged with increasing public awareness of women's health issues and identifying opportunities for improving their health and quality of life.

TCF, founded in 1918, currently conducts national health programs that emphasize prevention and promotion of health-promoting behavior. TCF's Commission on Women's Health was a response to the recognition in the early 1990s that numerous health issues are unique to women and that differences exist in health and health-care experiences between women and men. According to TCF, "The emphasis on women's health stems from a concern that it has been an important social issue often hidden by popular misconceptions, research neglect, or women's own silence."

The Commission began its work with a national survey on women's health, which provided baseline data and information about significant health concerns. A follow-up survey in 1998, *The Commonwealth Fund 1998 Survey of Women's Health*, found that, among the 2,800 women interviewed, a "mixed story" about their health emerged, and that "significant gaps remain in access to essential care. Violence persists as a significant factor in the lives of women—lifetime rates of violent or abusive events are disturbingly high." In addition the survey found that more women were uninsured in 1998 than in 1993, even though the economy had improved. Lack of insurance creates barriers to health care.

Other findings from the 1998 survey show that preventive care measures such as screening for breast and cervical cancer have changed little, with low-income and less-educated women less likely than higher income and more-educated women to receive regular preventive services. Smoking rates among women also remained about the same as in 1993.

The survey indicated a close relationship between economic security and health. "Good health and access to health care often depend on having a good job, while keeping a job depends on staying healthy. Poor health or family caregiving responsibilities can reduce opportunities to work, adding to economic stress. Half of all non-working women with incomes of $16,000 or less have a disability limiting their capacity to work or are caring for a sick or disabled child, spouse, parent, or other family member." *See also* Domestic Violence; Family Caregiving; Health Insurance

Further Reading

Collins, Karen Scott, Cathy Schoen, Susan Joseph, Lisa Duchon, Elisabeth Simantov, and Michele Yellowitz. *Health Concerns across a Woman's Lifespan: The Commonwealth Fund 1998 Survey of Women's Health.* (May 1999) <http://www.cmwf.org/programs/women/ksc_whsurvey99_332.asp>

Complementary and Alternative Medicine

Complementary and alternative medicine (CAM), sometimes called "integrative medicine" or, more commonly, "alternative medicine," is often controversial because it embraces unorthodox or nontraditional philosophies, approaches, and treatments for a great variety of health problems. Since the 1960s, CAM has been increasingly popular, growing rapidly in the 1990s. Complementary medicine usually refers to treatments that are in addition to traditional health care,

while alternative medicine usually suggests treatments used instead of conventional care. The National Institutes of Health (NIH), which maintains a national center to provide information about CAM, defines these health-care practices as those "not taught widely in medical schools, not generally used in hospitals, and not usually reimbursed by medical insurance." NIH further states:

> Many therapies are termed "holistic," which generally means that the health-care practitioner considers the whole person, including physical, mental, emotional, and spiritual aspects. Many therapies are also known as "preventive," which means that the practitioner educates and treats the person to prevent health problems from arising, rather than treating symptoms after problems have occurred. (NIH)

In the United States, approximately one in three adults uses nontraditional treatments for health problems, but women, especially aging women, are the primary consumers of alternative medicine. Women often resort to CAM when suffering from the debilitating effects of autoimmune diseases and life-threatening diseases such as cancer. The industry generates at least $4 billion annually from the sale of vitamin and mineral supplements, soy-protein powders, topical creams and salves made with "natural" ingredients, special foods touted as "nutritional support" (particularly for menopausal women), and herbal solutions for diseases; and from treatments such as acupuncture, chiropractic adjustments, hypnosis, energy healing, and massage. The *New York Times* reported that "patients make more visits each year to alternative care practitioners than to primary care physicians, and most of them pay out of their own pockets for the care they receive." Even alternative medicine advocates express concern about the increasing cost of nontraditional health care. (Brody, 1998)

In 1998, "Americans spent $27.2 billion . . . on providers of alternative health care, including those in chiropractic, traditional Chinese medicine, homeopathy, naturopathy and massage therapy." Sales of herbs also increased "from nearly $2.5 billion in 1995" to $4.4 billion in 1998. (Stolberg)

Until 1994, the federal government categorized vitamin, mineral, and herbal supplements as food additives, and manufacturers had to prove to the Food and Drug Administration (FDA) that their products were safe. But with passage of the Dietary Supplement Health and Education Act of 1994 (DSHEA), "dietary supplements are no longer subject to the premarket safety evaluations required of other new food ingredients or for new uses of old food ingredients. They must, however, meet the requirements of other safety provisions," according to the FDA.

Although the law does not allow manufacturers of dietary supplements to use labels claiming cures, prevention, or treatments of specific diseases (such as a cancer cure), products must contain a list of ingredients and information on nutrition. Nevertheless, most alternative medicine products and treatments have not been scientifically tested for quality, potency, or effectiveness. Unlike prescription drugs, alternative medicines are not strictly regulated. Some manufacturers of alternative medicines use misleading and confusing advertising to tout their products. Hundreds if not thousands of Internet Web sites on health care also may contain misleading or dangerously inaccurate information about CAM treatments for various diseases, according to a *New York Times* report. (Brody, 1999)

Integrative or alternative treatments for diseases are on the rise, because many female patients especially are dissatisfied with conventional health care, which they believe to be ineffective and too expensive. Patients also believe that alternative medicine can be used to augment conventional health care because it emphasizes the whole person rather than focusing entirely on a cure for a disease.

One such complementary treatment is acupuncture, which originated in China more than 2,500 years ago, and makes use of ultrafine needles to stimulate certain points on or under the skin. In some cases experimental methods involve the use of herbs, heat, and/or laser beams at acupuncture points. An independent panel of experts concluded in 1997 that acupuncture is a safe and effective practice that should become part of conventional health care for such conditions as pain and nausea. "Currently more than one million Americans are believed to be relying on acupuncture to treat a wide range of ailments, from headache and bowel disorders to arthritis and stroke." (Brody, 1997)

Although acupuncture may be increasingly accepted in the medical establishment, other CAM practices have long been shunned or denigrated by medical practitioners and academicians as absurd or dangerous quackery. In 1999, during a debate on integrative medicine at the University of Arizona, Arnold S. Relman, professor emeritus at Harvard Medical School and editor emeritus of the *New England Journal of Medicine*, declared that "Integrating alternative medicine with mainstream medicine, as things stand now, would not be an advance but a return to the past . . .. Alternative medicine stands apart from modern science, challenging many of its assumptions and methods and depending for its verification largely on personal belief and subjective experience." ("Teaching Alternative Treatments in Medical School")

Nontraditional, unproven remedies may be touted as cures but can cause great harm. Cancer patients, for example, may delay or refuse conventional treatments that could be of help. Concerns have also been raised about the use of alternative remedies (such as the use of herbs) that could cause harm during pregnancy or adversely affect the use of anesthesia during surgery.

In spite of the many objections to CAM, medical educators and practitioners have realized in recent years that there is widespread popular interest in alternative medicine, and that consumers want valid information on the efficacy and safety of CAM. As a result, say medical experts, the whole field requires serious study and evaluation.

One major source of information is the online database of the NIH's National Center for Complementary and Alternative Medicine. Medical journals such as the *Journal of the American Medical Association* and the *New England Journal of Medicine* are also publishing articles on the topic. In addition, more and more medical schools are adding CAM elective courses and CAM topics that are part of required courses. In the fall of 1999, the University of Minnesota began offering the nation's first graduate-level minor in "complementary healing." The first annual conference and course of study on CAM sponsored by Stanford University School of Medicine and the Center for Alternative Medicine Research and Education (an affiliate of Harvard Medical School) was held in San Francisco. Included in the agenda was the development of scientifically sound research concepts necessary to evaluate CAM, a review of costs of and insurance coverage for CAM therapies, and discussion of legal and regulatory issues pertaining to alternative medicine.

Even as evaluations and research continue, complementary and alternative medicine practices remain controversial, and many health-care experts are dubious about the touted benefits of CAM. *See also*

Aging; Autoimmune Diseases; Online Medicine

Further Reading

Brody, Jane E. "Panel Lauds Acupuncture as Effective Therapy for Some Ailments." *New York Times* (November 6, 1997).

Brody, Jane E. "Alternative Medicine Makes Inroads, but Watch Out for Curves." *New York Times* (April 28, 1998).

Brody, Jane E. "Point-and-Click Medicine: A Hazard to Your Health." *New York Times* (August 11, 1999).

Cassileth, Barrie R. *The Alternative Medicine Handbook: The Complete Reference Guide to Alternative and Complementary Therapies.* New York, W.W. Norton, 1998.

Druss, Benjamin G., and Robert A. Rosenheck. "Association between Use of Unconventional Therapies and Conventional Medical Services." *Journal of the American Medical Association* (August 18, 1999).

"Medicine & Health Perspectives: The Long Winding Road To Integration." *Medicine & Health* (May 24, 1999).

National Institutes of Health, National Center for Complementary and Alternative Medicine. "What Is CAM?" <http://altmed.od.nih.gov/nccam/what-is-cam/faq.shtml>.

Spencer, John W., and Joseph J. Jacobs, eds. *Complementary/Alternative Medicine: An Evidence-Based Approach.* St. Louis, Mosby, 1999.

Stabiner, Karen. "With Alternative Medicine, Profits Are Big, Rules Are Few." *New York Times* (June 21, 1998).

Stolberg, Sheryl Gay. "Folk Cures on Trial, Alternative Care Gains a Foothold." *New York Times* (January 31, 2000).

"Teaching Alternative Treatments in Medical School." *Los Angeles Times* (May 31, 1999).

Wetzel, Miriam S., David M. Eisenberg, and Ted J. Kaptchuk. "Courses Involving Complementary and Alternative Medicine at US Medical Schools." *Journal of the American Medical Association* (September 2, 1998).

"'U' to Teach Alternative Medicine." *Star-Tribune* (June 4, 1999).

U.S. Food and Drug Administration, Center for Food Safety and Applied Nutrition. "Dietary Supplement Health and Education Act of 1994." (December 1, 1995). <http://vm.cfsan.fda.gov/~dms/dietsupp.html>.

Comstock Law

The federal statute known as the Comstock Law, passed in 1873 during a period when censorship in the United States was at its height, criminalized the distribution of obscene material through the U.S. mails, and labeled birth control and abortion information as obscene. In part, it stated

Every obscene, lewd, or lascivious and every filthy book, pamphlet, picture, paper, letter, writing, print, or other publication of an indecent character, and every article or thing designated, adapted or intended for preventing conception or procuring abortion, or for any indecent or immoral use; and every article, instrument, substance, drugs, medicine, or thing which is advertised or described in a manner calculated to lead another to use or apply it for preventing conception or producing abortion, or for any indecent or immoral purpose; and every written or printed card, circular, book, pamphlet, advertisement or notice of any kind giving information, directly, or indirectly, where or how, or by what means any of the hereinbefore mentioned matters, articles or things may be obtained or made, or where or by whom any act or operation of any kind for the procuring or producing of abortion will be done or performed, or how or by what means conception may be prevented or abortion produced, whether sealed or unsealed, and even letter, packet or package or other mail matter containing any filthy, vile or indecent thing, device or substance; and every paper, writing, advertisement or representation that any article, instrument substance, drug, medicine or thing may, or can be used or applied for preventing conception or producing abortion, or for any indecent or immoral purpose; and every description calculated to induce or incite a person to so use or apply any such article, instrument, substance, drug, medicine or thing, is hereby declared to be non-mailable matter and shall not be conveyed in the

mails or delivered from any post office or by any letter carrier. Whosoever shall knowingly deposit or cause to be deposited for mailing or delivery, anything declared by this section to be non-mailable, or shall knowingly take, or cause the same to be taken, from the mails for the purpose of circulating or disposing thereof, or of aiding in the circulation or disposition of the same, shall be fined not more than $5000, or imprisoned not more than five years, or both.

The law was named for its chief lobbyist, Anthony Comstock, a zealous Christian and dry goods salesman. Comstock, who considered himself the moral guardian of the U.S. mails, was also instrumental in persuading most states and many municipalities to pass Comstock-type legislation. In New York, for example, Comstock hounded book dealers, bought their books, and then made citizen's arrests "under New York's obscenity statutes. He managed to persuade the businessmen who bankrolled the YMCA to fund 'The New York Society for the Suppression of Vice.' He gave up his job and pursued his smut-destroying campaign full time." (Weisberger)

The U.S. Post Office Department appointed Comstock a Special Agent to enforce anti-obscenity laws. In that role, he crusaded against birth control advocates such as Margaret and William Sanger, and Mary Ware Dennett, a little-known crusader for birth control. In 1914, Margaret Sanger was arraigned on eight counts of violating the Comstock Law and publishing articles on birth control. Her husband, William, served a jail term for selling a copy of *Family Limitation*, a pamphlet on birth control written by his wife. Mary Ware Dennett was tried and convicted of violating the Comstock Law, a decision that was later reversed.

As a result of the Comstock Law, publishers were forced to delete birth control information from their scientific and physiological materials, including major medical textbooks, and pharmacists were not allowed to provide information about contraception. Few Americans had any access to reliable information about contraceptive methods.

Comstock also attacked artists and writers, accusing them of producing obscene materials and driving some to commit suicide. But when Comstock assailed George Bernard Shaw and his play *Mrs. Warren's Profession*, Shaw fired back. In 1905, Shaw coined the term "Comstockery," which now means strict censorship of materials labeled obscene or in opposition to so-called immoral material.

In a 1914 interview with Comstock, *Harper* magazine reported that up to that time "Comstock had caused to be arraigned in state and federal courts 3,697 persons, of whom 2,740 were either convicted or pleaded guilty. On these were imposed fines to the extent of $237,134.30 and imprisonments to the length of 565 years, 11 months, and 20 days." (Hopkins)

By 1915 Comstock was boasting that he had helped convict enough people to fill a 61-coach passenger train. The Comstock Law, known as the Comstock Act, remains on federal statute books today, although in slightly modified form. In 1971, Congress deleted the prohibition on birth control; but retained the ban on information about abortion. However, First Amendment free speech rights prevent most censorship on abortion information. *See also* Birth Control; Dennett, Mary Ware; Sanger, Margaret

Further Reading

Chen, Constance M. *"The Sex Side of Life"*: *Mary Ware Dennett's Pioneering Battle for Birth Control and Sex Education*. New York: The New Press, 1996.

Hopkins, Mary Alden. "Birth Control and Public Morals: An Interview with Anthony Comstock." *Harper's Weekly* (May 22, 1915).

Weisberger, Bernard A. "Chasing Smut in Every Medium." *American Heritage* (December 1997).

Contraceptives

See **Birth Control**

Cosmetic Surgery

See **Plastic Surgery**

D

Death

See **Life Expectancy**

Dennett, Mary Ware (1872–1947)

Mary Ware Dennett's efforts on behalf of the birth-control movement were an important contribution to women's health. Although not as well known as Margaret Sanger and other activists in the early 1900s who fought to make birth-control information and devices legal in the United States, Dennett was a crusader for the rights to obtain and distribute information about contraception and to provide sex-education for young people. Birth control and sex education materials were banned under the Comstock Law passed in 1873 during a period when censorship in the United States was at its height.

Dennett, not Sanger as is commonly believed, was the first to establish a birth-control organization in the United States (the National Birth Control League) in 1915, according to Constance M. Chen, who wrote the first full-length biography of Dennett. Chen based her book on archival materials, including primary sources, recently donated to Radcliffe's Schlesinger Library.

Born into a middle-class, church-going family in Worcester, Massachusetts, Mary Ware "showed signs of a precocious intellect" from a very early age. (Chen, 16) Her father, George Ware, was a traveling merchant who died when she was 10 years old, forcing her resourceful mother, Vonie, to take in boarders to earn a living.

The Wares later moved to Boston, where they lived near relatives, and Vonie began a business taking young women on European tours. While their mother was away, Mary and her siblings, Willie and Clara, stayed with their two aunts. One of the aunts, Lucia, was a social reformer, and Mary's mentor, guiding and influencing Mary as her social consciousness developed.

Joining the Arts and Crafts movement of the 1890s, Mary Ware, like other advocates, attempted to combine the joy of nature, spirituality, and art, and to create "handiwork that elevated the human spirit." (Chen, 20) Mary studied at the School of Art and Design at the Boston Museum of Fine Arts and went on to a teaching position at the Drexel Institute of Art in Philadelphia, where she was appointed head of the department of design and decoration.

Mary Ware Dennett and her two sons, Devon (left) and Carlton, Dec. 25, 1919. The Schlesinger Library, Radcliffe Institute, Harvard University.

While in Philadelphia, Mary began corresponding with a fellow Arts and Crafts enthusiast in Boston, William Hartley Dennett, a budding architect. The two developed a more serious relationship when Mary Ware took a summer job at Boston's Museum of Fine Arts to work alongside Hartley, as he was called. The couple married in January 1900, and by the end of 1903 had two children, Carleton and another son who died shortly after birth. A third child, Devon, was born in 1905.

Five years later, the family was split when Hartley's romantic involvement with one of his married clients while his wife was recuperating from serious surgery, created a scandal in the community. After bitter divorce proceedings, Mary retained legal custody of the two boys, which was an unusual decision at this time in the na-

tion's history when women had few rights or financial means to raise a family.

To earn a living and to sublimate her feelings of loss because of her failed marriage, Mary Dennett took a salaried position with the Massachusetts Suffrage Association. Her organizing, campaigning, and speaking skills led to a job in 1910 with the National American Woman Suffrage Association in New York City. She enrolled her sons in boarding school and lived frugally in a small apartment near Greenwich Village.

Over the next few years, Mary Dennett was involved with artists, writers, social workers, students, and others who met in the village to discuss the radical ideas of the day, including the philosophy of free love, anarchist views, and birth control. During this time, Dennett met Margaret Sanger and was impressed with the birth-control information that Sanger shared with her.

As the Dennett boys grew older, they began to ask questions about sex and "Mary, as conscientious in her child rearing as she was in her social activism, wanted to do her best to answer them." (Chen, 171) She could communicate best by writing, so in 1915 she produced a straightforward essay, using scientific terminology for the sex organs and illustrating her text with her own drawings. Mary titled the essay "The Sex Side of Life: An Explanation for Young People," and sent a copy of it to her sons. The essay later became a pamphlet that was widely distributed by a variety of groups championing women's health and women's rights.

In 1915 Mary Dennett also became convinced that, along with sex education, information about birth control needed to be legalized. She established the National Birth Control League. Unlike Sanger, who constantly sought publicity regarding birth control and escaped to Europe to avoid a trial under the Comstock Law, Mary

Dennett's efforts were directed toward obtaining for women the legal right to birth-control information.

Throughout 1915, due in part to Dennett's dogged campaigns, the public became more aware of birth-control issues. Over the next few years, however, Dennett's enemies, including Anthony Comstock for whom the Comstock Law was named, did everything in their power to bring about an indictment of Dennett for publishing her sex education pamphlet and sending it through the mail. After many postponements Dennett's case went to trial in 1929. Her conviction on obscenity charges prompted a major public outcry across the United States. A defense fund was formed to pay for an appeal, which Dennett won, and eventually the National Council on Freedom from Censorship was established.

As a result of Dennett's efforts, women gained better access to birth-control information. She continued until the last few years before her death in 1947 to write on the subject and conduct letter-writing campaigns to overturn the Comstock Law. Although the law was not actually repealed, contraceptive devices and information about birth control were finally established as a constitutional right with a U.S. Supreme Court decision (*Griswold v. Connecticut*) in 1965. *See also* Birth Control; Comstock Law; Sanger, Margaret

Further Reading

Chen, Constance M. *"The Sex Side of Life"*: *Mary Ware Dennett's Pioneering Battle for Birth Control and Sex Education.* New York: The New Press, 1996.

Heins, Marjorie. "A Birth-Control Crusader." *Atlantic Monthly* (October 1996).

Depression

Depression—pervasive sadness—has long been considered a woman's issue because twice as many American women as American men are diagnosed as having this mental health problem. Men are as likely as women to become depressed, but they are "less likely to recognize and seek help for depression, and they have different ways of dealing with it." (Lanzillo, 1999)

The term "depression" is frequently misunderstood because it is used so often to describe the occasional "blues" or sadness that most people feel at one time or another. As an illness, however, depression encompasses a wide variety of conditions that may overlap and be diagnosed with a label such as clinical depression (meaning a person requires treatment), bipolar depression, dysthymia, or major depression.

The most common type of depression among women is dysthymia, which usually begins before adulthood and involves long-term, chronic symptoms that are not disabling but that prevent a woman from functioning at full capacity and often create social and economic problems. Major depression is manifest in a variety of symptoms that interfere with a woman's ability to perform daily functions at home or at work or to enjoy once-pleasurable activities. Bipolar disorder (or manic depression) occurs less often, but it is more debilitating and affects social behavior and judgment.

Symptoms of depression vary greatly and may be accompanied by such problems as anxiety, sleep disorders, panic attacks, and eating disorders. People suffering from depression may not only experience pervasive sadness, but also

may feel helpless, hopeless, and irritable. For many victims of depression, these mental and physical feelings seem to follow them night and day, appear to have no end, and are not alleviated by happy events or good news. Some people are so disabled by feelings of despair that they cannot even build up the energy to call a doctor. (Johns Hopkins, 430)

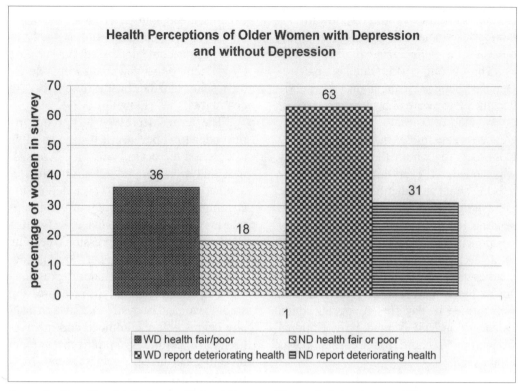

Health Perceptions of Older Women with Depression and without Depression

Legend:
- WD health fair/poor
- ND health fair or poor
- WD report deteriorating health
- ND report deteriorating health

Source for Data: Brandeis University National Center on Women & Aging Survey, 1998.

No one knows for certain the actual cause of depression or why more women than men appear to be afflicted with some form of the illness. The gender difference may be due to the way males are raised. As one male practitioner noted, men are taught "to be in control, independent, strong and rational... [and] trained to see life as a constant battle for what we consider our just rewards—a good job, a nice house and car, a fit body. Our machinelike mentality leaves little room for difficult emotions like confusion or sadness. It's considered unmanly to even admit these feelings, which we believe will slow us down or, even worse, break us down." (Lanzillo 1999)

Genetics—a history of depression or other forms of mental illness in the family—may be a factor in depression. There may be a chemical imbalance in the brain—a deficiency of serotonin or norepi-

nephrine, which are neurotransmitters that allow brain cells to transmit messages. Among women, another cause could be related to hormonal changes, particularly those that occur during life-cycle changes from puberty to menopause. Various diseases, alcohol and other drug abuse, and certain cultural issues may be factors in the high incidence of depression among women.

Some experts contend that women are more prone to depression because of such factors as marital problems, a history of sexual abuse, poverty, and reactions to stressful situations that have particular impact on women throughout their lives. The authors of *The Harvard Guide to Women's Health* explain that some feminist psychologists contend women have a tendency to interpret the world in terms of personal relationships, whereas men rely more on abstract laws and rules. From an early age women generally seek to cultivate and maintain their connections with others, but their lifelong quest for intimacy is viewed as a weakness in a culture that values self-sufficiency and independence. The discrepancy between the behavior of most women and the values of the culture leads to a loss of self-esteem, a feeling of "just not being good enough." Moreover, because of a power imbalance between the sexes, this argument goes,

it is hard for a woman to establish and maintain connections with others while preserving her inner or "true" self.... Depression may occur because women feel they cannot be themselves in their relationships and must conform to someone else's idea of what a good woman, partner, or mother should be. Even when they accept the standard, many women become depressed when they discover that they are simply unable to live up to it. Throughout the life span, according to this theory, the priority that women give to maintaining personal connections can lead to stresses that precipitate depression. (*Harvard Guide* CD-ROM)

While menopause does not increase the risk of depression, women who have had depression previously may develop symptoms at this time. Among older women, depression is a common problem, but it frequently is not recognized or is misdiagnosed. In 1998, Brandeis University's National Center on Women & Aging (NCWA) reported that researchers interviewed more than 700 women between the ages of 45 and 75, and found that only 41 percent of doctors asked their female patients about their emotional or psychological concerns, even though two out of five of these patients had suffered from depression.

Yet, 93 percent of all women surveyed said they would be comfortable discussing emotional problems such as depres-

sion with a doctor, leading the researchers to wonder why these difficulties are not being addressed by health care providers. Even more alarming is the fact that even women who have suffered clinical depression are not asked about their mental health by their providers. Two out of five such women reported that their doctors had not raised these questions. The survey showed that women who reported being diagnosed with clinical depression are more likely to say they have little or no control over their own health. (NCWA press release)

Educating health-care providers and the general public about issues surrounding depression is one of the efforts of the NCWA and is the focus of NMHA. Such organizations as the National Institute of Mental Health, the National Alliance for the Mentally Ill, the National Depressive and Manic Depressive Association, and the National Foundation for Depressive Illness also inform the public about symptoms and treatment of depression and other forms of mental illness. *See also* Alzheimer's Disease; Homeless Women; Mental Illness; National Center on Women and Aging

Further Reading
Carlson, Karen J, Stephanie A. Eisenstat, and Terra Ziporyn. *The Harvard Guide to Women's Health* (also The Harvard Guide to Women's Health-CD-ROM). Cambridge, MA: Harvard University Press, 1996.

Editors of the *Johns Hopkins Medical Letter, Health After 50. The Johns Hopkins Medical Handbook: The 100 Major Medical Disorders of People over the Age of 50.* New York: Rebus,1992.

Lanzillo, Anthony. "Men and Depression: It's Not Just a Woman's Problem." *WebMed* (1999). <http://my.webmd.com/content/article/1685.50047>.

National Center on Women and Aging, "National Study Shows Doctors Neglecting Emotional Health of Older Women." Press Release (October 8, 1998).

Sargent, Marilyn for the National Institute of Mental Health, National Institutes of Health. "Plain Talk about Depression." Pamphlet (1994).

DES

See **Diethylstilbestrol**

Diethylstilbestrol

Between 1941 and 1971, up to six million American women used a potent synthetic hormone called diethylstilbestrol, or DES, as a contraceptive and for reproductive and menopausal problems. Administered in pill or suppository forms or by injection, DES was considered a "wonder drug" that scientists theorized acted in the same biological manner as natural estrogens. By 1971, however, children of DES users were facing serious health problems, creating guilt feelings among some mothers and raising numerous questions and debates regarding DES use.

More than two million American women whose mothers took DES may be at risk for problems of the reproductive, cardiovascular, and immune systems. Some have been diagnosed with a rare type of vaginal or cervical cancer linked to DES exposure. Before the 1970s, the cancer, called clear-cell adenocarcinoma, had never been seen in women between the ages of 15 and 22 and had been described only rarely in medical literature. In 1991, it was estimated that one out of every 1,000 DES daughters would develop clear-cell cancer, although the number of cases began to decline after DES use was curtailed in the 1970s. Some DES daughters also suffer such adverse effects as difficult pregnancies and premature delivery. Nevertheless, an estimated 80 percent of DES daughters have few or no problems with their pregnancies.

About the same number of DES sons as daughters have reported health problems that range from reduced fertility to testicular cancer. Yet, little research has been done in recent decades on the links between the drug and serious disease or abnormalities. As a result, organizations such as DES Action, which has East and West Coast offices, and the DES Cancer Network are set up to educate at-risk persons and some uninformed medical practitioners about the special problems and medical findings regarding DES. *See also* Cervical Cancer; Hormone Replacement Therapy; Menopause

Further Reading

Boston Women's Health Book Collective. *The New Our Bodies, Ourselves.* New York: Simon & Schuster, 1992.
"DES: The Controversy about Hormone Replacement." *The DES Action Voice* (Spring 1994).
Planned Parenthood Federation of America. *The Planned Parenthood Women's Health Encyclopedia.* New York: Crown Trade Paperbacks, 1996.

Dieting and Diet Drugs

Dieting and taking diet drugs to lose weight are so common in the United States, particularly among teenage girls and women, that numerous health experts have called this phenomenon a national obsession. This dieting obsession stems in part from health considerations and also from countless media images that emphasize thinness as a physical ideal necessary for economic success and social acceptance. Although some women's activists and health practitioners are challenging the cultural stereotype of what beauty should be, at any given time at least half of American women are dieting to lose weight; an estimated 90 percent of high school junior and senior girls regularly diet.

In spite of the high incidence of dieting since the 1960s, health experts have contended for decades that 95 percent of those who lose weight gain it back and usually more within five years. Yet two researchers conducting an ongoing project known as the National Weight Control Registry, which they began in 1995, have found that about 50 percent of the long-term dieters

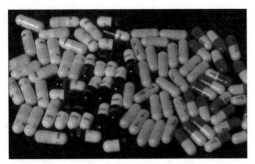

Diet pills. ©The Terry Wild Studio, Inc.

they have surveyed have been able to maintain their weight loss of at least 30 pounds for 12 months or more. According to Professor Rena King at Brown University School of Medicine, she and James Hill of the University of Colorado, with little effort, "identified 2,500 people who have succeeded" in their weight loss programs. (in Fritsch)

Obesity experts point out that millions of Americans are overweight primarily because they eat too much and do not exercise enough. According to Mayo Clinic, "36 percent of American women and 33 percent of American men are overweight," which helps fuel weight-loss dieting programs and the use of diet drugs. While extremely obese people may need diet drugs to help them shed pounds and improve their health, diet drugs are not risk-free. The widely popular appetite suppressants fenfluramine and dexfenfluramine (known as fen-phen), for example, were banned in 1997 because of the risk of heart-valve damage.

New drugs are on the market, however, such as Meridia, an appetite suppressant, and orlistat, a pill that blocks fat absorption and is marketed under the brand name Xenical. The use of orlistat concerns many health specialists, who argue that the drug can easily be abused. Even though Xenical is a prescription drug, a company known as Direct Response Marketing is selling the drug "over the Internet to just about any-body who electronically fills out a medical questionnaire that is reviewed by a company doctor who then 'prescribes' the drug," the *New York Times* reported.

Although new weight-loss drugs appear to have no adverse side effects, neither are they quick fixes. The drugs work in combination with low-calorie diets and exercise. Some health-care practitioners warn that diet drugs may be combined with other medications, causing adverse reactions. In addition people with eating disorders may obtain the diet drugs, intensifying their problems. *See also* Eating Disorders; Obesity; Weight Discrimination

Further Reading

Canedy, Dana. "Regulators Worry over Easy Access to New Diet Drug." *New York Times* (May 11, 1999).

Fritsch, Jane. "95% Regain Lost Weight. Or Do They?" *New York Times* (May 25, 1999).

Hoffman, Eileen, M.D. *Our Health, Our Lives: A Revolutionary Approach to Total Health Care for Women.* New York: Simon & Schuster, 1995.

Horiuchi, Vince. "Eating Disorders Not Going Away." *Salt Lake Tribune* (April 2, 1998).

"Weight Control: What Works and Why" (Medical Essay). *Supplement to Mayo Clinic Health Letter.* Rochester, MN: Mayo Foundation for Medical Education and Research, 1997.

Domestic Elder Abuse or Mistreatment

Domestic elder abuse or mistreatment is a form of domestic violence that has been increasingly recognized and identified since the 1980s. Although often hidden, domestic elder abuse includes physical assaults, verbal insults or threats, financial exploitation, and neglect of persons ages 60 and over living in their own homes or other non-institutional settings. Their abusers are predominantly family members—adult children, spouses, or other relatives or close companions. Male abusers outnumber women by nearly two to one.

Elderly women are mistreated at a higher rate than men, even after factoring in the larger proportion of females in the older population. The oldest of the elderly, those ages 85 and above (primarily women), are the most vulnerable. The number of abuse cases is expected to increase as the older population grows to an expected 39.4 million by 2010, an increase of 17 percent from the 35.5 million elderly in 1995, according to the U.S. Census Bureau. The group over age 85 will more than double by 2010 and will continue to expand in future decades. Thus the potential for elder abuse in domestic settings is an issue that will confront health-care professionals, social service agencies, law enforcement, and government well into the future.

While severe cases of elder abuse have been exposed in the news media, mistreatment of the elderly often goes undetected, especially when victims are afraid or ashamed to share information about their condition. To more accurately determine the incidence of domestic elder abuse, the U.S. Congress in 1992 mandated a study of the problem nationwide. As a result, the National Center on Elder Abuse (NCEA) conducted the National Elder Abuse Incidence Study (NEAIS), which was published in 1998. The NEAIS concluded that approximately 450,000 elderly Americans suffered domestic abuse in 1996; when the elderly who experienced self-neglect were counted, the estimate increased to 551,000. The study did not cover elderly abuse in nursing homes, group homes, or other institutional facilities.

Since the 1980s when domestic elder abuse was identified as a significant social problem in the United States, NCEA and an increasing number of Adult Protective Services (APS) agencies across the United States plus community programs assisting the elderly have become more aware of maltreatment. Some states have passed laws mandating that health-care professionals and social workers report suspected cases of domestic elder abuse to county departments of social services, an Area Agency on Aging, or APS. These agencies then investigate elderly abuse. In states that do not have reporting statutes, laws provide immunity from prosecution for persons who infringe on confidentiality to report situations in which elderly people are endangered. In addition, various local and state coalitions as well as the National Center for Prevention of Elder Abuse conduct conferences on domestic elder abuse and help raise funds to create shelters for abused elderly. Many groups and agencies also maintain Web sites to disseminate information about prevention measures, services for abused elderly, and lists of toll-free, elder-abuse hotlines. *See also* Domestic Violence

Further Reading

National Center on Elder Abuse. *The National Elder Abuse Incidence Study.* Washington, DC: U.S. Department of Health and Human Services, the Administration on Aging, September 1998.

Rogers, Albert R., ed. *Battered Women and Their Families.* New York: Springer Publishing Company, 1998.

Domestic Violence

Violence committed by men against women (and sometimes by women against men) with whom they are intimate and by homosexuals (male and female) against their partners is known as domestic violence. Depending on when and how surveys have been made, an estimated 4 to 8 million women each year are victims of physical domestic violence—punching, kicking, choking, beating, or battering. Millions more women are abused verbally or emotionally, which is often the forerunner of repeated battering. At least 95 percent of all domestic violence is committed by men and the abusive behavior occurs among all age, ethnic, racial, religious, and socioeconomic groups, most often within the nuclear family.

Domestic Violence—A National Problem

- In 1996, approximately 840,000 women were victimized by violence perpetrated by an intimate. [U.S. Bureau of Justice Statistics, 1998]
- About 30% of female murder victims are killed by current or former partners. [U.S. Bureau of Justice Statistics, 1998]
- Companies lose 1,751,100 days a year due to violence in the workplace—10% of that absenteeism, or 175,000 days is due to domestic violence. [Workplace Violence—U.S. Department of Justice, 1994]
- From 1987 to 1992, workers were the victims of nearly a million crimes a year, on average, at a variety of public and private workplaces. And when the victim was a woman, she was much more likely than a man to know the attacker. [U.S. Justice Department, 3/10/96]

Source: White House Press Release, 1998.

Domestic violence is a major public health problem that is not adequately addressed. Many medical personnel may ignore the problem because they do not want to open up the proverbial "Pandora's box" of broader and more complex social issues stemming from past laws and moral codes giving men the "right" to control women's behavior with violent actions. It was once legal, for example, for a husband to beat his wife with a stick that was no thicker than a thumb, from which comes the common "rule-of-thumb" saying.

Another factor contributing to the problem of domestic violence is the patronizing or uninterested approach of male clergy, counselors, and others to whom battered women go for help. Some shrug off the problem as insignificant or none of their business and find excuses for the actions of abusers. Battered women also are reluctant to discuss their problems because they often are not believed, they fear reprisals, or they erroneously assume that the abuse will somehow stop.

Because of the widespread impact of domestic violence, the U.S. Congress passed the Violence Against Women Act of 1994 and the Justice Department established an Office on Violence Against Women. In early 1999, the U.S. Centers for Disease Control and Prevention announced that it would spend up to $2.7 million over five years to fund the establishment of the National Violence Against Women Prevention Research Center. Wellesley Centers for Women at Wellesley College, the Medical University of South Carolina (Charleston), and the University of Missouri at St. Louis have been selected to run the center.

Nevertheless, in spite of federal and state laws, numerous news accounts, and highly publicized statistics about domestic violence, the problem is perpetuated for numerous reasons, primarily the long-held belief that women provoke the beatings or emotional abuse they endure. Another common myth is that women like to be battered; otherwise they would get away from the abusive situation. Yet many battered women have such low self-esteem that they believe they are responsible for their own abuse. They also may stay with their abusers because they have no other economic means to survive and care for their children.

Victims of domestic violence also fear that if they leave their partners will kill them. The fear is well-founded. According to homicide statistics collected by the Federal Bureau of Investigation (FBI), 32 percent of the 3,419 women killed in the United States in 1998, the latest year for which data are available, died at the hands of a husband, a former husband, a boyfriend, or a former boyfriend.

On the basis of smaller, regional studies and the limitations of the data-gathering methods used by the FBI, however, many experts believe that the true figure is much higher, perhaps 50 percent to 70 percent. In comparison, 4 percent of 10,606 male homicide victims in 1998 were killed by current or former intimate partners. (Goode)

Domestic violence continues generation after generation because many battered women and their male batterers abuse their children and the children repeat the behavior. Boys learn to be batterers and girls become intimidated and degraded, which in turn sets the stage for victimization. However, since the 1960s when feminist and civil rights movements got underway, broad public awareness of domestic violence has grown. Political advocates of the 1970s supported legislation to fund shelters for battered women and children. Since the 1980s, numerous academic texts have been published and seminars have been presented for clinicians, emergency-room personnel, primary physicians, nurses, social workers, and other caregivers likely to deal with domestic violence cases. Information covers crisis intervention, wife-battering prevention, treatment of children in violent families, community response to domestic violence, elder abuse (a form of domestic violence), the higher incidence of domestic violence among immigrant populations, and other related subjects.

In 1996, the Spring issue of the *Journal of the American Medical Women's Association* was devoted to domestic violence; articles covered numerous aspects of the problem. One article, for example, explains how emergency departments can intervene in domestic-violence cases. Others deal with legal issues of domestic violence; how physicians can help batterers; and how clinicians can intervene to help prevent domestic violence.

Business and industry have also been focusing on domestic violence prevention programs in order to ameliorate financial losses. Battered women frequently are late for work, are harassed at work by batterers, or lose their jobs because of abuse. Corporation leaders claim that loss of productivity due to domestic violence costs up to $5 billion annually. A variety of groups and organizations have established educational programs, shelters, and other facilities to help victims of domestic violence. Among them are the American Bar Association's Commission on Domestic Violence; Battered Women's Justice Project; the National Domestic Violence Resource Center; and the National Domestic Violence Hotline (1-800-799-SAFE). Other groups include statewide coalitions against domestic violence and local domestic violence programs. *See also* Domestic Elder Abuse; Lesbian Health; Rape and Sexual Assault; Violence Against Women Act of 1994

Further Reading
Boston Women's Health Book Collective. *Our Bodies, Ourselves for the New Century.* New York: Simon & Schuster, 1998.
Bureau of Justice Statistics Special Report: National Crime Victimization Survey, Violence Against Women. Washington, DC: U.S. Department of Justice, January 1994.
"Domestic Violence and Women's Health." *Journal of the American Medical Women's Association* (May–July 1996).
Goode, Erica. "When Women Find Love Is Fatal." *New York Times* (February 15, 2000).
Hoffman, Eileen, M.D. *Our Health, Our Lives: A Revolutionary Approach to Total Health Care for Women.* New York: Simon & Schuster, 1995.
Rogers, Albert R., ed. *Battered Women and Their Families.* New York: Springer Publishing Company, 1998.
U.S. Senate, Committee on the Judiciary. Hearings on Women and Violence. "Ten Facts about Violence against Women." (August 29 and December 11, 1990).

Doula

Doula is an ancient Greek word meaning handmaiden or servant. Today it refers to a trained and experienced woman who helps other women during labor with continuous physical and emotional support. A doula serves as a nonmedical adjunct to a doctor or midwife; she does not take the place of the woman's partner or a doctor, nurse, midwife, or other health-care provider.

Although doulas assist at only one percent of births in the United States, their numbers are growing. The use of a doula is both a personal and a health-care issue for pregnant women who want choices in the way they experience childbirth, the methods they use during labor, and how they manage pain—with or without drugs.

A number of clinical studies indicate that women who have the help of doulas are likely to have shorter labor and less medication for pain as well as higher self-esteem than those laboring without such support. A doula helps a woman focus on managing labor pain with relaxation and breathing techniques, massage, hydrotherapy in a tub or shower, or other methods. Often referred to as the person who mothers the mother, a doula can assist a woman in childbirth at home, in a freestanding birthing center, or in a hospital. She is trained in the physiology of birth and the emotional needs of a woman in labor and stays with her throughout labor and during the postpartum period. Women who want the assistance of a doula can find

Mother and her doula sharing a momment of gratitude, relief, and appreciation moments after birth. ©1999, Patti Ramos Photography, Tacoma, Washington.

someone certified by Doulas of North America (DONA), an international organization founded in 1992, through its Web site <http://www.dona.com> or through a childbirth center, health-care providers, or La Leche League members. *See also* Childbirth Practices; Midwifery; La Leche League

Further Reading
DONA Press Kit <http://www.dona.com>.
Gilbert, Susan. "Benefits of Assistant for Childbirth Go Far beyond the Birthing." *New York Times* (May 19, 1998).
Kohn, Anna. "Mothering the Mothers: Meet the Doulas." *Chatelaine* (October 1997).

Drug Abuse and Addiction

Drug abuse and addiction include the use of and addiction to illegal drugs as well as overuse of and addiction to legal substances such as tobacco, alcohol, and prescription medications. Drug abuse and addiction are frequently referred to as substance abuse. A major health issue, substance abuse creates social, economic, and legal problems that affect millions of women as well as their family members and communities in the United States. According to a 1996 report on a two-year study conducted by the National Center on Addiction and Substance Abuse (CASA), 3.5 million women misuse prescription drugs and 3.1 million report using illicit drugs. The direct and indirect costs of drug abuse total more than $58 billion annually in the United States.

In a 1997 report, the Substance Abuse and Mental Health Administration (SAMHA) noted that, even though more men than women in the United States report drug abuse,

> substance abuse is a significant problem for women. Research has demonstrated that abuse, or problem use, of alcohol or illicit drugs by women is a risk factor for unprotected intercourse, sexually trans-

mitted disease and HIV infection, unintended pregnancy, poor birth outcomes, child abuse and neglect, criminal activities, mental health disorders, and other adverse health and social consequences.... Substance use and abuse among women of child-bearing age are especially problematic, because they not only pose hazards to their long-term health, but also endanger the well-being of their children.

Substance abuse among women is not a new phenomenon. During the 1800s medications were limited and those containing opium were used to treat a variety of diseases from cholera to syphilis. Because Victorian women were seen as weak and unable to bear pain, doctors overmedicated women with opiates. Doctors also prescribed addictive drugs such as cocaine and cannabis for many female conditions. As a result many women became addicted; women made up the majority of drug addicts during the nineteenth century.

Even though physicians became more aware of the dangers of drug use and safer medications were more readily available by the early 1900s, U.S. society, in general, denied that women were drug abusers and needed treatment. During the 1960s that attitude began to change; since the 1970s a variety of drug treatment programs have been established for women. Yet until recent years, little data were available on women who abuse drugs because, as with other health research, studies focused exclusively on male subjects.

During the 1990s, the National Institute on Drug Abuse (NIDA) and other federal agencies and private organizations conducted laboratory, clinical, and field research to determine gender differences in drug abuse and addiction. According to the NIDA, childhood sexual abuse is a major factor in female drug abuse. Some studies indicate that up to 70 percent of women in drug treatment programs report physical

and sexual abuse beginning before 11 years old.

Female drug abuse also is associated with anxiety, depression, eating disorders, and other psychiatric problems that affect women predominantly. Gender differences show up in the progression of drug abuse, with abuse of illegal drugs following a more complex pattern for females than for males. Women become drug dependent more rapidly than men. There are also gender differences in treatment for drug abuse—adult females are less likely to receive treatment than adult males. However, among adolescents just the opposite is true. More girls than boys (ages 12–17) are treated for alcohol and illicit drug abuse.

Gender is also a factor in abuse of legal drugs. Women are much more likely than men to abuse prescription medications and over-the-counter drugs such as tranquilizers, sedatives, antidepressants, and painkillers. The two-year study of substance abuse by CASA found that mature women—those ages 60 and over—are especially susceptible to abuse of medications along with the abuse of alcohol, which hastens addiction. Yet drug abuse among mature women is often hidden because women seldom report or admit their problems to family, friends, or caregivers. The problem is also exacerbated by the fact that few physicians expect mature women to abuse drugs and so do not recognize and treat the condition.

Public health campaigns to raise awareness of drug abuse and addiction among women are the mission of CASA at Columbia University and government agencies such as NIDA. Numerous published materials are available from CASA and NIDA as well as from the National Clearinghouse for Alcohol and Drug Information (NCADI), a service of the SAMHSA. A Web site sponsored by NCADI and SAMHSA called Prevline offers a variety of free research reports, fact sheets, and other publications that can be downloaded or ordered in print form. *See also* AIDS; Alcohol Abuse and Alcoholism; Drug-Dependent Mothers; Sexually Transmitted Diseases

Further Reading

National Center on Addiction and Substance Abuse. "CASA Releases Report, Substance Abuse and the American Woman." Press Release, New York: National Center on Addiction and Substance Abuse at Columbia, June 5, 1996.

Substance Abuse and Mental Health Services Administration, Office of Applied Studies. *Substance Use among Women in the United States.* Rockville, MD: National Institute on Drug Abuse, September 1997.

U.S. Department of Health and Human Services, National Institutes of Health, National Institute on Drug Abuse. *Drug Addiction Research and the Health of Women.* Rockville, MD: National Institute on Drug Abuse, 1998.

Drug-Dependent Mothers

Drug-dependent mothers—women who are addicted to drugs—certainly have a health problem, but only in recent years have they been the focus of some research on their addiction. Past studies of drug abuse among women frequently centered on the effects of drugs on a pregnant woman's fetus or the children of drug-dependent mothers.

Many legal battles have been fought over maternal rights versus fetal rights, and some states have attempted to protect a fetus by passing laws that make drug use by a pregnant woman a form of child abuse. Addicted mothers or pregnant women may be arrested and jailed for illegal drug use, but imprisonment prevents women from getting the health care and drug treatment they need. "The vast majority of addicted inmates lack access to drug treatment programs, and studies show that women continue to obtain drugs behind bars." (Haack, 17) Imprisoned mothers also may lose custody of their children.

Much media attention during the 1980s was given to children born of cocaine- and heroin-addicted mothers, which has fostered the belief that all children prenatally exposed to drugs will have development and behavior problems. While children born of drug-dependent pregnant women are at risk for numerous health problems, recent research has shown that the developmental outcomes of these children depend more on the home environment than on prenatal exposure to drugs.

Since the early 1990s, the issue of drug addiction research and the health of women has received special attention from the U.S. Department of Health and Human Services and its National Institute on Drug Abuse and the Substance Abuse and Mental Health Services Administration (SAMHSA) as well as numerous healthcare groups in the private sector. The American Medical Association, for example, has long urged "federal, state, and local governments to increase funding for drug treatment so that drug abusers can have immediate access to appropriate care, regardless of ability to pay. This is the most important step that can be taken to reduce the spread of human immunodeficiency virus (HIV) infection among intravenous drug abusers."

Substance abuse is a major public-health problem that affects millions of people and places enormous financial and social burdens on society. Addiction can be a chronic, life-threatening condition. Most people whose drug use has progressed to addiction cannot simply stop using alcohol or drugs, no matter how strong their inner resolve, without one or more courses of structured substance abuse treatment.

Even if a person never achieves perfect abstinence, addiction treatment can reduce the number and duration of relapses, minimize related problems such as crime and poor overall health, reduce the impact of parental addiction on children, and improve the individual's ability to function in daily life. Nearly one-third of substance abuse treatment clients achieve sustained abstinence from their first attempt at recovery. An additional one-third have a period of relapse episodes but eventually achieve long-term abstinence. The remaining one-third have chronic relapses that result in eventual death from complications of their addiction, according to SAMHSA.

In its 1999 report to the U.S. Congress, the National Clearinghouse for Alcohol and Drug Information (NCADI) of SAMHSA noted that fathers are just as likely to abuse drugs as are mothers, but drug-dependent mothers are much more likely than fathers to be reported to child protective services. African-American women with substance abuse problems are more likely to be involved with child welfare agencies than are similar women of other races. Many parents, especially mothers, who enter substance abuse treatment are motivated to do so out of concerns about their parenting and how their substance abuse is affecting their children.

SAMHSA has developed a treatment guide for drug-dependent women that can be adapted by communities and used to build comprehensive programs over time. Because alcohol- and drug-dependent women tend to have few economic and social resources, comprehensive treatment that addresses the full range of a woman's needs is advised. The purpose of comprehensive treatment, SAMHSA points out, is to address a woman's substance abuse in the context of her health and her relationship to family, community, and society. Such treatment is associated with increasing abstinence and improvement in other measures of recovery, including parenting skills and overall emotional health. Treatment that only addresses drug abuse is likely to fail and contribute to a higher potential for relapse. *See also* Alcohol Abuse and Alcoholism; Drug Abuse and Addiction

Further Reading

American Medical Association Council on Scientific Affairs. "The Reduction of Medical and Public Health Consequences of Drug Abuse." *Report 8* (June 1997).

Barth, Richard P. "Revisiting the Issues: Adoption of Drug-Exposed Children." *The Future of Children* (Spring 1993).

Chasnoff, Ira J., Griffith, D. R., et al. "Cocaine/ Polydrug Use in Pregnancy: Two Year Follow Up." *Pediatrics* (February 1992).

Franck, Ellen J. "Prenatally Drug-Exposed Children in Out-of-Home Care: Are We Looking at the Whole Picture?" *Child Welfare* (January–February 1996).

Haack, Mary R., ed. *Drug-Dependent Mothers and Their Children,* New York: Springer Publishing Company, 1997.

National Clearinghouse for Alcohol and Drug Information, The Substance Abuse and Mental Health Services Administration. *Blending Perspectives and Building Common Ground: A Report to Congress on Substance Abuse and Child Protection* (April 1999).

Wetherington, Cora Lee, and Adele B. Roman, eds. U.S. Department of Health and Human Services, National Institutes of Health, National Institute on Drug Abuse. *Drug Addiction Research and the Health of Women, Executive Summary.* Rockville, MD: National Institute on Drug Abuse, 1998.

Zuckerman, Barry. "Effects on Parents and Children." In *When Drug Addicts Have Children.* Douglas Besharov, ed. Washington, DC: Child Welfare League of America/American Enterprise Institute, 1994.

E

Eating Disorders

Since the 1980s, the health and social issues related to eating disorders have gained much public attention. The most prevalent eating disorders among American women are anorexia nervosa, a fear of gaining weight which leads to self-starvation, and bulimia, in which victims purge their bodies of food by induced vomiting or use of laxatives. Another type of eating disorder is binge eating, which is similar to bulimia except that binge eaters do not "purge" themselves of excess food. Binge eating occurs most often among women who are in weight control programs and have trouble losing weight and keeping it off.

Anorexia and bulimia are frequently stress-related and are an indication of psychological problems. Bulimia may also be caused by abnormal levels of the neurotransmitter serotonin in the brain, according to a study published in 1998 in the *Archives of General Psychiatry*. Anorexia and bulimia also stem from the American obsession with weight loss and the desire to mirror the wispy thin body images of most fashion models and TV and movie actresses. Some models and actresses are themselves anorexic or bulimic. The disorders are also common among dancers, fig-ure skaters, gymnasts, and other athletes whose performance depends on weight control.

Anorexia and bulimia eventually cause physical ailments and can shorten lives and kill victims. A woman afflicted with an eating disorder is likely to weigh 15 percent

A very thin young woman critically appraising herself in the mirror. ©1992 George White Jr.

below what is considered normal for her age and height. She may not menstruate for several months. Some anorexic women also develop growths of baby-fine hair on their bodies; their nails may become brittle and they may have swollen joints. Nearly 20 percent of anorexics die from physical complications brought on by the affliction. Bulimics may develop heartbeat irregularities, chronic sore throat, and dental problems from vomiting and digestive problems from the use of laxatives.

When singer Karen Carpenter died in 1983 from complications of anorexia, eating disorders were brought to public attention; ever since they have been the subject of hundreds of magazine articles, dozens of books, and thousands of Internet Web sites. Eating disorders also afflicted famous gymnasts Kathy Johnson, Nadia Comaneci, and Cathy Rigby. For 12 years Rigby battled anorexia and bulimia, and because of the disorders twice suffered cardiac arrest. Christy Henrich, one of the world's top gymnasts, was told to lose weight and resorted to anorexia and bulimia; she died of multiple organ failure in 1994 at the age of 22. An estimated 5 to 10 million young women and an increasing number of young men (about one million) are afflicted with anorexia.

Large numbers of young people with eating disorders are college students, many of whom are driven to excel in academics, sports, and other activities. Eating disorders are so common on college campuses that most schools have programs to counter the problem. Hundreds of colleges also have taken part in the National Eating Disorders Screening Program (NEDSP), which was implemented during the first annual National Eating Disorders Awareness Week on 600 campuses in 1996 and expanded in 1998 to include the general public. High school screening began in 2000. The NEDSP includes educational materials on eating disorders, opportuni-

ties to meet with health professionals, and information on how to encourage friends or family members to seek treatment for eating disorders.

Help also is available from such groups as the Anorexia Nervosa and Related Eating Disorders, Inc. of Eugene, Oregon; National Eating Disorders Organization of Tulsa, Oklahoma; the National Association of Anorexia Nervosa and Associated Disorders in Highland Park, Illinois; and the American Anorexia/Bulimia Association in New York City. *See also* Dieting and Diet Drugs; Weight Discrimination

Further Reading

"Disappearing Act." *Time* (November 2, 1998).

"Explorations: Treating Eating Disorders." *Scientific American* (March 2, 1998).

Halmi, Katherine A. "A 24-Year-Old Woman with Anorexia Nervosa." *The Journal of the American Medical Association* (June 24, 1998).

Horiuchi, Vince. "Eating Disorders Are Not Going Away." *Salt Lake Tribune* (April 2, 1998).

"Out of Control: Weight-Obsessed, Stressed-Out Coeds Are Increasingly Falling Prey to Eating Disorders." *People Weekly* (April 12, 1999).

Egg Donors

During the last two or three decades an increasing number of women in their prime child-bearing years have become oocyte, or egg, donors. Oocyte donors provide eggs for women who have very little chance of getting pregnant with their own eggs or who are unable to produce any eggs. The practice of donating eggs, however, has prompted ethical questions as well as concerns about the health of donors.

A female is born with all of the eggs she will ever have and that number diminishes as she ages, at a rate that is different for every woman. Because more and more women are waiting until they are in their thirties and forties to try to conceive, they may discover that they have "unhealthy" eggs when they want to become pregnant.

Some women search on their own for egg donors among relatives or friends. Most couples, however, turn to fertility clinics or reproductive centers for help in finding egg donors. Some clinics are set up especially to help nontraditional couples-lesbians, for example—to find donors.

Ideally egg donors are between 21 and 30 years old. Medical personnel at clinics screen women who apply as donors, reviewing their medical histories for inheritable diseases, genetic conditions, or birth defects. Donors are also tested for hepatitis, syphilis, HIV (the AIDS virus), cytomegalovirus (CMV, a common viral infection which can cause birth defects), and Rh status. If accepted into a donor program, a woman takes hormones to stimulate her ovaries to produce oocytes, which carries some risk since the medication can have side effects, such as bleeding, infections, and swollen, painful ovaries. After several days, her eggs are surgically removed. The oocytes are artificially inseminated through in vitro fertilization (IVF) and the embryos that result are transferred into the recipient's uterus, or womb. Theoretically the recipient woman can then achieve a normal pregnancy and delivery.

Reproductive centers or clinics frequently place ads for egg donors in magazines and newspapers, offering sums ranging from several thousand dollars up to $50,000. In March 1999, for example, an advertisement ran in the newspapers of top universities asking for an egg donor who was athletic, 5-foot-10, and had scored at least 1400 on her Scholastic Achievement Test. Another stipulation was that the donor's family had to be free of major medical problems. In return for providing eggs, she would receive $50,000. Several hundred women responded to the advertisement, the *New York Times* reported. Critics claim that offering such high fees to egg donors makes eggs a "hot commodity," not a gift of fertility as proponents of assisted reproductive technologies call egg donations.

Commercializing egg donations became an issue once more in 1999 when an Internet Web site called Ron's Angels offered to auction eggs from beautiful models with bids beginning from $15,000 to $150,000 in increments of $1,000. The American Society for Reproductive Medicine (ASRM) responded with a statement from its Ethics Committee saying that

reasonable compensation is justified for the time and trouble of both sperm and egg donors. Compensation should not vary based on attributes that a child may have. The 'Ron's Angels' Web site is essentially a donor egg 'auction' to sell human eggs to the highest bidder in the hopes of providing potential parents with more attractive—and therefore desirable—children. We believe that the 'Ron's Angels' Web site violates the ethical principles outlined by the Committee, promotes unrealistic expectations to potential parents, commercializes what is otherwise a voluntary donation process, offers undue enticement to potential donors, and has great potential to exploit highly vulnerable people. Donor egg programs exist to help this nation's infertile couples have the children they very much want to have—even if it means using another woman's eggs to do so. (American Society for Reproductive Medicine, 1999)

Traditionally in the United States payments are not made for body parts (such as kidneys), but the Society for Assisted Reproductive Technology defines eggs as body products, like blood. Because blood donors do receive some limited compensation, the society declares that egg donors also "should be compensated for the direct and indirect expenses associated with their participation" but that "financial payments should not be so excessive as to constitute undue inducement." The society's goal is to prevent "the enticement or exploitation of young women."

During the 1990s, legal issues became a concern for egg donors and recipients. Many states do not have laws dealing with egg donations or surrogacy, but throughout the United States some law firms have begun to specialize in egg-donor contracts (as well as surrogate mother contracts). These contracts usually address such issues as the risks involved in being a donor, fees to be paid by recipients, and ownership rights of eggs produced. A contract may also cover multiple oocytes that are retrieved during the egg-donation process. Surplus eggs that have been fertilized are usually frozen, providing embryos for a recipient if she does not become pregnant during the first cycle of treatment. But the number of frozen embryos has been growing and "it has become obvious that a sizable fraction of them will never be required, and no one knows what to do with them," Gina Maranto reported in *Scientific American*.

Because a federal court decision in 1989 held that laboratories are not the owners but are merely custodians of embryos, many embryologists are reluctant to dispose of embryos, even those that have been preserved for years. Some couples also are extremely reluctant to permit disposal. Some have strong feelings about the embryos' sanctity; some view them as "children" or "family," an attitude that makes sense, infertility counselors say, given that these couples may already be raising one or more children conceived from stored embryos. Even patients who regard embryos as potential beings, rather than fully human, may hold on for long periods, regardless of whether or not they intend to continue with IVF. Because of these conflicts, laboratories provide consent forms that address the disposal of unused embryos and also charge fees for lengthy preservation.

Other issues regarding egg donation have yet to be addressed. Little is known about the psychological effects of being an egg donor and what effect donating eggs has on a donor's fertility. Questions arise also about whether to tell children about the role egg donors have played in their conception. *See also* Artificial Insemination; American Society for Reproductive Medicine; Infertility; Surrogate Mother

Further Reading

American Society for Reproductive Medicine. "ASRM Statement on 'Ron's Angels' Website." Press Release (October 26, 1999). <http://www.asrm.com/Media/Press/ronsangels.html>

Kolata, Gina. "$50,000 Offered to Tall, Smart Egg Donor." *New York Times* (March 3, 1999).

Kolata, Gina. "Soaring Price of Donor Eggs Sets Off Debate." *New York Times* (February 25, 1998).

Maranto, Gina. "Embryo Overpopulation." *Scientific American* (April 1996).

Ron's Angels <http://www.ronsangels.com>.

Elder Abuse

See **Domestic Elder Abuse**

Elder Care

See **Aging**

Emergency Contraception

See **Birth Control**

Emma Goldman Clinic

The Emma Goldman Clinic, a free-standing clinic on the campus of the University of Iowa in Iowa City, is named for the famed Emma Goldman, who not only championed women's rights in the early 1900s but also campaigned extensively for women's reproductive health issues, particularly birth control. When it was founded in 1973, the Emma Goldman

The Emma Goldman clinic, established in 1973, moved into this building. Courtesy of The Emma Goldman Clinic, Photograph by Dawn R. Newbill.

Clinic was the first women's health-care center in the Midwest and first outpatient abortion clinic in Iowa. Operated by women, the clinic exists "to empower women in all life stages through the provision of quality reproductive health care, active education, and the promotion of women's voices in public policy." (Emma Goldman Clinic Web site)

On its Web site, clinic operators state their purpose: "We believe that controlling our bodies and health is integral to establishing the quality of our lives. We promote participatory health care, informed decision making, client rights, advocacy for women, and expansion and support of women's choices" <http://www.emmagoldman.com>.

The Emma Goldman Clinic is affiliated with a number of national public policy organizations including the National Abortion Federation (NAF), National Abortion Rights Action League (NARAL), and the National Coalition of Abortion Providers

(NCAP). The clinic also serves as a training site for medical students and residents from the University of Iowa, supplementing their hospital-based training. In 1998, the university physicians and the clinic began a collaborative service, providing second trimester abortions up to the twentieth week of pregnancy. As the clinic's newsletter explained: "Although there are slightly higher risks associated with second trimester abortions, the procedure is still safe for most women in an outpatient setting." The arrangement allows "the University to concentrate their attention on providing services to women who need hospital-based care because of specialized health concerns. This...relationship between the clinic and the university highlights the commitment of both institutions to continue to bring the highest standard of care to the next generation of women and families in the Midwest." (*Emma's Journal*)

Another major effort of the clinic is promoting self-health care, that is, showing women how to perform their own breast and cervical examinations to learn what is healthy and normal. "While this does not replace the need for routine exams from a health care provider, it is another way women can take responsibility for their own health." ("Advocacy for Women")

Along with the medical services it provides, the clinic advocates for women by lobbying legislators at all levels of government for equitable health-care policies for women and by challenging such medical practices as breast implants. The clinic also challenged the use of Norplant as a form of birth control and would not offer it to their clients for two reasons. "First, enough research had not been done on its side effects and removal. Second, some legislators and law enforcement officials proposed uses of Norplant that had the potential of mandating birth control in a way that would disproportionately affect young women, low-income women, and women of color. The Clinic is opposed to legislated birth control, and was unwilling to participate in oppression through coercive birth control tactics." ("Advocacy for Women") *See also* Abortion; Abortion Providers; Birth Control; Women's Health-Care Advocates

Further Reading

"Advocacy for Women." Emma Goldman Clinic Web site <http://www.emmagoldman.com>.

"Emma and University of Iowa Launch New Era of Collaboration." *Emma's Journal: Newsletter of the Emma Goldman Clinic* Special Edition (November 1998).

"Our Commitment to Women." *Emma's Journal* <http://www.emmagoldman.com/journal/ 98_nov/committment.html>.

Endometriosis

Endometriosis is named for the endometrium, tissue that is similar to the lining of the uterus. A woman diagnosed with endometriosis usually has tissue implanted outside the uterus on organs ranging from the uterus itself to the ovaries, bowel, bladder, and other surfaces. The disease has no known cure, and "is without question one of the most puzzling conditions that affect women," according to the Endometriosis Association. (Ballweg, 13)

Endometriosis can be devastating for many of the 5,000,000 female Americans—from all age groups, races, and classes—with the condition. Because endometriosis primarily affects the reproductive organs, infertility may result, causing not just physical problems but also emotional difficulties. Most women spend frustrating years trying to get diagnoses, which in turn create economic burdens. Many doctors do not know much about the disease, and, writes Eileen Hoffman, M.D., there is also an

artificial "turf" separation that doctors have established when dealing with the abdominal cavity. Neither the gynecologist nor the internist will take full responsibility for the area.... internists never adequately learn about endometriosis, and gynecologists have little training in bowel disease. (Hoffman, 212)

Effective treatment for endometriosis is also difficult to determine. It can range from prescription drugs to radical surgery.

One of the basic problems for women with endometriosis is the fact that most must cope with chronic and debilitating pain. Endometriosis sufferers may be stereotyped as people who need psychiatric treatment. They are sometimes treated like hypochondriacs or thought to be suffering from factitious disorders. A woman who experiences chronic pain may be told she is "acting like a baby" and should be more stoic, or she may be perceived as someone trying to gain an advantage by "playing a sick role." As a result many women feel they are alone with their problems and that they are not supported by intimate partners, families, friends, employers, medical insurance providers, or even health-care practitioners. However, in recent years research on chronic pain and professional articles on the subject have helped dispel some of the myths and misconceptions about chronic pain patients, including women with endometriosis.

The Endometriosis Association (EA), with headquarters in Milwaukee, Wisconsin, is the leading international organization educating the public about all aspects of endometriosis. Founded by women for women, the EA has published a sourcebook, which includes advice for coping physically and emotionally with endometriosis and describes various types of theories for causes and treatments of the disease. Some animal studies funded by the EA as well as by federal agencies have linked endometriosis to environmental toxins such as dioxins and polychlorinated biphenyls (PCBs). The EA maintains an Internet Web site with current information on endometriosis research <http://www. endometriosisasn.org>.

The Institute for the Study and Treatment of Endometriosis (ISTE) located in Chicago, Illinois, also supports and conducts research on endometriosis. The ISTE hopes to "clarify the association between endometriosis and infertility...develop new, non-invasive diagnostic techniques...and test new preventative and therapeutic measures, and identify medical and societal barriers to the diagnosis of endometriosis." (ISTE home page) Like EA, the ISTE maintains a Web site to disseminate information on endometriosis and also conducts lectures, seminars, courses, and workshops for medical personnel and patient education activities. ISTE staff members publish articles in the professional journals and the press on the subject of endometriosis, and they regularly appear on educational TV and radio shows.

Physicians at the National Institutes of Health (NIH) are also conducting clinical studies of women experiencing pain due to endometriosis. The NIH study tests whether laproscopic surgery followed by daily doses of the drug raloxifene is effective in reducing pain for longer periods than standard medications and laproscopic surgery, which involves only a tiny incision. Laproscopy has proven to be one of the most effective surgical approaches. "NIH researchers believe that the drug raloxifene (approved by the Food and Drug Administration for preventing bone loss in postmenopausal women) will block estrogen action in the lining of the uterus of reproductive age women, thereby limiting growth of endometriosis and preventing the return of pain." (NIH study) *See also* Environmental Health Hazards; Factitious Disorders

Further Reading
Ballweg, Mary Lou, and the Endometriosis Association. *The Endometriosis Sourcebook*. Lincolnwood, IL: Contemporary Books, 1995.
Endometriosis Association ENDOOnline. <http://www.endometriosisasn.org>.
Hoffman, Eileen, M.D. *Our Health, Our Lives: A Revolutionary Approach to Total Health Care for Women*. New York: Simon & Schuster, 1995.
Institute for the Study and Treatment of Endometriosis home page. <http://www.endometriosisinstitute.com>.
NIH Endometriosis Study. National Institutes of Health <http://clinicalstudies.info.nih.gov>.

Environmental Health Hazards

Since the 1960s and 1970s women have been in the forefront of grassroots efforts to eliminate environmental health hazards such as toxic waste sites and emissions from industries in their communities. The issue of environmental health hazards has created controversy across the United States and around the world, particularly among those who argue for and against

A protest sign stands in front of an evacuated and boarded-up house in the Love Canal neighborhood in Niagara Falls. The area was abandoned after it was learned that tons of toxic waste were dumped in the canal behind the houses. ©Bettmann/CORBIS.

multiple chemical sensitivity, various ailments attributed to low-level exposure to the many toxic chemicals in the environment. Some of those toxins include dioxins, lead, polychlorinated biphenyls (PCBs), and dichlorodiphenyltrichloroethane (DDT).

Some environmental activists are convinced that various human-made chemicals used in manufacturing, agriculture, and daily living cause serious diseases such as cancer, respiratory disorders, and reproductive health problems, including endometriosis. Manufacturers, on the other hand, frequently argue that they provide jobs and other economic benefits which should be weighed against any health hazards their facilities might pose to the environment.

One of the earliest activists against environmental health hazards was Rachel Carson, whose 1962 book, *Silent Spring,* called attention to dangerous pesticides and led to a ban on DDT, known to cause cancer. Carson's work helped prompt other women to become activists in a burgeoning environmental movement.

An early grassroots campaign against environmental pollutants was organized by Lois Gibbs and her neighbors, who lived near a toxic dump site called Love Canal in Niagara Falls, New York. From 1978 to 1980 the group struggled to obtain public funds to move from the contaminated area. Many families reported health problems ranging from birth defects to respiratory problems. Eventually families were evacuated. Several studies published during the 1980s in *Science, Human Biology,* and other scientific journals confirmed that children in Love Canal suffered adverse health effects linked to toxic chemicals.

In 1987, two New York City women, Vernice Miller and Peggy Shepard, cofounded West Harlem Environmental Action (WHE ACT) to combat myriad contaminants in their predominantly African-American community, including a huge

sewage treatment plant that emitted nox-
ious fumes. The sewage plant was first
planned for a white neighborhood, but af-
fluent residents were able to organize opposition and convince officials to site the
facility in west Harlem. WHE ACT eventually won a court case that forced the city
to repair the sewage plant and ameliorate
the bad odors, and the organization continues its efforts to alleviate other environmental health hazards in the community.

In 1990, Joann Tall, who lives on the
Lakota tribe's Pine Ridge Reservation in
South Dakota, began a campaign to prevent Amcor, a waste-disposal company
based in Connecticut, from dumping trash
on the reservation. A long-time environmental activist, Tall persuaded tribal leaders that Amcor was attempting to buy them
off with promises of jobs and cash payments for use of their land. She convinced
Lakota leaders to protect tribal rights and
reject the waste company's proposal.

Countless other women and men have
organized to investigate, monitor, and protest against dangerous chemicals in water
supplies, poisonous emissions from industries, workplace health hazards, and contamination from waste sites for toxic and
radioactive materials. Nevertheless, the
health hazards from environmental pollutants are an ongoing issue in the United
States, particularly for dozens of private
activist organizations such as the Citizens'
Clearinghouse for Hazardous Wastes
(founded by Lois Gibbs), the Environmental Defense Fund, Silent Spring Institute,
and the Society for Occupational and Environmental Health. Government agencies
concerned with environmental health hazards include the Environmental Protection
Agency; the U.S. Department of Health
and Human Services; the Occupational,
Safety, and Health Administration; and the
Consumer Product Safety Commission.
See also Endometriosis; Multiple Chemical Sensitivity; Silent Spring Institute;
Women's Health Movement; *Women:
Work and Health*

Further Reading
Boston Women's Health Book Collective. *The New
Our Bodies, Ourselves,* Chapter 7, "Environmen-
tal and Occupational Health." New York: Simon
& Schuster, 1992.
Carson, Rachel. *Silent Spring.* Greenwich, CT:
Fawcett Crest, 1962.
Gay, Kathlyn. *Pollution and the Powerless.* New
York: Franklin Watts, 1994.
Kenen, Regina. *Reproductive Hazards in the Work-
place: Mending Jobs, Managing Pregnancies.*
Binghamton, NY: Haworth Press, 1992.
Nelson, Lin, Regina Kenen, and Susan Klitzman.
*Turning Things Around: A Woman's Occupa-
tional and Environmental Health Resource
Guide.* Washington, DC: National Women's
Health Network, 1990.

Environmental Illness

See **Multiple Chemical Sensitivity**

Epilepsy

More than one million women and girls in
the United States have seizure disorders
known as epilepsy, according to the Epilepsy Foundation, formerly the Epilepsy
Foundation of America (EFA). Although
epilepsy affects both genders, women and
girls with epilepsy face many unique
health and social problems that were
largely ignored until recent years. The female menstrual cycle may trigger seizures,
for example, and many women with epilepsy fear they will have seizures that
could do harm during pregnancy or while
caring for their children, or that could be
complicated by hormonal changes and
menopause.

Women with epilepsy are vulnerable
to discrimination in the workplace, although the civil rights of people with epilepsy are protected under the Americans
with Disabilities Act. One of the most difficult issues for a person with epilepsy is

coping with social situations, such as going on dates or to parties or taking trips. Many girls and women try to hide their disorder because they fear they will be ostracized if others know about their seizures.

The Epilepsy Foundation advocates for all people with epilepsy, but lack of information specifically geared toward women prompted the foundation to develop its Women and Epilepsy Initiative campaign. The campaign includes information sheets on the specific issues that affect women with epilepsy. These are available on the foundation's Internet Web site as well as in print format. *See also* Menstruation; Pregnancy

Further Reading

Epilepsy Foundation Web site. <http://www.efa.org/>.

Hopkins, Anthony, and Richard Appleton. *Epilepsy: The Facts*, Second Edition. Oxford: Oxford University Press, 1996.

Estrogen Replacement

See **Hormone Replacement Therapy**

Exploitative Labor

See **Sweatshops**

F

Factitious Disorder

People who have a mental illness known as factitious disorder fabricate ailments or symptoms of disease ("play sick") in order to gain medical attention. They usually have a need to be nurtured and may exhibit mild symptoms brought on with no malicious intent. Or they may deliberately fake a disease or create self-induced health problems. Factitious disorders can baffle physicians trying to find the real causes of their patients' problems. People with this disorder also defraud family, friends, employers, and others around them.

Although patients suffering from factitious disorders represent all walks of life and can be adults or children, adult women account for the largest number of diagnosed cases. Yet "the prevalence of factitious disorders is difficult to determine" because sufferers who report their symptoms are not always recognized as having disorders. (Feldman, Ford, and Reinhold) On the other hand, some health-care practitioners may suspect that their patients with chronic symptoms are faking health problems, but the health-care practitioners may not be able to diagnose a mental disorder and help patients get the treatments they need.

An extreme type of a factitious disorder is called Munchausen syndrome, which is characterized in part by self-induced symptoms requiring frequent hospitalization and by the patient's moving from place to place in order to obtain medical care. A tragic and deadly factitious disorder is a form of child abuse: Mentally ill adults with Munchausen by proxy (MBP), usually mothers, create signs of illness in their children, which may prompt doctors to perform invasive treatments or unnecessary surgeries to find the causes of the mysterious symptoms. Adults with MBP use a variety of means to fabricate illnesses in their children, including injecting substances such as bacteria into their children, inducing vomiting and diarrhea, and administering poisons and harmful over-the-counter medications. Although cases of MBP are not common, they often are publicized because of the bizarre and cruel behavior inflicted on young children. *See also* Mental Illness; Women as Patients

Further Reading

Feldman, Marc D., and Charles V. Ford with Toni Reinhold. *Patient or Pretender: Inside the Strange World of Factitious Disorders.* New York: John Wiley & Sons, 1994.

Family Caregiving

Family caregiving has long been considered a woman's "duty." Until about the 1960s, caring for a family's well-being was the primary occupation—albeit unpaid—of most women in the United States. Today, even those who work outside the home are expected to also be responsible for family caregiving. Between 75 and 80 percent of all family caregiving is performed by women.

According to a study published in 1999 by the *New England Journal of Medicine,* women make up 72 percent of caregivers for the chronically ill—frail adults who suffer from illnesses such as heart and lung disease. Terminally ill cancer patients, on the other hand, frequently are cared for in hospices or are able to make use of a variety of services designed for their care. The number of women caring for the terminally ill is likely to grow as the managed health-care system in the United States forces shorter hospital stays and in turn requires relatives to take responsibility for the dying. In addition, the aging "baby boom generation" (born during the 1950s) means that larger numbers of chronically ill patients will need care, placing even greater stress on women as family caregivers. (Stolberg)

With changing family structures, many woman in their fifties and sixties who are free of the child-rearing demands of their own families may suddenly find themselves caring for their grandchildren. Grandparents become primary caregivers for a variety of reasons: the children's parents have divorced or separated, have neglected or abused their children, have serious illness such as AIDS, are substance abusers, or are imprisoned. The U.S. Administration on Aging reported that an estimated four million children live in households headed by grandparents, and the grandmother is usually the primary caregiver.

A family caretaker celebrates with her relative. ©Barros & Barros/The Image Bank.

Certainly some men are caregivers for their children, disabled or ill spouses, and elderly relatives. However, women and men approach family caregiving in different ways. Since most women are taught from an early age to be responsible for the care of others, they often take on caregiving as a personal obligation. As a result women may immerse themselves in caregiving and neglect their marital and social relationships and leisure activities. Stress and/or depression may result if caregiving duties cannot be juggled satisfactorily with other activities. Generally, men approach caregiving in a more task-oriented way and do not suffer as much distress as women if they cannot personally perform all the caregiving duties. Men, in fact, are more likely than women to seek outside help for family caregiving needs.

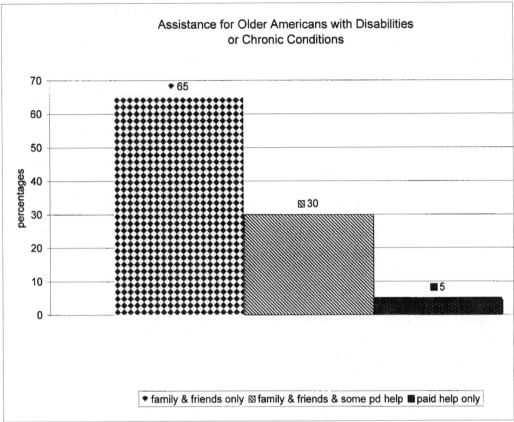

Source of Data: U.S. Administration on Aging, National Long Term Care Survey, 1994. Website: www.aoa.dhhs.gov/May 2000.

According to the nonprofit National Family Caregivers Association (NFCA), at least 25 million Americans provide primary care for relatives (usually a spouse or elderly parents) or close friends. These unpaid caregivers provide services estimated at $196 billion annually. The number of family caregivers is expected to increase dramatically as people in the United States live longer and age-related disabilities such as Alzheimer's disease, Parkinson's disease, and stroke affect an increasing number of family members. The number will increase even more as health-care providers continue to cut costs. Yet services and education for caregivers are not increasing proportionally. NFCA, the Older Women's League, and other organizations are attempting to raise public consciousness regarding the emotional, physical, and financial costs of caregiving.

Family caregivers must sometimes make difficult decisions such as whether to give up a job in order to provide home care for a family member. More than 50 percent of the women between the ages of 45 and 65 are in the workforce and some have reached senior or executive positions in their companies. But this is also the time in their lives when they are more likely to be faced with family caregiving responsibilities. It is not unusual for a woman in her sixties to be caring for a parent in her or his eighties or nineties.

Some companies provide assistance for workers, such as flextime and job-sharing, personal leave of absence for caregiving responsibilities, social workers to provide consultation with families, and seminars for caregivers. However, most caregivers must find help in other ways, such as hiring part-time in-home services, or using community support services or out-of-home institutional services. Most states and counties have Departments of Aging that can help caregivers locate service agencies in their areas. Hospitals also maintain lists of local services. Hundreds of self-help books and articles aimed at family caregivers have been published since the 1980s.

In addition, helpful information for caregivers and numerous lists of resources available can be found on Internet Web sites. Some sites have been created by unpaid family caregivers who simply want to help others facing similar problems and issues. Others offer commercial services and products; still others deal with ways caregivers can support family members who have specific diseases such as AIDS, Cancer, and Multiple Dystrophy, or with information that focuses on such caregiving concerns as legal issues in the care and treatment of family members with Alzheimer's disease.

Advocates for family caregivers and caregivers themselves would like to see some type of long-term national healthcare system established. The system would include a comprehensive network of resources in the United States, according to Suzanne Mintz, president and co-founder of the NFCA. She notes that the United States has a patchwork of programs and resources but no continuous link to bring them together. For example

hospitals hand back our loved ones, after treating the latest medical crisis, with a list of instructions told to tired ears, a fist full of prescriptions and not much else to ease the transition back home to a new routine. Forget actual training or ongoing support. A care counseling network could really help to fill some of these gaps and bridge the transitions. (Mintz)

Groups like NFCA and OWL point to the fact that people over 85 years of age are the fastest growing segment of the U.S. population, and many will need long-term care. Contrary to popular belief most elderly will be cared for at home. But as the population ages, the number of family caregivers is dwindling. Thus, advocates say, family caregiving issues should become a national priority. *See also* Alzheimer's Disease; National Family Caregivers Association; Older Women's League

Further Reading

Administration on Aging. "Grandparents as Caregivers" (May 1997). <http://www.aoa.dhhs.gov/May97/grandparents.html>.

Emanuel, Ezekiel J., Diane L. Fairclough, Julia Slutsman, Hillel Alpert, DeWitt Baldwin, and Linda L. Emanuel. "Assistance from Family Members, Friends, Paid Care Givers, and Volunteers in the Care of Terminally Ill Patients." *The New England Journal of Medicine* (September 23, 1999).

Field, Susan, and Ros Bramwell. "An Investigation into the Relationship between Caregiver Responsibilities and the Levels of Perceived Pressure Reported by Female Employees." *Journal of Occupational and Organizational Psychology* (June 1998).

Garrett, Carol B. "The Majority of Family Caregivers of the Elderly Are Women." *Womansword* (November 1997).

Mintz, Suzanne. "Family Caregivers Want Real Help from Real People." (1999) <http://www.nfcacares.org>.

National Family Caregivers Association. "The Status of Family Caregivers in America." <http://www.mediconsult.com/associations/nfca/status/index.html>.

Sommers, Tish, and Laurie Shields. *Women Take Care: The Consequences of Caregiving in Today's Society.* Gainesville, FL: Triad Publishing Co., 1987.

Stolberg, Sheryl Gay. "Study Finds Shortcomings in Care for Chronically Ill." *New York Times* (September 23, 1999).

Female Genital Mutilation

Female genital mutilation (FGM), often called female circumcision, includes the removal of the clitoris to decrease a woman's ability to achieve orgasm. The rite may also include removal of the labia minora and a portion of the labia majora, sewing up what remains, and leaving only a small opening to allow urine and menstrual blood to flow through. A federal crime in the United States, FGM has become a health and woman's rights issue because it has been practiced by immigrants from some African countries, parts of Asia, and the Middle East to protect a young girl's virginity and decrease her ability to enjoy sex. This practice at the time of the procedure can be life threatening due to hemorrhage, shock, or infection. FGM also can result in urilogical complications, severe pain during childbirth, and numerous chronic problems.

In 1994, U.S. Congresswoman Patricia Schroeder introduced a bill to outlaw FGM and to initiate educational programs for immigrant communities on the health risks and legal liabilities of the practice. At the time, some critics asserted that American values should not be imposed on immigrants. But Shroeder disagreed, arguing

There are a number of practices that immigrants are required to leave at home when they move here. Polygamy and slavery are two obvious examples.

Even when religions and strong cultural factors are involved, the courts have been clear: parents cannot endanger the lives or physical and mental well-being of their children simply to raise them within the confines of their own culture. Although parents have a fundamental right to raise and educate their children (guaranteed under the due-process clauses of the Fifth and Fourteenth Amendments), a long history of case law has established that the government can

intervene if there is a compelling reason to do so. (Schroeder, Editorial page)

In 1996, the U.S. Congress passed legislation known as the "Federal Prohibition of Female Genital Mutilation Act," which amends the U.S.Code to make FGM a federal crime, that can result in a prison term of up to five years. Still, the rite prevails in some U.S. immigrant communities, and physicians may be asked to perform the ritual cutting on infant girls and female adolescents. The American Association of Pediatrics (AAP) has alerted doctors to this life-threatening health risk and stated firmly that "AAP opposes all forms of FGM, counsels its members not to perform such ritual procedures, and encourages the development of community educational programs for immigrant populations." (American Academy of Pediatrics Committee on Bioethics, 153)

The American Medical Association, the American College of Obstetricians and Gynecologists, the College of Physicians and Surgeons of Ontario, Canada, and other groups also oppose FGM, as do the World Health Organization and the International Federation of Gynecology and Obstetrics.

Some young women have fled their countries of origin to avoid genital circumcision, asking for asylum in the United States, Canada, Great Britain, France, and other European nations. Several U.S. cases during the 1990s not only called public attention to FGM but also raised the question of whether the fear of FGM constituted a reason to grant asylum. In one 1997 case, the U.S. Immigration and Naturalization Services (INS) denied asylum to Adelaide Abankwah, who fled her tribe in Ghana. Abankwah claimed that she could not return to Ghana for fear of being killed or genitally mutilated after losing her virginity. Her deportation was blocked until an appeals court heard her case. In 1999 the court decided that the woman's health and life could be endangered and that she should not be sent back to Ghana.

Support and advocacy groups have formed to help young women learn about their legal rights and find medical care for health problems stemming from FGM. One group based in Oakland, California, is called Rising Daughters Aware (RDA), formerly known as the Female Genital Mutilation Network and Message Board. The RDA maintains an extensive Internet Web site and provides free information and services for FGM-affected women, their physicians, other health-care providers, social workers, counselors, and attorneys. *See also* Sexuality

Further Reading

American Academy of Pediatrics Committee on Bioethics. "Policy Statement, Female Genital Mutilation." *Pediatrics* (July 1998).

Dugger, Celia M. "Tug of Taboos: African Genital Rite Vs. American Law." *New York Times* (December 28, 1996).

International Planned Parenthood Federation. "Statement by the International Medical Advisory Panel" (November 1991).

Schroeder, Patricia. "Female Genital Mutilation—A Form of Child Abuse." *The New England Journal of Medicine* (September 15, 1994).

Female Migrant/Seasonal Farm Workers

Female migrant or seasonal farm workers move from place to place with their families, traveling from home bases in the south to the north during the growing and harvesting seasons. Migrant farm workers plant crops, cultivate them, apply chemicals (fertilizers and pesticides), irrigate fields, harvest, and pack for shipping more than 85 percent of the fruits and vegetables produced in the United States. These seasonal farm workers are employed by multibillion-dollar agricultural corporations or by individual farm owners who produce row crops or fruits in orchards and citrus groves. Of the estimated three to five

million migrant and seasonal farm workers in the United States, between 16 and 19 percent of them are women and girls.

Contrary to the common belief that migrant workers are primarily illegal immigrants, most migrant farm workers either are American citizens or are working in the country legally. Although the migrant population is diverse, most are of Latino or Hispanic heritage.

Female migrant farm workers encounter many of the same health problems that other poor women face, but the nature of their work and their economic and social status present additional health issues as well. Some face language barriers to health services, but most problems are related to working and living conditions and low income. Most live at the poverty level, endure hard manual labor and lack of sanitary facilities, have no medical insurance, and have limited access to health care. Migrant

The families of migrant workers often go without adequate sanitary facilities. FLOC Archives, Farm Labor Organizing Committee, AFL-CIO, 1221 Broadway, Toledo, OH 43609 (419) 243-3456.

farm workers do not receive sick leave, so they are often afraid of losing wages or their jobs if they take time off to seek health care. Because of poor health care, farm workers suffer high rates of illness and early death.

A significant health hazard for field-workers—women, children, and men—is exposure to toxic pesticides. According to the U.S. Environmental Protection Agency (EPA), an estimated 300,000 farm workers each year suffer acute pesticide poisoning. Physical stress and strain, and extreme heat, cold, and dampness further affect their health. Lack of safe drinking water contributes to dehydration and heat stroke. The absence of toilet facilities leads to urinary retention, which in turn is linked to a higher rate of urinary tract infection than in the general population. Women in agriculture also are more likely than other women to experience difficulties in pregnancy and menstrual cycles.

Lack of housing or inadequate housing is an issue that impacts on health. Employers recognize the problem, but construction and maintenance of housing is expensive and costs rise when employers must abide by laws designed to improve housing standards. As a result, workers may share rooms with several other people, or be forced to sleep in tents, cars, ditches, or open fields. The National Center for Farmworker Health points out that

Conditions such as tuberculosis, diabetes, cancer, and HIV, which require careful monitoring and frequent treatment, pose a special problem for farm workers who must move frequently. As a predominantly Hispanic population, farm workers are particularly vulnerable to diabetes. The National Women's Health Information Center notes that "Mexican Americans and Puerto Ricans experience up to 112 percent higher diabetes rates, compared to whites...[and] have a two to three times greater risk of non-insulin dependent diabetes than non-Latinas."

Death rates for Latina women with diabetes is twice that of non-Latina whites.

Depression is common among farm worker adults, and is often related to isolation, economic hardship, and weather conditions. In addition, poverty, stress, mobility, and lack of recreational opportunities make farm workers (both women and men) vulnerable to substance abuse. Depression and other mental health problems for migrant women also are the result of domestic violence.

The U.S. Health Service funds some migrant health centers to help provide care to farm workers, but there is not nearly enough to meet the need. Various church groups and private organizations such as the National Center for Farmworker Health and its emergency Friends of Farmworker Families Fund assist farm workers who cannot afford needed health care. The NCFH notes:

Follow-up care and continuity of care for chronic conditions are serious problems. Mobile units are an effective means of reaching isolated clients, but too few health centers have the resources to establish mobile programs. Health-care planners and providers, as well as migrant farm workers themselves, have to be creative to ensure good health options.

The American Hospital Association (AHA) developed one innovative project—taking health care directly to farm workers. Hospitals, clinics, food growers, doctors, and local health departments join together to provide nursing services, prenatal care, and transportation to clinics. *See also* Domestic Violence; Latina Women's Health; Poor Women's Health Care; Pregnancy; Working Women

Further Reading
Centers for Disease Control and Prevention. "Pregnancy-Related Behaviors among Migrant Farm Workers—Four States, 1989–1993." *Journal of the American Medical Association* (May 21, 1997).

Fleischhauer, Carl, and Beverly Brannan, eds. *Documenting America, 1935–1943.* Berkeley: University of California Press, 1988.

Manly, Libby, Alejandra Okie, and Melinda Wiggins, eds. *Fields without Borders/Campos Sin Fronteras: An Anthology of Documentary Writing.* Durham, N.C.: Student Action with Farm Workers, 1998.

National Center for Farmworker Health. "Farm Worker Health—About America's Farmworkers." <http://www.ncfh.org/aboutfws.htm>.

National Women's Health Information Center. "Minority Women." <http://www.4women.gov/faq/minority.htm>.

Fertility Drugs

See **Infertility**

Fetal Alcohol Syndrome

When a woman uses alcohol during pregnancy, the fetus she carries is at risk for fetal alcohol syndrome (FAS), a disorder characterized by growth retardation, facial abnormalities, and central nervous system dysfunction. Children with FAS suffer lifelong consequences, such as mental retardation, learning disabilities, and serious behavioral problems. The issue has raised numerous concerns in the United States as frequent drinking among pregnant women increased fourfold between 1991 and 1995.

The National Organization on Fetal Alcohol Syndrome (NOFAS) estimates that "at least 5,000 infants are born each year with FAS, or approximately one out of every 750 live births." Estimates of FAS vary, however, because many children with FAS or FAE are not diagnosed. In its special 2000 report to the U.S. Congress on alcohol and health, the Department of Health and Human Services notes:

Estimates of FAS prevalence vary from 0.5 to 3 per 1,000 live births in most populations, with much higher rates in some communities.... However, the diagnosis

of FAS identifies only a relatively small proportion of children affected by alcohol exposure before birth. Children with significant prenatal alcohol exposure can lack the characteristic facial defects and growth deficiency of FAS but still have alcohol-induced mental impairments that are just as serious, if not more so, than in children with FAS.

The term "alcohol-related neurodevelopmental disorder" (ARND) has been developed to describe this condition. In addition, prenatally exposed children without FAS facial features can have other alcohol-related physical abnormalities of the skeleton and certain organ systems; these are known as alcohol-related birth defects (ARBD).

In its fact sheet on FAS, the CDC's National Center for Environmental Health notes that no amount of alcohol is safe for a woman to drink while pregnant. "When a pregnant woman drinks alcohol, so does her fetus, because alcohol crosses the placenta freely."

Not only are FAS and other alcohol-related disabilities health issues but they also pose economic concerns. Individuals lose income and families incur high costs, including legal expenses and health care, to raise and care for FAS children. "The institutional and medical costs for one child with FAS are $1.4 million over a lifetime," according to the NOFAS. Those costs for the nation total billions of dollars annually due to health problems, special education, psychotherapy and counseling, welfare, crime, and encounters with the justice system.

Although FAS is 100 percent preventable if pregnant women do not drink alcohol, there is "no single, organized discipline within medicine that can, at this time, logically be held responsible or accountable for the development of a comprehensive approach to preventing and treating fetal alcohol syndrome," the Institute of Medicine reports, adding that there is not a single discipline in the broader arena of health and health care appropriate for this role.... Because the disorders pose health and developmental problems over the life span, they have been variably managed after the newborn period by pediatric subspecialists such as clinical geneticists, developmentalists, child neurologists, and others. No group has yet shown any interest in the management of FAS, ARBD [alcohol-related birth defects], or ARND patients as adults. Families affected by FAS frequently require the services of specialists in substance abuse, developmental disabilities, and education. Therefore, these disorders lie within the purview of many groups but are clearly not the full responsibility of any one. All groups will accept, or have accepted, an interest in handling an appropriate piece of the problem, but no one is in a position to lead and coordinate. Hence, there is no group to which government can look for leadership, and no group is focused on advocacy. (Stratton, et al, 194)

Yet groups in the private sector and within government (at the federal and state level) are attempting to educate the public about the health, economic, and social issues associated with FAS. These include the Centers for Disease Control and Prevention, the National Institutes of Health, the National Clearinghouse for Alcohol and Drug Information, the National Organization on Fetal Alcohol Syndrome, and the National Center on Addiction and Substance Abuse at Columbia University.

Federal and state laws also attempt to deal with the hazards of drinking during pregnancy. Alcoholic beverages must carry warnings that drinking during pregnancy can cause birth defects. In some states, warning signs must be posted in places where liquor is served. Some legislators want to ban alcohol use by pregnant women altogether. However, civil libertarians say that such regulations would violate a woman's right to make her own choices.

The issue is often intertwined with broader social issues on women's reproductive rights versus "fetal rights" and personhood. *See also* Alcohol Abuse and Alcoholism; Drug-Dependent Mothers; Pregnancy; Prenatal Testing

Further Reading

Jacobson, Joseph L. "Drinking Moderately and Pregnancy." *Alcohol Research & Health* (Winter 1999).

Jacobson, Sandra W. "Assessing the Impact of Maternal Drinking During and After Pregnancy." *Alcohol Health & Research World* (Summer 1997).

National Center for Environmental Health, Centers for Disease Control and Prevention. "Fetal Alcohol Syndrome." Fact Sheet (August 1999).

National Organization on Fetal Alcohol Syndrome. "What Is FAS?" (no date). <http://www.nofas.org/what.htm>.

Stratton, Kathleen, Cynthia Howe, and Frederick Battaglia, Eds., for the Institute of Medicine. *Fetal Alcohol Syndrome: Diagnosis, Epidemiology, Prevention and Treatment.* Washington, DC: National Academy Press, 1996.

United States Department of Health and Human Services. *Tenth Special Report on Alcohol and Health* (to the U.S. Congress, June 2000). <http://silk.nih.gov/silk/niaaa1/publication/10report/10-order.htm>.

Freedom of Access to Clinic Entrances Act of 1994

The U.S. Congress enacted the Freedom of Access to Clinic Entrances Act, often called the Abortion Clinic Access bill or the FACE law, in May 1994. The law was supported by numerous women's health-care advocates and women's rights groups, who were concerned about protection for pregnant women and health-care providers at reproductive health service clinics. Anti-abortion activists frequently attempted to prevent pregnant women from entering such clinics, threatened clinic staff, and in some cases injured or killed doctors and health-care workers.

FACE amends the federal criminal code and makes it illegal to intentionally injure, intimidate, or interfere with a per-

Little Rock police begin removing handcuffed members of Rescue America, a prolife group, after they were arrested for blocking the entrance to a women's clinic, Little Rock, Arkansas, July 8, 1994. ©Reuters/Vidal Medina/Archive Photos.

son trying to obtain reproductive health services. The law also prohibits intentional damage or destruction of clinic property and sets fines and prison terms for offenders. However, the law does not prohibit peaceful demonstrations by antiabortionists or others at reproductive healthcare clinics. Such protests are protected by the First Amendment to the U.S. Constitution. *See also* Abortion; Abortion Providers

Further Reading

Bill Summary and Status for the 103rd Congress, Summary of S.636, Public Law 103-259 <http://thomas.loc.gov>.

G

Gender-Based Biology

Gender-based biology is a relatively new field of inquiry that is gaining widespread acceptance in the scientific and academic communities. According to the Society for Women's Health Research (SWHR), it is defined as

> the field of scientific inquiry committed to identifying the biological and physiological differences between men and women. Gender differences that are found at the system, organ, tissue, cellular, and sub-cellular level, as well as gender differences in response to pharmaceuticals, are considered gender-based biology. The findings from gender-based biology explain many of the known gender differences in disease epidemiology and health outcomes. Gender-based biology has the potential to revolutionize the way in which we understand health and disease for both men and women. (SWHR Fact Sheet)

Courses on gender-based biology have been generated because of the fact that, like gender-biased research, human biology has focused on the male anatomy—physiological, blood composition, lung capacity, and other measurements—as the norm. Gender-based biology courses were initiated at women's colleges or former women's colleges; they are also being taught at university medical schools or as component parts of regular biology courses.

Although researchers have long studied differences in the male and female anatomies, only in recent decades have studies uncovered distinct biological differences in the ways women and men respond to treatment for various diseases and health conditions. Women, for example, have less of the gastric enzyme that breaks down alcohol than men do; thus after drinking the same amount of alcohol, women have higher alcohol blood content, even when size differences are taken into account. Women also are likely to absorb more toxic chemicals than men, so are at a higher risk when exposed to the same environmental hazards. Some pain medications do not have the same effect on women as on men. Ibuprofen, for instance, provides less pain relief for women. Other types of medications, such as antibiotics, can create different reactions in women and men. Higher bone density and bone mineral content in men than in women account for the higher rates of osteoporosis among women. The 52 percent higher rate of serotonin synthesis in men than in women could explain the higher rate of depression among women. Women have stronger immune systems than men, but are more likely to get autoimmune diseases, in which the body attacks its own tissues, such as rheumatoid arthritis and multiple sclerosis. *See also* Autoimmune Diseases; Depression; Environmental Health Hazards; Gender-Biased Research and Treatment; Osteoporosis; Society for Women's Health Research

Further Reading

Lewis, Ricki. "Gender-Based Biology Courses Take Diverse Forms." *The Scientist* (November 9, 1998).

Society for Women's Health Research. "Just the Facts: Gender-Based Biology" (1999).

Society for Women's Health Research. "10 Differences between Men and Women That Make a Difference in Women's Health." <http://www. womens-health.org/insertB.htm>.

Gender-Biased Research and Treatment

Gender-biased research and gender-biased treatment refer to the fact that government-funded researchers (as well as most privately sponsored researchers) studying health problems, diseases, and the effects of medications and treatments have, until the 1990s, concentrated solely or overwhelmingly on male subjects in clinical trials. The conclusions drawn from this male-dominated biomedical research have long been applied to women, even though women experience health problems and react to treatments differently than men. Gender bias and outright discrimination against women also extend to research communities where women frequently are hindered from doing meaningful scientific investigations and face numerous obstacles, including low and unequal pay, disparagement of their abilities, and sexual harassment. In addition, studies of women's health issues have been woefully underfunded or not funded at all.

Historically women's health research was linked primarily to their reproductive systems; during the late nineteenth and early twentieth centuries women were advised to "take particular care of themselves lest they injure their reproductive organs. Vigorous activity, especially during menstruation, or exposure to physical or mental stress could create irreparable damage," practitioners believed. (LaRosa and Pinn, 145) By the 1960s and 1970s, activists involved in the women's health movement were demanding that medical practitioners and researchers pay more attention to health-care issues specific to women, such as breast cancer and menopause, and those issues affecting both women and men but predominantly impacting on women; domestic violence and eating disorders are examples.

During the 1980s various government agencies, congressional members, and women's health-care organizations—including the Society for the Advancement of Women's Health, Research, the American Medical Women's Association, the Boston Women's Health Book Collective, Jacobs Institute of Women's Health, and minority women's health groups—began to issue an increasing number of reports and information on gender differences in health care. The National Women's Health Information Center of the U.S. Department of Health and Human Services pointed out:

Women often face a fragmentation of health care services to meet their reproductive and other health needs, and make more visits than men to the doctor. Women are also highly interested and informed about health care issues, but reliable health information needed for informed choices about health care has not been widely available. National studies have indicated that women may not be as satisfied as men with the information they receive from their health care providers or the level of communication with their provider. Furthermore, several studies have found that health care providers treat women differently from men. Compared with treatment given to men, health providers may give women less thorough evaluations for similar complaints, minimize their symptoms, provide fewer interventions for the same diagnoses, prescribe some types of medications more often, or provide less explanation in response to questions.

In the late 1980s, a U.S. Public Health Service task force investigating women's health issues found that knowledge about health care specific to women was inadequate or completely lacking. A U.S. Government Accounting Office (GAO) report issued in 1990 lent support to these findings by showing that male scientists at the prestigious National Institutes of Health (NIH) had for years systematically excluded women from medical studies. Women were not asked to participate because of the belief that their hormone fluctuations and the possibility of pregnancy would interfere with medical investigations. The GAO report included numerous examples of how women's health issues had been ignored and neglected. For one, a five-year NIH study concluded that one aspirin a day could reduce heart attacks, but the more than 27,000 subjects in the study were all men, who experience heart attacks differently than women. Even though heart disease is the number one killer of women, no researcher knew whether the aspirin therapy would be effective for women.

Due to the efforts of Congresswomen Patricia Schroeder and Olympia Snowe and Congressman Henry Waxman, congressional hearings followed the GAO report. Since then the American public as well as some research scientists and medical practitioners have become more aware that women should be treated according to their specific health needs rather than the basis of what is or was known about male health. As Beryl Lieff Benderly for the In-

stitute of Medicine explained, there is now an "effort...to see and treat the female person as a whole and normal human being in her own right, rather than as a subsidiary or deviant version of the dominant male.... The need to incorporate female experience and perceptions into medical thinking has become obvious across the heath care community." (Benderly, 6) She writes further that

Women's life experiences and social roles differ from men's in ways that affect physical and mental health. These differences bear heavily on many aspects of health, including such diverse issues as what and how much a woman eats, how and where she gets medical care, and whether the factors affecting her health get appropriate attention in research. (Benderly, 10)

If biological differences between women and men are not taken into account, treatment for women's health problems may be inadequate or even life-threatening. One research finding, for example, shows that women are more likely than men to have a second heart attack within a year of the first heart attack, and they reject heart transplants more frequently than men. Among smokers who smoke the same number of cigarettes, from 20 to 70 percent more women than men are likely to develop lung cancer.

Other studies indicate that the types and dosage amounts of medication prescribed should be based on gender. Dr. Raymond Woosley of Georgetown University "examined 40 drugs that sometimes cause irregular heartbeats. For almost a dozen of the drugs, women have twice the risk of developing this potentially life-threatening side effect." (Associated Press) Woosley reported his findings during a May 1999 scientific meeting sponsored by the NIH Office of Research on Women's Health. The two-day conference was called to alert doctors to gender differences in reactions to medications, which may be related to hormones and proteins that help the body assimilate drugs. Scientists, however, could provide few reasons for the differences, primarily because of a paucity of scientific investigations. Drug manufacturers refused to include women of childbearing age in drug studies, fearing that if a woman became pregnant her fetus would be harmed. The U.S. Food and Drug Administration forced a change in that practice during the early 1990s.

In spite of all the public pronouncements, new studies released in 2000 show that "medical researchers who receive federal money often flout a federal law that requires them to analyze the effects of new drugs and treatments on women," according to a report in the *New York Times*. The studies were issued by the GAO and the *Journal of Women's Health.* According to the *Times,* the General Accounting Office found that while the National Institutes of Health "has made substantial progress in ensuring inclusion of women in studies," it has not enforced the requirement for researchers to examine whether women and men fare differently in such clinical studies. Moreover, it said, the N.I.H., the government's main sponsor of biomedical research, has done a haphazard job of tracking data on research involving women. (Pear) *See also* American Medical Women's Association; Boston Women's Health Book Collective; Jacobs Institute of Women's Health; National Women's Health Information Center; Society for Women's Health Research; Women's Health Movement

Further Reading

Associated Press. "Decisions on Medication Can Hinge on Patient's Gender." (May 16, 1999).
Benderly, Beryl Lieff. *In Her Own Right: The Institute of Medicine's Guide to Women's Health Issues.* Washington, DC: National Academy Press, 1997.
Hicks, Karen M., ed. *Misdiagnosis: Woman as a Disease.* Allentown, PA: People's Medical Society, 1994.
LaRosa, Judith H., and Vivian W. Pinn. "Gender Bias in Biomedical Research." *Journal of the American Medical Women's Association* (September/October 1993).
Laurence, Leslie, and Beth Weinhouse. *Outrageous Practices: The Alarming Truth about How Medicine Mistreats Women.* New York: Fawcett Columbine/Ballantine, 1994.
National Women's Health Information Center. "Priority Women's Health Issues." <http://www.4woman.org/owh/pub/womhealthissues/whipriority.htm>.
Nechas, Eileen, and Denise Foley. *Unequal Treatment: What You Don't Know about How Women Are Mistreated by the Medical Community.* New York: Simon & Schuster, 1994.
Pear, Robert. "Research Neglects Women, Studies Find." *New York Times* (April 30, 2000).
Smith, John M. *Women and Doctors: A Physician's Explosive Account of Women's Medical Treatment—and Mistreatment—in America Today and What You Can Do about It.* New York: The Atlantic Press, 1992.

Genetic Testing

Genetic testing in medicine involves using genetic information to help diagnose diverse health problems in individuals and sometimes to determine the health of a fetus or the paternity of a child. Genetic research and genetic testing have made it possible to identify genes that could cause breast cancer, Alzheimer's, and other serious diseases, many of which affect women in large numbers. Genetic testing reveals whether newborns have or could develop diseases that can be treated such as phenylketonuria (PKU), congenital hypothyroidism, and cystic fibrosis. However, warns the National Institutes of Health (NIH),

> Caregivers will need to know not only about the medical benefits and risks of genetic technologies, but also about the psychosocial and legal implications of these technologies in the public arena.

Bacteria for human genome research. ©James King-Holmes/Photo Researchers, Inc.

Until these issues are resolved, the technical ability to perform tests for DNA mutations should not be confused with a mandate to offer them. Safeguards must be in place to ensure that these tests are used wisely, maximizing their potential benefits to patients and minimizing their potential risks. (Fink and Collins, abstract)

Since the mid-1990s, rapid developments in the field of genetics and the Human Genome Project of the NIH have raised concerns about testing for genetic abnormalities. A couple might decide not to have children if genetic testing suggests the possibility of producing offspring with a genetic abnormality. As several publicized cases have shown, a pregnant woman may be faced with potentially embarrassing legal ramifications (and marital and relationship problems) if genetic testing reveals that she has borne a child whose DNA does not match her partner's. She could also be faced with the choice of ter-

minating a pregnancy if a test shows a genetic disorder in the fetus.

Testing for adverse genetic conditions is not new. For years, women in the United States and other countries have undergone amniocentesis to determine whether the fetus has inherited a genetic abnormality such as Down's Syndrome. Patients also are tested for Tay-Sachs disease (a nerve disorder that is often fatal), sickle cell anemia, and other genetic irregularities.

Because of rapid advances in genetic research, testing for suspected genetic disorders is becoming increasingly commonplace. The procedure involves a blood test, which is relatively simple and risk-free. But the results could have profound effects on patients. The American Nurses Association (ANA), the Institute of Medicine (IOM), the NIH, and other medical groups recommend that patients be given more information than the purpose, risks, and benefits of genetic testing. Before patients sign "informed consent" forms for genetic testing, they should be told how severe a genetic condition can be and what can be done to treat it. Patients also should know that genetic tests are not infallible, what the rates of false positives and negatives are, and when the disease might manifest itself. For example, the test for Huntington's disease, which causes abnormal body movements and mental deterioration, is 99 percent accurate, but there is great variation in when and how the disease impacts on an individual. Learning about the possibility of such a disease could cause emotional distress; thus a patient should receive information about support groups and counseling, experts say.

Another important issue raised in regard to genetic testing is confidentiality. Keeping test results confidential is one way to assure that genetic data will not be used to discriminate against those who are likely to inherit debilitating diseases. Laws are in place in some states to prevent the release of information about genetic data without a patient's written authorization. In California, for example, seven employees sued Lawrence Berkeley National Laboratory after the workers discovered that during their pre-employment medical examinations black applicants' blood samples were tested for sickle cell anemia and female applicants were tested for pregnancy. A California appeals court ruled in favor of the employees, saying that such tests are an invasion of privacy and illegal unless an employee or applicant gives consent or a person is unable to do her or his job.

Whether or not to disclose positive test results to family members is one more troubling genetic testing issue. For example, a pregnant woman who learns that her fetus carries the gene responsible for cystic fibrosis may decide not to tell her sister, immediate family members, or others because of possible adverse consequences, such as negative impacts on employment and insurance. While some ethicists contend that a woman or couple has a right to privacy and has no moral obligation to share the information, most argue that genetic information is a family matter and should be shared with those who might be affected.

Discrimination in health insurance and the fear of potential discrimination threaten society's ability both to use new genetic technologies to improve human health and to conduct the very research needed to understand, treat, and prevent genetic disease, notes the U.S. Department of Health and Human Services. Genetic testing has created dilemmas for those whose family histories predispose them to illness. Of particular concern, the department states,

is the fear of losing or being denied health insurance because of a possible genetic predisposition to a particular disease. For example, a woman who carries a genetic alteration associated with breast cancer, and who has close relatives with the disease, has an increased risk of developing breast and ovarian cancer. Knowledge of this genetic status can enable women in high-risk families, together with their health care providers, to better tailor surveillance and prevention strategies. However, because of a concern that she or her children may not be able to obtain or change health insurance coverage in the future, a woman currently in this situation may avoid or delay genetic testing.

Because of the widespread fear among Americans that private genetic information will be used against them, President Bill Clinton signed an executive order in February 2000 that prohibited the federal government and its agencies from using genetic testing in any employment decision. It prevented federal employers from requesting or requiring that employees undergo genetic tests of any kind. It strictly forbade employers from using genetic information to classify employees in such a way that deprives them of advancement opportunities. *See also* Alzheimer's Disease; Breast Cancer; Pregnancy

Further Reading

Fink, Leslie, and Francis S. Collins, M.D. "The Human Genome Project: View from the National Institutes of Health." Abstract. *Journal of the American Medical Women's Association* (Winter 1997). <http://jamwa.amwa-doc.org/vol52/52_1_1.htm>

Finger, Anne L. "How Would You Handle These Ethical Dilemmas?" *Medical Economics* (October 27, 1997).

Kirby, Michael. "Genetic Testing and Discrimination: The Development of Genetic Testing Confronts Humanity with Urgent Challenges." *UNESCO Courier* (May 1998).

Scanlon, Colleen. "The Legal Implications of Genetic Testing." *RN Magazine* (March 1998).

Griswold v. Connecticut

In 1965 the U.S. Supreme Court decided the case known as *Griswold v. Connecti-*

cut, which helped establish the individual right to privacy in regard to the use of contraceptives. The case involved Estelle Griswold, who was the executive director of the Planned Parenthood League of Connecticut. Griswold and Planned Parenthood's medical director, a licensed physician, were convicted as accessories for giving married persons information and medical advice on how to prevent conception and, following examination, for prescribing a contraceptive device or material for the wives to use. At the time a Connecticut law made it a crime for any person to use any form of birth control to prevent conception. The case was appealed to the State Supreme Court and upheld. But the U.S. Supreme Court reversed the decision in 1965. Justice William O. Douglas wrote the opinion for the Court, noting:

> We deal with a right of privacy older than the Bill of Rights—older than our political parties, older than our school system. Marriage is a coming together for better or for worse, hopefully enduring, and intimate to the degree of being sacred. It is an association that promotes a way of life, not causes; a harmony in living, not political faiths; a bilateral loyalty, not commercial or social projects. Yet it is an association for as noble a purpose as any involved in our prior decisions.

The High Court's decision in Griswold and another contraceptive case, *Eisenstadt v. Baird*, in 1972 helped to establish a basic privacy principle. The *Eisenstadt* decision struck down a Massachusetts law banning the sale of contraceptives to unmarried people. The Court ruled that the right of privacy applied not only to married couples but also to individuals. People were free to make decisions about their private lives without government interference. This led to the Supreme Court's 1973 ruling in *Roe v. Wade*, declaring that the constitutional right to privacy extends to decisions regarding whether or not to have children. *See also* Birth Control; Planned Parenthood Federation of America; *Roe v. Wade*

Further Reading
Griswold v. Connecticut, 381 U.S. 479 (1965).

H

Hair Loss

Hair loss, or balding, is a health and social concern for an estimated two million American women. Hair loss is usually associated with medical treatments and is often a side effect of chemotherapy and radiation therapy for various forms of cancer. In addition, "more than 290 medications are known to cause hair loss in women, including beta blockers and ace inhibitors that are used to treat hypertension; lithium and other antidepressants; blood-thinning agents, and amphetamines like phentermine, which was half of the recently banned fen-phen diet drug combination." (Fritsch) Lupus, a form of arthritis that affects more women than men, may also cause hair loss. Genetics, hormones, and pregnancy are other factors related to hair loss in women.

Both women and men lose some hair due to heredity or changing hormones as they age. However, hair loss in women

is far less prominent than it is in men. It also occurs in a different pattern. Most women first experience hair thinning and hair loss where they part their hair and on the top of the head, but don't have a receding hairline. (Mayo)

Social attitudes in regard to balding also reflect gender differences. Balding women are often viewed as unattractive and unacceptable or seen as abnormal. Bald men, on the other hand, may be seen as distinguished or virile. In some cases, sports and film celebrities deliberately shave their heads for "sex appeal." Although both women and men attempt to hide baldness, women who lose their hair are more likely than men to use wigs, hair pieces, or treatments for hair regrowth or retention. *See also* Dieting and Diet Drugs; Genetic Testing; Pregnancy

Further Reading
Fritsch, Jane. "The Secret Loss That Women Try to Keep under Their Hats." *New York Times* (June 21, 1998).

Mayo Health Clinic. "Hair Loss in Women." *Mayo Clinic Health Letter* (February 1997).

Hamilton, Alice (1869–1970)

Alice Hamilton is considered the matriarch of occupational medicine, and is honored by women's health organizations and labor groups for her major contributions to improving working conditions for factory employees. She is also remembered for her work at Hull House, the settlement house

Alice Hamilton, Hull House resident, and specialist in industrial disease. Jane Addams Memorial Collection (JAMC neg. 398), Special Collections, The University Library, University of Illinois at Chicago.

in Chicago founded by social reformer Jane Addams.

Born in New York City, Alice was the daughter of Montgomery and Gertrude Hamilton and sister of Edith, a well-known classicist. She grew up in Indiana, where she was educated at home. She attended a finishing school in Connecticut and then the Fort Wayne, Indiana, College of Medicine. She earned her medical degree at the University of Michigan in 1893, and interned in Minneapolis and Boston. With her sister she spent a year in Germany, attending the universities of Munich and Leipzich, which previously had not allowed women to enroll. Hamilton was allowed to attend bacteriology and pathology lectures with the condition that she not be conspicuous to male students and professors. After returning to the United States, Hamilton conducted research at Johns Hopkins University in Baltimore, Maryland. In 1897 she became professor

of pathology at Northwestern University's Women's Medical School in Evanston, Illinois, and in 1902 she accepted a bacteriologist position at the Memorial Institute for Infectious Diseases in Chicago.

During the late 1800s and early 1900s, many workers—countless women and children among them—became ill from toxic materials such as lead in workplaces. Or they were injured due to lack of safety measures. Because no laws were in place to protect workers from such hazards, when they became ill or injured, they lost their jobs and employers found others to replace them.

In Chicago, Dr. Hamilton lived in Hull House, which served the working poor. There, while operating a baby clinic and treating widows of poor immigrant workers, she acquainted herself with the families in the neighborhood. She learned about their health problems, strange deaths, and the high numbers of widows. As she wrote in her autobiography:

> I could not fail to hear tales of the dangers that workingmen faced, of...carbon-monoxide gassing in the great steel mills, of painters disabled by lead palsy, of pneumonia and rheumatism among the men in the stockyards. Illinois then had no legislation providing compensation for accident or disease caused by occupation. (There is something strange in speaking of "accident and sickness compensation." What could "compensate" anyone for an amputated leg or a paralyzed arm, or even an attack of lead colic, to say nothing of the loss of a husband or son?) (Hamilton, 114)

When the typhoid fever epidemic hit Chicago in 1902, Hamilton concluded that improper sewage disposal attracted flies, which in turn spread the disease. About this time she also found that lead dust and other toxic materials were affecting the health of many poor immigrant workers. Due to Dr. Hamilton's findings, the governor of Illinois created the world's first Occupational Disease Commission and appointed her as its director. The commission called attention to the need for legislation to protect workers, and Illinois passed several laws compensating workers for health problems and injuries due to work-related conditions.

In 1919, Dr. Hamilton became the first female professor at Harvard Medical School in Boston, a position she held until she retired in 1935. She conducted industrial research and published several books, among them *Industrial Poisons in the United States* (1925), *Industrial Toxicology* (1934), and her autobiography, *Exploring the Dangerous Trades* (1943). She was also a consultant for the Division Of Labor Standards and president of the National Consumers' League. *See also* Environmental Health Hazards; Public Safety; Women in Medicine; *Women: Work and Health*

Further Reading

Centers for Disease Control and Prevention. "Alice Hamilton, M.D." *Morbidity and Mortality Weekly Report* (June 11, 1999).

Hamilton, Alice. *Exploring the Dangerous Trades: The Autobiography of Alice Hamilton, M.D.* Boston: Little, Brown and Company, 1943.

Read, Phyllis J., and Bernard L. Witlieb. *The Book of Women's Firsts: Breakthrough Achievements of Almost 1,000 American Women.* New York: Random House, 1992.

Harvard Nurses' Health Study

The *Harvard Nurses' Health Study* (NHS) is one of the largest, long-term studies of women ever to be compiled and has resulted in important data on women's health. When the study began in 1976, a Harvard Medical School professor, Frank Speaker, wanted to learn about the long-term effects of oral contraceptives. He and his colleagues sent questionnaires to 370,000 registered nurses and received responses from about one-third of them. An expansion of the study began in 1989 (Nurses' Health Study II), and since then nurses have been asked every other year to respond to questions about their health and lifestyle, such as eating habits, past illnesses, whether and what medications and vitamins they took, and whether they have exercised, smoked, or drank. Because the respondents are nurses trained to provide accurate information, their answers to questions are considered highly reliable. Periodically, the women in the study have also provided blood and other samples for researchers. As the *New York Times* reported: "By knowing these women's experiences, researchers can look at the histories of those who have contracted diseases and compare them with those who have not and begin teasing out the important factors in determining a woman's risk for a particular illness." The *Times* report notes that

> Researchers have been able to identify risk factors for more common diseases, like breast, colon and lung cancer, diabetes and heart disease. In the future, researchers say they will be able to identify risk factors for rarer conditions, like lymphoma, kidney cancer and bladder cancer, as well as afflictions more common later in life, such as stroke and senility. (Yoon)

One aspect of the NHS was to determine whether women's exposure to environmental pollutants such as dichlorodiphenyltrichloroethane (DDT) and polychlorinated biphenyls (PCBs) could put women at risk for breast cancer. Although banned since the 1970s, the chemicals stay in the environment for decades, have an adverse effect on wildlife, and accumulate in the human body. Nearly all North Americans have some residues of these pollutants in their bodies. Some past studies suggested that the toxins acted as environmental estrogens. However NHS researchers analyzed blood samples provided by participants in the nurses' study and concluded that no evidence existed to link the chemicals to the increasing breast cancer rates in the United States, according to a 1997 report in the *New England Journal of Medicine*.

The success of the long-term study has prompted other researchers to attempt similar projects. One study that began in 1989 involves nurses who enrolled in the project at an earlier age than those in the NHS. Researchers are also studying children of the participants in order to identify factors leading to adolescent obesity. These and other investigations will contribute to understanding of how such factors as diet and lifestyle changes can help prevent disease in women. *See also* Environmental Health Issues

Further Reading

Hunter, D.J., S.E. Hankinson, F. Laden, G.A. Colditz, J.E. Manson, W.C. Willet, F.E. Speaker, and M.S. Wolff. "Harvard Study Refutes Link between 'Environmental Estrogens' and Breast Cancer." *New England Journal of Medicine*, Research Highlights, Harvard University Kresge Center for Environmental Health Science. <http://www.niehs.nih.gov/centers/hilites/97hilite/hvd.htm>.

Yoon, Carol Kaesuk. "In Nurses' Lives, a Treasure Trove of Health Data." *New York Times* (September 14, 1998).

Health-Care Access

Many groups of women in the United States encounter barriers to health care, and health-care access is a significant economic issue for millions of American women and their families. Race, gender, sexual orientation, and socioeconomic status determine whether women will have access to health-care delivery systems, which include the varied institutions and personnel that provide health care in the United States, from hospitals and clinics to health-care practitioners and medical researchers.

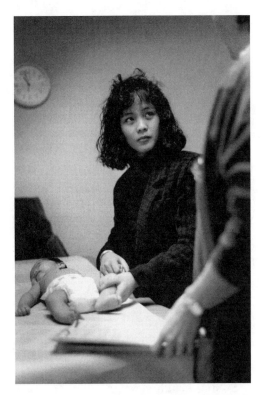

Mother with baby at clinic. ©Dean Wong/CORBIS.

For women, one underlying factor that creates a barrier to good health care is the fact that until the 1990s little medical research included women in clinical trials and studies. Women's health problems were frequently related to their reproductive functions and their problems were seen as deviations from the male-defined model. In addition, women who complained about their health were viewed as being emotionally unstable or having mental health problems. Although medical researchers and practitioners are beginning to recognize that gender differences exist in treatment, many health-care professionals fail to take into account the

major psychosocial issues that traditionally exist outside the framework of the primary care disciplines: depression, anxiety, the effects of sexual abuse and domestic violence, eating disorders, chemical dependency, and life cycle transitions like menopause. Failure to recognize the impact of these issues on how women commonly use health services leads to inappropriate diagnosis and treatment. (Hoffman, 16)

Poverty, lack of medical insurance, aging, and the geographic location of health-care providers are some other major barriers to health-care access. Pregnant women without insurance, for example, frequently cannot afford prenatal care. Because most women earn less than men, they are less able to afford health care or insurance that provides medical benefits, particularly if they are single mothers with children, elderly, or part of the working poor. Many disabled, elderly, and low-income women lack transportation access to hospitals, clinics, and other health-care providers. Adolescents encounter similar problems in accessing health care; in addition, many young girls (as well as boys) do not get the health care they need because they are afraid to confide in their parents or physicians. Adolescent girls may be too embarrassed or intimidated to report sexual or physical abuse, or to seek help for eating disorders, depression, and other mental health problems.

Other diverse groups of women face barriers to health care. Among them are HIV-positive women. The AIDS Legal Referral Panel of California researched hundreds of medical articles and studies related to HIV-positive women's access to health care. They found that the

relationship of HIV-positive women to health care services is intricately connected to historic and current institutionalized racism and sexism; the providers who administer care to positive women; past and persistent HIV-related discrimination; coercive practices; and breaches of privacy/confidentiality.

The pervasive and ongoing alienation of women, people of color and poor people from medical structures is the context within which women with HIV attempt to access the health care system.

Women with HIV are overwhelmingly poor women and women of color, and therefore face a more complex spectrum of barriers to care. It is well established that the social dimensions of gender have been overlooked in determining an individual's health care utilization and outcomes. Additionally, inequalities in the health outcomes of many communities of color have been well documented, and attitudes about HIV among communities of color have been affected by a protracted history of discriminatory practices and experimentation on people of color. (AIDS Legal Referral Panel, 1998)

Health-care access is also a major problem for lesbian women. Whatever their economic status or racial heritage, many lesbian and bisexual women do not seek help from medical providers because they fear they will not be treated with respect, that their sexual orientation will not be kept confidential, and that they will not receive adequate care. *See also* Adolescent Girls' Health; AIDS; African-American Women's Health; Asian-American Women's Health; Eating Disorders; Latina Women's Health; Lesbian Women's Health; Menopause; Native American Women's Health; Poor Women's Health Care

Further Reading

AIDS Legal Referral Panel. "Barriers to Health Care for HIV-Positive Women: Deadly Denial." (1998) <http://www.alrp.org/barriers.html>

Benderly, Beryl Lieff for the Institute of Medicine. *In Her Own Right: The Institute of Medicine's Guide to Women's Health Issues.* Washington, DC: National Academy Press, 1997.

Commonwealth Fund. "Facts on Access to Health Care" (September 1997). <http://www.cmwf.org/programs/women/acesfact.asp>.

Hoffman, Eileen, M.D. *Our Health, Our Lives: A Revolutionary Approach to Total Health Care for Women.* New York: Simon & Schuster, 1995.

Health-Care Delivery Systems

See **Health-Care Access**

Health Insurance

Health insurance is a prominent economic issue affecting the health of many women in the United States. Insurance coverage for health care is not readily available for many groups of women, particularly those of working age between 18 and 64. A report from The Commonwealth Fund, a private research foundation based in New York City, found that, from 1993 to 1998, the percentage of women covered by private insurance fell from 77 percent to 72 percent. Many uninsured women forego medical care, or they encounter problems accessing the health-care system. Their health may be compromised when, for example, they do not seek preventive care such as Pap smears and mammograms and do not see their doctors except in emergency situations. Chronic or life-threatening conditions may develop. According to The Commonwealth Fund report, a major concern

is that women ages 25 to 34 are least likely to have health insurance. Further, women in this age group who do not have employer-sponsored insurance when they start working are not getting coverage as they grow older, even when they stay in the workforce. From 1986 to 1996, the coverage rate for women in this age group fell from 80 percent to 75 percent. Among working women in their early forties, employer-sponsored coverage fell from 72 percent in 1981 (when they were in their mid- to late-twenties) to 62 percent in 1996.

Of the approximately 55 percent of women who are in the labor force today, about 30 percent are employed in the retail and service sectors—sectors where women have typically earned low wages and have limited health insurance options. Younger women are 50 percent more likely than older women to be working in sales and service occupations, making them even more likely to lack health coverage.

Low-income women who have federally funded Medicaid health-care insurance may face obstacles as well. A review of 11 state Medicaid managed-care plans conducted by the Center for Women Policy Studies in 1998 found that these plans "create barriers to care." Women living with HIV/AIDS or suffering from other chronic illnesses are forced to go to health-care providers outside the plan for many critical Medicaid-covered services because the plans do not "require contractors to provide a comprehensive package of Medicaid-covered health and social services." In addition, the state plans "do not require formal referral structures of comprehensive case management services to help people enrolled in plans navigate the health care system." (Center for Women Policy Studies, 3)

As more people live longer, costly and fragmented long-term care will become an even greater problem than it is at present. Because women have a longer lifespan than men, they are more likely to need long-term care. Over half of American women who reach age 65, the age at which they become eligible for Medicare, can expect to spend part of their remaining years in assisted living, adult daycare, home care, or a nursing home. But few have insurance policies covering such care. Many women mistakenly believe that Medicare, the federal insurance program, will cover nursing home care, but the insurance provides only skilled nursing services, not the daily maintenance that many elderly patients need. With the average annual cost of long-term care now $51,100 and home care often just as expensive, older women need to plan ahead for long-term care insurance. *See also* AIDS; Mammogram; National Center on Women and Aging; Pap Smear; Sexually Transmitted Diseases

Further Reading
Center for Women Policy Studies. "Health Policy Update." *State Legislative Report* (Spring 1998).
Commonwealth Fund. "Losing Ground: Working-Age Women Increasingly Likely to Lack Health Insurance." Press Release (September 16, 1999).
Commonwealth Fund. "Health Insurance Coverage and Access to Care for Working-Age Women." Fact Sheet from The Commonwealth Fund 1998 Survey of Women's Health (May 1999).
National Center on Women and Aging. "Challenges to Women in the 21ˢᵗ Century." *Women and Aging Letter* (December 1998).

Healthy People 2000 and *Healthy People 2010*

Healthy People 2000 and its follow-up, *Healthy People 2010*, constitute a set of national health targets for the United States, including numerous issues associated with women's health. The first set of national health targets was published in 1979 in *Healthy People: The Surgeon General's Report on Health Promotion and Disease Prevention*. Goals for the 1980s were to reduce death rates among four age groups: infants, children, adolescents and young adults, and adults; and to increase independence among older adults, the majority of whom are women. In 1990, *Healthy People 2000: National Health Promotion and Disease Prevention Objectives* presented a comprehensive agenda for the next ten years: to increase the years of healthy life, reduce disparities in health among different populations such as minority women and older women, and achieve access to preventive health services.

Healthy People 2010 is a ten-year plan based on previous initiatives. Like its predecessors, *Healthy People 2010* provides information about how to improve health in a format that enables diverse groups to combine their efforts and work as a team. The Office of Disease Prevention and Health Promotion in the U.S. Department of Health and Human Services calls *Healthy People* "a road map to better health for all that can be used by many different people, states and communities, businesses, professional organizations, groups whose concern is a particular threat to health, or a particular population group. *Healthy People* is based on scientific knowledge and is used for decision making and for action." The office maintains an Internet Web site with details about this health initiative and its goals. Along with offering print materials, the Web site presents information that is in the public domain and encourages civic groups to integrate *Healthy People* facts and concepts into current programs, special events, publications, and meetings. Businesses use the framework to guide worksite health-promotion activities as well as community initiatives. Schools and colleges undertake activities to further the health of children, adolescents, and young adults. By selecting among the national objectives, individuals and organizations can build an agenda for community health improvement and monitor results. *See also* U.S. Department of Health and Human Services

Further Reading
Chrvala, Carole A., and Roger J. Bulger, eds. *Leading Health Indicators for Healthy People 2010: Final Report.* Washington, DC: National Academy Press, 1999.
Office of Disease Prevention and Health Promotion, U.S. Department of Health and Human Services. "Healthy People 2000 Fact Sheet" <http://odphp.osophs.dhhs.gov/pubs/hp2000/hp2kfact.htm>.
Office of Disease Prevention and Health Promotion, U.S. Department of Health and Human Services; "Healthy People 2010 Fact Sheet." <http://www.health.gov/healthypeople/2010fctsheet.htm>.

Healy, Bernadine (1944–)

A cardiologist and the first woman to head the National Institutes of Health (NIH), Bernadine Healy has been a strong advocate for women's health and women's health research. She has spent much of her career attempting to convince the medical establishment that coronary heart disease is a major health problem for women and not just a man's disease as had been believed for many years.

Healy was born in New York City, the second of Michael J. and Violet (McGrath) Healy's four daughters. She grew up in Queens and attended Hunter College High School, a prestigious public school in Manhattan, graduating first in her class. At Vassar College she majored in chemistry, minored in philosophy, and graduated summa cum laude. When she applied for medical school and was invited to her first interview, she wrote years later, she

> ran head-on into the way the world of the sixties operated. The man interviewing me held a powerful position—he helped determine who would be admitted into one of the top medical schools in the country. At the time, while colleges were filled with women who wanted to train as physicians, the medical schools maintained an unofficial "quota"—they admitted as few women as possible, and those women who did get in had to be much more qualified than any male candidate. My interviewer obviously felt that even this unspoken quota was too high. He asked me little about my scholastic interest or future plans, but he did want to know more about my mother: Was she menopausal and therefore frustrated? Had she inspired my clearly deviant life choice? Was my neurosis caused by the fact than my parents hadn't graduated from high school? (Healy, 6)

Healy withdrew her application and was accepted at Harvard, one of ten women in a class of 120. She received her M.D. cum laude in 1970, and eventually became a professor on the medical school faculty of Johns Hopkins University. In 1985 she was appointed head of the Research Institute of the Cleveland Clinic Foundation.

Healy married cardiologist Floyd D. Loop in 1985 and the couple have a daughter, Marie McGrath Loop; Healy's other daughter is Bartlett Ann Bulkley from her previous marriage to surgeon George Bulkley, whom she divorced in 1981.

From 1988 to 1989, Healy was president of the American Heart Association. In addition she led a wide variety of government advisory committees on health and science policy and economics. Following her nomination by President George Bush, she became, from 1991 to 1993, the first female director of the National Institutes of Health, which at the time included 13 institutes and 16,000 employees. She became known for establishing the Women's Health Initiative, a $625 million study, "the largest clinical research study of women

Bernadine Healy, M.D., President and CEO of the American Red Cross. Courtesy of the American Red Cross.

and their health ever undertaken in the United States or elsewhere." (Healy, 10)

Healy's book, *A New Prescription for Women's Health,* was published in 1995. In 1999, she was appointed director of the American Red Cross. *See also* Cardiovascular Disease; Women's Health-Care Advocates; Women's Health Initiative

Further Reading

"Dr. Bernadine Healy Named Red Cross President." U.S. Newswire (July 8, 1999).

Healy, Bernadine. *A New Prescription for Women's Health.* New York: Viking, 1995.

Healy, Bernadine. Gale Group: Women's History <http://www.gale.com/library/resrcs/womenhst/ healyb.htm>.

Heart Disease

See **Cardiovascular Diseases**

Hispanic Women's Health

See **Latina Women's Health**

HIV-Positive Women

See **AIDS**

Homeless Women

The homeless in the United States are defined by the Stewart B. McKinney Homeless Assistance Act of 1987 as people who do not have "a fixed, regular, and adequate nighttime residence" and who do have a "primary nighttime residence that is a supervised publicly or privately operated shelter designed to provide temporary living accommodations (including welfare hotels, congregate shelters, and transitional housing for the mentally ill)." Although five times more men than women are homeless, single women head more than 80 percent of homeless families, who comprise the fastest growing segment of the homeless population. Frequently the women and their children suffer health problems that cannot be addressed because of lack of income. According to the federal government,

By the middle of the 1980s, the number of homeless people had surpassed anything seen since the Great Depression. Disability, disease, and even death were becoming regular features of life on the streets and in shelters. For the first time, women and children were occupying quarters formerly "reserved" for skid-row men. Psychiatric hospitals continued to discharge people with little hope of finding, let alone managing, housing of their own. Crack cocaine emerged as a drug of choice for those on the margins of society. A new scourge—HIV/AIDS—joined an old one—tuberculosis—to become a major affliction of the homeless poor. (U.S. Housing and Urban Development)

It is impossible to accurately measure the total number of homeless Americans because they frequently are transient, periodically homeless, or not easily located, especially in rural areas. Estimates of the homeless have varied considerably, because people are counted in different ways—by a specific night, by the week, or by the year. The National Law Center on Homelessness and Poverty in Washington, DC, estimates that 700,000 people are homeless on any given night and up to two million people are homeless annually. One study during the 1990s found that 12 million Americans had been homeless at some point in their lives.

As the number of homeless people in the United States (no matter what the gender or age) has increased, so have the public health, economic, social, and ethical issues, which are often intertwined. This reality raises questions about how well the nation cares for its weak and vulnerable members. Often cited are such issues as the

Invisibility—a homeless woman on a Manhattan street unnoticed by crowds. ©Photos—Bettye Lane.

widespread need for affordable housing and the waits of up to three years for federal assistance from the U.S. Department of Housing and Urban Development (HUD). Other concerns include the need for health care and education for the homeless; the passage of punitive local laws that attempt to keep homeless people "out of sight, and out of mind"; and the legal, social, and health obstacles activists face when trying to feed and shelter homeless people.

For women, homelessness frequently occurs because of extreme poverty and domestic violence, which in themselves underscore major health issues. In 1996, the federal program Assistance for Families with Dependent Children (AFDC) was replaced by the Temporary Assistance for Needy Families (TANF) program. As a result of TANF, thousands of former welfare recipients—the majority of them single

women with children—are required to abide by strict conditions to receive benefits from federal block grants to states. For example, a beneficiary must get a job after receiving financial aid for a set time (from two months to several years, depending on the state). Yet since the 1970s, changes in the U.S. economy from the manufacture of goods to service industries have adversely affected wage-based workers, particularly women who lack appropriate skills or adequate schooling. If women are unable to get jobs that provide income above the poverty level, they likely will be unable to pay for basic necessities for themselves and their children. At least one-third of female-headed families live below the poverty line.

Poverty not only leads to homelessness, but it also can contribute to violence, authorities say, which forces women to leave their homes. Among homeless women, 63 percent have been violently abused by an intimate male partner, according to the National Coalition for the Homeless (NCH). Some of these women find refuge in women's shelters or other facilities, frequently with their children.

The health effects of homelessness are multiple. A high percentage of homeless women suffer from such problems as asthma, anemia, and major depressive disorders. Although many of them receive emergency help from privately funded groups that provide and support homeless shelters and shelters for battered women in most major cities, the number of homeless far exceeds the facilities available.

The National Law Center on Homelessness and Poverty in Washington, DC, files lawsuits to aid homeless people, such as "enforcing homeless children's right to a public education; converting vacant federal property into housing, job training, and child care sites for homeless people; and defending homeless Americans from unconstitutional arrests and harassment." The Law Center also provides educational materials and reports on the homeless (National Law Center). Government programs such as those administered by the federal Department of Health and Human Services (DHHS) include Health Care for the Homeless; Projects for Assistance in Transition from Homelessness (PATH); Access to Community Care and Effective Services and Supports (ACCESS); Homelessness Prevention Program (substance abuse and mental illness); Housing Initiative for Homeless Persons with Mental Illness; Runaway and Homeless Youth; Head Start for the Homeless; and Battered Women's Shelters. *See also* Domestic Violence; Drug-Dependent Mothers; Poor Women and Health Care

Further Reading

Aron, Laudan Y., and Janet M. Fitchen. "Rural Homelessness: A Synopsis." In *Homelessness in America,* edited by Jim Baumohl for the National Coalition for the Homeless. Phoenix, AZ: Oryx Press, 1996.

Browne, Angela, Amy Salomon, and Shari S. Bassuk. "The Impact of Recent Partner Violence on Poor Women's Capacity to Maintain Work." *Violence Against Women* (April 1999).

Burt, Martha. *Practical Methods for Counting Homeless People: A Manual for States and Local Jurisdictions.* 2d ed. Washington, DC: The Urban Institute, 1996.

Goldberg, Joan E. "A Short Term Approach to Intervention with Homeless Mothers: A Role for Clinicians in Homeless Shelters." *Families in Society: The Journal of Contemporary Human Services* (March/April 1999).

Momeni, Jamshid A. *Homelessness in the United States.* New York: Greenwood Press, 1990.

National Law Center on Homelessness and Poverty. *Out of Sight - Out of Mind? A Report on Anti-Homeless Laws, Litigation, and Alternatives in 50 United States Cities.* Washington, DC: National Law Center on Homelessness and Poverty, 1999.

U.S. Conference of Mayors. *A Status Report on Hunger and Homelessness in America's Cities: 1998.* Washington, DC: U.S. Conference of Mayors, 1998.

U.S. Housing and Urban Development. *Priority Home!: The Federal Plan to Break the Cycle of Homelessness.* Washington, DC: Interagency Council on the Homeless, March 1994.

Hormone Replacement Therapy

Hormone replacement therapy (HRT) is a drug treatment that combines estrogen and progestin, a synthetic version of progesterone; it is prescribed for some women who experience symptoms of menopause, such as "hot flashes" and depression, and for women who have had hysterectomies, or are at risk for developing osteoporosis, heart disease, or endometriosis. Because hormones are not actually replaced in the body but technically are added, HRT is sometimes referred to as hormone-additive therapy or simply hormone therapy. Many women may derive health and fitness benefits from hormone therapy, but there is conflicting evidence on whether the benefits of HRT outweigh the risks.

During the 1960s doctors prescribed estrogen alone for menopausal symptoms, but throughout the next decade the rate of cancer of the endometrium (lining of the uterus) rose tenfold. When doctors added progestin to the regimen, endometrium cancer risks appeared to diminish. Nevertheless, some practitioners question the safety and long-term effects of HRT on women who have taken a variety of hormonal medications over several decades. Women born in the 1920s and 1930s, for example, may have taken a hormonal drug called diethylstilbestrol, better known as DES, which once was thought to be a "wonder drug" for reproductive problems, cancer, and other diseases; they also may have taken birth control pills that when first introduced contained high dosages of estrogen.

Hormonal preparations are usually taken orally in pill form. They may also be administered through injections or adhesive patches that transfer a small amount of the hormones through the skin. The drug treatment can provide some protection from osteoporosis, a disease affecting bone density, and perhaps Alzheimer's disease.

Some studies suggest that HRT can reduce the risk of heart disease and stroke, but other studies find no beneficial reduction in heart disease from HRT. One recent study, completed in 1998 and called the Heart and Estrogen-progestin Replacement Study (HERS), shocked doctors with the conclusion that "four years of treatment with estrogen and progestin pills failed to lower the risk of heart attacks in women who already had heart disease." A second study, of more than 300 women with heart disease, sponsored by the National Institutes of Health and released in 2000, supports the HERS' findings. After four years, researchers "found no difference in the progression of their disease." (Associated Press)

Other conflicting studies conclude that HRT may also help prevent breast cancer and that estrogen-related cancers have increased in women over 50 years of age. In a study published in *Cancer* in June 2000, for example, scientists of the Fred Hutchinson Cancer Research Center in Seattle, Washington, reported that the incidence of one form of breast cancer was 2.6 times higher in women who used HRT than in women who did not.

The cumulative effect of high doses of hormones is unknown, but as a report in the *New York Times* notes, researchers are

> studying how women on hormone therapy respond to reductions of 50 percent or more in the standard prescription of estrogen.... The picture that is emerging from this research is intriguing, suggesting that a woman's need for estrogen shifts as she ages. As the investigators acknowledge, women experiencing a turbulent change of life frequently do require full-strength H.R.T. for symptom relief. But women whose symptoms have subsided or who are not bothered by menopause may be able to gain long-term benefits with fewer side effects by switching to a half-dose regimen.
>
> This approach appears to maintain sufficient bone mass to stave off fractures of osteoporosis, an often crippling disease that affects 22 million American women. (McAuliffe)

The differing medical reports confuse many menopausal women, as well as their doctors; some women choose not to take the drugs, while others opt for alternative treatment, such as acupuncture and the use of herbs. *See also* Alzheimer's Disease; Cardiovascular Diseases; Diethylstilbestrol; Endometriosis; Menopause

Further Reading

Associated Press. "Another Study Disputes Estrogen Heart Benefit." *New York Times* (March 14, 2000), electronic version.

Boston Women's Health Book Collective. *The New Our Bodies, Ourselves.* New York: Simon & Schuster, 1992.

Hoffman, Eileen, M.D. *Our Health, Our Lives: A Revolutionary Approach to Total Health Care for Women.* New York: Simon & Schuster, 1995.

Howard, Beth. *Mind Your Body: A Sexual Health and Wellness Guide for Women.* New York: St. Martin's Press, 1998.

McAuliffe, Kathleen. "For Hormone Replacement Therapy, One High-Dose Size May Not Fit All." *New York Times* (June 25, 2000).

Notelovitz, Morris, M.D., and Diana Tonnessen. *Menopause and Midlife Health.* New York: St. Martin's Press, 1993.

Planned Parenthood Federation of America. *The Planned Parenthood Women's Health Encyclopedia.* New York: Crown Trade Paperbacks, 1996.

Hospice Care

As is true with most types of caregiving in the United States, women supply most hospice care, which is a special concept of providing compassionate care and comfort for the dying and their families. "Hospice" is a term used in medieval times to describe a place for tired or sick travelers. Today, the term does not refer to a particular place—hospice care can be provided in a hospital, a continuing care facility, a nursing home, or a dying person's own home. If care is provided for a patient at home, a nurse may visit to offer pain-control medication or help with medical equipment. A home health-care aide may bathe a patient or help with other personal services. A member of the clergy might provide counseling, and a volunteer might visit to relieve the family caregiver for a few hours. Specialized hospice care attempts to improve the quality of a patient's final days with an emphasis on controlling pain and discomfort.

Although hospice care is not just a women's health issue, women have been at the forefront of this kind of care. The concept developed with the work of Cicely Saunders, a British physician, who opened the Saint Christopher's Hospice outside

Florence Wald, dean of Yale School of Nursing, 1959–1966. Photograph by Stephanie Welsh. Courtesy of Yale School of Nursing.

London in 1967 to help people die confidently rather than fearfully. Florence Wald, who served in the Signal Corps during World War II and eventually became dean of Yale's School of Nursing, studied the hospice movement in Europe and in 1971 established the first hospice unit in the United States. She also worked to set up hospice units in U.S. prisons.

The American hospice movement was supported by the ideas of psychiatrist Elisabeth Kübler-Ross. During the late 1960s, Kübler-Ross began to conduct seminars on confronting death in a realistic but sensitive manner and helping people cope with their fears of death. The first U.S. hospice facility opened in Connecticut in 1974. Since then more than 3,000 hospice programs across the nation and in Puerto Rico and Guam have provided services for the terminally ill.

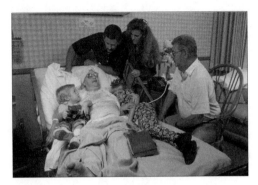

Family visits hospice patient, California.
©Grantpix/Photo Researchers, Inc.

Hospice care is sometimes controversial because it is mistakenly viewed as a form of "mercy killing." But hospice organizations and programs oppose legalization of euthanasia, aid in dying, and physician-assisted suicide. The role of hospice care is frequently misunderstood by the general public because of widespread resistance to realistic discussions about matters related to death. National organizations attempting to educate the public about hospice care include the American Hospice Foundation, the Hospice Foundation of America, and the National Hospice and Palliative Care Organization. *See also* Family Caregiving; Kübler-Ross, Elisabeth

Further Reading

Gay, Kathlyn. *The Right to Die*. Brookfield, CT: The Millbrook Press, 1993.

Naierman, Naomi. "American Hospice Foundation: Debunking the Myths of Hospice." <http://www.americanhospice.org/debunking.htm>.

Naierman, Naomi, and Jo Turner. "Demystifying Hospice." *AAPA News* (July 15, 1997).

Hospital Mergers

Hospital mergers, in which several hospitals join together in a consortium to cut costs and improve quality care, have occurred at a fairly rapid pace throughout the United States since the early 1990s. These mergers have created controversy when they have been perceived as affecting women's reproductive rights. Such mergers include those between nonprofit community hospitals strapped for funds and religiously affiliated hospital networks.

While hospital alliances such as those operated by Baptists and Adventists have restrictions on abortion and other reproductive services, Roman Catholic hospitals have the most stringent rules in regard to these issues. Because hospital unions governed by Catholic dogma far outnumber those with other religious affiliations, they have caused the greatest furor among women's and civil rights groups.

In 1994 the National Conference of Catholic Bishops issued Ethical and Religious Directives (ERDs) for Catholic Health Care Services. Although the directives apply only to Catholic hospitals, partner hospitals usually are induced to follow them, including those which affect reproductive health care services. Some community hospitals that have merged with Catholic hospitals will no longer perform sterilizations, provide fertility treatments that involve sperm and egg donors and surrogate mothers, or carry out elective abortions for pregnant women who choose to abort fetuses with severe genetic defects. According to Catholics for a Free Choice, which opposes mergers because of limits on reproductive services, in 100 out of 127 mergers between Catholic and secular hospitals, reproductive services were cut or "greatly restricted in 48 cases." (O'Donnell)

Yet the rules are sometimes bent in Catholic-dominated consortia so that a secular affiliate can offer some reproductive services. "Around the country, there's no fixed approach to the bishops' directives—every hospital must work out for itself what services to allow." (McCollum)

In 1997, Bayfront, a non-sectarian community hospital in Tampa Bay, Florida, joined the BayCare consortium, which includes four Catholic-dominated hospitals; the public was told little about the merger—only that no policy changes would occur. Two years later, news reports indicated that Bayfront would be required to follow Catholic religious guidelines. When this information became public, a philosophy professor at the University of South Florida, who was on the ethics committee for Bayfront, pointed out that, by not informing the public, BayCare had created a "real ethical issue" because the public had a right to know what the effects of the merger would be. The chair of the consortium's ethical committee countered that there was nothing "improper or unusual" about discontinuing any kind of service or procedure at any of the hospitals. He noted that "when considering a partnership between a secular hospital and a Catholic hospital, the secular hospital needs to decide if the benefits [economic survival] of the partnership outweigh the changes in services that may need to be made to accommodate the partners." (Miller)

In 1998, the Greater Baltimore (Maryland) Medical Center (GBMC), which was managed by the Hospital for the Women of Maryland (HWM), planned to join the Catholic-affiliated St. Joseph Medical Center, until the board for HWM threatened to withdraw its financial support if the merger took place. For over a century, HWM had provided services for women; in the board's view such services as abortion, sterilization, and in-vitro fertilization would be banned if the hospital were Catholic-owned and required to follow the church's ERDs. Instead of the merger, the GBMC board chose to operate under a joint agreement with a board made up of equal numbers of representatives from GBMC and St. Joseph. In addition, GBMC established a subsidiary office to provide abortion and fertility services on the GBMC campus.

Whatever arrangements are made, women's rights groups and women-centered health organizations as well as the American Civil Liberties Union and other groups advocating the separation of church and state have protested what they perceive as the loss of unqualified access to reproductive services. Activists also complain that "the government hasn't treated some of the mergers as violations of anti-trust laws. They also wonder why federal and state laws allow church hospitals to have 'conscience clauses' that permit them to opt out of procedures on religious or moral grounds." (Conklin) Although most women's health advocates appreciate the free medical care that Catholic hospitals provide for indigents, they maintain that reproductive health is basic to women's health and that imposing a religious perspective on health care threatens public health. (O'Donnell) *See also* Abortion; Artificial Insemination; Birth Control; Surrogate Mother

Further Reading

Baumgardner, Jennifer. "Immaculate Contraception." *The Nation* (January 25, 1999).

Conklin, Melanie. "Blocking Women's Health Care: Your Hospital May Have a Policy You Don't Know About." *The Progressive* (January 1998).

Lipton, Eric. "In Houses of Healing, an Uneasy Alliance; Worried by Church Rules, Hospital May End Union with Catholic Facility." *Washington Post* (April 3, 1998).

Miller, Robert, M.D. "Bayfront Sought Greatest Good for the Community." *St. Petersburg Times* (August 31, 1999).

McCollum, Monica J. "Spirited Controversy: Reproductive Services Force Executives to Weigh Church Teaching vs. Community Good." *Hospitals and Health Networks* (June 20, 1998).

O'Donnell, Jayne. "Antitrust Health Fight: Catholic Hospital Deals Limit Access, Activists Say." *USA Today* (April 8, 1999).

Hysterectomy

Each year about 600,000 American women pay several thousand dollars to undergo a hysterectomy, a surgical procedure to remove the uterus, frequently along with the ovaries. It is the second most common surgery among American women, after cesarean section. Although hysterectomy rates have been declining since the 1980s, by age 65 more than 37 percent of all U.S. women will have had hysterectomies, according to the Agency for Healthcare Research and Quality of the U.S. Department of Health and Human Services. The total cost for hysterectomies each year is about $5 billion.

Often, women are led to believe that a hysterectomy is inevitable in midlife. But female medical professionals in recent years have questioned the need for hysterectomies among so many women, claiming that less expensive and less risky means could be used to treat some pelvic disorders. In addition, life-threatening complications such as hemorrhaging can develop.

Another issue of concern is the well-entrenched attitude among many male physicians that a woman should have a hysterectomy along with removal of her ovaries after menopause because the organs are no longer needed. Women-centered practitioners, however, contend that the uterus holds other organs in place and that ovaries should remain intact because they "continue to produce an array of hormones well past menopause." (Hoffman, 220)

Although a hysterectomy with removal of the ovaries may be recommended because of uterine or ovarian cancer risks, the lifetime risk of, for instance, ovarian cancer is low—1.2 percent in 50-year-old women. Paradoxically, doctors do not generally recommend that the male prostate be removed even though "more than 165 thousand older men get prostate cancer every year." (Hoffman, 220) *See also* Cesarean section; Menopause; Ovarian Cancer

Further Reading

Boston Women's Health Book Collective. *The New Our Bodies, Ourselves* New York: Simon & Schuster, 1992.

Hoffman, Eileen, M.D. *Our Health, Our Lives: A Revolutionary Approach to Total Health Care for Women.* New York: Simon & Schuster, 1995.

Notelovitz, Morris, M.D., and Diana Tonnessen. *Menopause and Midlife Health.* New York: St. Martin's Press, 1993.

Planned Parenthood Federation of America. *The Planned Parenthood Women's Health Encyclopedia.* New York: Crown Trade Paperbacks, 1996.

I

In Vitro Fertilization

See **Artificial Insemination**

Infertility

Infertility is a disease of the reproductive system. It is usually defined as the inability to conceive after a year of frequent intercourse without contraception or the inability to carry a child to term. Contrary to popular belief, infertility is not primarily a female problem—it affects an equal number of women and men. More than six million American couples are considered infertile, a condition that sometimes creates psychological problems due to the social pressure on couples to bear children. Economic burdens often plague those who opt for expensive treatments to correct infertility problems.

Male infertility is usually due to poor sperm quality or low sperm count. Alcohol and other drug use and exposure to some environmental toxins can reduce sperm quality. Female infertility can be caused by a number of factors, such as blocked fallopian tubes, ovulation disorders, endometriosis and other chronic diseases, hormonal imbalances, or a misshapen uterus.

Fertility in both genders can be impaired because of sexually transmitted diseases, environmental hazards, the aging process, or a combination of factors. In some infertility cases no specific cause is identified.

In attempts to conceive, many infertile women seek medical help. A doctor may suggest self-help procedures such as carefully documenting the ovulation time—when a woman is fertile and able to conceive. Or a doctor may prescribe fertility drugs, which may result in multiple births and health risks. As a *Newsweek* report noted:

> Women carrying multiple fetuses risk anemia, hypertension and labor complications that can require cesarean delivery. And their babies are often born prematurely. On average, each additional fetus shortens the usual 40-week gestation period by three and one-half weeks. A pair of twins born at 86 weeks may do fine. But as the number of fetuses increases, the kids' gestation times and birth weights decline. (Cowley, 66)

Another procedure, called intrauterine insemination, requires a woman's partner or anonymous donor to provide sperm that can be inserted into the uterus with a syringe or through a small tube. However,

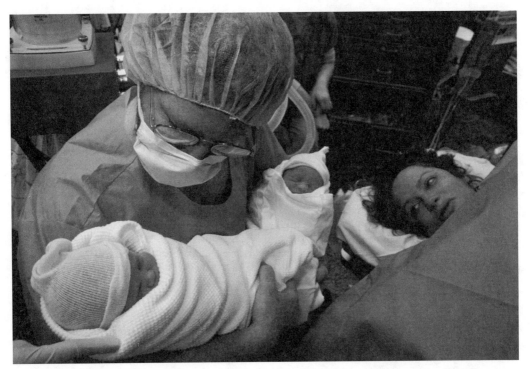

A woman gives birth to triplets after fertility treatments. The father holds two of his three new children. ©Annie Griffiths Belt/CORBIS.

some religious groups label the use of sperm from an anonymous donor as adultery. Men may object to having children not connected biologically.

Some infertile women seek the help of fertility clinics and medical specialists trained in assisted reproductive technology (ART), which includes various forms of *in vitro* fertilization (IVF). However, not all fertility clinics have the same percentage of successes (babies born after ART); organizations such as the American Society for Reproductive Medicine, RESOLVE (which sponsors an annual National Infertility Awareness Week), and Planned Parenthood Federation of America provide information on how to rate clinics. These organizations also have begun to address the issue of the increasing incidence of multiple births that result from IVF, which has become a public health issue and social concern. According to a report in the *Journal of the American Medical Association*

One common practice that aims to increase the likelihood of pregnancy is to transfer multiple embryos (often more than 3) into the uterine cavity. This treatment approach also presents an important drawback, however, because it increases the risk for multiple birth. Multiple-birth infants are at significant risk for a number of adverse outcomes including preterm delivery, low birth weight, congenital malformations, fetal and infant death, and long-term morbidity and disability among survivors (Schieve, et al. 1,832)

Another option for infertile women is surrogacy. A fertilized egg is transferred from a woman unable to carry a child to term to a surrogate mother who carries and delivers the child. Surrogacy, however, is highly controversial because of the legal and ethical issues surrounding the practice. *See also* American Society for Reproductive Medicine; Artificial Insemination; Assisted Reproductive Technologies; Egg Donors; Endometriosis; Environmental Hazards; RESOLVE; Surrogate Mother

Further Reading

Carson, Sandra, and Peter Casson, eds. *Complete Guide to Fertility.* Chicago, IL: Contemporary Books, 1999.

Cohen, Elizabeth. "Moms at Last: How 8 Friends Faced Infertility." *Family Circle* (September, 15 1998).

Cowley, Geoffrey. "Multiplying the Risks: More Group Births Mean More Preemies and, Often, More Problems." *Newsweek* (December 1, 1997).

Henry, Ed. "Covering the Cost of Fighting Infertility." *Kiplinger's Personal Finance Magazine* (August 1999).

Hope, Toni Gerber. "The Ultimate Fertility Guide." *Redbook* (November 1998).

Meilaender, Gilbert. "Biotech Babies." *Christianity Today* (December 7, 1998).

Miller, Annetta, and Joan Raymond. "The Infertility Challenge." *Newsweek* Special Issue (Spring/Summer 1999).

Nordenberg, Tamar. "Overcoming Infertility." *FDA Consumer* (January–February 1997).

Schieve, Laura A., Herbert B. Peterson, Susan F. Meikle, Gary Jeng, Isabella Danel, Nancy M. Burnett, and Lynne S. Wilcox. "Live Birth Rates and Multiple-Birth Risk Using In Vitro Fertilization." *Journal of the American Medical Association* (November 17, 1999)

Tielemans, E. "Pesticide Exposure and Decreased Fertilization Rates In Vitro." *The Lancet* (August 7, 1999).

Zouves, Christo, and Julie Sullivan. *Expecting Miracles: On the Path of Hope from Infertility to Parenthood.* New York: Holt, 1999.

J

Jacobs Institute of Women's Health

Founded in 1990 by the American College of Obstetricians and Gynecologists (ACOG), Jacobs Institute of Women's Health (JIWH) was named for its benefactor, J. Bay Jacobs, M.D. (1898–1989), a specialist in obstetrics-gynecology in the Washington, DC area. The JIWH promotes the study and dissemination of information on women's health issues. One important goal is to identify women's health issues in terms of the interrelationship between medical and social systems and improve women's access to health care.

The institute publishes *Women's Health Issues*, a bimonthly, peer-reviewed journal for health professionals, social scientists, policy makers, and others concerned with the complex and diverse facets of health-care delivery to women. Other publications include *In Touch*, a quarterly newsletter, which reports on the current activities of the JIWH; *State Profiles on Women's Health*, which outlines the status of women's health in all 50 states and the District of Columbia; and *The Women's Health Data Book*, which contains statistics on a wide variety of women's health topics.

Each year, JIWH holds an annual Excellence in Women's Health Awards Luncheon to honor individuals who have made noteworthy contributions to the field of women's health. In 2000 awards were presented to Jeannie Rosoff, immediate past president of the Alan Guttmacher Institute; Jane Brody, *New York Times* health columnist and best-selling author; and Sylvia Drew Ivie, executive director of T.H.E. (To Help Everyone) Clinic, which serves the uninsured and poor women of the inner city. In addition the institute awards an annual grant of $30,000 to a selected applicant to conduct a research study that results in a publishable manuscript on a topic that relates to women's health. *See also* Alan Guttmacher Institute; American College of Obstetricians and Gynecologists; Health Care Access

Further Reading
"About the Jacobs Institute of Women's Health." <http://www.jiwh.org/aboutus.htm>.

Journal of the American Medical Women's Association

See **American Medical Women's Association**

K

Kübler-Ross, Elisabeth (1926–)

Elisabeth Kübler-Ross is known internationally for her medical and psychiatric work with and for the dying and her seminal book, *On Death and Dying*. Although not focused strictly on women's health issues, she battled the prejudice against women in medicine and became a pioneer in the field of helping the terminally ill face death. Her work helped break the silence about death that prevailed among hospital staff.

Elisabeth was the smallest of triplets born to Emma and Ernst Kübler in July 1926 in Switzerland. The first born of the three identical girls, Elisabeth was des-

Elizabeth Kübler-Ross. ©Reuters/Ken Ross/Archive Photos.

tined to be a pathfinder, her mother's obstetrician predicted. While the other triplets, Eva and Erika, grew up abiding by Ernst Kübler's wishes and demands, Elisabeth was an independent soul who defied her father and other authoritative figures on a number of occasions. She refused to become a secretary and bookkeeper for her father's business, and was forced to take a demeaning job as a maid with an abusive employer rather than submit to a life for which she felt unsuited. In spite of her father's opposition and other obstacles, she was able to obtain a medical degree, become a psychiatrist, and throughout most of her adult life pursue her mission of helping people face the reality and fear of death.

Elisabeth earned her medical degree at the University of Switzerland, where at one time a professor tried to discourage her by insisting that women belonged "at home cooking and sewing rather than studying medicine." (Kübler-Ross, 1997, 92) At the university, she met fellow student Emanuel (Manny) Ross, an American who would become her husband in 1958. They moved to the United States, completed their internships in New York, and were offered residencies in Manhattan. Kübler-Ross began a three-year residency in 1959 at Manhattan State Hospital for the mentally ill. During that time, Kübler-Ross gave birth to a son, Kenneth. She wrote that some of her greatest accomplishments while in residence at Manhattan State

> included ending the most sadistic punishments [for severely disturbed patients] and the discharge of 94 percent of my "hopeless" schizophrenics into productive, self-sufficient lives outside the hospital.

In 1963, Elisabeth Kübler-Ross earned her psychiatric degree and she and Manny found positions at the University of Colorado's medical school. At the end of that year, a baby girl, Barbara, was born to the couple. Two years later the family moved to the Chicago area, where Manny accepted a position at Northwestern University Medical Center and Elisabeth joined the faculty in the psychiatric department at Billings Hospital, part of the University of Chicago hospitals. Kübler-Ross was also the liaison between the psychiatric department and sick patients, some of them terminally ill. She eventually began to talk honestly with dying patients, helping them to express their feelings, much against hospital and medical practice. As she explained:

> In this modern hospital, dying was a sad, lonely and impersonal event. Terminally ill patients were routed to back rooms. In the emergency room, patients lay in total isolation while doctors and their families debated whether or not they should be told what was wrong. To me, only one question ever needed asking: "How do we share the information?"....Truth was always the best.
>
> The great advances in medicine had convinced people that life should be pain-free. Since death was only associated with pain, people avoided it. Adults rarely mentioned anything about it. Children were sent into other rooms when it was unavoidable. But facts are

facts. Death was a part of life, the most important part of life. Physicians who were brilliant at prolonging life did not understand death was a part of it. (Kübler-Ross, 1997, 141)

As Kübler-Ross became more and more involved with dying patients, she asked them to take part in seminars in which students asked questions about the patients' feelings. Although medical personnel accused Kübler-Ross of being sordid and sadistic and exploiting the dying, all but one of the terminally ill patients were eager to participate in the seminars, releasing pent-up feelings that their doctors and nurses would not allow them to express. Kübler-Ross' work led to the publication of her first book, *On Death and Dying,* in 1969. Other publications followed and she continued to lecture, teach, and help people deal with and accept death in a realistic manner. Her work has brought her much fame and continual controversy, particularly when she began working with AIDS patients, but she has received numerous honorary doctorates from major universities and humanitarian awards. Her last book, *The Wheel of Life,* was published in 1997 after she had suffered a massive stroke. *See also* AIDS

Further Reading
Gill, Derek. *Quest: The Life of Elisabeth Kübler-Ross.* New York: Harper & Row, 1980.
Kübler-Ross, Elisabeth. *On Death and Dying.* New York: Macmillan Publishing, 1969.
Kübler-Ross, Elisabeth. *The Wheel of Life: A Memoir of Living and Dying.* New York: Scribner, 1997.

Kuhn, Margaret (Maggie) (1905–1995)

Margaret Elisa Kuhn, better known as Maggie Kuhn, worked for more than three decades to educate the public on the concept that old age is a triumph, not a "disease," as many Americans, particularly women, are prone to believe. Kuhn became a role model for women who wanted to become activists in the fight against ageism as well as other social and health problems affecting women. She maintained that old and young should join together as activists seeking to combat sexism, racism, and other social stereotypes and injustices.

In 1970, Kuhn with five other women formed the Consultation of Older and Younger Adults for Social Change, which a television producer later dubbed the Gray Panthers after the militant civil rights group, the Black Panthers. The term stuck and the organization is still one of the leading forces in efforts to change public attitudes about older people.

Kuhn was born in Buffalo, New York, and spent her childhood in Cleveland, Ohio, and Memphis and Louisville, Tennessee. She graduated from the College for Women in Cleveland, and in the 1920s while working for the YMCA began advocating for working women. The "Y" sent her to Columbia University to take courses in social reform. During World War II, Kuhn worked with the United Service Organization (USO) helping women who worked in defense plants. She joined the national office of the Presbyterian Church in the 1940s and became involved in a variety of social causes over the next two decades, including racial justice, desegregation, affordable housing, national health care, peace, and antipoverty efforts. She was an outspoken opponent and activist against the Vietnam War.

After Kuhn was forced to retire at the age of 65 from her career with the Presbyterian Church, she began to speak out publicly, demanding that mandatory retirement be abolished because, as she noted, "it is socially wasteful and often personally devastating." She declared that "an institution that forces older people out of their work roles requires perpetuation of an ageist belief system. This system requires that

Maggie Kuhn, founder of the Gray Panthers, at an anti-nuclear rally in Washington, DC. ©Photos—Bettye Lane.

all groups buy into the concept that old people are less able than young and ought to enjoy leisure time, even if they don't want it." (Hessel, 66, 70) Under Kuhn's leadership the Gray Panthers eventually helped end most if not all mandatory retirement provisions. The Gray Panthers and organizations such as the Older Women's League founded by Tish Sommers also urged that older people become activists for health care, social security, and other issues affecting seniors.

Throughout her 25 years as a Gray Panthers activist, Kuhn lived in her own home in Philadelphia, Pennsylvania, sharing it with housemates in their twenties and thirties, who provided companionship and helped with chores in exchange for a place to live at a reasonable rent. She never married, but made no secret of her affair with a married man and a man 50 years her junior. She noted that sexuality is part of life "and to deny it in old age is to deny life itself." (Folkart)

Although Kuhn suffered from severe arthritis and osteoporosis, she traveled thousands of miles across the United States, giving speeches and organizing. She and the Gray Panthers never advocated only for seniors, however; they consistently refused to pit the interests of the old against those of the young. As the Gray Panthers Web site now states: "From ages 9 to 93, we are *Age and Youth in Action*, activists working together for social and economic justice." (Gray Panthers)

For years the Gray Panthers also espoused the concept of Living Wills, which, now commonplace, allow terminally ill people to decide for themselves whether they want to prolong their lives by artificial means. Other targets of the Gray Panthers have been funeral practices that exploit survivors and derogatory media images of the elderly. In 1998, Maggie Kuhn was inducted into the National Women's Hall of Fame, which maintains an Internet Web site that includes brief biographical sketches of inductees. *See also* Older Women; Older Women's League; Sexuality

Further Reading

Folkart, Burt A. Obituary. *Los Angeles Times* (April 23, 1995).

Gay, Kathlyn, and Martin K. Gay. *Heroes of Conscience: A Biographical Dictionary.* Santa Barbara, CA: ABC-CLIO, 1996.

Gray Panthers home page. <http://www.graypanthers.org/>.

Hessel, Dieter T., ed., and Margaret E. Kuhn. *Maggie Kuhn on Aging.* Philadelphia, PA: Westminster Press, 1977.

Kuhn, Maggie, with Christina Long and Laura Quinn. *No Stone Unturned: The Life and Times of Maggie Kuhn.* New York: Ballantine Books, 1991.

L

La Leche League International

La Leche League International (LLLI) began in the 1950s as simply La Leche (the milk) League—a group of women who hoped to share with others their knowledge about the health benefits of breastfeeding their children. Breastfeeding became an issue in the mid-1950s as most babies—between 75 and 80 percent—were bottlefed. Bottle feeding with formula milk was considered the most "scientific" method of nourishment. In addition, there was much social criticism of women who breastfed in public—mothers were expected to feed their infants in a private place, a "back room," restroom, car, or some place out of sight. Thus bottlefeeding became the most accepted and convenient method of nourishing infants.

At the same time, however, during the late 1950s, "natural" childbirth practices began to become popular. These childbirth practices included the concept that women should, when possible, breast-feed their infants as the natural and healthy way to nourish their babies. La Leche League worked to spread this message and to help women overcome their aversion or lack of confidence in breastfeeding.

La Leche League was incorporated in 1958 and published its first edition of *The Womanly Art of Breastfeeding*. The group officially became an international organization in 1964 with groups in Canada, Mexico, and New Zealand. Groups have formed in many other countries since, and LLLI has held numerous international conferences on the merits of breastfeeding. In its statement of purpose, LLLI notes

> While complementing the care of the physician and other health care professionals, it recognizes the unique importance of one mother helping another to perceive the needs of her child and to learn the best means of fulfilling those needs. LLL believes that breastfeeding, with its many important physical and psychological advantages, is best for baby and mother and is the ideal way to initiate good parent-child relationships. The loving help and support of the father enables the mother to focus on mothering so that together the parents develop close relationships which strengthen the family and thus the whole fabric of society.

Some 3,000 La Leche League groups meet regularly in the United States, and hundreds of thousands of American mothers call LLLI's toll-free number to ask questions and seek advice on such health issues as whether a breastfed baby receives enough to eat; how to store breast milk; how to increase the supply of breast milk; when and how to wean a baby from breast-feeding; and whether lactation is an effective birth control method. Many women simply want instructions or encouragement on breastfeeding procedures, and some are surprised to learn that human milk is, as one writer put it,

> the ultimate in renewable resources. It's there as soon as the baby arrives, in the quantity the baby needs, for as long as the mother and baby want it. Not only that, but in most cases it doesn't require any preparation on the mother's part. The baby is put to the breast and the milk starts to flow. I heard that one pregnant mother, unaware of this simplicity, called La Leche League International Head-quarters to ask when she should get the holes poked in her nipples so that she could breastfeed her baby....Western society has become so mechanized that the question makes a weird sort of sense. The birth process seems to require so much technological paraphernalia...that it doesn't seem possible that breastfeeding should work without machinery. (Smith, 68)

LLLI also maintains an extensive library of breastfeeding literature and regularly posts information on its Internet Web site. Articles cover such topics as the cultural differences in breastfeeding practices around the world and the health benefits of lactation for mother and child. *See also* Birth Control; Childbirth Practices

Further Reading

Booksh, Alicia Clemens. "Getting Off the Back Room Team." *New Beginnings* (March–April 1994).

Gotsch, Gwen. *Breastfeeding Pure and Simple.* La Leche League International: Franklin Park, IL: 1994.

La Leche League International. *The Womanly Art Of Breastfeeding,* 35th Anniversary ed. Franklin Park, IL: La Leche League International, 1991.

Smith, Mark Eddy. "Nursing the World Back to Health." *New Beginnings* (May–June 1995).

Latina Women's Health

Latina women, or Hispanic women, are a diverse group in the United States and include Mexican Americans, Central and South Americans, Puerto Ricans, Cuban Americans, and Spanish Americans. Most of the issues affecting Latina women's health are similar to those of other minority groups, such as African-American women. Like all U.S. populations, the socioeconomic status and employment of Latinas determine access to health insurance, and thereby to health care. According to the National Women's Health Information Center (NWHIC) of the U.S. Department of Health and Human Services (DHHS), when Latina women are employed, they tend to hold jobs with low pay and are more likely than other Americans to be among the working poor. Among the estimated 14 million Latina women are those who are part of the farm labor population whose life expectancy is 49 years and infant mortality rates are 25 percent higher than the United States average. The NWHIC's *Women of Color Health Data Book* reports that

> Hispanic households also are more likely than non-Hispanic white households to be headed by females; these female-headed households also are more likely to have incomes below the federal poverty line than other types of households.... Overall, nearly half (47 percent) of poor Hispanic families are female-headed and are likely to face the combined stresses of poverty, lack of health insurance, lack of health care for themselves and their children, and lack of social support.... This arsenal of stressors places these women at risk for mental

health problems as well as for substance and alcohol abuse. The lack of citizenship may be an added stressor for poor Hispanic women and may make them unwilling to use public clinics and other health facilities for fear of detection and deportation. (NWHIC, *Women of Color Health Data Book*)

Latina women also face health problems created by environmental hazards. For instance, agricultural workers are exposed to pesticides, which can contribute to a range of health problems, from skin diseases to reproductive disorders.

Cultural factors play a major role in the health of many Latina women. Religion, folk healing, and family mores and traditions sometimes interfere with preventative health practices. Hispanic women who rely on indigenous healers and folk medicines often do not disclose these practices and thus delay professional medical care that could help prevent serious health problems such as cancer, heart disease, and diabetes. Diabetes, including gestational diabetes that occurs during pregnancy, is two to three times more common in some Latina groups than in non-Hispanic whites. Following tradition, many Hispanics also seek advice of family members before getting medical help, which delays the use of health-care services and preventive tests such as the Pap smear and mammography.

Other health issues facing the Hispanic population are associated with the rapid growth in the number of Hispanic elderly, with a 555 percent increase expected by the year 2030. To date, 57 percent of older Hispanics are females and many have language, educational, and financial barriers to quality health care. Being old, poor, and members of a minority group, they live in "triple jeopardy," the Office of Minority and Women's Health reports. Chronic diseases such as diabetes and cardiovascular diseases are common among 85 percent of older Latina women, and heart disease, cancer, and stroke are the three main causes of death.

To encourage the use of health-care services and improve Latina women's health, the DHHS has initiated the Hispanic Agenda for Action. DHHS agencies must ensure that the workforce and programs of HHS are reflective of and sensitive to Hispanic customers and that historical systematic barriers, which have negatively affected Hispanic Americans as employees and participants in HHS programs, are removed.

Another organization is the National Association of Hispanic-Serving Health Professions Schools, formed in 1996. The association's goal is to help rectify the underrepresentation of Hispanics in the health professions, which adversely affects the health status of Hispanic Americans. The national association focuses its efforts on expanding the pool of Hispanics in the health professions.

The National Hispanic Religious Partnership for Community Health (NHRP) was also established in 1996. The organization represents approximately 2,000 U.S. churches that have a unique access to the nation's poor and minority Hispanic community. The NHRP helps these churches develop a network of comprehensive health services targeted to Hispanic communities. They include AIDS programs; women's centers; youth projects; child abuse prevention; health education; mental health services; rehabilitation programs; and community centers. *See also* African-American Women's Health; Cardiovascular Diseases; Environmental Hazards; Mammogram; National Women's Health Information Center; Pap Smear

Further Reading
National Women's Health Information Center. "Latina Women's Health." <http://www.4woman.gov.faq/latina.htm>.
National Women's Health Information Center. *Women of Color Health Data Book.* "Factors Af-

fecting the Health of Women of Color." <http://www.4women.org/owh/pub/woc/hispanic.htm>.

Office of Minority and Women's Health, Bureau of Primary Health Care. "Health Status of Racial/Ethnic Older Women." <http://bphc.hrsa.gov/omwh/OMWH_9.htm>.

Perez, James P. "Black and Latino Doctors Are in Short Supply in the Chicago Area." *The Chicago Reporter* (July–August 1998).

Lesbian Health

In early 1999, the National Institutes of Health (NIH) published a report titled "Lesbian Health: Current Assessment and Directions for the Future," which called attention to the paucity of reliable information on the health of lesbian women. A committee of experts was formed in 1977 to investigate the issue of lesbian health in the medical literature and hold workshops with clinicians and researchers. The panel found a deploring lack of understanding about the health of homosexuals in general and numerous myths and misconceptions about lesbians and their health. For example, health-care practitioners have long treated same-sex orientation as a psychological disorder that can be "cured." During the 1970s the American Psychiatric Association acknowledged that no rigorous scientific evidence proved that homosexual orientation was pathological. In 1996 the American Medical Association's Council on Scientific Affairs dropped its recommendation to try to "reverse" sexual orientation.

Research on lesbian health has been limited because of numerous factors, the most basic of which is society's ingrained prejudice against homosexual activities. Such prejudice has prompted many hate crimes against lesbian women and gay men. Discrimination and abuse have kept many lesbians from revealing their sexual orientation and cooperating with researchers. Research has also been hampered by lack of funding and limited initiatives on the part of the federal government and the private sector. Another research obstacle is the politically sensitive nature of the topic and the controversy it generates. In addition, lesbians are a highly diverse but small group within the population, making it difficult to find a probability sample for research.

The health risks that are associated with various groups of women, such as women of color, poor women, and older women, are compounded in lesbian women, who frequently do not seek health care because they justifiably believe practitioners will not be objective. Surveys have shown that "most lesbians avoid going to the doctor for routine checkups—especially gynecological exams—because of hostility from doctors, or because they are uncomfortable talking about issues that may reveal their sexual orientation" (Thompson). Lesbian women also drop out of the health-care system because they fear their medical records will not remain confidential, and that revelations about their sexual orientation could adversely affect employment, insurance coverage, relationships with family members, and many other aspects of their lives. By avoiding health care, lesbians are at risk for diseases that could be life-threatening because they are not diagnosed and treated early.

In recent years lesbian health-care providers and political advocates have tried to address the negative impacts that stereotyping and stigmatizing have on lesbian health. As a result lesbian health-care centers have been set up in New York City, Boston, Los Angeles, San Francisco, and other large cities.

Another type of advocacy was spearheaded by a coalition representing the American Academy of Pediatrics, the National Education Association, the American Psychological Association, and other organizations. The coalition mailed a 12-page booklet titled *Just the Facts About*

Sexual Orientation & Youth to all public school districts in the United States. The booklet emphasizes that there is no medical support for the concept that homosexuality is abnormal or a psychological disorder. It includes sections on how sexual orientation develops, problems with religious groups that attempt to change the sexual orientation of lesbians and gays, and laws protecting homosexuals. According to a *New York Times* report, the coalition contends that the booklet "will help school administrators and educators to create safe and healthy environments in which all students can achieve to the best of their ability." (Goode) *See also* Poor Women's Health Care

Further Reading

France, David. "Fact, Fiction and the Health of Lesbians." *New York Times* (January 19, 1999).

Goode, Erica. "Group Sends Book on Gay Tolerance to Schools." *New York Times* (November 23, 1999).

Lynch, Margaret A., and Richard S. Ferri. "Health Needs of Lesbian Women and Gay Men." *Clinician Reviews* (January 1997).

Solarz, Andrea L., ed. *Lesbian Health: Current Assessment and Directions for the Future.* Washington, DC: National Academy Press, 1999.

Thompson, Ginger. "Trend Is Seen of Clinics Catering to Lesbians, Who Often Shun Health Care." *New York Times* (March 30, 1999).

Life Expectancy

The life expectancy of U.S. women today—the number of years they can expect to live—has nearly doubled since the turn of the century. In 1900 women lived to age 47; now they can expect to live until age 79 or 80, and possibly beyond to well over 90 years. However, women of color have a lower life expectancy than Caucasian women. In 1991, life expectancy for Caucasian women was 79.6 years; for Latina/Hispanic women, it was 77.1 years; for American Indian women it was 74.4 years; and for African-American women it was 74.1 years. Although women overall live

seven to eight years longer than men, they do not necessarily live those extra years in good physical and mental health, the U.S. Agency for Health Care Policy and Research (AHCPR) reports.

The longevity of women in American society is one of many differences between men and women that make the study of gender a focus of public policy in the United States, notes the National Aging Information Center (NAIC). Numerous health issues are raised for women. For instance, while a great number of women have good health during their elderly years, chronic conditions of cardiovascular disease, cancer, and stroke account for 65 percent of American women's deaths. In addition, women usually have heart attacks at an older age than men.

Other health-related issues for women include the possibility of social, economic, and psychological adjustments to widowhood. In 1998, nearly half of women aged 65 years were widowed and 70 percent of them lived alone. Many had inadequate or no insurance coverage for health care. They also lacked access to health care because of disabilities, low income, and few or no transportation facilities. In some cases, aging women also are at risk of physical or emotional abuse by family caregivers or hired caregivers. The NAIC reports:

By 2005, 70 percent of the nearly 5 million older adults age 85 and over in the United States will be women. The majority of this age group will need assistance in more than one activity of daily living. A significant number will have or be at risk of some form of dementia. To meet these challenges, older women will need substantial increases in assets to generate income to maintain independence. *See also* African-American Women's Health; Aging; Domestic Elderly Abuse; Family Caregiving; Health-Care Access; Latina Women's Health; Native American

Total Life Expectancy in Years by Race and Sex, 1989, 1991–1993, 1994

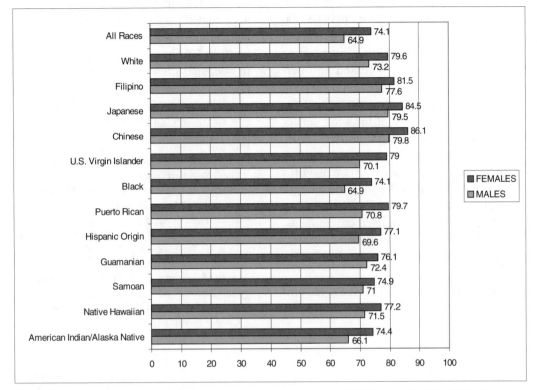

Sources: National Center for Health Statistics, Health United States, 1995, Hyattsville, MD: US Public Health Service, 1996. National Institutes of Health, Report of the National Institutes of Health: Opportunities for research on women's health, Bethesda, MD: Office of Research on Women's Health, 1991. Indian Health Service, Regional differences in Indian health 1996, Rockville, MD: US Public Health Service, 1997. Braun KL, Yang H, Onaka AT, Horiuchi BY, Life and death in Hawaii: Ethnic variations in life expectancy and mortality, 1980 and 1990, Hawaii Med J 1996; 55(12):278–283, 302. Honorable D Christian-Green, Member of Congress, personal communication, February 1997. U.S. National Women's Health Information Center, http://www.4woman.gov/owh/pub/woc/figure1.htm.

Women's Health; Nursing Home and Long-Term Care; Widowhood

Further Reading

Agency for Health Care Policy and Research. "AHCPR Women's Health Highlights." Fact Sheet. Rockville, MD: Agency for Health Care Policy and Research. (May 1998). <http://www.ahcpr.gov/research/womenh1.htm>.

Benderly, Beryl Lieff for the Institute of Medicine. *In Her Own Right: The Institute of Medicine's Guide to Women's Health Issues.* Washington, DC: National Academy Press, 1997.

National Aging Information Center. "Internet Information Note: Older Women." <http://www.aoa.gov/naic/notes/olderwomen.html>.

Love, Susan M.

See Breast Cancer

Lung Cancer

Lung cancer was once thought to be a "man's disease" but it is a major health concern for tens of thousands of women. Although more men than women die of lung cancer, in 1987 lung cancer surpassed breast cancer as the leading cause of cancer deaths among women in the United States.

Smoking is directly responsible for 87 percent of all lung cancer cases in America, claiming the lives of approximately 68,000 women annually, more than breast cancer and ovarian cancer combined. Lung cancer deaths among women increased 150 percent between 1974 and 1994, compared to just 20 percent for men over the same period. Experts predict that the lung cancer mortality rate will continue to rise sharply among women, despite an overall decline in U.S. cancer death rates. One reason for the high mortality rate may be due to women's higher susceptibility to the harmful effects of tobacco-related carcinogens, according to a study published in a 1999 issue of the *Journal of the National Cancer Institute*.

The lung cancer health issue is also related to a social concern: Since the 1920s, the tobacco industry has targeted women and adolescent girls with advertising images that depict female smokers as liberated, glamorous, slim, feminine, and attractive. Critics claim that such advertising has boosted smoking among women, helping to increase the lung cancer rates. *See also* Adolescent Girls' Health; Breast Cancer; Ovarian Cancer; Smoking

Further Reading

Brody, Jane. "A Fatal Shift in Cancer's Gender Gap" *New York Times* (May 12, 1998).

Brown, Ellen. "Waging War on Lung Cancer." *FDA Consumer* (May–June 1999).

Wingo, Phyllis A., Lynn A. G. Ries, Gary A. Giovino, Daniel S. Miller, Harry M. Rosenberg, Donald R. Shopland, Michael J. Thun, and Brenda K. Edwards. "Annual Report to the Nation on the Status of Cancer, 1973–1996, with a Special Section on Lung Cancer and Tobacco Smoking" (Special Issue). *Journal of the National Cancer Institute* (April 21, 1999).

M

Mammogram

A mammogram, or x-ray of the breast, is a preventive health measure for many American women ages 40 and older. Despite increases in mammography rates over the past two decades, large numbers of midlife and older women have never had mammograms and are not aware that such screening can help detect early cancerous nodules or lumps. Women's health-care practitioners and organizations such as the American Cancer Society, AARP (formerly called the American Association of Retired Persons), the National Cancer Institute (NCI) of the National Institutes of Health, and the National Breast Cancer Coalition (co-founded by breast cancer surgeon Susan Love) have consistently emphasized the importance of mammography in early detection of breast cancer. An estimated 180,000 women are diagnosed with breast cancer each year, and 44,000 die from the disease. Although little is known about how to prevent breast cancer, finding it early may give a woman more treatment options and a better chance for survival.

A debate over whether a woman in her forties should have a yearly mammogram has been ongoing for years, primarily be-

cause breast cancers in women in this age group are not readily detected with mammography. Younger women's breasts are more dense than older women's; as women age, their breasts become more fatty, making it easier to detect cancerous tumors. The debate intensified in 1997 when the National Institutes of Health (NIH) announced there was not enough scientific evidence to warrant routine mammography screening for women ages 40 to 49. However, the American Cancer Society (ACS), which previously had advised women in their forties to have mammograms every two years, declared that its

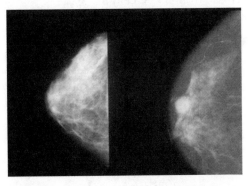

The image shows a comparison between mammograms of a normal breast (left) and one with cancer (right). The cancer shown as a whitish area was diagnosed as colloid carcinoma. National Cancer Institute.

scientific findings indicated these women should have annual mammograms. The National Cancer Institute (NCI) countered that regular screening of women could prolong the lives of as many as ten women or none at all in their forties. But NCI advised women at risk for breast cancer to consult with their doctors and make up their own minds about whether or not to have mammograms. To date, the debate remains ongoing.

Because the risk of breast cancer increases with age, mammography screening has become an important health issue for midlife and older women. But more than one-third of women ages 65 and older are not as concerned about getting breast cancer as they were when they were younger, according to a 1999 survey by NCI. Although the vast majority (88 percent) of women ages 65 and older have had at least one mammogram in their lifetimes, only 57 percent of the nationally representative sample of 814 women ages 65 and older knew they should have screening mammograms every one or two years, the NCI survey found. Nevertheless, this total represented a 25 percent increase from a similar survey conducted by AARP in 1992. The majority of women over age 65 (70 percent) have received mammograms within two years, which is also a substantial increase from 35 percent in 1992.

In 1998, the NCI and the U.S. Health Care Finance Administration formed a partnership to raise awareness of the importance of regular mammography screening among women ages 65 and older. The agencies also emphasized the expanded mammography screening benefit for Medicare beneficiaries. The U.S. Department of Health and Human Services provides screening services for low-income and medically underserved women in all 50 states, six U.S. territories, the District of Columbia, and 12 American Indian/Alaska Native organizations through the National Breast and Cervical Cancer Early Detection Program of the Centers for Disease Control and Prevention. Hospitals and clinics across the United States periodically offer free mammogram screening, particularly during Breast Cancer Awareness Month.

Although most facilities providing mammography notify women of results, the Food and Drug Administration (FDA) strengthened its rules for mammography centers in 1999. The FDA requires centers to send written notice of results to all women who have mammograms. The provision, as added to the Mammography Quality Standards Act (MQSA) of 1992, ensures that written notification occurs promptly, in easy-to-understand language, and that it is provided by all the 10,000 mammography facilities in the United States. *See also* Breast Cancer; Midlife Women; United States Department of Health and Human Services

Further Reading

Begley, Sharon. "The Mammogram War." *Newsweek* (February 24, 1997).

Love, Susan M. *Dr. Susan Love's Breast Book*, 2d ed. Reading, MA: Addison-Wesley, 1995.

National Cancer Institute. "Despite Increases in Mammography among Older Women, Misperceptions Persist." Press Release (October 20, 1999). <http://www.nci.nih.gov>.

Wolfe, Suzanne. "The Great Mammogram Debate." *RN* Magazine (August 1997).

U.S. Department of Health and Human Services. "Mammogram Law Takes Effect." Press Release (April 27, 1999).

Mastectomy

Mastectomy, or surgical removal of a breast, is one form of breast cancer treatment that has a relatively long and controversial history. Today, there are several types of mastectomy, from removal of a lump in the breast to removal of the entire breast and underlying muscle and lymph nodes. But for most of the twentieth century, "there was but one surgical approach to treating breast cancer—the *Halsted radical mastectomy*," named for Stewart Halsted, the surgeon who advocated the method during the 1880s. (Healy, 242)

Radical mastectomy was based on the theory that cancer spreads in a predictable manner and that the more tissue removed the better the chance of arresting the disease and saving women's lives. However, over the years the data did not support this view. Halsted radical mastectomy not only was disfiguring but it did not improve survival rates. During the 1960s and 1970s, doctors began to question radical surgery, and in 1979, the National Cancer Institute declared that, except for a few rare cases, the Halsted radical mastectomy was not the best procedure to use. Since then surgery has been more conservative, and a number of studies have shown that breast-conserving surgery is as effective as mastectomy. Procedures include a lumpectomy, removing a lump in the breast; a partial mastectomy, removing a lump plus nearby breast tissue; removing the entire breast and in some cases all the lymph nodes under the arm; and modified radical mastectomy, which "removes the breast and underlying tissue and some lymph nodes but preserves the chest muscles." (Healy, 242)

With more choices in breast cancer treatment, women frequently seek a number of medical opinions before making decisions about surgery. In 1997, the National Cancer Institute noted that

diagnosis of breast cancer at a smaller size or earlier stage will allow a woman more choice in selecting among various treatment options. For example, more women with cancer detected by mammography have the option of lumpectomy, rather than mastectomy, compared with women whose cancers are detected by palpation. Studies also show that the rate of axillary dissection or chemotherapy may be reduced among women who have smaller or earlier stage cancer. This choice in type of treatment allows a woman a measure of control over treatment decisions.

If mastectomy is performed, some women decide to have reconstructive surgery. For some women reconstruction is essential to rebuilding self-esteem and for psychological healing after losing a breast. The reconstruction may involve using tissue from other parts of the woman's body or an implant filled with a silicone gel or saline solution. Silicone gel implants were withdrawn from the market because of health problems linked to the devices, but the Food and Drug Administration allows their use under controlled clinical studies for reconstruction after mastectomy. Because of concerns about the possible adverse effects from an implant, women may opt instead to wear prostheses, external breast forms. Others shun the use of any type of artificial breast after mastectomy. *See also* Breast Cancer; Breast Implants

Further Reading
Boston Women's Health Book Collective. *Our Bodies, Ourselves for the New Century: A Book by and for Women.* New York: Touchstone/Simon & Schuster, 1998.
Gross, Amy, and Dee Ito. *Women Talk about Breast Surgery.* New York: HarperPerennial, 1990.
Healy, Bernadine. *A New Prescription for Women's Health.* New York: Viking, 1995.
National Cancer Institute. National Institutes of Health Consensus Development Conference Statement (January 21–23, 1997).

Maternal and Child Health Bureau

The Maternal and Child Health Bureau (MCHB) of the U.S. Health Resources and Services Administration is responsible for promoting and improving the health of the nation's mothers and children. Its predecessor, the Children's Bureau, was established in 1912; in 1935 Congress authorized the MCHB to provide health services, which today help communities meet critical issues and challenges in maternal and child health. These include:

- Significantly reducing infant mortality
- Providing comprehensive care for women before, during, and after pregnancy and childbirth
- Providing preventive and primary-care services for children and adolescents
- Providing comprehensive care for children and adolescents with special health needs
- Immunizing all American children
- Reducing teenage pregnancy
- Putting into community practice national standards and guidelines for prenatal care; for healthy and safe child care; and for the health supervision of infants, children, and adolescents
- Assuring access to care for all mothers and children
- Meeting nutritional and development needs of mothers, children, and families

The MCHB has outlined other health objectives of concern to women and their families. These include reducing fetal alcohol syndrome, cesarean deliveries, severe complications of pregnancy, and alcohol and substance abuse. Additional goals include increasing breastfeeding, screening, and counseling on detection of fetal abnormalities and genetic disorders. *See also* Adolescent Girls' Health; Breastfeeding; Cesarean Section; Fetal Alcohol Syndrome; Genetic Testing; Health Resources and Services Administration; Pregnancy; Teenage Pregnancy and Childbearing

Further Reading

HRSA's Maternal and Child Health Bureau, Fact Sheet (September 1999). <http://www.mchb.hrsa.gov>.

Melanoma

Melanoma is a cancer of pigment-producing skin cells called melanocytes, and is frequently caused by repeated exposure to ultraviolet (UV) radiation of the sun. While farmers, construction workers, lifeguards, and others who spend most of the daylight hours outdoors may be at risk for skin cancers, light-skinned Caucasians who deliberately expose themselves to the sun or use tanning beds and sun lamps also place themselves at risk for melanoma. The main risk factor in the development of melanoma, however, is having many moles or atypical moles on the skin and being badly sunburned during childhood. Genetics may also play a role in the disease.

In recent years the incidence of melanoma has increased at an alarming rate, according to the American Cancer Society. Since 1973, the number of new melanomas diagnosed per 100,000 people each year has doubled from 6 to 13 with an estimated 44,200 new melanomas diagnosed in the United States during a single year. The increase of melanoma cases and the more than 7,000 deaths from the disease each year have brought some public attention to this health issue.

Melanoma is more common in the elderly than in other age groups and "As the baby-boomer generation gets older and becomes at risk for melanoma, rates are expected to increase even more." (Dennis, 1,037) Far more fair-skinned men than women are likely to have this type of skin cancer, but malignant melanoma is the most common cancer among women be-

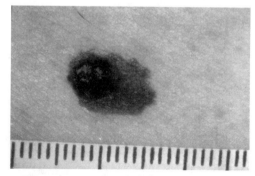

Melanoma. National Cancer Institute.

tween the ages of 25 and 29, exceeding the number of cases in men by a ratio of 3:2. Women 30 to 34 years of age outnumber men in that age group by a ratio of 2:1 in the incidence of melanoma, according to the Society for the Advancement of Women's Health Research, which holds a Scientific Advisory Meeting (SAM) each year on gender differences in health.

In spite of the health risks, Caucasian women, young people of both genders, and those living in areas with relatively few sunny days, are influenced by the perception that sun-worshiping and using tanning booths are healthy activities; they intentionally expose themselves to UV radiation. Media advertisements encourage this behavior by showing tanned models representing the "good life" and apparently enjoying the benefits of a robust lifestyle.

To counteract such misconceptions, dermatologists, primary-care physicians, and other health-care providers are trying to educate the public about cancer prevention and the risks of ultraviolet exposure. They admit that they must intensify their efforts to encourage changes in behavior that will lower the risks and incidence of skin cancer. Cancer experts advise people to wear hats and protective clothing and to use sunscreens when being exposed to the sun. They also recommend limiting sun exposure between 10 a.m. and 4 p.m. when UV radiation is strongest. A great deal of information about melanoma and cancer prevention can be found on Internet web sites maintained by the American Cancer Society, Memorial Sloan-Kettering Cancer Center, American Academy of Dermatology, American Medical Association, and similar groups. *See also* Scientific Advisory Meeting

Further Reading

Dennis, Leslie K. "Increasing Risk of Melanoma with Increasing Age." *Journal of the American Medical Association* (September 15, 1999).

"Detecting Melanoma." *Harvard Health Letter* (May 1999).

Goff, Karen Goldberg. "A Safe Place in the Sun." *Insight on the News* (August 30, 1999).

Mooney, Linda. "The Cancer Your Doctor May Miss." *Prevention* (May 1999).

Poole, Catherine M., and DuPont Guerry. *Melanoma: Prevention, Detection, and Treatment.* Yale University Press, 1998.

Menopause

A midlife concern for many women is menopause, a word that comes from the Greek *mens* for monthly and *pausis*, cessation, and commonly called the "change of life." Menopause is the point when menstruation stops permanently, the last stage of a biological process called perimenopause that occurs on average over a two- to six-year period when a woman's ovaries gradually reduce their production of the hormones estrogen and progesterone; when estrogen and progesterone production ends, menopause is over. Although some medical experts contend that there is also a male menopause, the "change" is usually associated with women between the ages of 45 and 55, with the average menopausal age about 51. About five percent of women experience menopause before age 40.

Until recent years, the menopausal and midlife years were often misunderstood. Little scientific research focused on this particular stage of life, primarily because menopause was linked to old age and in the past the process occurred near the end of life. Today women generally live several decades beyond menopause. In 2000, more than 31 million women began the change, and by 2020 nearly 46 million will be in this transition stage.

With the increase in menopausal women, attention has focused on dismantling the stereotypes of menopause that have developed. Some of the menopausal stereotypes stem from studies of dysfunctional women, particularly studies based on Sigmund Freud's portrayal of midlife women as pathological. Stereotypes have also developed because menopause has long been considered a disease rather than a natural process.

Surveys have shown that physiological and psychological changes that women expect are based more on myth than on reality. One common myth is that once the reproductive years are over the "beginning of the end" is at hand. Others believe they will experience depression and be unable to cope with stress.

Studies conducted at the Women's Medical and Diagnostic Center in Gainesville, Florida, and others at the New England Research Institute in Watertown, Massachusetts, have "found that menopause has no significant effect on depression." In addition, "not all changes resulting from menopause are perceived as negative....women reported they felt relief or neutral feelings about the cessation of menstruation. And the biggest source of frustration for menopausal women was *not* having their children leave home but *having their grown children return to the roost*." Other research has shown "numerous positive counterbalances at this time in a woman's life: the arrival of grandchildren, freedom from unwanted pregnancy, and the chance to pursue other activities, such as finishing an education or reentering the work force." (Notelovitz, 6)

Nevertheless, the menopausal years can pose health risks, such as heart disease, breast cancer, and ovarian cancer; but 60 percent of women between 45 and 75 years of age are unaware of these risks. According to a 1998 study by the National Center on Women and Aging at Brandeis, University, nearly 8 out of 10 women understand the need for exercise, good eating habits, and regular cancer screenings to reduce risks associated with aging, but "they do not realize that the end of estrogen produc-

tion puts them at risk for some serious conditions regardless of their daily habits." Although 64 percent of women understood the relationship between menopause and osteoporosis, 56 percent of women surveyed did not know that menopause affects the risk of heart disease and breast cancer and 61 percent did not realize that menopause affects the risk of ovarian cancer. This gap in knowledge sometimes prevents women from considering hormone replacement therapy (HRT) or alternative therapies to protect themselves from declining levels of estrogen.

Since the 1970s, there has been an ongoing debate on whether menopausal women should undergo hormone replacement therapy to restore the estrogen that is no longer being produced. Advocates for hormone replacement therapy contend that it diminishes the risk of a great variety of health problems from bone fractures to ovarian cancer. A major argument for HRT has been the medical doctrine that estrogen reduces heart disease risks. But two studies in recent years have concluded that there is no evidence to support the use of estrogen supplements to lower risks of heart disease. Others argue against hormone replacement, saying that menopause has been so "medicalized" that little emphasis is placed on a healthy lifestyle to reduce health risks.

A nonprofit organization called the North American Menopause Society (NAMS) was established in 1989 to promote understanding of menopause, and thereby improve the health of women as they approach menopause and beyond. The NAMS has a multidisciplinary membership of 2,000, including clinical and basic science experts from medicine, nursing, sociology, psychology, nutrition, anthropology, epidemiology, and education. *See also* Hormone Replacement Therapy; Midlife Women

Further Reading

Associated Press. "Another Study Disputes Estrogen Heart Benefit." *New York Times* (March 14, 2000).

Jacobson, Joan Mathews, Ph.D., R.N. *Midlife Women Contemporary Issues.* Boston: Jones and Bartlett, 1995.

National Center on Women and Aging, Brandeis University. "Women Unaware of Serious Health Risks Associated with Aging." Press Release (September 14, 1998).

North American Menopause Society. <http://www.menopause.org>.

Menstruation

During menstruation, which is part of an ovulation cycle that occurs approximately once a month in fertile women, the lining of the uterus that had been preparing for the implantation of a fertilized egg breaks down and is discharged from the body. The discharge, known as menstrual blood, and the process of menstruation have generated countless myths, superstitions, rituals, and taboos over the ages, contributing to many of the negative cultural attitudes about menstruation that prevail today. Even though many modern American women understand that menstruation is a natural function, they still struggle to live with what has been called "the curse." Such a concept affects women at home, in the workplace, and in the general society, which stereotypes menstruating women as dysfunctional and creates what the authors of *The Curse: A Cultural History of Menstruation* call "menstrual politics." The authors contend that

> Practitioners of menstrual politics...are convinced that women are naturally and irrevocably limited by the menstrual function. Since the early nineteenth century, menstrual politics has taken two positions with regard to menstruation and economic life: first, that factories and businesses pose a fatal threat to women's reproductive life; second, that the menstrual cycle threatens the health of American capitalism. (Delaney, et al., 55)

Such ideas have been repudiated by numerous women who have succeeded in business, politics, and the military over the past few decades. However, the negative stereotypes have not disappeared. In fact, menstruating girls and women are the butt of numerous denigrating jokes, cartoons, and remarks. Physical and emotional difficulties that accompany menstruation also play a role in the negative attitudes about the ovulation cycle. Some women suffer from cramps and backache during menstruation, or a few days before menstruation they experience a range of symptoms known as Premenstrual Syndrome (PMS). The symptoms, which vary greatly from one woman to another, include depression, tension, bloating, and cravings for certain foods. The causes of PMS are not well understood, although many medical researchers and practitioners view PMS as a hormonal disorder.

In spite of problems and stereotypes associated with menstruation, young girls (and boys, too) can develop a positive attitude about the process, if they receive accurate information about what to expect and are taught that menstruation is healthy and natural. In some families, parents or other relatives celebrate menarche (a girl's first menstrual period) as a rite of passage with a special dinner or symbolic gestures such as presenting a red rose or a glass of red wine.

Since the 1970s, the topic of menstruation has been more openly discussed and more positive attitudes about menstruation have been reflected in various art forms, from the graphic arts to literature. Manufacturers of menstrual products frankly describe and depict napkins and tampons in their advertising. Products developed over the years and other menstruation memorabilia became part of the Museum of Menstruation (MUM), which was open between 1994 and 1998 in the home of its creator, Harry Finley, a graphic designer in Landover, Maryland. Finley had to close the museum because visitors were reluctant to go to a private home, but Finley maintains a Web site (http://www.mum.org) that depicts some of his collection and describes his plans for a public museum, which would focus on women's health and menstruation. *See also* Premenstrual Syndrome; Toxic Shock Syndrome

Further Reading

Delaney, Janice, Mary Jane Lupton, and Emily Toth. *The Curse: A Cultural History of Menstruation.* Rev. ed. Urbana and Chicago: University of Illinois Press, 1988.

Howard, Beth. *Mind Your Body: A Sexual Health and Wellness Guide for Women.* New York: St. Martin's Press, 1998.

Planned Parenthood Federation of America. *The Planned Parenthood Women's Health Encyclopedia.* New York: Crown Trade Paperbacks, 1996.

Mental Illness

Mental illness encompasses many maladies and is defined by the National Mental Health Association (NMHA) as "a disease that causes mild to severe disturbances in thinking, perception and behavior." The disease ranges from anxiety disorders to the most serious and disabling disorder, schizophrenia. Overall nearly the same number of females and males in the United States suffer from mental illness, but during a lifetime women are more prone than men to certain afflictions. The National Women's Health Information Center of the U.S. Public Health Service's Office on Women's Health points out that women are two to three times more likely to have certain types of depression and anxiety disorders, including panic and phobic disorders. Ninety percent of all cases of eating disorders, which are closely related to depression and substance abuse, occur in women. After childbirth, between 70 and 80 per-

cent of women have feelings of anxiety and depression for several days. Marked feelings of anxiety and despair, called postpartum depression, affect about 10 percent of women who give birth. Untreated disorders can lead to death (usually from suicide), particularly among women between the ages of 15 and 24.

The gender differences in some types of mental illness may stem from the male tendency to externalize mental distress by "acting out" disorders, using violence, crime, chemicals, or some other generally risky behavior to transform their feelings into action. "Females tend to pull their anguish into themselves—to 'internalize' it—in abnormal states of anxiety or mood. Depression, which in its various forms strikes about 10% of women during their lifetimes but fewer than 5% of men, in many ways typifies this pattern of difference." (Benderly, 23)

Mentally ill women as well as men must face major concerns about getting proper health care—often they are afraid or embarrassed to discuss their problems because of the social stigmas attached to mental disorders. Those stigmas are perpetuated by long-held misconceptions and media images, such as portrayals of mentally ill people as violent, suicidal, women with multiple personalities, and delusional homeless women and men. As the National Mental Health Association (NMHA) points out:

> It is sometimes easy to forget that our brain, like all of our other organs, is vulnerable to disease... because people with mental illnesses often suffer from symptoms which are behavioral, they are sometimes thought of differently than people with physical ailments. Instead of receiving compassion and support, people with mental illnesses may be greeted by unsympathetic, unfair or hostile responses. (NMHA Fact Sheet)

Those responses can lead to discrimination on the job and little or no medical insurance coverage. While medical science has begun to unravel some of the mysteries of the brain, researchers do not fully understand many of the brain's functions or why it malfunctions. However, experts have found that chemical imbalances in the brain probably cause some disorders. Today many people with mental illness are treated successfully with medications to correct chemical imbalances, helping them to live active and productive lives. Along with a variety of mental health organizations, a number of well-known individuals who have suffered from mental disorders have helped to educate the public about mental illness. Among the prominent women who have spoken out are Alma Powell, wife of General Colin Powell; comedienne Joan Rivers; Kitty Dukakis, wife of former presidential candidate Michael Dukakis; actress Patty Duke; and Tipper Gore, wife of Vice President Al Gore. Rosalynn Carter, first lady from 1977 to 1981 and head of the Mental Health Task Force at the Carter Center in Georgia, frequently delivers speeches and appears on television shows to assail the stigma of mental illness. Carter wrote *Helping Someone with Mental Illness: A Compassionate Guide for Family, Friends and Caregivers*, published in 1998. *See also* Depression; Eating Disorders; Homeless Women

Further Reading

Carlson, Karen J., Stephanie A. Eisenstat, and Terra Ziporyn. *The Harvard Guide to Women's Health.* Cambridge, MA.: Harvard University Press, 1996.

Editors of the *Johns Hopkins Medical Letter, Health After 50. The Johns Hopkins Medical Handbook: The 100 Major Medical Disorders of People over the Age of 50.* New York: Rebus, 1992.

Krueger, Curtis. "Rosalynn Carter Attacks Stigma of Mental Illness." *St. Petersburg Times* (May 26, 1999).

National Mental Health Association. "Mental Illness and the Family-Stigma: Building Awareness and Understanding about Mental Illness." Fact Sheet (1996).

Midlife Women

Many midlife women—those between the ages of 45 and 64—are at a stage in their lives when they enjoy good health and secure financial status. But a significant number are faced with diverse health, economic, and social issues. For some American women, their middle years pose risks for the onset of chronic health problems, which can lead to the loss of a job and employer-based health insurance, factors that can have lasting impact. The Commonwealth Fund (TCF), a philanthropic organization based in New York City, commissioned a survey of more than 5,000 adults ages 18 to 64 during the first five months of 1999, and found that 30 percent of Americans ages 55 to 64 rate their health as fair or poor. Those with health problems are more likely to have difficulty meeting their health-care needs. Fifty-three percent of midlife adults who rate their health status negatively could not pay medical bills. One of eight lacks health insurance. Those who have retired for health reasons or are unemployed are at even greater risk. More than one of five with incomes less than $35,000 is uninsured.

Some midlife women in the United States dread menopause and consider this transition a traumatic issue, but for many others the end of menstrual periods is not as grim as they are often led to believe. Physically, women at midlife may have some adverse conditions such as hot flashes and irritability linked to "the change," but there are beneficial psychological and social factors that many midlife women experience. At this time of their lives, some women become more liberated and assertive. If they are free of family caregiving responsibilities, they are likely

A workshop for "midlife" women meets. ©Photos—Bettye Lane.

to be more zestful, and may even achieve social, political, or economic power.

At midlife, a sexual relationship may be an issue for some women. A special report by AARP and its magazine *Modern Maturity* shows that approximately "half of 45- through 59-year-olds have sex at least once a week" but as women age, they have fewer opportunities for sexual activity because fewer male partners are available.

A common health issue facing women at midlife is whether or not to have a hysterectomy, surgery to remove the uterus and frequently the ovaries. Many women believe this is a necessary procedure at midlife, even though only a small percentage of hysterectomies are performed because of serious health problems such as cancer.

A significant concern for women at midlife is health education—being informed consumers about their own health care and what measures they can take to prevent cardiovascular disease, breast cancer, and other diseases that are leading causes of death among midlife women. "Too many women submit to the opinion of a single physician without question. They are often forced to make decisions with too little information about their condition and the wide range of options available. It is essential for women to be aware of the principles of self-care as they educate themselves about health problems and all available choices," notes one health-care practitioner. (Jacobson, 39) *See also* Hysterectomy; Menopause; Menstruation; Sexuality

Further Reading

Brotman, Barbara. "(The) Change Is Good." *Chicago Tribune* (July 21, 1999).

Commonwealth Fund. "Health Care Hazards for Midlife Americans." Press Release (January 27, 2000).

Jacobson, Joan Mathews. *Midlife Women: Contemporary Issues.* Boston: Jones and Bartlett Publishers, 1995.

Jacoby, Susan. "Great Sex—What's Age Got to Do with It?" Special Report, *Modern Maturity* (September–October 1999).

Komesaroff, Paul A., Philipa Rothfield, and Jeanne Daly. *Reinterpreting Menopause: Cultural and Philosophical Issues.* New York: Routledge, 1997.

Midwifery

Midwifery is a childbirth practice that treats pregnancy and birthing as normal bodily functions. It is an alternative to the "medicalization" of childbearing, which approaches childbearing as an illness that requires drugs and medical care. Although midwifery is practiced extensively in many parts of the world, including European countries and Japan, it is not common in the United States where physicians attend the vast majority of deliveries. Encouraging and making women aware of the midwifery alternative is an issue that a variety of women's groups champion as does a Taskforce on Midwifery made up of members of the Pew Health Professions Commission and the Center for the Health Professions at the University of California, San Francisco. In its joint 1999 report on *The Future of Midwifery,* the taskforce found that "the midwifery model of care is an essential element of comprehensive health care for women and their families that should be embraced by, and incorporated into, the health care system and made available to all women." (Dower, i)

Those who practice midwifery in the United States are either nationally certified nurse-midwives (CNMs) licensed to practice nursing as well as midwifery or are direct-entry midwives whose education focuses only on midwifery. The latter may become nationally certified professional midwives or certified midwives, or they may work independently without national certification. CNMs may have private practices, or work with physicians in their private practices, in hospitals, or in birth centers. "They always practice in conjunction with physicians, referring women who have problem pregnancies to them and calling upon them in situations and emergencies which require medical care, advice and/or surgical attention." (BWHBC, 410)

Although the art of midwifery stems from ancient practices, midwives were discouraged or prevented from attending deliveries when the U.S. medical profession determined decades ago that doctors, particularly obstetricians, could best assure the safety of mother and child at birth. Many midwives who served specific communities, such as the "granny" midwives among rural African-Americans, faced numerous obstacles set up to prevent them from practicing, even though they assisted women living in areas where no hospitals or doctors existed. The bias against midwifery is fairly widespread in the United States today, although a recent study by the National Center for Health Statistics (NCHS) published in 1998 shows that the number of births attended by midwives grew from three percent in 1989 to six percent of total births in 1995. The study also indicates that nurse-midwives have an excellent record of deliveries. Even though they attend a greater proportion of women at high medical or social risk for problems at childbirth (women of color and teenagers, for example), "the risk of experiencing an infant death was 19 percent lower for births attended by certified nurse-midwives than for births attended by physicians." The NCHS pointed out some reasons for successful deliveries:

Certified nurse-midwives generally spend more time with patients during prenatal visits and put more emphasis on patient counseling and education, and providing emotional support. Most certified nurse-midwives are with their patients on a one-on-one basis during the entire labor and delivery process providing patient care and emotional support, in contrast

A midwife weighs a pregnant woman. ©Jennie Woodcock; Reflections Photolibrary/CORBIS.

with physician's care which is more often episodic. (NCHS Press Release)

According to the California Taskforce report, midwifery is also cost-effective; charges for midwives are usually much less than physician costs. Still many women in their childbearing years presume that their only birthing option is the medical model, and they do not have easy access to information about midwifery. Pregnant women who do opt for midwifery are not necessarily able to find suitable midwives since the demand exceeds the supply of qualified practitioners. The California Taskforce and other groups such as the Boston Women's Health Book Collective have made recommendations on a variety of midwifery issues, including more educational programs in the field of midwifery, more analysis of the cost benefits of midwifery, and more unified standards

for midwives in the United States. *See also* Childbirth Practices; Prepared Childbirth

Further Reading

Boston Women's Health Book Collective. *The New Our Bodies, Ourselves.* New York: Simon & Schuster, 1992.

Dower, C.M., J.E. Miller, and E.H. O'Neil, and the Taskforce on Midwifery. *Charting a Course for the 21ˢᵗ Century: The Future of Midwifery.* San Francisco, CA: Pew Health Professions Commission and the UCSF Center for the Health Professions, April 1999.

Foreman, Judy. "The Midwives' Time Has Come—Again." *Boston Globe* (November 2, 1998).

National Center for Health Statistics, Centers for Disease Control and Prevention. "New Study Shows Lower Mortality Rates for Infants Delivered by Certified Nurse Midwives." Press Release (May 19, 1998).

Rooks, Judith. *Midwifery and Childbirth in America.* Philadelphia, PA: Temple University Press, 1997.

Mifepristone (RU-486)

Used safely and effectively in more than 20 European countries, mifepristone is a drug (also known as RU-486) that blocks the action of progesterone, a hormone necessary to sustain pregnancy. Mifepristone is combined with a prostaglandin called misoprostol to abort pregnancies, much like a spontaneous miscarriage, during the first seven weeks after conception. RU-486 also has been tested in the Netherlands and Canada as a possible treatment for some forms of breast cancer. Women in the United States, however, have only been able to obtain the drug at clinical trial sites in such states as California, Montana, Nebraska, New Jersey, New York, Ohio, Vermont, and Washington.

Mifepristone was first developed in 1980 by Dr. Etienne-Emile Baulieu of the French pharmaceutical company Roussel-Uclaf. The medication name RU-486 came from the company's initials and laboratory serial number. Since its introduction in France, the drug has been used to induce abortions in about 400,000 European women. But the United States Food and Drug Administration (FDA) banned the import of RU-486, an action that many members of Congress, medical research groups, and prochoice advocates declared was politically motivated. The Center for Reproductive Law and Policy filed a lawsuit in 1992 in an attempt to overturn the ban, but was unsuccessful. In 1993, President Bill Clinton rescinded the ban, and in 1996 the FDA gave temporary approval for the drug's manufacture, withholding final approval until information became available on how mifepristone would be manufactured and labeled. Antiabortion groups organized to boycott Roussel-Uclaf and its parent company, Hoechst A.G. of Germany, plus its American affiliates, calling RU-486 the "French death pill." As a result no major U.S. company would distribute RU-486, and Canada refused to allow its use because of political opposition. But an abortion rights group formed a small manufacturing facility to produce mifepristone and provide it free to doctors who are researching the drug's effects.

By 1997, under pressure from the Clinton administration, Roussel-Uclaf, which had stopped manufacturing RU-486, donated its U.S. patent rights to the nonprofit Population Council, an organization promoting reproductive health. The Population Council made arrangements with a marketing firm, Danco, to distribute RU-486, but the council would not reveal the name of the manufacturer for fear of backlash and intimidation from antiabortionists. The drug was distributed to physicians and clinics only.

In September 2000, the FDA announced approval of RU-486, which brought pro and con reactions from politicians, the general public, health-care advocates, and activists. Responses to the FDA action were evenly split between prochoice and antiabortionist positions.

Prochoice activists applauded the action. They believe the use of RU-486 will change the abortion debate significantly because the drug will be dispensed in the privacy of a doctor's office, removing the spotlight from abortion clinics. In addition, proponents believe the drug will reduce surgical abortions.

Antiabortionists denounced the FDA approval of RU-486, claiming that the drug's use will lead to an increase in abortions. Some members of the U.S. Congress who oppose the drug vowed to introduce legislation to strictly limit the use of mifepristone to doctors who now perform abortions. Other politicians called for a review of the FDA decision.

Although the FDA would not reveal the name or location of the drug's manufacturer, several days after its decision the *Washington Post* reported that Hua Lian Pharmaceutical Company in China will manufacture RU-486 for the United States. The drug has been used for years in China as part of its strategy to control population. According to the *Post,* "FDA inspectors spent a week at the factory in July [2000] and agreed to allow Hua Lian to produce RU-486 in bulk amounts for export to the United States," where the drug will be produced in pill form. (Pan, A1)

Surveys of doctors show that they are willing to use the FDA-approved drug. But if the use of RU-486 is strictly regulated to use only by physicians who perform abortions, the primary advantage of the drug—its availability for prescription by family physicians, gynecologists, and other doctors who do not perform abortions—will be negated. *See also* Abortion; Birth Control

Further Reading
Blumenthal, Paul, Jane Johnson, and Felicia Stewart. "The Approval of Mifepristone (RU-486) in the United States: What's Wrong with This Picture?" Medscape <http://www.nhtp.org/news_archive/news_early_approval.htm>

Feminist Majority Foundation. "Feminist Majority Foundation Reports on Mifepristone." <http://www.feminist.org/gateway/ru486one.html>.

Krieger, Lisa M. "U.S. Drug Makers in No Hurry to Make Abortion Pill RU-486." Detroit News (February 1, 1998).

Pan, Philip P. "Chinese to Make RU-486 for U.S." Washington Post (October 12, 2000).

Talbot, Margaret. "The Little White Bombshell." The New York Times Magazine (July 11, 1999).

Migraine

Migraine, a word that comes from the Greek term for half a head, refers to a type of headache that may range from mild to severe and affects one side of the head for several hours to two or three weeks. A migraine headache attack includes nausea and sometimes vomiting, sensitivity to sound, and in some cases neurological symptoms such as visual disturbances (flashing lights, bright spots, distorted vision) or numbness in a hand, side of the face, or other part of the body. About three-fourths of the estimated 24 to 26 million migraine sufferers in the United States are women, but headache experts point out that there is little understanding of how migraine affects women. Many U.S. practitioners believe migraine is imagined—an emotional or a psychological problem. However, it is a significant disease often associated with a woman's reproductive life, including the menstrual cycle, contraceptive use, pregnancy, and menopause.

The disabling effects of migraine attacks lead to economic costs, a concern for both migraine sufferers, particularly women who incur the most costs, and their employers. Yet the issue "has not received adequate attention as a public health priority because its impact on society has been underestimated," one study concluded. When workers become bedridden with migraine attacks, employers lose productivity, costing "American employers about $13 billion a year because of missed workdays and impaired work function.... Annual direct medical costs for migraine care were about $1 billion and about $100 was spent per diagnosed patient." (Hu, et al., 813)

In order to inform doctors and the general public about migraine, the *Journal of the American Medical Association* has created a Web site called the Migraine Information Center, which includes a page debunking some of the common myths about headache patients and a variety of medical reports on migraine. The World Headache Alliance (WHA) also has developed an information and awareness program. Aimed at physicians, the program focuses on a treatment approach for women that is different from that used with men and emphasizes management of the disease as opposed to simply reacting to it. Although there is no proven cause for migraine, physicians advise various methods to manage headaches, such as identifying factors from alcohol and certain foods to hormone changes and stress that can provoke attacks; using medication to reduce inflammation of the blood vessels and nerves around the brain; and learning biofeedback, a method of concentration to reduce

Woman suffering from a headache. ©Sheila Terry/Photo Researchers, Inc.

muscle tension. The American Osteopathic Association recommends osteopathic manipulative treatment as one method among others to stop or reduce the severity of migraine attacks.

Other help for migraineurs (migraine sufferers) is available from organizations such as the American Council for Headache Education in Mount Royal, New Jersey; MAGNUM (Migraine Awareness Group: A National Understanding for Migraineurs) in Alexandria, Virginia; the National Headache Foundation in Chicago, Illinois; and the National Institutes of Health Neurological Institute in Bethesda, Maryland. All of these organizations maintain Internet Web sites with current information on migraine. *See also* American Osteopathic Association Women's Health Initiative; Menopause; Menstruation; Pregnancy

Further Reading

Editors of the *Johns Hopkins Medical Letter, Health After 50. The Johns Hopkins Medical Handbook: The 100 Major Medical Disorders of People over the Age of 50*. New York: Rebus, 1992.

Freitag, Frederick G. "Manage Your Migraines." *The DO* (June 1999). <http://www.aoa-net.org/Consumers/WomensHealth/migraines.htm>.

Hu, X. Henry, Leona E. Markson, Richard B. Lipton, Walter F. Stewart, and Marc L. Berger. "Burden of Migraine in the United States." *Archives of Internal Medicine* (April 26, 1999).

Nordenberg, Tamar. "Heading Off Migraine Pain." *FDA Consumer Magazine* (May–June 1998).

Phillips, Pat. "Migraine as a Woman's Issue—Will Research and New Treatments Help?" *Journal of the American Medical Association* (December 16, 1998).

Mood Disorders

See Depression; Mental Illness

Mothers and Daughters

The health issue for many mothers and daughters today is how to develop good exercise and eating habits—together. "Many adolescent girls develop negative habits like physical inactivity and destructive eating patterns: only two thirds of high school girls exercise the recommended three times a week. More than half diet frequently; nearly 20 percent binge and purge." (Clemetson, 16)

Health-conscious mothers are attempting to provide positive examples for their daughters, taking part in sports and fitness programs with their daughters or participating in physical activities and sending a message about the health benefits of exercise. Some mothers also influence their teenage daughters' dietary habits by preparing calcium-rich foods and other nutritious items for meals and snacks.

Some health experts believe that mothers who are not health-conscious begin to mold their daughters' health in the womb, programming them for chronic diseases

Mothers and daughters in Los Angeles, California. ©Joseph Sohm; ChromoSohm, Inc./CORBIS.

such as diabetes, heart disease, and other problems. But such programming can be reversed, the experts say, if mothers set examples of good exercise and diet habits for their daughters, who, in turn, will pass on healthy lifestyles to their daughters. Yet, many mothers concentrate more on thinness than on fitness. Debra Waterhouse, a nutritionist who has written several books on women and weight obsession, notes:

Weight-loss behaviors are so firmly integrated into our daily lives that mothers diet without thinking about it and pass along their weight preoccupations to their daughters without realizing it. By modeling these behaviors and setting the standard for female identity:

- a mother's dieting history becomes her daughter's dieting future
- a mother's eating habits are passed on to her daughter
- a mother's poor body image is mirrored by her daughter (Waterhouse, xv)

In some cases, the reverse is true, and daughters provide positive health examples for their mothers. Health-conscious daughters have helped and encouraged their mothers to begin exercise programs, walk regularly, and avoid fad diets. *See also* Adolescent Girls' Health; Dieting and Diet Drugs

Further Reading
Clemetson, Lynette. "Our Daughters, Our Selves." *Newsweek* Special Issue (Spring/Summer 1999).
Waterhouse, Debra. *Like Mother, Like Daughter.* New York: Hyperion, 1997.

Mothers' Voices United to End AIDS

A nonprofit, grassroots organization, Mothers' Voices United to End AIDS began in 1991 with a small group of women and has grown to include a membership of 40,000 mothers and supporters nation-

wide. "As more families confront the reality of the disease, Mothers' Voices has steadily grown to meet an expanding need," notes the organization's president.

Mothers' Voices addresses the public health issue of HIV and other sexually transmitted diseases (STDs), focusing in particular on the rise in STDs among teenagers. The organization mobilizes mothers to become educators and advocates for improved HIV prevention, expanded research, and better medical treatments for people with HIV. In a policy statement adopted in 1996, Mother's Voices declares:

the rise of HIV and other sexually transmitted infections can best be stemmed in a climate of healthy sexuality. Research shows that children are strongly influenced by their parents, and Mothers' Voices acknowledges that mothers are primary educators to promote healthy sexuality and behavioral choices for children. Today, the AIDS epidemic poses an urgent challenge to mothers as they guide their children through this important aspect of human development.

Mothers' Voices believes that sexuality education need not be difficult if started early and as a natural part of parenting. By educating themselves, mothers can take the lead in developing a positive approach to communicating a healthy and responsible understanding of sexuality to their children and families.

The policy statement also emphasizes that "sexuality education is a lifelong process and that mothers are in a singularly unique position to encourage healthy sexuality by promoting values that positively support children's understanding of their body, their gender, their sexual orientation, their social role, and their interactions with others." In addition, the organization points out that mothers outside the home "can be a voice of reason for policies and programs that promote healthy sexuality. Recognizing that development extends beyond the home environment, it is vital that schools, religious and community groups, media, business and government accept responsibility in reinforcing healthy attitudes." *See also* AIDS; Sexuality; Sexually Transmitted Diseases

Further Reading

Mothers' Voices United to End AIDS. <http://www.mvoices.org/index_new.html>.

Multiple Chemical Sensitivity

Multiple chemical sensitivity (MCS) is a term used to describe a syndrome thought to be caused by low-level exposure to pollutants and toxins in the environment, including exposure to aerosol air fresheners, household cleaners, laundry detergents, gasoline exhaust, insecticide sprays, perfumes, and cigarette smoke. MCS has also been given numerous other names such as environmental illness (EI), sick-building syndrome, toxic-carpet syndrome, total immune disorder syndrome, and twentieth century disease. An estimated 37 to 75 million Americans report that they are sensitive to chemicals in common household products and pesticides. Up to 13 million are extremely sensitive and have such symptoms as severe allergies, depression, and respiratory illness. MCS has become a women's health issue over the past few decades primarily because women make up 85 to 90 percent of patients who seek treatment for it. However, much of the established medical community does not recognize MCS as a verifiable syndrome. In fact, "MCS syndrome has led to great controversy among clinicians, researchers, patients, lawyers, legislators and regulatory agencies. The absence of scientific agreement on MCS has contributed to the development of emotionally charged, extreme and entrenched positions." (Magil and Suruda, 721)

Nevertheless an increasing number of doctors in recent years have declared that MCS, like the mysterious Gulf War Syndrome that has debilitated military personnel who served in the Persian Gulf during 1990–1991, is a new ailment whose cause is yet to be determined. In 1998, a federal interagency workgroup issued a report on MCS, stating:

> It is currently unknown whether MCS is a distinct disease entity and what role, if any, the biochemical mechanisms of specific chemicals have in the onset of this condition. The workgroup finds that MCS is currently a symptom-based diagnosis without supportive laboratory tests or agreed-upon signs of clinical manifestation. The workgroup knows of no reports in the literature of definite end-organ damage attributable to MCS. However, scientific knowledge changes over time as additional findings are reported. It is therefore important not to lose sight of lessons from the past in which suspected health effects of environmental exposures were verified at a later date through scientific research. (Interagency Workgroup)

In 1999, a group of 34 researchers, physicians, and clinicians with diverse experience treating MCS patients signed a consensus statement on six criteria for the clinical diagnosis of MCS. Five of the criteria had been published previously (in 1989), and the sixth was added in 1999. The experts recommended that "MCS be diagnosed whenever all 6 of the consensus criteria are met, along with any other disorders that also may be present, such as asthma, allergy, migraine, chronic fatigue syndrome (CFS), and fibromyalgia (FM)." The consensus, which was published in the *Archives of Environmental Health* and made available for free distribution on the Internet (http://heldref.org/html/Consensus.html), includes these criteria:

1. The symptoms are reproducible with repeated [chemical] exposure.

2. The condition is chronic.

3. Low levels of exposure [lower than previously or commonly tolerated] result in manifestations of the syndrome.

4. The symptoms improve or resolve when the incitants are removed.

5. Responses occur to multiple chemically unrelated substances.

6. Symptoms involve multiple organ systems. (Bartha, et al., 1999)

Medical experts certainly do not discount environmental health hazards such as the metals lead and mercury, the banned pesticide dichlorodiphenyltrichloroethane (DDT), and insidious gases like carbon monoxide. But some health practitioners contend that MCS victims with multiple symptoms could be suffering from mental disorders, even factitious disorders, which nevertheless manifest as real physical illnesses or a combination of chronic ailments. A few argue that EI patients are manipulated by charlatans. One outspoken critic is Stephen Barrett, M.D., founder of Quackwatch, a member of Consumer Federation of America, which attempts to combat health-related frauds, myths, fads, and fallacies. In Barrett's opinion, many who say they suffer environmental illnesses "are seeking special accommodations, applying for disability benefits, and filing lawsuits claiming that exposure to common foods and chemicals has made them ill. Their efforts are supported by a small cadre of physicians who use questionable diagnostic and treatment methods." (Barrett, 1999)

Experts on the other side of the argument include Professor Nicholas Ashford at Massachusetts Institute of Technology (MIT) and Claudia Miller, M.D., who teaches at the University of Texas Health Science Center in San Antonio. Ashford and Miller have studied MCS since the 1980s; they charge that chemical compa-

nies fund their own research to discount MCS symptoms. As Ashford and Miller note:

Many of those who advocate psychological explanations in government-sponsored meetings and in the scientific literature are paid corporate spokespersons or consultants with financial conflicts of interest. Yet these conflicts generally are not revealed when these individuals appear in scientific meetings, author scientific articles, serve on official panels or boards, or serve as reviewers of grant proposals. Policymakers and publishers of scholarly journals need to recognize and remedy this appalling injustice. (Ashford and Miller, 256)

Those who believe they suffer from EI continue to seek treatment and turn to practitioners of environmental medicine or alternative medicine. To protect themselves from environmental pollutants, some EI sufferers with severe symptoms go out only when they can wear oxygen masks. Some move out of their apartments or houses to live in porcelain-lined mobile homes, or they live in rooms lined with aluminum foil or plastic. Others live in makeshift huts or other shelters in isolated rural areas. Still others try to find relief from their symptoms in ultra-clean apartments in places like Ecology House in California and the Natural Place hotel in Florida.

True believers of EI accuse critics of trying to cover up serious health conditions, and they band together for support. Hundreds of Web sites offer advice and suggest treatments for EI victims. One site is maintained by MCS Referral & Resources, Inc., founded by Grace Ziem, who has a medical degree in occupational and environmental medicine, and Albert Donnay, who has a master's degree in environmental engineering. According to the organization, its "mission is to further the diagnosis, treatment, accommodation and prevention of multiple chemical sensitivity disorders." (MCS Referral & Resources) *See also* Alternative Medicine; Environmental Health Hazards; Factitious Disorders

Further Reading

Ashford, Nicholas A., and Claudia S. Miller. *Chemical Exposures; Low Levels and High Stakes*. 2nd Ed. New York: Van Nostrand Reinhold, 1998.

Barrett, Stephen, M.D. "Multiple Chemical Sensitivity:A Spurious Diagnosis." Quackwatch home page (July 24, 1999). <http://www.quackwatch.com/01QuackeryRelated Topics/mcs.html>.

Barrett, Stephen, and Ronald E. Gots. *Chemical Sensitivity: The Truth about Environmental Illness*. Amherst, NY: Prometheus Books, 1998.

Bartha, Liliane, et al. "Multiple Chemical Sensitivity: A 1999 Consensus." *Archives of Environmental Health* (May–June 1999). <http://www.heldref.org/html/Consensus.html>.

Futrelle, David. "Making Ourselves Sick." *Salon* (August 6, 1997).

Goldberg, Burton, and *Alternative Medicine Digest* eds. *Alternative Medicine Guide to Chronic Fatigue, Fibromyalgia and Environmental Illness*. Tiburon, CA: Future Medicine Publishers, 1998.

The Interagency Workgroup on Multiple Chemical Sensitivity. *A Report on Multiple Chemical Sensitivity*. Atlanta: Agency for Toxic Substances and Disease Registry, August 24, 1998.

Magill, Michael K., and Anthony Suruda. "Multiple Chemical Sensitivity Syndrome." *American Family Physician* (September 1, 1998).

MCS Referral & Resources. "What Is MCS Referral & Resources?" <http://www.mcsrr.org/whoweare.html>.

Radetsky, Peter. *Allergic to the Twentieth Century: The Explosion in Environmental Allergies—From Sick Buildings to Multiple Chemical Sensitivity*. Boston: Little Brown, 1997.

Staudenmayer, Herman. *Environmental Illness: Myth and Reality*. Boca Raton, FL: Lewis, 1999.

N

National Abortion and Reproductive Rights Action League

The National Abortion and Reproductive Rights Action League (NARAL) has promoted reproductive freedom for women and their families since 1968. Calling itself a prochoice not a pro-abortion organization, NARAL does not encourage abortions but recognizes that ending a pregnancy is a choice that women should have, not government. The league's mission is to secure safe and legal abortion and to make abortion less necessary through sexuality education, improved use of birth control, teen pregnancy prevention, and family planning.

In 1974 the NARAL Foundation, a charitable organization, was set up to support in-depth research and legal work, publish policy reports, conduct public education campaigns on reproductive freedom, and provide leadership training for grassroots activists across the United States. Today NARAL has more than 30 state affiliates and more than 500,000 members nationwide.

Part of the NARAL effort is campaigning to elect prochoice candidates and lobbying for prochoice legislation to secure a woman's freedom to choose. The NARAL was part of the successful lobbying effort for the 1994 Freedom of Access to Clinic Entrances Act (FACE). Along with its affiliates, the NARAL has fought efforts to pass laws that criminalize abortion and demonize abortion providers. *See also* Abortion; Abortion Providers; Birth Control; Freedom of Access to Clinic Entrances Act of 1994; Teenage Pregnancy and Childbearing

Further Reading
NARAL Mission. <http://www.naral.org/naral/about.html>.

National Abortion Federation

The National Abortion Federation (NAF) calls itself "the voice of abortion providers" and is the professional association of abortion providers in the United States and Canada. Founded in 1977, NAF's mission "is to preserve and enhance the quality and accessibility of abortion services." NAF members include nonprofit clinics, private physicians' offices, for-profit surgical centers, feminist women's health centers, Planned Parenthood affiliates, and hospital-based clinics.

The National Abortion Federation sets standards for quality care, provides accredited continuing medical education, develops innovative training materials, offers accurate medical information about abortion, and provides details about funding sources and referrals to qualified abortion providers through its national, toll-free hotline. The organization also produces informational and educational materials on abortion and fights against antiabortion restrictions in the U.S. Congress and in state legislatures. NAF advocacy for abortion includes materials for television, radio, newspapers, and magazines to bring the providers' perspective into the abortion debate.

When MAF members are harassed or attacked by antiabortion activists, they receive legal guidance from NAF's Legal Clearinghouse and assistance with responding to anti-choice violence from its Clinic Support program. Because of the practitioner shortage in abortion care, NAF works to expand abortion training opportunities, develops new training materials and sources, fosters the professional development of new providers, and educates the medical community about reversing the isolation of abortion practice and making it a part of mainstream medical care. *See also* Abortion; Abortion Providers; Planned Parenthood Federation of America

National Asian Women's Health Organization

See **Asian-American and Pacific Islander Women's Health**

National Center on Women and Aging

The National Center on Women and Aging at Brandeis University in Massachusetts was established in 1995 to focus national attention on the special problems of women as they age, including health and financial security issues. The center develops strategies for dealing with problems women face as they age and reaches out to women and organizations across the United States, promoting the changes necessary to improve older women's lives.

Health issues are a major focus of the center; activities include identifying barriers to preventive health care and combating gender bias in medical research and practice. In addition, the center attempts to find better ways to assist women who are the primary family caregivers.

One current activity of the center is focusing on income security with the goal of reducing poverty in old age. In early 1999, the center received a grant from the U.S. Department of Health and Human Services to set up a Program on Women's Education for Retirement (POWER) to help remedy an alarming gender gap in retirement preparation that leaves many women indigent in their older years. POWER teaches women—especially those at risk of falling into poverty in their later years—how to plan for long-term financial security, which in turn can assist in preventive or chronic health care.

The center publishes a newsletter six times a year titled *Women and Aging*, which provides information on women's health, pensions, living options, caregiving, financial planning, and many other topics. Excerpts from the newsletter, press releases, and updates on current research and activities of the center are available on its Internet Web site <http://www.heller.brandeis.edu/national/ind.html>. *See also* Aging; Family Caregiving

Further Reading
National Center on Women and Aging. *Women and Aging* newsletter, various issues (1998–2000).

National Centers of Excellence in Women's Health

In 1996 the Office on Women's Health in the U.S. Department of Health and Human Services established National Centers of Excellence in Women's Health. These centers have set up a new model health-care system that combines women's health research, medical training, clinical care, public health education, community outreach, and the promotion of women in academic medicine. All deal with a basic woman's health-care issue and common goal: to improve the health status of diverse women across the life span.

Located in renowned academic health centers across the United States, the first centers were established at Allegheny University of the Health Sciences in Philadelphia, Pennsylvania; Magee Women's Hospital, Pittsburgh; Ohio State University Medical Center in Columbus; University of California San Francisco; University of Pennsylvania in Philadelphia; and Yale University in New Haven, Connecticut. A second group of centers, established in 1997, includes Boston University Medical Center in Massachusetts; University of California at Los Angeles; Indiana School of Medicine in Indianapolis; University of Michigan in Ann Arbor; and Wake Forest University Baptist Medical Center, Winston-Salem, North Carolina. The third generation of centers, established in 1998, includes Harvard University, in Boston, Massachusetts; University of Illinois at Chicago; University of Puerto Rico, San Juan; Tulane University and Xavier University of New Orleans, Louisiana; University of Washington in Seattle; and University of Wisconsin-Madison in Madison.

The University of Illinois center at Chicago is an example of how the program works. It is designed to integrate biomedical expertise with the grassroots women's health vision, emphasizing cooperation across disciplines and professions, academic with community, and health-care provider with patient. Gender-based biology is a key component of the center's health model. There is also a focus on gender in social context because gender has so many consequences that are not biologically based, including social expectations and access to resources. The center addresses the needs of underserved groups of women, recognizing that "race, ethnicity, sexual orientation, age, or (dis)ability can have an impact on health and well-being." In addition, the center focuses on the many dimensions of women's health issues, including "killer" diseases, chronic conditions more prevalent in women, health behaviors, environmental/occupational health, mental health, and women's health policy. *See also* Environmental Health Hazards; Gender-Based Biology; U.S. Department of Health and Human Services

Further Reading

National Women's Health Information Center. "University of Illinois at Chicago, Center of Excellence in Women's Health." <http://www. 4woman.gov/x/owh/coe/UI_C.htm>.
Office on Women's Health. "National Centers of Excellence in Women's Health." Flyer. <http://www.4woman.gov/owh/coe/flyer.htm>.

National Cervical Cancer Coalition

The National Cervical Cancer Coalition (NCCC) is a grassroots effort that addresses an important women's health issue: preventing deaths from cervical cancer. The coalition includes health-care providers, pathologists, patients, women's groups, and technology and research organizations. An aspect of the coalition's mission is to educate the public about the need for the Pap smear screening test to help detect cervical cancer early and to inform women that many insurance companies and the government-funded Medicare and Medicaid programs reimburse for the test.

One NCCC program is the free Pap smear initiative that began in 2000. Health-care providers across the United States promoted the initiative, waiving the fee for the test and office visit for women who had not had Pap smears for three years. The NCCC plans to expand the effort to include additional clinicians, hospitals, laboratories, clinics, managed care organizations, medical universities, news media, advocacy groups, medical organizations, and all others that can help encourage women to come in for their free Pap smears.

Along with increasing awareness of how the cervical cancer screening program helps battle the disease, the NCCC also assists in efforts related to cervical cancer disease research; is active in helping to battle cervical cancer disease for uninsured and underserved women; works to assure that women have access to cervical cancer screening; acts as a clearinghouse in distributing information on cervical cancer for women and family members; and provides support services for women and their family members who are dealing with cancer issues. In addition, the coalition reviews and helps develop national and international cervical screening and treatment programs. *See also* Cervical Cancer

National Council on Women's Health

Founded in 1979, the National Council on Women's Health (NCWH) is a nonprofit women's health organization based in New York City. Its mission is "to advance the cause of women's health by bringing together professionals and consumers to learn from each other, and to increase public awareness of women's health needs." Some of the women's health issues that the organization addresses include outreach programs to help meet the needs of underserved women and efforts to inform the public and policy makers about women's health conditions.

The NCWH maintains an Internet Web site (http://www.womens-health.com/index.phtml), called Women's Health Interactive (WHI), a learning center that allows women to access information and be proactive on such health issues as migraine headache, which is much more common in women than in men; gynecologic health care; midlife health; mental health; and wellness. With the aid of online technology, WHI's Consumer Research Center focuses on women's attitudes, behavior, and needs as related to health information, education, products, and services, and publishes such data. In addition, the interactive center provides names and addresses of women's health providers and services. *See also* Mental Illness; Midlife Women; Migraine

National Family Caregivers Association

The National Family Caregivers Association (NFCA) "is the only national, charitable organization dedicated to making life better for all America's family caregivers," according to its Web site statement. In a 1997 survey of its members, NFCA found that 82 percent were women; as the total number of family caregivers grows nationwide, NFCA is designed to focus on their health and well-being. The NFCA helps family caregivers—who frequently express feelings of isolation, frustration, and anxiety—to take charge of their lives and be effective caregivers for their loved ones. The NFCA provides educational, support, and advocacy information through an Internet Web site, a quarterly newsletter, and a resource guide called *The Resourceful Caregiver: Helping Family Caregivers Help Themselves.* As a voice for caregivers, the organization lobbies the U.S.

Congress and other officials regarding caregivers' rights. Each year, NFCA also organizes National Family Caregivers Week, which is celebrated during Thanksgiving week. Events are devoted to raising public awareness of family caregiver issues. *See also* Family Caregivers

Further Reading
National Family Caregivers Association home page. <http://www.nfcacares.org>.

National Institutes of Health Office of Research on Women's Health

Established in 1990, the National Institutes of Health (NIH) Office of Research on Women's Health (ORWH) was set up in response to a United States General Accounting Office report showing that women were routinely excluded from clinical studies funded by the NIH. Consequently, the purpose of the ORWH is to ensure that NIH-supported research addresses issues regarding women's health and that women participate appropriately in clinical trials. The ORWH was given a mandate to

> Strengthen, develop, and increase research into diseases, disorders, and conditions that affect women, determine gaps in knowledge about such conditions and diseases, and establish a research agenda for NIH for future directions in women's health research; Ensure that women are appropriately represented in biomedical and biobehavioral research studies, especially clinical trials, that are supported by NIH; Create direct initiatives to increase the number of women in biomedical careers and to facilitate their advancement and promotion. (ORWH Overview)

In 1993, a Coordinating Committee and an Advisory Committee on Research on Women's Health were formed. The ad-

visory committee is made up of private sector physicians and other health experts who advise on appropriate research that should be undertaken regarding women's health and disease. The ORWH has sponsored regional and national public meetings and scientific workshops to continually update the women's health research agenda. That agenda focuses on a multidisciplinary approach and, ORWH states, "addresses sex and gender perspectives of women's health, as well as differences among special populations of women. The agenda encompasses the entire life span of women, from birth through adolescence, reproductive years, menopausal years, and the more advanced, elderly years. Included are studies to better define normal development, physiology, and aging in women. The agenda includes conditions that are unique to women, as well as those that affect both men and women."

In addition, the ORWH has sponsored activities designed to identify and break down barriers that women confront in biomedical careers, which are included in a report titled *Women in Biomedical Careers: Dynamics of Change; Strategies for the 21st Century*. Information about the research studies and initiatives of ORWH can be obtained from the Office of Research on Women's Health, NIH, Building 1, Room 201, Bethesda, MD 20892 or on the ORWH Web site <http://www4.od. nih.gov/orwh/index.html>. *See also* Gender-Biased Research and Treatment

Further Reading
"Office of Research on Women's Health Overview" <http://www4.od.nih.gov/orwh/overview.html>.

National Women's Health Information Center

The National Women's Health Information Center (NWHIC) is a project of the Office on Women's Health of the U.S. Department of Health and Human Services. NWHIC is a free information and resource service on the Internet, providing hundreds of articles on women's health issues designed for students, educators, health-care professionals, and researchers. Anyone accessing the site at <http://www.4woman.gov> can link to, read, and download a wide variety of women's health-related material developed by the Department of Health and Human Services, the Department of Defense, other Federal agencies, and private sector resources. The site includes links to numerous medical dictionaries and glossaries, medical journals, editorials by medical experts, and information on minority women's health issues (African-American Women's Health, Asian-American Women's Health, Latina Women's Health, Native American Women's Health), as well as health issues affecting all American women, a *Women of Color Health Data Book*, a handbook on eating disorders, calendars of women's health events across the nation, and many current reports on women's health. *See also* African-American Women's Health; Asian-American Women's Health; Eating Disorders; Latina Women's Health; Native American Women's Health

National Women's Health Network

Founded in 1975, the National Women's Health Network (NWHN) is a nonprofit feminist organization that testifies for women's health issues before the U.S. Congress, the Food and Drug Administration (FDA), and the National Institutes of Health. The five women who founded the organization are Barbara Seaman, author of the *Doctor's Case Against the Pill*, and Belita Cowan, both of whom envisioned a women's health movement with a full-fledged lobby in Washington, DC; Alice Wolfson, a health activist living in Washington, DC; Mary Howell of the Boston

Women's Health Book Collective; and Phyllis Chesler, an activist on women's mental health issues. Among the early efforts of the NWHN was a protest at the FDA regarding the cancer risks of taking menopausal estrogens, which helped prompt the agency to inform women of these health risks. At the same time, the NWHN held a demonstration and memorial service for all of the women who had died because of estrogen replacement therapy and use of diethylstilbestrol (DES), which at the time was being prescribed as a birth control pill.

As a health advocacy organization, the NWHN gives women a greater voice in the U.S. health-care system, and through its Information Clearinghouse provides women with information and resources to assist them in making better health-care decisions. The Network does not accept funding from either pharmaceutical or medical device manufacturers, and is supported by a membership of 12,000 individuals and 300 organizations. *See also* Boston Women's Health Book Collective; Women's Health Movement

National Women's Health Organization

The National Women's Health Organization (NWHO) was founded in 1976 to provide abortion services "in a safe and comfortable environment" for women. Headquartered in North Carolina, NWHO is made up of clinics in eight states: North Carolina, Mississippi, Georgia, Florida, Indiana, Wisconsin, North Dakota, and Delaware. Violence against abortion providers has been a major issue with NWHO, whose clinics have suffered some of the most severe antiabortion terrorism in the United States, including arsons, bombings, and massive harassment. One NWHO provider, Dr. David Gunn, was murdered in front of the Pensacola, Florida, clinic in 1993.

In testimony before the U.S. House of Representatives Committee on Judiciary, Susan Hill, head of NWHO, asked panel members "to throw away their biases and understand that...abortion providers were under siege." She expressed her belief that "women should be allowed to obtain abortion services in a dignified manner...that doctors should be able to practice medicine safely and with dignity."

Hill testified further that abortion providers are dedicated health-care professionals who, under great duress, have provided services for 1.5 million American women each year. As she noted:

Not only have we been threatened, stalked, bombed, burned, and shot at, we also have been continuously and systematically extorted. I have compared this history of extortionate acts against our businesses as similar to the corner grocery store owner who is visited by a man who tells him: if he will pay up every Friday, he will not be hurt; his store will not be burned; his family will not be threatened; and he will not be killed. As providers of abortion services, we have been visited each week for years by people associated with an enterprise, and have been told in different ways that we would not be harmed, our families would not be threatened, our clinics would not be burned, if we would pay the price. In our case, the price was our profession and our business. If we would cease providing abortion services, we would not be bothered. (Hill)

Hill had testified before Congress twice before and in 1986 NWHO became a co-plaintiff with the National Organization for Women (NOW) in a class-action suit against antiabortion activist Joseph Scheidler and an antiabortion group Operation Rescue. The plaintiffs alleged that there was a nationwide organized conspiracy to illegally close family planning, abortion, and women's reproductive health clinics. In 1994 the U.S. Supreme Court ruled that the plaintiffs had the right to sue under the Federal Racketeer Influenced and Corrupt Organizations (RICO) statute. In 1998, a jury found Joseph Scheidler, Operation Rescue, and others liable for terrorist and extortionist acts against abortion clinics and providers. *See also* Abortion; Abortion Providers

Further Reading

Booth, William. "Doctor Killed during Abortion Protest." *Washington Post* (March 11, 1993).

Feminist Majority Foundation. "National Feminist Leader Eleanor Smeal Calls for Use of Criminal RICO to End Violence" Press Release (April 20, 1998).

Hill, Susan. "On the Racketeer Influenced Corrupt Organization Act." Testimony before the U.S. House of Representatives Committee on Judiciary (July 17, 1998).

National Women's Health Resource Center

The nonprofit National Women's Health Resource Center (NWHRC) is a national clearinghouse for information on a variety of women's health issues, which it provides through its newsletter, fact sheets, national HealthyWomen Database, Women's HealthInfo Search Program, and its Internet Web site. Established in the 1980s, the center is located in New Brunswick, New Jersey. Focusing on prevention and wellness, NWHRC is committed to helping women make informed decisions about their health. One of the center's main efforts, called A Partnership for Long-Term Health for Women, addresses post-menopausal women whose risks for cardiovascular disease, certain cancers, osteoporosis, diabetes, and other chronic diseases increase significantly. The partnership is a national campaign to bring together diverse women's groups and encourage them to take proactive measures to guard their health.

NWHRC publishes *National Women's Health Report* six times a year. The publication includes articles on such issues as breast help, depression, eating disorders, and a woman's guide to influenza. NWHRC's *Book of Women's Health* emphasizes disease prevention and the steps women can take to maintain healthy lives. NWHRC's Web site <http://www.healthywomen.org> contains information on a variety of health topics, health services, and health news of interest to women. *See also* Cardiovascular Diseases; Depression; Eating Disorders; Menopause; Osteoporosis

National Women's Heart Health Day

National Women's Heart Health Day is observed on the first day of February each year. Founded by women's health advocate Charlotte Libov, National Women's Heart Health Day provides an opportunity to promote heart health in women by focusing attention on risk factors for cardiovascular diseases in women and what women can do to reduce their risk. Another focus is on the need for more research on heart disease in women and on the differences between women and men in diagnostic tests and cardiac treatments.

Each year across the United States, Heart Health Day events include screening programs for women that focus on heart disease; blood pressure and cholesterol checks; cooking demonstrations on how to create low-fat meals; walkathons; and distribution of materials about such risk factors as diabetes, obesity, smoking, and a sedentary lifestyle. During the event, there is also emphasis on such statistics as these:

- Heart disease is the number one killer of American women.
- Every year, an estimated 485,000 American women die of cardiovascular disease (heart disease and stroke), more than twice the number who die of all forms of cancer combined.
- An estimated 240,000 women die annually of heart disease, five times the number who die of breast cancer.
- Women suffer nearly half (49 percent) of the 480,000 heart disease deaths that occur each year.
- More women than men die of heart attacks within the first year of their first heart attacks (44 versus 27 percent).
- More women than men will suffer heart attacks within four years after their first heart attack (20 percent versus 16 percent).
- Black women have a 33 percent higher death rate from coronary heart disease than white women, and a 77 percent higher death rate from stroke.

Coronary heart disease is a major risk factor for stroke, which kills over 87,000 women each year. *See also* African-American Women's Health; Cardiovascular Diseases; Obesity; Smoking; Women's Health Care Advocates

Further Reading
Libov, Charlotte. *Beat Your Risk Factors: A Woman's Guide to Reducing Her Risk for Cancer, Heart Disease, Stroke, Diabetes, and Osteoporosis.* New York: Plume, 1999.
National Women's Heart Health Day Statistics <http://www.libov.com/womens_h_h_stat.html>.
Notelovitz, Morris, M.D., and Diana Tonnessen. *The Essential Heart Book for Women.* New York: St. Martin's Griffin, 1996.

Native American Women's Health

Native American women's health is affected by the fact that there are higher rates of poverty and unemployment among Native Americans than among other ethnic groups in the United States. Native Americans include more than 550 recognized tribes in 34 states. Under the 1975 Native American Programs Act, the following groups are defined as Native Americans:

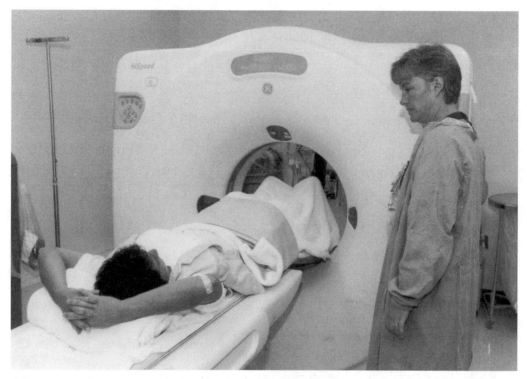

Patient undergoing an MRI at Alaska Medical Center, Anchorage, Alaska. Courtesy of the Indian Health Service (Dept. of Health and Human Services, Public Health Service).

American Indians, Alaska Natives (Eskimos and Aleuts), Native Hawaiians, Samoans, and other native Pacific Islanders. Descending from the original inhabitants of North America, Native American women face health risks associated with cultural dislocation, poverty, and the historical neglect of Indian rights and treaties.

Cardiovascular disease is a major health issue among all American women, but Native American women are at a particularly high risk for heart disease because of high rates of diabetes, obesity, and binge drinking. "Sixty percent of American Indian women are overweight, have a sedentary lifestyle, eat relatively high-fat diets and experience cigarette and alcohol abuse," according to the National Women's Health Information Center of the U.S. Department of Health and Human Services (DHHS). Some other major health issues

for Native American women include the following:

- Accidental deaths are nearly three times the national average. Many are associated with a lack of seat belt use and drunk driving.

- Diabetes rates range from five percent to as much as 50 percent in different Indian tribes. Diabetes is the fourth-ranked cause of death in Native American women.

- Native American women die from alcoholism at five to six times the national rate. Drinking during pregnancy is three times the national average. Deaths from tuberculosis are five times the national rate.

- Native American women have some of the highest smoking rates in the country compared to white, African-American, Latino, and Asian-American women.

- Suicide death rates for young Native American women are nearly twice the national average, but are lower than average in older women.

- The average infant mortality rate among Native American women is 30 percent higher than the national average, and sudden infant death syndrome (SIDS) is nearly two times higher.

- Native Americans have the highest prevalence of gallstones in the United States. Among the Pima Indians of Arizona, 70 percent of women have gallstones by age 30.

As a group, Native American women also have poor access to obstetric and gynecological health care. The Indian Health Service (IHS) of the DHHS is responsible for providing health services to approximately 1.5 million American Indians and Alaska Natives, as required by hundreds of treaties and agreements between tribal leaders and the U.S. government. But the location and the small number of facilities on tribal lands and in urban areas account in part for American Indian women having both greater difficulties in obtaining access to prenatal care and less likelihood of getting such care than either black or white women. For example, there are only two IHS health units east of the Mississippi River to serve all the American Indians from Maine to Florida. The Native American Women's Health Education Resource Center notes that many American Indian women are suspicious of the IHS and federal government agencies upon which they depend for health-care services. The Native American Women's Health Education Resource Center charges HIS and federal agencies with such abuses as "forced sterilization, unsafe use of Depo-Provera and Norplant [contraceptives], and destructive alcohol-related policies."

The Indian Health Service, which became part of the United States Public Health Service in 1955, developed an In-dian Women's Health Initiative in 1994 to heighten awareness of American Indian and Alaska Native women's health status. The IHS reorganized the Indian Women's Health Steering Committee (IWHSC), which is composed of 16 tribal representatives and four federal employees. The goal of the committee is to establish a national Indian women's health network that promotes advocacy, education, policy development, increased access to health promotion and disease prevention activities, and healthy lifestyle behavioral changes. The committee is community-driven and success is the result of the strength, ability, and determination of Indian women to promote healthy lifestyles in Indian communities.

Centers for American Indian health and research have been established in numerous states to work with major universities and state health-care agencies to help prevent disease and dysfunction, provide health services, and conduct research in chronic disease, particularly diabetes and cardiovascular disease. Native American groups also address women's health issues. For example, the Native American Community Board of the Yankton Sioux in South Dakota developed a Women and Children in Alcohol project in 1986 to address fetal alcohol syndrome and in 1988 opened the Native American Women's Health Education Resource Center, the first resource center located on a reservation in the United States. In 1991, after a long legal battle, the Domestic Violence Program of the Resource Center opened a shelter for battered women a few blocks away from the Resource Center, which has expanded to include many programs such as the AIDS Prevention Program, Environmental Awareness and Action Project, Cancer Prevention, Diabetic Nutrition Program, Reproductive Health and Rights, and Community Health Fairs.

Dozens of Web sites provide resources on Native American health, including such government sites as the Administration on Aging: Programs and Resources for Native American Elders, the American Indian Environmental Office, and the Office of Minority Health Resource Center. Among the nongovernmental organizations that maintain sites are the Alaska Women's Network; American Indian Tobacco Education Network; Association of American Indian Physicians; Association of American Indian Natural Healthcare Practitioners; and the Hanford Health Information Network. The latter network was created by nine Indian Nations and the health agencies of Washington, Oregon, and Idaho to provide information on the known and potential health effects of the radioactive releases from the Hanford Nuclear Reservation in south central Washington state from 1944 to 1972. Many other nongovernmental sites are listed on a Web site maintained by American Indian Health Resources at <http://www.ldb.org/vl/geo/america/indi_hn.htm>. *See also* Alcohol Abuse and Addiction; AIDS; Environmental Health Hazards

Further Reading

American College of Obstetricians and Gynecologists. "ACOG Works to Improve Health among Native American Women." *ACOG Today* (March 1999).

Gay, Kathlyn. *Pollution and the Powerless.* New York: Franklin Watts, 1994.

Heavner, Jay. "Broken Treaties, Empty Promises." <http://www.rcrc.org/wocp/native.html>.

Joe, Jennie R. "The Health of American Indian and Alaska Native Women." *Journal of the American Medical Women's Association* (August–October 1996).

Noren, Jay. "Challenges to Native American Health Care." *Public Health Reports*, (January–February 1998).

Novello, Antonia (1944–)

Puerto Rican–born Antonia Novello was the first Latina to serve as U.S. Surgeon General (1990–1993). In that role, she was committed to addressing women's health issues as well as the health of all Americans. When she was appointed by President George Bush in 1990, she said she hoped to "reach many individuals with my message of empowerment for women, children, and minorities." In her remarks after being sworn in on March 9, 1990, she said:

> When I was a little girl attending public schools in Puerto Rico...all I wanted to do...was to become a pediatrician, a doctor for the little kids in my hometown. I never told anyone that I wanted to be that. It seemed too grand of a notion. Well, dreams sometimes come true in unexpected ways, and today I stand before you with pride and humility as the first Puerto Rican, Hispanic, female Surgeon General of this country.
>
> ...I do not aspire to be the Surgeon General of the Hispanics, or the Surgeon General of the women, or the Surgeon

Antonia Novello. Courtesy of Dr. Antonia Novello.

General of the children. I aspire to be the Surgeon General of every American of this great country. As a practicing physician, I learned what patients want from their doctor. They don't care if the doctor is male or female, if the doctor is black or white, if the doctor is Anglo or Hispanic, or even how they voted in the last election. What they do care is that the doctor has compassion, scientific excellence, availability at all times—the good ones and the bad ones. That's the definition of a good doctor.

Once a dream, it is now my pledge to be a good doctor for all who live in this great country. My motto as your Surgeon General will be "good science and good sense."

Born in Fajardo, Puerto Rico, to Antonio Coello and Ana Delia Coello, Antonia suffered from a chronic colon condition that required hospitalization every summer. Her condition was not corrected until she was a young adult. By that time, her experiences as a patient had motivated her to choose a career in medicine. She earned her undergraduate and medical degrees in Puerto Rico, and became a pediatrician. In 1970 she married Joseph Novello, a U.S. Navy flight surgeon, and the couple moved to Ann Arbor, Michigan, where they continued their medical training at the University of Michigan Medical Center. Antonia also attended Georgetown University in Washington, DC, and Johns Hopkins University in Baltimore, Maryland, where she earned a degree in public health. She became deputy director of the National Institute of Child Health and Human Development in 1986.

After she became surgeon general of the United States, Novello often spoke out about serious health issues affecting women, such as domestic violence, which she labeled an epidemic, and the rising lung cancer rates among women. She also called attention to HIV-infected women and AIDS-infected children, and the perils of smoking and teenage drinking.

In 1999 Dr. Novello was confirmed as New York's health commissioner. Her appointment was highly criticized by some prochoice groups who opposed Novello's antiabortion stance. *See also* AIDS; Lung Cancer; Smoking

Further Reading

Hawxhurst, Joan C. *Antonia Novello: U.S. Surgeon General.* Brookfield, CT: Millbrook Press, 1993.
"Remarks at the Swearing-In Ceremony for Antonia Novello as Surgeon General." (March 9, 1990). <http://bushlibrary.tamu.edu/papers/1990/90030900.html>.

Nurse Midwives

See **Midwifery**

Nurse Practitioners

Nurse practitioners (NPs), along with physician assistants (PAs) and certified nurse midwives, are nonphysicians who provide primary care for millions of Americans. Most nurse practitioners and midwives are women who, women's health advocates contend, are more in tune with women's health issues than male doctors. Since the 1950s and 1960s, nonphysician practitioners have increasingly provided health services in clinics, hospitals, health departments, private practice offices, nursing homes, freestanding birth centers, and school-based clinics. NPs take health histories, perform physical exams, diagnose and treat common illnesses and injuries, manage chronic health problems, order and interpret lab tests and x-rays, and provide preventive services and health education. They frequently provide care for underserved populations, such as people in rural areas where there are no physicians or only one doctor.

NP and PA training programs were started in the 1960s in response to short-

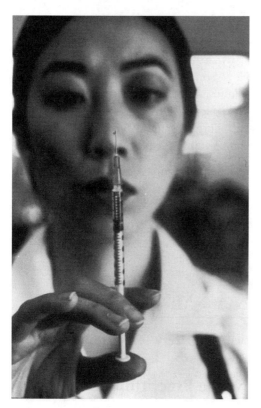

Nurse practitioner prepares to give treatment.
©Xavier Bonghi/The Image Bank.

bursement. States with restrictive laws discourage nurse practitioners from practicing, although physician shortages and inadequate access to primary-care services have forced many states to revise their practice regulations to better utilize NPs and other nonphysician practitioners. According to a 1996 report by the U.S. Congress' Office of Technology Assessment (OTA), the care provided by NPs, PAs, and nurse midwives is equivalent in quality to the care of physicians. Moreover, OTA's report noted that nurse practitioners and midwives are "more adept than physicians at providing services that depend on communication with patients and preventive actions." (OTA, 5) *See also* Childbirth Practices; Midwifery; Women's Health Education

Further Reading

Zimmerman, Joy, and the Rural Information Center Health Service. "Nurse Practitioners, Physician Assistants and Certified Nurse-Midwives: Primary Care Providers in Rural Areas." (July 1994).

Nurse Practitioners, Physician Assistants, and Certified Nurse-Midwives: A Policy Analysis. Washington, DC: Office of Technology Assessment, U.S. Congress, 1986.

Nursing Home Care and Long-Term Care

Nursing home care is usually long-term health and custodial care provided in facilities that serve as permanent or temporary residences for people who are too frail or sick to live at home or need care during a recovery period (such as after a stroke or accident). Nursing home care provides each resident with a room, meals, recreational activities, and help with daily living. Generally, nursing home residents have physical disabilities or mental impairments, such as Alzheimer's disease, that prevent them from living independently.

About 1.6 million elderly and disabled Americans, the majority of them women, receive care in approximately 16,800 nurs-

ages of primary-care physicians. These early programs trained nurses to become nurse practitioners and medical corpsmen to become physician assistants. Since the late 1980s, numerous organizations have advocated for increased utilization of NPs and PAs, including the National Advisory Committee on Rural Health, the National Advisory Council of the National Health Service Corps, the Federal Office of Rural Health Policy, the Institute of Medicine, the Physician Payment Review Commission, and the Rural Health Care Advisory Panel of the Office of Technology Assessment, U.S. Congress.

An issue that many nurse practitioners must face is whether state laws allow them to be licensed and to write prescriptions. Some states have strict limitations on nonphysicians' scope of practice, prescriptive authority, and eligibility for reim-

Nursing home residents with caregiver. ©Will and Deni McIntyre/Photo Researchers, Inc.

ing homes across the United States. Although the need for long-term care is tied to aging and deteriorating health, "the factor that determines who moves into an institution and who gets to stay at home is marital status.... And women constitute the great bulk of elderly persons without spouses." (Benderly, 171) Thus older women who are widowed or single may have to hire people to care for them—either in or out of nursing homes.

Nursing home care has long been controversial. For decades news stories have focused on inadequate care and abuses in nursing homes, fueling public fears about the safety of such facilities. But the U.S. government, through the Medicare and Medicaid programs, provides funding to the states to conduct on-site inspections of nursing homes participating in Medicare and Medicaid and to recommend sanctions against those homes that violate health and safety rules.

During the late 1990s, the Health Care Financing Administration (HCFA) established a Nursing Home Database (http://www.medicare.gov/nursing/home.asp) that provides information about the performance of every Medicare- and Medicaid-certified nursing home in the United States. While the HCFA emphasizes the importance of visiting nursing homes under consideration, the database is a preliminary way to see the results of state inspections of nursing homes. The database also provides information on the characteristics of nursing home residents, such as the number of residents with urinary incontinence, the need for restraints, or feeding problems.

Nursing home care is a health and economic issue that more women than men face because they live longer than men and are more likely to have chronic illnesses. Because of the high cost of nursing home care—about $40,000 per year—some women prepare for the possibility that they will need it by buying long-term care insurance. Yet such insurance is expensive, and many women lack the income to pay for it. Some hope they will have coverage under Medicare, the federal insurance program for people age 65 and older. But Medicare benefits for long-term care are limited, set specific requirements, and cover skilled nursing only. Medicaid, a federal program covering impoverished people, pays nursing home costs for those who qualify.

For people who require less than skilled care, most communities offer a variety of living arrangements and services that might make nursing home care unnecessary. Home services include Meals-on-Wheels programs, friendly visiting and shopper services, and adult day-care. Nursing homes may provide respite care and admit persons in need of care for short periods of time to relieve family caregivers or professional caregivers. Federal and state programs that help pay for housing for older people with low to moderate incomes may assist residents with certain tasks, such as shopping and laundry.

Assisted living, or nonmedical senior housing, provides help for residents who can live independently if they have help with a small number of tasks, such as cooking and laundry, or reminders to take medications. Board and care homes offer a wider range of services than independent living options. Most provide help with activities of daily living, including eating, walking, bathing, and toileting.

Continuing care retirement communities (CCRCs) are housing communities that provide different levels of care based on residents' needs. These range from independent living apartments to skilled nursing care in an affiliated nursing home. Residents move from one setting to another based on their needs, but continue to remain part of their CCRC communities. However, many CCRCs require large payments prior to admission and also charge monthly fees. Thus they may be too expensive for older people with modest incomes. *See also* Aging; Alzheimer's Disease; Family Caregiving; Health Insurance; Widowhood

Further Reading
Benderly, Beryl Lieff for the Institute of Medicine. *In Her Own Right: The Institute of Medicine's Guide to Women's Health Issues.* Washington, DC: National Academy Press, 1997.
Health Care Financing Administration. "Problem Nursing Homes to Face Immediate Sanctions." Press Release (December 14, 1999).
"Should I Buy Long Term Care Insurance?" *Women and Aging Letter.* Waltham, MA: Brandeis University National Policy and Resource Center on Women and Aging, November 1996.

Nutrition

Nutrition is important in the health of all people, but women face more nutritional challenges and needs than men do. Nutrients in the diet are particularly consequential for premenopausal women, because the monthly menstruation

taxes their stores of iron. Pregnancy and lactation place immense burdens on both women's bodies and their ability to consume the nutrients they need to create and nourish a new life without depleting the nutritional stores they need to maintain their own health. Then, after menopause, due to the drop in estrogens and the protection they impart, a variety of chronic diseases apparently related at least in part to diet choices made during earlier decades arise: osteoporosis, cardiovascular disorders, and reproductive cancers. (Benderly, 120)

In the United States, women make most of the food and nutrient choices for themselves and their families, but determining what constitutes a nutritious diet can be confusing, because of many conflicting opinions about what nutritional factors should be considered for a healthy diet. For example, numerous scientific studies link dietary fat to breast cancer, but the well-publicized *Harvard Nurses' Health Study* found no relationship between fat and breast cancer. Some studies suggest that fruits and vegetables are important in reducing the risk of breast cancer, and other research indicates that alcohol consumption and a person's diet in early life may be factors in breast cancer risks. Actually a combination of nutritional factors may be beneficial or detrimental to women at risk for breast cancer.

Food processing and food supplement companies with claims about the health benefits of their products add to the confusion over nutritional factors, as do popular weight loss "gurus" such as Robert C. Atkins, author of *Dr. Atkins' New Diet Revolution*; Dean Ornish, author of *Eat More, Weigh Less;* and Barry Sears, author of *The Zone,* who sponsor diets that claim to be nutritionally sound. Nutritionists such as Keith-Thomas Ayoob of Albert Einstein College of Medicine and Denise Bruner, president of the American Society of Bariatric Physicians (who deal with obesity) argue that these diets jeopardize health in the long run.

New scientific studies are frequently released about dietary factors and their role in health. But reliable information on nutritional factors means little if a woman cannot afford to buy nutritious food products or because of disabilities is unable to obtain or prepare healthful foods. Government agencies have played a role in that regard with programs such as the federal government's Nutrition Program for the elderly, which sponsors the Meals-on-Wheels program. Other examples include the federal Food Stamp program, National School Breakfast and Lunch programs, and the Special Supplemental Nutritional Program for Women, Infants and Children. The U.S. Department of Agriculture (USDA) also pub-lishes dietary guidelines for Americans and the food pyramid group.

Weight-loss diets and eating disorders are other issues that affect nutritional factors related to women's and adolescent girls' health. Frequently women and girls attempting to lose weight are more concerned about body image than about the nutrients needed for good health. A wide variety of educational programs and projects sponsored by government agencies and private organizations attempt to deal with these problems.

Another concern is whether vegetarian diets meet nutritional standards. Some Americans are vegetarians for reasons of culture, belief, or health; most eat dairy products and eggs; and, as a group, lacto-ovo vegetarians enjoy excellent health. According to the USDA, vegetarian diets are consistent with their dietary guidelines and can meet recommended dietary allowances for nutrients. Protein is not limited in vegetarian diets as long as the variety and amounts of foods consumed are adequate. Meat, fish, and poultry are major contributors of iron, zinc, and B vitamins in most American diets, and vegetarians should pay special attention to these nutrients, the USDA advises. *See also* Adolescent Girls' Health; Cardiovascular Diseases; Dieting and Diet Drugs; Eating Disorders; Menopause; Menstruation; Osteoporosis; Pregnancy

Further Reading

Benderly, Beryl Lieff for the Institute of Medicine. *In Her Own Right: The Institute of Medicine's Guide to Women's Health Issues.* Washington, DC: National Academy Press, 1997.

Margen, Sheldon, and the Editors of the University of California at Berkeley Wellness Letter. *The Wellness Encyclopedia of Food and Nutrition.* New York: Rebus, 1992.

Mark, Saralyn, and Carol Krause. "Federal Role in Nutrition Education, Research, and Food for Women and Their Families." *Journal of the American Dietetic Association* (June 1, 1999).

United States Department of Agriculture. "Dietary Guidelines for Consumers" (1995). <http://www.nal.usda.gov/fnic/dga/dguide95.html>.

O

Obesity

Obesity is the condition of being over-weight. In 1999 the U.S. Centers for Disease Control and Prevention (CDC) released a long-term study showing that the number of overweight Americans is reaching epidemic proportions. One in five American adults is now considered obese, compared to about one in eight in the early 1990s. According to CDC, more than half of U.S. women are overweight and nearly one-fourth are considered obese.

Obesity statistics create what some see as a significant women's health issue while others view obesity as a societal prejudice related to the American obsession with dieting and trying to emulate fashion and advertising models. Women are encouraged by advertising, health experts, and medical practitioners to lose weight in order to be accepted in society and to be healthy.

Some medical studies do show that obese women are more likely than non-obese women to die from cancer of the gallbladder, breast, uterus, cervix, and ovaries. Obesity in women also places them at risk for such health conditions as osteoarthritis and rheumatoid arthritis, cardiovascular disease, infertility, and urinary incontinence.

Doctors generally agree that women with more than 30 percent body fat are obese. To determine body fat, medical practitioners frequently use the body-mass index (weight in kilograms divided by the square of the height in meters). In a study of more than one million adults in the United States, researchers found that the "risk of death from all causes, cardiovascular disease, cancer, or other diseases increases throughout the range of moderate and severe overweight for both men and women in all age groups. The risk associated with a high body-mass index is greater for whites than for blacks." (Calle, et al., 1,097) Yet groups at high risk for obesity include African-American women, Latina women, middle-aged women of all races, and women of low socioeconomic status.

Health care for obese women is another issue. When they need health-care services or emergency hospitalization,

they don't always receive appropriate care, because many providers aren't prepared to meet their special clinical needs. Skin and wound care, airway management, drug administration, and the delivery of adequate nutrition all present unique challenges in the hospital setting. (Gallagher, 43)

Obese women (and men) are prone to skin problems, slow healing of wounds, breathing problems, inability to absorb medications effectively, and poor dietary habits. One of the most painful aspects of obesity may be the emotional suffering it causes. American society places great emphasis on physical appearance, often equating attractiveness with slimness, especially in women. Thus obese women frequently believe they are unattractive. Obese people are thought to be gluttonous, lazy, or both, although more and more evidence contradicts this assumption. Other problems surface in the workplace, at school, and in social situations where obese people frequently face discrimination. As a result feelings of rejection, shame, or depression are common.

Economic costs associated with obesity create another issue. In the United States, billions of dollars are spent each year due to health problems among overweight and obese workers. Most of the costs are related to health insurance for medical conditions associated with coronary heart disease, high blood pressure, diabetes, high cholesterol, stroke, gall bladder disease, and endometrial cancer.

Numerous government and private sector organizations are attempting to call attention to the health issues associated with obesity. Among them is the American Obesity Association (AOA), a nonprofit organization that conducts a national campaign to educate the public and provide current information on obesity. The AOA maintains an Internet Web site that includes a fact sheet on women and obesity. The CDC, the U.S. Department of Health and Human Services, and other government agencies also inform women about obesity-related health problems on their Internet sites. *See also* Breast Cancer; Cardiovascular Diseases; Dieting and Diet Drugs; Incontinence; Infertility; Weight Discrimination

Further Reading

American Obesity Association. "The Facts about Women and Obesity." <http://www.obesity.org/Obesity_Women.htm>.

Calle, Eugenia E., Michael J. Thun, Jennifer M. Petrelli, Carmen Rodriguez, and Clark W. Heath, Jr. "Body-Mass Index and Mortality in a Prospective Cohort of U.S. Adults." *The New England Journal of Medicine* (October 7, 1999).

Department of Health and Human Services, National Institutes of Health, National Institute of Diabetes and Digestive and Kidney Diseases. "Understanding Adult Obesity" (November 1993). <http://www.niddk.nih.gov/health/nutrit/pubs/unders.htm>

Gallagher, Susan. "Tailoring Care for Obese Patients." *RN* (May 1999).

Hwang, Mi Young. "Are You Obese?" *Journal of the American Medical Association* (October 27, 1999).

Must, Aviva. "The Disease Burden Associated with Overweight and Obesity." *Journal of the American Medical Association* (October 27, 1999).

Obstetrics and Gynecology

Obstetrics and gynecology (ob/gyn) is a combined medical specialty that focuses on the care of pregnant women and female reproductive disorders. Many American women consult ob/gyn specialists for their primary health-care needs, an issue that has concerned some women's health-care advocates since the 1970s. As ob/gyn specialists have taken control of women's reproductive health and childbirth, these advocates have criticized the "medicalization" of pregnancy, arguing that a woman's health must be viewed in a holistic manner, not just as a reproductive issue. As Eileen Hoffman, M.D., points out:

The myth of pregnancy is that it is strictly a gynecological event. In this century, the medical specialty of OB/GYN has controlled reproduction, and a rigid barrier has developed between it and other health issues. Based on the way our health care system is structured, one would think that pregnancy confined itself to the uterus. But the opposite is true.

Pregnancy (and the potential for pregnancy) has a systemic influence throughout a woman's life. (Hoffman, 230)

On the other hand, ob/gyn specialists point to the many developments in obstetrics and gynecology that have occurred during the past millennium, such as

the spectacular reduction in maternal mortality, particularly in developed nations. Most of these gains were achieved during the last few decades. At the beginning of the 20th century, for every 1000 live births, 6 to 9 women in the United States died of pregnancy-related complications, and approximately 100 infants died before age 1 year. From 1915 through 1997, the infant mortality rate declined...to 7.2 per 1000 live births, and from 1900 through 1997, the maternal mortality rate declined almost 99%...7.7 deaths per 100,000 live births in 1997. And although much of the decline can be attributed to the improvement in social and economic conditions, medical discoveries played a crucial role....

However, these benefits have accrued predominantly to the privileged, leaving large disparities between rich and poor nations and between social or ethnic groups within nations.... The challenge of the new millennium will be to ascertain that these gains are shared equitably among all the mothers of the nation and the world. (Ncayiyana)

Whatever the benefits of reproductive advances, the controversy over the "medicalization" of childbearing continues, and some women seek alternative health care during pregnancy and childbirth. The doula and midwife are practitioners who complement or take the place of ob/gyn specialists in some instances. *See also* Childbirth Practices; Doula; Midwifery; Pregnancy

Further Reading
Boston Women's Health Book Collective. *The New Our Bodies, Ourselves.* New York: Simon & Schuster, 1992.
Ncayiyana, Daniel J. "Millennial Landmarks in Obstetrics and Gynecology." *Medscape General Medicine* (February 28, 2000). <http://womenshealth.Medscape.com/Medscape/GeneralMedicine/journal/2000/v02.n01/mgm0228.ncay/mgm0228.ncay.html>.

Occupational Safety and Health Administration

The Occupational Safety and Health Administration (OSHA), an agency of the U.S. Department of Labor, was established following passage of the federal Occupational Safety and Health Act of 1970. Congress passed the Act to "assure safe and healthful working conditions for working men and women." OSHA, for example, prohibits exposure to noise above 115 decibels and limits the noise levels above 85 decibels in most workplaces. Employers are required by OSHA regulations to provide ear protection for employees when necessary and provide hearing tests for workers routinely exposed to high noise levels.

Since its inception, OSHA has been highly controversial, with businesses accusing regulators of harmful meddling in operations and labor leaders arguing that workers do not have adequate protection. As female workers have increasingly entered the labor force over the years, OSHA has attempted to address health and safety issues of particular concern to women. For instance, a study prepared for OSHA found that, while construction work is hazardous for both male and female workers, women face unique health and safety problems that create barriers to their entering and remaining in this field. Those problems include "a hostile workplace, restricted access to sanitary toilets, protective clothing and equipment in the wrong sizes, and poor on-the-job training."

Hostile workplace environments are frequently caused by gender and sexual harassment. Female workers may be isolated or ostracized by male co-workers on the job site, which can evoke fear of assault and lead to stress. Some female construction workers have been threatened with physical harm or have received death threats.

Among its many recommendations, the workgroup preparing the report on women in construction urged much more OSHA surveillance of construction sites, confidential interviews with female workers, and more emphasis on training programs that deal with the importance of not lifting weight beyond an individual's capacity to do so in a safe manner. As the report points out:

Women's size and body build require reconsideration of techniques for lifting and material handling. Not only do women come in all sizes and with varying degrees of muscular strength, their pelvic structure is different and their center of gravity is lower than men's. This would impact jobs that require standing at a work station. Lower equipment handles would facilitate the use of body weight in pushing and pulling tasks. Women's muscular strength is more equal to men's in their legs. Women would be on more equal footing with men if the work load could be transferred downward, with less reliance on the strength of hands and arms.

Another contentious issue in recent years has been OSHA's proposed mandatory ergonomic programs that would require employers to make workplaces fit workers rather than forcing workers to adjust to equipment or conditions that routinely lead to musculoskeletal disorders (MSD). These disorders, often due to heavy lifting and repetitive motion, are the most widespread occupational health hazards in the United States, according to OSHA testimony during a congressional committee hearing in Spring 2000. Nearly two million workers suffer job-related musculoskeletal disorders every year at a direct cost of between $15 billion and $20 billion annually. OSHA testified that

Women disproportionately suffer some of the most debilitating types of MSDs, such as carpal tunnel syndrome. This is not because women are more vulnerable to MSDs, but because a large number of women work in jobs associated with heavy lifting, awkward postures or repetitive motions. They hold a disproportionate number of jobs as nurses, cashiers, packagers, maids and house staff, assemblers and office workers. Consequently, women suffer 70 percent of the carpal tunnel syndrome cases and 62 percent of the tendonitis cases that are serious enough to warrant time off work.

Some industries have opposed mandatory ergonomic standards, claiming that their voluntary ergonomic programs are sufficient and that more regulations would add substantial costs to manufacturing, processing, or other business operations. Yet some of the OSHA suggestions for ergonomic workplaces are relatively inexpensive, such as "purchasing ergonomic chairs for production employees; providing back safety training; installing robot presses to eliminate the need for production employees to reach for parts; and making pallet jacks available for metal bins to allow height adjustments." OSHA contends that companies "with sound ergonomics programs have often improved productivity, drastically reduced workers' compensation costs, and improved job satisfaction." (Statement of Charles N. Jeffress) *See also* Carpal Tunnel Syndrome; Sexual Harassment; Sweatshops; Working Women

Further Reading

Occupational Safety and Health Administration Advisory Committee on Construction Safety and Health (ACCSH), U.S. Department of Labor. *Women in the Construction Workplace: Providing Equitable Safety and Health Protection for Health and Safety of Women in Construction.* (June 1999). <http://www.osha-slc.gov/doc/accsh/haswicformal.html>.

Statement of Charles N. Jeffress, Assistant Secretary for Occupational Safety and Health, U.S. Department of Labor, before the Subcommittee on Regulatory Reform and Paperwork Reduction of the House Small Business Committee, April 13, 2000. <http://www.osha-slc.gov/OshDoc/Testimony_data/T20000413.html>

Older Women's League

The Older Women's League (OWL) was founded in 1980 by Trish Sommers, who had been active during the 1970s as chair of the National Organization of Women's Task Force on Older Women and organizer of the Displaced Homemaker campaign advocating for older women. Today OWL is a national organization with more than 70 chapters nationwide. Its primary purpose is to improve the status and quality of life for midlife and older women through a grassroots network. Some of the women's health issues that OWL has undertaken call attention to the managed health-care system and its effect on older women; family caregiving, a responsibility that falls disproportionately on older women; and domestic violence, a major problem for women of various age groups and walks of life.

OWL conducts national campaigns on key women's health issues, such as heart disease, menopause, osteoporosis, and urinary incontinence. The organization also reports on health-care access and provides women with the tools to negotiate the healthcare system effectively. In its effort to influence public policy at the state and national levels, OWL voices its concerns on a variety of issues, including Social Security, Medicare, health-care access and quality, and age discrimination. *See also* Aging; Cardiovascular Diseases; Domestic Violence; Family Caregiving; Health-Care Access; Menopause; Midlife Women; Osteoporosis

Further Reading

Huckle, Patricia. *Tish Sommers, Activist: and the Founding of the Older Women's League.* Knoxville, TN: University of Tennessee Press, 1991.

Shields, Laurie. *Displaced Homemakers: Organizing for a New Life.* NY: McGraw-Hill, 1981.

Online Medicine

Online medicine, or accessing information about health care and medical treatments on the Internet, is a rapidly growing practice among America's women. For decades, more women than men have sought information about health care, but they have relied on medical practitioners or other women for advice. Today, online medicine is a source of information for one out of three women (compared to one in four men). As consumers increasingly search the Internet for medical information, some experts are raising serious questions about the accuracy, credibility, and objectivity of online medicine.

They cite numerous problems. For one, the vast number of Internet Web sites that focus on women's health issues can make searching for specific information online a daunting task. Many sites are maintained by commercial companies selling health-care products or medical treatments, ranging from acupuncture and other alternative medicine practices to women's health care. Hundreds of others are set up by medical practitioners to advertise their specialties. The *New York Times* reported in mid-1999 that some online medical sites were set up

for the sole purpose of prescribing and selling hot-ticket prescription drugs like Viagra to patients they have not met—a practice that has drawn the attention of state and Federal regulators, who regard it as unethical, though not illegal. The American Medical Association says doctors who prescribe drugs to people they have never physically examined should face disciplinary action.

A Web site called cyberdocs.com charges a fee for anyone wanting to have a private electronic chat session with a board-certified specialist.

> The doctors can prescribe any drugs except controlled substances, including narcotics. Dr. Tom Caffrey, who founded the company in 1996, five years after graduating from medical school, said he has diagnosed a case of shingles, sent someone to the emergency room for heart disease and refilled blood pressure medication—all online. (Stolberg)

The issue of online medicine has been the basis for much criticism, especially by practitioners who contend that patients should be examined, tested, and monitored, not treated sight unseen in a virtual reality situation. Investigations of online medicine have also been conducted by medical and research groups, ranging from the American Academy of Pediatrics to cancer clinics to the famed Mayo Clinic. A study by a University of Michigan team analyzed 371 Web sites on an uncommon bone cancer called Ewing Sarcoma and found information that was not only outdated but also incorrect or misleading, sometimes dangerously so. (Brody)

"Government and professional organizations...[are] good places for both physicians and patients to commence a search," according to Dr. Helene Cole, medical editor for the *Journal of the American Medical Association*. (Cole, 1,211) The most reliable sites contain information reviewed for publication in reputable medical journals or posted by established medical schools or health-care institutions, govern-

ment agencies (such as the Public Health Service's National Women's Health Information Center, the Department of Health and Human Services, or the Centers for Disease Control and Prevention), professional medical associations (like the American Medical Association, the American Medical Women's Association, or the American College of Obstetricians and Gynecologists), or national disease-centered research organizations, such as the American Cancer Society or the American Heart Association. Among other recommended and reliable sites are Medscape, Healthfinder, InteliHealth (John Hopkins University), National Institutes of Health, National Library of Medicine, HealthGate Healthy Woman, PharmInfoNet (a comprehensive guide to drugs), Reuters Health Information Services, and Mayo Clinic. Other suggestions for those seeking online medical information were included in a *New York Times* article:

> Steer clear of sites that ask for a lot of personal information. If you need to register to access information, study the site's privacy policy.
>
> ...Health information changes rapidly, particularly in fields like cancer and heart disease, in which new research findings abound. Reputable Web sites will include a date for each article that is posted.
>
> ...Web sites usually have a policy on how they establish links to other sites. Don't assume that links from a reputable site will always lead to other reputable organizations. If the link is unfamiliar to you, use common sense in evaluating its information.
>
> ...Running a Web site costs money. The source of funds should be stated clearly. The best sites also clearly separate advertisements, sponsorships and online stores from content. (Coburn)

Many women also use online healthcare sites to locate doctors in their local areas, to share information (on chat lines and by e-mail) with people suffering similar health problems, and to find support groups. The Internet is also useful to search medical journals such as the *Journal of the American Medical Association, The New England Journal of Medicine, Cancer* (journal of the American Cancer Society), and the *Annals of Internal Medicine*. Medical experts advise that any information found on the Internet should be discussed with a trusted medical practitioner, who hopefully can determine how up-to-date and reliable it is. *See also* American Medical Women's Association; Complementary and Alternative Medicine; National Institutes of Health Office of Research on Women's Health; Public Health Service's Office on Women's Health

Further Reading

Biermann, J. Sybil, Gregory J. Golladay, Mary Lou V.H. Greenfield, and Laurence H. Baker. "Evaluation of Cancer Information on the Internet." *Cancer* (August 1, 1999).

Brody, Jane. "Point-and-Click Medicine: A Hazard to Your Health." *New York Times* (August 31, 1999).

Coburn, Susan. "Turning a Medical Mountain into a Manageable Molehill." *New York Times* (June 25, 2000).

Cole, Helene M. "Women's Health on the Web." *Journal of the American Medical Association* (October 6, 1999).

Grady, Denise. "Sorting Health Facts from Fiction." *New York Times* (July 9, 1998).

Henson, Donald Earl. "Cancer and the Internet." *Cancer* (August 1, 1999).

Public Health Service's National Women's Health Information Center. "PHS Offers One-Stop Shopping for Women's Health." *Public Health Reports* (March 1999).

Stolberg, Sheryl Gay. "Need a Doctor in a Hurry? How about MD.com?" *New York Times* (July 4, 1999).

Osteoporosis

A debilitating disease, osteoporosis literally means bone that is porous. The condition leads to loss of bone mass and deterioration of bone tissue, causing bones to break or fracture easily. Osteoporosis frequently occurs without noticeable symptoms until bones break or a vertebra collapses, resulting in loss of height, stooped posture, or rounded shoulders (frequently called dowager's hump). The disease affects 28 million Americans, 80 percent of whom are women. As women live longer than ever before and the group ages 85 and older increases, the risk of osteoporosis also increases. However, the disease is not an inevitable part of aging, as was once thought. Today people at risk for osteoporosis can take preventive measures to stop bone loss, such as supplementing the diet with calcium and in some cases for post-menopausal women taking estrogen to prevent fractures from osteoporosis. At issue is the need to alert the public to facts about the disease and what actions people can take to improve bone health.

Osteoporosis creates not only physical problems but also social and economic concerns. People with osteoporosis may lose their independence because of crippling hip and spinal fractures. Overall more than 1.5 million fractures occur each year due to osteoporosis. More than $14 billion is spent annually for direct expenses such as hospital and nursing home care due to fractures and related problems. Those who have suffered fractures may live with constant fear of further incidents, thus hindering their normal activities.

Women are four times more likely than men to develop osteoporosis, because generally they have 30 percent less bone mass than men. Their bone mass builds until about age 30 to 35, then remains stable until after menopause when estrogen levels drop and bone mass begins to deteriorate. According to the National Osteoporosis Foundation (NOF) in Washington, DC, one in two women over the age of 50 is at risk for osteoporosis-related bone fractures, commonly of the hip, ribs, spine, and wrist, although any bones can be affected. Caucasian and Asian women have less bone mass than African-American women and thus are at greater risk of bone fractures.

The NOF reports that 86 percent of women with the disease are not being treated. Physicians usually advise persons at risk for osteoporosis to undergo bone-density tests (low- radiation x-ray) to determine whether treatment is needed. Although there is no cure for osteoporosis, a number of organizations, such as the Foundation for Osteoporosis Research and Education (FORE) in California, osteoporosis centers in various states, and NOF, alert the public about risk factors and preventive measures. These measures include eating a balanced diet rich in calcium and vitamin D, getting plenty of exercise, maintaining a healthy lifestyle, limiting alcohol intake, and getting a bone-density test.

In September 1999, *The Lancet*, a British medical journal, published a study suggesting that another preventive measure is reducing high blood pressure. Of the 3,676 elderly women in Britain and the United States who were studied over a three-and-one-half-year period, those with high blood pressure also suffered bone-density loss—the higher the pressure, the greater the bone mineral loss. The study concluded that high blood pressure was a major factor in the onset of osteoporosis regardless of other preventive measures.

The FORE and NOF organizations maintain Web sites on the Internet, which provide information on the causes, prevention, and treatment of osteoporosis. The NOF also conducts an annual National Osteoporosis Prevention Month Campaign. *See also* Alcohol Abuse and Addiction; Eating Disorders; Smoking

Further Reading

Healy, Bernadine. *A New Prescription for Women's Health.* New York: Viking, 1995.

National Osteoporosis Foundation. "Osteoporosis: What Is It?" <http://www.nof.org/osteoporosis/osteoporosis.htm>.

Notelovitz, Morris, M.D., and Diana Tonnessen. *The Essential Heart Book for Women.* New York: St. Martin's Griffin, 1996.

Pollak, Michael. "High Blood Pressure and Osteoporosis." *New York Times* (September 21, 1999).

Our Bodies, Ourselves

See **Boston Women's Health Book Collective**

Ovarian Cancer

Ovarian cancer, a malignant tumor that begins on the surface of the ovaries, is the most common type of cancer of the ovaries. The ovaries, one on each side of the pelvis, produce eggs and are the main source of the female hormones estrogen and progesterone.

While public campaigns to warn women about breast and lung cancer are widespread, only in recent years have women's health-care advocates called attention to the issue of ovarian cancer and attempted to educate women about possible risks. In addition, advocates are calling for more research on the disease.

According to the National Cancer Institute (NCI) of the National Institutes of Health (NIH), about 1 in every 57 women in the United States will develop ovarian cancer. Although most cases occur in women over the age of 50, the disease can also affect younger women. The major concern for this type of cancer is diagnosing the disease before it spreads beyond the ovaries and becomes incurable. Ovarian cancer is often called a silent killer because it is difficult to detect—the symptoms are not easily recognized as ovarian abnormalities. In its booklet on ovarian cancer, the NCI explains:

Ovarian cancer cells can break away from the ovary and spread to other tissues and organs in a process called shedding.

When ovarian cancer sheds, it tends to seed (form new tumors) on the peritoneum (the large membrane that lines the abdomen) and on the diaphragm (the thin muscle that separates the chest from the abdomen). Fluid may collect in the abdomen... [and] may make a woman feel bloated, or her abdomen may look swollen.

Ovarian cancer cells can also enter the bloodstream or lymphatic system (the tissues and organs that produce and store cells that fight infection and disease). Once in the bloodstream or lymphatic system, the cancer cells can travel and form new tumors in other parts of the body. Some symptoms of the disease include

- General abdominal discomfort and/or pain (gas, indigestion, pressure, swelling, bloating, cramps)
- Nausea, diarrhea, constipation, or frequent urination
- Loss of appetite
- Feeling of fullness even after a light meal
- Weight gain or loss with no known reason
- Abnormal bleeding from the vagina (National Cancer Institute)

Along with the NIH, the American Cancer Society, the Ovarian Cancer National Alliance, and the Women's Cancer Network are among the groups trying to raise awareness of the disease. These groups maintain Internet Web sites with information about ovarian cancer symptoms and risks. Women at risk for ovarian cancer should request a combination pelvic-rectal exam and a transvaginal sonogram, the experts say. Some of the risks outlined by the American Cancer Society include the following:

Age: Most ovarian cancers develop after menopause. Half of all ovarian cancers are found in women over 65. Fertility drugs: Some studies have found that long-time use of the fertility drug clomiphene citrate, without achieving pregnancy, may increase a woman's risk for having a type of

tumor called LMP tumor (low malignancy potential). A woman taking this drug should discuss the issue with her doctor.

Menstrual history: Women who started having periods at an early age (before age 12), who go through menopause late, or who have no children (or who had their first child after age 30), may have an increased risk of ovarian cancer. There seems to be a relationship between the number of menstrual cycles in a woman's lifetime and her risk of developing ovarian cancer. More monthly periods may be related to an increased risk. Breastfeeding may lower the risk since menstrual periods often stop during breastfeeding.

Family history of ovarian cancer: Having a mother, sister, or daughter with ovarian cancer increases the risk, especially if they developed the cancer at a young age. A woman can inherit a higher risk for ovarian cancer from either her mother's or her father's side of the family. About 7% of ovarian cancers result from inherited risks. Gene changes (mutations) are involved in these cancers.

Breast cancer: Women with breast cancer are more likely to have ovarian cancer.

Diet: The American Cancer Society recommends choosing most foods from plant sources (fruits, vegetables, whole grain products) and limiting intake of high fat foods, especially those from animal sources. (American Cancer Society)

The NCI is conducting research on the causes and prevention of ovarian cancer, and reports: "Researchers have discovered that changes in certain genes...are responsible for an increased risk of developing ovarian and breast cancers. Members of families with many cases of these diseases may consider having a special blood test [called CA125] to see if they have a genetic change that increases the risk of these types of cancer. Although having such a genetic change does not mean that a woman is sure to develop ovarian or breast cancer, those who have the genetic change may want to discuss their options with a doctor." (National Cancer Institute)

Further Reading

American Cancer Society, ACS Ovary Cancer Resource Center. "Ovarian Cancer Overview." <http://www3.cancer.org>.

Lowry, Vicky. "Researchers Fix Their Sights on an Elusive Silent Killer." *New York Times* (June 25, 2000).

National Cancer Institute. *What You Need to Know about Ovarian Cancer.* Booklet. <http://cancernet.nci.nih.gov/wyntk_pubs/ovarian.htm>.

P

Pap Smear

See **Cervical Cancer**

Partial-Birth Abortion Ban Act of 1995

See **Abortion**

Planned Parenthood Federation of America

The largest and oldest family planning organization in the United States, Planned Parenthood Federation began in 1916 when Margaret Sanger and her sister, Ethel Byrne, both nurses, and a third woman, Fania Mindell, opened the first birth control clinic in Brooklyn, New York. Sanger organized the American Birth Control League in 1921, and the Birth Control Clinical Research Bureau in 1923. The two organizations merged in 1939 to become the Birth Control Federation of America, which was later renamed the Planned Parenthood Federation of America.

Planned Parenthood (PP) believes that every individual has a fundamental right to decide when or whether to have a child, and that every child should be wanted and loved. Planned Parenthood affiliates are located across the United States, and each one is a unique, locally governed health services organization that reflects the diverse needs of its community.

Planned Parenthood was led by Faye Wattleton from 1978 to 1992. Wattleton was the first African-American and the youngest president in the organization's history, and she became well known for her activism. Wattleton had observed first-hand the adverse consequences of poor health care for pregnant women and their newborn children. Under her leadership, PP developed a national grassroots network that has been able to prevent efforts to overturn women's legal right to reproductive choices. Wattleton also helped broaden PP's reproductive health-care services to reach an increasing number of women and their families across the United States.

According to Planned Parenthood's Internet Web site, its health centers offer a wide range of services that may include

- family planning counseling and birth control
- pregnancy testing and counseling

- gynecological care, Pap tests, breast exams
- emergency contraception
- HIV testing and counseling
- comprehensive, age-appropriate sex education
- screening and treatment for sexually transmitted infections
- infertility screening and counseling
- voluntary sterilization for women and men
- male reproductive medical exams
- safe-sex counseling
- midlife services
- abortions or abortion referrals
- prenatal care
- adoption referrals
- primary care

Over the years, Planned Parenthood has gone to court in attempts to protect women's reproductive freedom. Affiliates of the Planned Parenthood Federation have been involved in nearly a dozen Supreme Court cases involving contraception, family planning counseling, and abortion. For example, in a 1965 U.S. Supreme Court case, *Griswold v. Connecticut*, a Planned Parenthood appeal overturned Connecticut's ban on the use or prescription of contraception. Today, the organization, through its Legal Action for Reproductive Rights, continues to file suits against government efforts to deny access to reproductive health care. Such actions have frequently been assailed by groups aligned with the prolife movement. *See also* Abortion; African-American Women's Health; Birth Control; *Griswold v. Connecticut; Planned Parenthood of Southeastern Pennsylvania v. Casey;* Prolife Movement; Sanger, Margaret; Sexually Transmitted Diseases

Further Reading
Chesler, Ellen. *Woman of Valor: Margaret Sanger and the Birth Control Movement in America.* New York: Simon & Schuster, 1992.

Planned Parenthood Federation of America. "About Us." <http://www.plannedparenthood.org/about/index.html>.

Planned Parenthood of Southeastern Pennsylvania v. Casey

In *Planned Parenthood of Southeastern Pennsylvania v. Casey,* the U.S. Supreme Court in 1992 upheld most of a state law that requires a woman to give her informed consent prior to an abortion procedure, and "specifies that she be provided with certain information at least 24 hours before the abortion is performed." The Court also ruled that a state may assert its interest in potential human life throughout pregnancy and adopted the "undue burden" standard; state laws could be designed to dissuade women from having abortions but the law could not "place a substantial obstacle in the path of a woman seeking an abortion before the fetus attains viability." At the same time the Court declared unconstitutional a requirement that a woman notify her husband before having an abortion, recognizing that a married woman could be physically abused by a husband opposed to abortion.

The case before the High Court was the result of a Pennsylvania law signed by then-Governor Robert P. Casey in 1990. Before any of the provisions took effect, five abortion clinics, a physician representing himself, and a class of doctors who provide abortion services brought suit, charging that each of the provisions was unconstitutional. The District Court found all the provisions unconstitutional, but the state of Pennsylvania appealed and an appellate court upheld the law. Attorneys for Planned Parenthood and other prochoice groups petitioned the High Court to hear the case.

Since the Supreme Court's decision in 1992, the case has been controversial.

Women's health-care advocates and reproductive rights groups such as the National Abortion and Reproductive Rights Action League, Planned Parenthood Federation of America, and the Center for Reproductive Law and Policy contend that the "undue burden" test can be interpreted in many ways. This in turn greatly weakens women's reproductive rights. Antiabortion groups, on the other hand, praised the ruling as one more step toward overturning laws that allow a woman to end her pregnancy. *See also* Abortion; Center for Reproductive Law and Policy; National Abortion and Reproductive Rights Action League; Planned Parenthood Federation of America; Pregnancy; Prolife Movement; *Roe v. Wade*

Further Reading

Gay, Kathlyn. *Pregnancy: Private Decisions, Public Debates.* New York: Franklin Watts, 1994.

U.S. Supreme Court. *Planned Parenthood of Southeastern Pennsylvania v. Casey.* <http://laws.findlaw.com/US/000/u10345.html>.

Plastic Surgery

Women by far make up the majority of today's patients who have plastic surgery, which includes a variety of medical procedures to change structures of the body for either reconstructive or cosmetic purposes. Reconstructive surgery is a physical and psychological issue for women who have congenital problems (such as one breast smaller than another) or have developed abnormalities from disease, infection, or tumors. More than one million reconstructive procedures were performed in 1998, with tumor removal constituting about half the surgeries.

One of the most common reconstructive surgeries for women is breast reconstruction after mastectomy. Cosmetic, or aesthetic, surgery, on the other hand, is primarily an issue of image and raises questions about whether women are unduly influenced by style setters and society's general notion of what is attractive. Women and girls who opt for cosmetic surgery usually want to improve their appearance and enhance their self-esteem.

Plastic surgery stems from ancient times when practitioners used skin grafts to treat facial injuries. Modern-day surgical procedures began during and after World War I when doctors had to repair terrible skull and facial injuries of war victims. At the same time physicians realized they could help people who hid from public view because of physical deformities. Plastic surgery continued to develop during other armed conflicts, but medical procedures for cosmetic purposes were especially enhanced with the development of silicone, a substance manufactured in solid, liquid, or gaseous forms. Silicone was created by the chemical industry about the time that plastics were invented during the late 1920s and early 1930s. Medical practitioners in the United States used liquid silicone for cosmetic purposes—primarily breast augmentation—from the late 1940s to the 1960s. But numerous women who were injected with liquid silicone suffered serious health problems, and the U.S. Food and Drug Administration (FDA) banned silicone injections in 1965.

Prior to the ban, Thomas Crooning, a plastic surgery professor at Baylor College of Medicine in Houston, and his student, Frank Gerow, experimented with the idea of using rubbery silicone for breast implants, presenting the possibility to Dow Corning. The company began manufacturing a model device in 1961, and the Dow implant became the model for at least 40 varieties of implants produced over the next three decades. Breast implants, however, became highly controversial in the early 1990s as women who had implants filled with silicone gel began to register complaints about health problems associated with the devices. The FDA banned the

Selected Plastic Surgery Procedures 1998

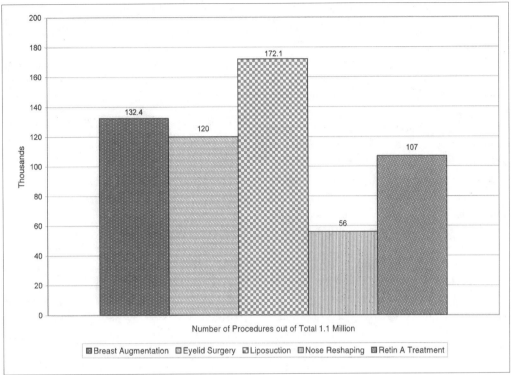

Source of Data: Plastic Surgery Information Service, 2000.

use of silicone gel–filled implants in 1992, although other types of implants are allowed.

Some health risks have been cited with other types of plastic surgery. A study in the *New England Journal of Medicine* in 1999, for example, noted that between 1993 and 1998 five patients who had undergone tumescent liposuction died from the procedure. Performed in a medical office, the surgery involves injecting fat cells with several quarts of a water solution containing lidocaine, a pain blocker, and other drugs; the fatty tissue in water is then sucked out through tiny incisions. Researchers concluded that tumescent liposuction could pose unpredictable life-threatening risks, "perhaps in part because of lidocaine toxicity or lidocaine-related drug interactions." (Rao, 1,471)

Because of the lucrative income cosmetic surgery provides, a great number of physicians without expertise and some without even backgrounds in surgery are entering a field with few regulations or licensing requirements, although surgeons and some others are board-certified. Most cosmetic procedures are not covered by insurance, so doctors do not have to file forms and patients pay up-front with credit cards or with cash that sometimes is borrowed from finance companies aggressively advertising for business.

The influx of doctors untrained in plastic surgery and its rapidly expanding technology raises concerns about safety and risks of procedures. An increasing number of patients are seeking help from established, board-certified cosmetic surgeons to repair damages or complications from botched surgeries. In spite of dangers associated with some cosmetic surgery, the procedures increased dramatically from 1992 through 1999. According to data compiled by the American Society of Plastic Surgeons, the top cosmetic surgeries in 1999 were liposuction, breast augmentation, and eyelid surgery. Liposuction procedures increased 389 percent from 47,212 in 1992 to 230,865 in 1999. Breast augmentation procedures rose from 32,607 in 1992 to 167,318 in 1999, a 413 percent increase. Eyelid surgery increased 139 percent over the eight-year period, from 59,461 in 1992 to 142,033 in 1999. Face-lift and nose reshaping were other popular procedures.

Qualified plastic surgeons certified by the American Board of Plastic Surgery or the Royal College of Physicians and Surgeons of Canada advise candidates for plastic surgery to seek out specialists by asking for referrals from family doctors or satisfied patients. Some experts warn people to be cautious of Internet Web sites—hundreds of these sites deal with plastic surgery and include home pages that essentially are advertisements for individual surgeons or plastic surgery centers. Various medical groups such as the American Academy of Cosmetic Surgery, American Society of Plastic Surgeons, Mayo Clinic, and the Foundation for Plastic Reconstruction Surgery also have Web sites and published information about the types of plastic surgery performed, average costs (in the thousands of dollars), and locations of plastic surgeons. *See also* Breast Cancer; Breast Implants

Further Reading

American Society of Plastic Surgeons, Plastic Surgery Information Service. "Most Popular Cosmetic Surgery Procedures Just Became More Popular." Press Release July 20, 2000. <http://www.plasticsurgery.org/mediactr/stats.htm>.

American Society of Plastic and Reconstructive Surgeons. "Cosmetic Surgery Jumps 50 Percent: Liposuction and Breast Augmentation Top Procedures." News Release (April 28, 1999).

Cowley, Geoffrey, and Karen Springen. "Lowdown on Liposuction." *Newsweek* (May 24, 1999).

Gay, Kathlyn. *Breast Implants: Making Safe Choices.* New York: New Discovery Books/Macmillan, 1993.

Gilbert, Susan. "Gauging the Risk Factors in the Search for a Perfect Face." *New York Times* (June 21, 1998).

Jacoby, Susan. "I Liked the Way I Looked, until I Talked to a Plastic Surgeon." *New York Times* (June 21, 1998).

Rao, Rama B., Susan F. Ely, and Robert S. Hoffman. "Deaths Related to Liposuction." *New England Journal of Medicine* (May 13, 1999).

Poor Women's Health Care

The poverty-stricken, no matter their age or gender, have always had to struggle to obtain minimum health care. But in the United States today poor women's health care encompasses multiple issues ranging over the lifespan, from birth to death. Inadequate health care for poor pregnant women and single women with families compounds the problems. Racism in society also works especially against poor women of color, who have historically been denied access to proper health care and currently are less likely than white women to receive the most modern medical treatments. Poor women are frequently blamed for not getting the medical care they and their children need, in spite of the fact that they cannot afford more than minimal access to health care and seek medical care primarily in crisis situations. In addition, many poor women suffer from health problems due to undernourishment, environmental and workplace hazards, and the extreme stress of trying to provide basic necessities.

Reproductive issues impact significantly on poor women's health care. Several widely published news stories in 1998 focused on poor women who were denied anesthesia during childbirth because they could not pay cash for the services of anesthesiologists. Poor women, including many pregnant teenagers, also are less likely than women with adequate financial means to receive proper prenatal care; thus they are likely to have children with low birth weights and health problems during childhood. (Alan Guttmacher Institute, September 1999)

Lack of access to abortion providers and birth control information and devices is another reproductive issue that adversely affects poor women. Since 1977, the U.S. Congress has banned the use of federal Medicaid funds (administered by states) for abortions, unless a woman's life is in jeopardy or if she has been the victim of incest or rape. While providing access to abortion services is a highly controversial issue, recent studies have shown that unplanned pregnancies, especially among women who cannot afford a child, will increase, adding not only to the abortion rate but also to the health-care problems of women and their children. (Alan Guttmacher Institute)

According to findings by Jean Schroedel, a Claremont (California) Graduate University researcher, there is a correlation between states with strict antiabortion laws and the amount of money they spend to aid poor women and children. These antiabortion states spend less on programs that, for example, help combat battering, or domestic violence against women, and programs for needy children such as education, foster care, and adoption of children with handicaps. "To put it simply, prolife states make it difficult for women to have abortions, but they do not help these women provide for the children once born," Schroedel concluded. (quoted in Claiborne)

Unless poor women are eligible for and able to obtain government-funded medical insurance such as Medicaid, they seldom receive early treatment for serious diseases, counseling for alcohol and other drug abuse, or protection from physical vi-

olence or sexual abuse by their intimate partners. Any of these health problems can prevent a woman from maintaining a job, completing an education, or competently caring for her children. The twin issues of poverty and violence also can lead to homelessness and even more severe health problems.

Elderly women who are poor face numerous health-care concerns. "Compared with men, elderly women are three times more likely to be widowed or living alone, spend more years and a larger percentage of their lifetime disabled, are nearly twice as likely to reside in a nursing home, and are more than twice as likely to live in poverty," according to the Administration on Aging of the U.S. Department of Health and Human Services. Some elderly poor must choose between using meager funds to pay for medicine or to buy food and other necessities. Since the 1980s, domestic elder abuse has become a significant social and health problem in the United States; victims frequently are those who do not have the financial resources to live independently and are forced to move in with family members.

Many voices have been raised in recent years to call attention to poor women's health-care issues. Among advocates are the Boston Women's Health Book Collective, which has published several editions of the famed health book for women, *Our Bodies, Ourselves;* the Children's Defense Fund, which is encouraging poor mothers to enroll their children in the federally funded Children's Health Insurance Program (CHIP); the Planned Parenthood Federation of America, which provides family planning and other health information for women and their families and is a strong supporter of reproductive rights; and the Health Care for the Homeless Clinicians' Network, a national association of nurses, physicians, nurse practitioners, psychologists, social workers, dentists, pharmacists, mental health therapists, substance abuse counselors, and other practitioners working to prevent homelessness and to improve the health and quality of life of homeless people. Programs at the U.S. Department of Health and Human Services focus on numerous health issues that affect not only women in general but also poor women in particular, such as a domestic violence hotline; elder nutrition programs; and free or low-cost mammography screening for low-income elderly, minority, and Native American women. *See also* Abortion Providers; Boston Women's Health Book Collective; Domestic Elder Abuse; Homeless Women; Teenage Pregnancy and Childbearing

Further Reading

Administration on Aging. "Older Women: A Diverse and Growing Population." Fact Sheet. Washington, DC: Administration on Aging, U.S. Department of Health and Human Services.

Alan Guttmacher Institute. "Induced Abortion." Facts in Brief (1998). <http://www.agi-usa.org/pubs/fb_induced_abort.html>.

Alan Guttmacher Institute. "Teen Sex and Pregnancy." (September 1999). <http://www.agi-usa.org/pubs/fb_teen_sex.html>.

Children's Defense Fund. "The Waiting Game." Focus group report on the Children's Health Insurance Program and Medicaid (March 1998).

Claiborne, William. "Study Links Abortion Laws, Aid to Children." *Washington Post* (October 9, 1999).

National Center on Elder Abuse. *The National Elder Abuse Incidence Study.* Washington, DC: U.S. Department of Health and Human Services, the Administration on Aging, September 1998.

Rogers, Albert R., ed. *Battered Women and Their Families.* New York: Springer Publishing Company, 1998.

Schroedel, Jean. *Is the Fetus a Person: A Comparison of Fetal Policies across the 50 States.* Ithaca, NY: Cornell University Press, 2000.

Sidel, Ruth. *Keeping Women and Children Last: America's War on the Poor.* Revised ed. New York: Penguin, 1998.

Pregnancy

Pregnancy, or the time period when a woman is pregnant and a fetus is developing in her uterus, is a biological process that primarily concerns a pregnant woman and her partner. But because human reproduction can have long-term impact on any society, childbearing is usually controlled by traditions and beliefs. In the United States, pregnancy has been surrounded for decades by controversial political, legal, social, medical, religious, and economic issues. Some of the most strident arguments have been over a woman's right to abort or terminate a pregnancy, but heated debates have also focused on the many other ways that public and private authorities intervene in the lives of pregnant women.

Some controversies have developed because of assisted reproductive technologies (ART), or artificial insemination techniques, that have helped women become pregnant but in some cases have resulted in legal battles over who owns the rights to artificially inseminated and preserved embryos. ART also has made it possible for a surrogate mother to carry and deliver a baby for another woman unable to bear children. Surrogates usually are paid fees for their services, a practice that critics charge is tantamount to renting out women's bodies and selling babies.

Because medical technology makes it possible to perform surgery on a fetus (fetal therapy), arguments arise over who should determine whether such a procedure should take place—medical practitioners or the woman carrying the fetus. Some women are opposed to fetal therapy or question its safety and believe they have the right to refuse such treatment; their opponents believe a pregnant woman's refusal to undergo surgery endangers the life of a fetus. In some cases, the courts have intervened and ordered a woman to accept fetal therapy.

Court-ordered interventions to protect a fetus have been applied to pregnant teenagers, women who abuse alcohol and other

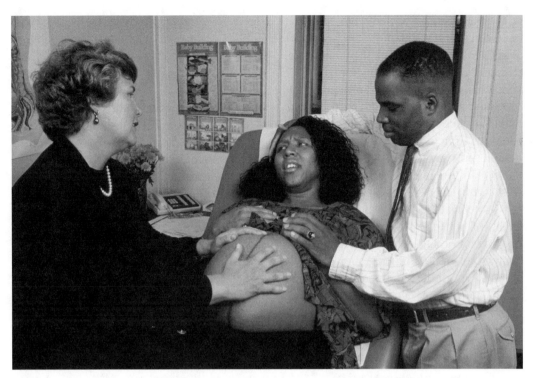

A man accompanies his pregnant wife to a prenatal checkup. ©James Marshall/CORBIS.

drugs, HIV-positive women who are pregnant, and pregnant women in the workplace. Legal action has been taken as well against medical practitioners and others (such as those responsible for vehicle accidents) who have caused prenatal injuries.

Increasingly over the past few decades some legal, medical, and religious authorities have been inclined to favor fetal protective measures, while others argue that the law should not be used to prevent harm to a fetus. These opposing views stem from conflicting ideas about "personhood"—when life begins and a fetus becomes a person. According to one view, life begins the moment the female egg is fertilized by the male sperm to form a single-celled organism. Others contend that personhood is not achieved until the fetus is viable or able to live outside the womb.

Another pregnancy issue has developed in recent years over genetic testing to detect the presence of genes that carry dis-orders. If a woman suspects that she or her partner is likely to reproduce children with an inherited disease, she may consider an abortion. Genetic testing might also prompt some couples to attempt *in vitro* fertilization techniques to develop an embryo using eggs or sperm from someone not at risk of passing on a hereditary disorder. Some experts predict that genetic and embryo research will lead to procedures that will encourage couples to try to reproduce "perfect" children. Yet, critics argue, no one can determine what characteristics would constitute a "perfect" individual.

Economics plays a major role in some pregnancy issues. Poor women frequently are unable to obtain adequate prenatal care, primarily because they lack medical insurance or are underinsured and few doctors practice in poverty-stricken areas. Thus poor women may suffer serious, undetected health problems that adversely affect their pregnancies and their newborns.

Perhaps the most basic reproductive issue centers on whether or not a woman is able to make her own choices during her pregnancy or be limited by socially constructed and accepted ideas and practices. She may, for example, want to seek midwifery services for childbearing but be discouraged from doing so by medical practitioners (primarily male) who dominate in the care of pregnant women. A pregnant woman might be prevented from working at a job considered too dangerous for the health of her fetus. Women who lack access to information about reproductive matters are limited in their knowledge of options. One of the main goals of women's health movement activists and women-centered medical practitioners is to help women make their own decisions about their pregnancies. See also Abortion; Artificial Insemination; Genetic Testing; Prepared Childbirth; Surrogate Mother; Teenage Pregnancy and Childbearing

Further Reading
Gay, Kathlyn. Pregnancy: Private Decisions, Public Debates. New York: Franklin Watts, 1994.
Healy, Bernadine. A New Prescription for Women's Health. New York: Viking, 1995.
Holmes, Helen Bequaert, and Laura M. Purdy, eds. Feminist Perspectives in Medical Ethics. Bloomington and Indianapolis, IN: Indiana University Press, 1992.

Premenstrual Syndrome (PMS)

Premenstrual syndrome, usually known as PMS or premenstrual tension, includes a variety of symptoms, but they differ with each woman who experiences them, ranging from irritability to fluid retention to violent behavior. Very little research has been done on PMS, so it is difficult to define. But the studies that have been conducted "have failed to define any biological abnormality in hormones or brain function to explain PMS or its variability." (Healy, 317)

Because of the paucity of research on PMS, many myths and misconceptions have developed. For many years, PMS was thought to be an imaginary problem, a mental health disorder; the American Psychiatric Association has classified some severe forms of PMS (which affect only a small percentage of women) as a psychiatric disorder that can become disabling.

While some health-care practitioners still treat all PMS sufferers as having a psychological illness, most doctors consider the syndrome a real physical problem related to hormonal changes before menstruation that can be treated with a variety of self-help techniques. Some women use complementary and alternative medicine, such as herbal remedies, to relieve symptoms.

Stereotyping is an issue of concern for women with PMS. They are frequently the brunt of jokes and negative images that portray them as abnormal, "bitchy," and mean. The negative images of PMS have been used as political attacks in attempts to show that women are not capable of holding positions of authority. At the same time, some feminist groups, women's organizations, and woman-centered health practitioners have countered the PMS stereotypes by emphasizing that tension or physical changes are symptoms of normal menstrual cycles. See also Depression; Menstruation; Mental Illness

Further Reading
Figert, Anne E. Women and the Ownership of PMS. Hawthorne, NY: Aldine de Gruyter, 1996.
Healy, Bernadine. A New Prescription for Women's Health. New York: Viking, 1995.
Hoffman, Eileen, M.D. Our Health, Our Lives: A Revolutionary Approach to Total Health Care for Women. New York: Simon & Schuster, 1995.
Planned Parenthood Federation of America. The Planned Parenthood Women's Health Encyclopedia. New York: Crown Trade Paperbacks, 1996.

Prenatal Testing

Prenatal testing is a way for a woman to monitor her pregnancy and determine whether there is a potential for abnormalities such as Down syndrome, hemophilia, Rh disease, and Tay-Sachs disease. An estimated 125,000 American women each year undergo amniocentesis, a procedure in which a doctor inserts a thin needle through a woman's abdomen to extract fluid from the amniotic sac that holds the fetus. The fluid is analyzed in a laboratory to examine chromosomes for disorders. Other tests include fetal blood tests and cell sampling to analyze for disorders.

Prenatal testing is not only a health issue for some women but also an ethical concern. Some prenatal tests cannot be performed until just before the second trimester. Amniocentesis, for example, cannot be done until after the fourteenth week of pregnancy because of the high risk of miscarriage and leaking amniotic fluid. In addition, fetal cells must grow in the laboratory so that there will be enough to analyze; thus results of the analysis are not known for two to three weeks. If the results of amniocentesis prompt a woman to terminate a pregnancy, she may face the physical, emotional, and ethical difficulty of a second-trimester abortion.

Fetal DNA analysis being developed raises even more ethical questions. Not only will parents learn about chromosomal abnormalities weeks earlier than they do now, but infertile couples using artificial insemination will learn whether embryos have defective genes. Thus it would be "possible to choose only healthy embryos for transfer to the uterus during in vitro fertilization. Moreover, couples at risk for giving birth to a child with a hereditary disease could use embryo testing and in vitro fertilization as a way to have a healthy baby." (Wymelenberg, 140) Some argue that such DNA testing would be a better alternative than fetal testing. But others consider it a type of ge-

Pregnant woman watching ultrasound exam. Tom and Dee Ann McCarthy/Unicorn Stock Photos.

netic breeding that raises numerous questions about the criteria for determining who is qualified to populate the earth. *See also* Artificial Insemination; Assisted Reproductive Technologies; Genetic Testing

Further Reading
Planned Parenthood Federation of America. *The Planned Parenthood Women's Health Encyclopedia.* New York: Crown Trade Paperbacks, 1996.
Springen, Karen. "A State of the Art: Pregnancy." *Newsweek* Special Issue (Spring–Summer 1999).
Wymelenberg, Suzanne for the Institute of Medicine. *Science and Babies Private Decisions, Public Dilemmas.* Washington, DC: National Academy Press, 1990.

Prepared Childbirth

See **Childbirth Practices**

Prolife Movement

The prolife political movement in the United States is made up of hundreds of local, state, and national organizations whose members believe that life begins at conception and that abortion is murder. Because the term "prolife" suggests that people with opposing views are against life, antiabortion advocates have used the prolife slogan for decades to counter prochoice arguments, or the view that it is a basic human right for a woman to make her own reproductive choices.

In the view of prolife advocates, the fetus is entitled to the same human rights as the mother. This stance spawned a movement in the 1960s to overthrow laws that legalize abortion. Some within the movement oppose abortion even in cases of rape and incest and to protect the health and life of a pregnant woman. Most prolife groups contend that legal abortion has not improved women's health and on the contrary has contributed to numerous physical complications and psychological problems among women who have had abortions, as well as higher incidences of serious diseases like breast cancer. No scientific data support those charges.

For the most part, organizations within the prolife movement base their views on religious doctrine and include members who are obstetricians, gynecologists, medical students, pharmacists, and other health-care professionals. Hundreds of prolife organizations maintain Internet Web sites to espouse their views. Among the main groups are American Life League (http://www.all.org); Feminists for Life (http://www.serve.com/fem4life); Human Life International (http://www.hli.org); Life Dynamics (http://www.ldi.org); Life Issues (http://www.lifeissues.org); LifeLinks (http://National Right to Life Committee (http://www.nrlc.org); People for Life (http://www.peopleforlife.org); Prolife America (http://www.prolife.com); Prolife Action League (http://www.prolifeaction. org); and Vida Humana Internacional (http://www.vidahumana.org). The latter organization's Web site contains links (but does "not necessarily endorse or condone the contents of the sites") to the main prolife organizations; post-abortion ministries; religious prolife organizations, including Baptist, Catholic, Lutheran, Methodist, and Presbyterian sites; state and local right-to-life organizations; medical and student prolife groups; political and legal prolife organizations; feminist prolife groups; dozens of pregnancy centers; and "organizations that study the myth of overpopulation." *See also* Abortion

Further Reading
Bender, David L., and Bruno Leone, eds. *Abortion: Opposing Viewpoints.* San Diego, CA: Greenhaven Press, 1991.

Public Health Service's Office on Women's Health

Established in 1991, the United States Public Health Service's Office on Women's Health (PHS OWH) is designed to "improve the health of American women by advancing and coordinating a comprehensive women's health agenda throughout the U.S. Department of Health and Human Services." According to its fact sheet, PHS OWH "works with numerous government agencies, nonprofit organizations, consumer groups, and associations of health-care professionals."

During its first decade, PHS OWH focused on developing women's health as a specialized issue for government action and attention. With women's health now firmly rooted in the national health landscape, PHS OWH is shifting women's health priorities to meet new demographic trends, one of which is the growing number of elderly women. "By the year 2030, one in four American women will be over the age of 65," OWH notes, adding:

> Another dramatic demographic trend is the racial and ethnic diversification of America. By the year 2030, one in five American women will be of Hispanic heritage, one in 11 will be Asian, and the number of African-Americans will grow steadily. In fact, by the year 2050, women of color will represent fully half of the adult female population in America. The result: women are living longer, facing more of the chronic diseases and conditions that accompany old age, and coming from an ever-increasing variety of cultural and economic backgrounds.

Although vast improvements in medicine have resulted in longer lives for women—they live 30 years longer on average than they did in 1900—many American women and their families still face economic, social, and cultural barriers to adequate health care. Thus the OWH is fo-

cusing "on two priority areas: 1) reducing racial and ethnic gaps in health care for women—many of which are influenced by social and economic conditions, and 2) supporting culturally sensitive educational and communications initiatives that encourage women to take an increasing role in their own health and wellness."

To meet its goals and priorities, PHS OWH coordinates women's health initiatives in various federal agencies and departments, including the National Institutes of Health, the Food and Drug Administration, and the Centers for Disease Control and Prevention. PHS OWH also stimulates the development and implementation of effective women's health policies at the highest levels of national, state, and local governments. In addition, the Office of Women's Health attempts to disseminate information about women's health policies and topics to every region of the United States, and develops mechanisms to give the private sector a voice in women's health policy. One more function of OWH is to foster the recruitment, retention, and promotion of women in health- care and biomedical careers. *See also* National Institute of Health Office of Research on Women's Health; Women in Medicine; Women in Science; "Women Living Long, Living Well"

Further Reading
Public Health Service's Office of Women's Health. "Fact Sheet: About the U.S. PHS Office on Women's Health."

Public Safety

Public safety is a prime concern for many American women, particularly for women alone, who are vulnerable to violent crimes ranging from robbery to sexual assault to murder. Newspapers and magazines have published hundreds of articles in recent years on women who have been brutally attacked during home invasions, or while running for fitness, traveling in cars, or tak-

Self-defense class for women. ©Photos—Bettye Lane. .

ment, sexual assault, and other violence against women in the workplace received special attention. Each year 13,000 acts of violence against women in the workplace are committed by former husbands or boy-friends. According to the National Institute for Occupational Safety and Health (NIOSH), homicide was the leading cause of death for women in the workplace in 1996. Some experts believe the violence is due to anxiety in the workplace

> where layoffs and downsizing run ram-pant, where company and worker loyalty is long forgotten, and where the typical employee feels like a disposable cog in a big machine that itself may soon be scrapped. In other words, for many work-ers, much of the dignity and humanity of work has been lost. And some are angry enough to strike back violently.
> Another theory is that violent behav-ior, reported day and night by the media, has now become a viable option in the minds of the more suggestible members of society. (Blythe, 43)

ing public transportation. The issue has prompted seminars and classes on mea-sures women can take to protect them-selves. Some learn martial arts or how to use firearms, tear gas, mace, pepper sprays, and other self-defense equipment. Others attempt to follow safety rules such as con-sistently locking windows and doors in their cars and homes and being alert to sus-picious strangers.

Women who are frequent business travelers also face safety issues. Most fol-low security procedures when they stay in hotels and motels, looking for brightly lighted parking garages and well-moni-tored lobbies. They also ask for rooms near elevators to avoid long walks alone down halls.

In the workplace women's safety is-sues have been a concern for decades; dur-ing the 1980s and 1990s, sexual harass-

In 1998 the Heinz Foundation commis-sioned a Women's Health in the Workplace survey of 1,000 women from all parts of the economy to learn the special risks women face while on the job. Women who participated in the survey reported job-re-lated health risks, frequently from working with or around hazardous materials, and 43 percent reported work injuries that resulted in five days off the job. Half of the respon-dents said they had not received informa-tion from employers about workplace risks, even though NIOSH requires that this information be readily available. *See also* Domestic Violence; Occupational Safety and Health Administration; Sexual Harassment; Rape and Sexual Assault; Working Women

Further Reading
Blythe, Bruce. "Eye on Workplace Violence." *Risk Management* (April 1999).

Hickins, Michael. "Docs Yawn at Women's Work." *Management Review* (April 1998).

Spano, Susan. "Hotels Get a Lot Wiser about Women Traveling on Business." *Los Angeles Times* (August 9, 1998).

R

Radiance

Radiance: *The Magazine for Large Women* has been published quarterly since 1984 to support and provide information for the Size Acceptance Movement. The magazine deals with the issue of American society's obsession with thinness and dieting crazes, eating disorders, and the prejudices and cruel harassment that fat women and girls face. One issue contained essays from teenage girls who recounted their experiences with size and weight discrimination and how they endured taunts from classmates about their size. The magazine's main purposes is to help readers gain or maintain self-respect and to obtain ideas and tools needed for a healthy life. *See also* Dieting and Diet Drugs; Eating Disorders; Weight Discrimination

Further Reading
Radiance: The Magazine for Large Women Online.
<http://www.radiancemagazine.com/>.

Rape and Sexual Assault

In the United States, federal and state laws define rape in diverse ways, but essentially it is sexual assault, an act of violence that is a criminal offense. A rapist forces or co- erces someone to have sexual intercourse or other sexual contact by physically over-powering a victim or by threatening a victim with physical injury or death. Laws usually stipulate that a non-consenting victim of rape includes persons who are mentally incapacitated, physically helpless (due to alcohol or other drugs), asleep, or less than 17 years of age. The rate of sexual assault in the United States is the highest of any industrialized nation; the majority of victims are women and girls, although men and boys are also rape victims.

Over the centuries men have seldom been harshly punished for sexually assaulting or raping women. Until the industrial revolution in the early 1900s, women had few if any rights and were considered no more than property owned by their fathers or husbands. The prevalence of rape against women stems from the oppression of women as well as the ancient belief that rape is an act of sexual passion and that men should be excused for being unable to control themselves. In addition many cultural attitudes perpetuate rape, such as the belief that a husband is entitled to have sex with his wife and can force her to do so and that "real men" should be able to have sex whenever they have the desire. Media images that depict violence against women or that suggest women like being forced to have sex may also promote rape. Only in recent years has a rape victim been recognized as a person whose human rights have been violated by a criminal assault. Even then, there is a widespread but erroneous belief that women who are raped "ask for it" or are somehow at fault for the crime against them.

Since about the mid-1970s in the United States, public attention has focused on rape and sexual assault as a women's health issue as well as a legal, social, and moral issue. The rate of sexual assault and rape in the United States is the highest of any industrialized country, and rape is the most underreported crime. Only about 10 to 15 percent of rape victims report the crime, due to fear of recrimination and concern about being stigmatized or not believed. As Senator Joseph Biden noted in an introduction to a 1993 Senate Judiciary Report:

Survivors of rape and family violence pay a double price: like other victims of violent crime, they suffer the terrible toll of physical and psychological injury. But, unlike other crime victims, they also suffer the burden of defending the legitimacy of their suffering. It is bad enough when friends or neighbors ask why a survivor "let it happen," or why the survivor was in the "wrong place at the wrong time." But, when the criminal justice system adopts these attitudes of disbelief and hostility, survivors' only recourse is to blame themselves.

Many rape victims are adolescent girls, with half of all sexual assault cases occurring before age 18. Thirty-two percent "of all rapes occur among girls between the ages of 11 and 17...[and] 15% of college women have experienced a sexual assault." (Kaplan, 42)

Some of the serious physical health effects of rape include injuries requiring hospitalization, sexually transmitted diseases, and pregnancy.

However, delayed physical and behavior outcomes are the more common and difficult results that need to be treated after a rape. These aftereffects include chronic pain syndromes, increased self-destructive behaviors.... Rape also can contribute to poor self-esteem, low sexual self-respect, loss of control over one's body, and feelings of powerlessness. Compared with nonvictims, rape victims experience more major depression, chronic fear and anxiety, substance abuse, and suicide. (Kaplan, 42)

When a woman is raped by a spouse or partner, she is likely to be victimized repeatedly and also to be beaten. Battered women sometimes must choose between staying with husbands or partners or leaving. Leaving and seeking refuge does not necessarily guarantee that a woman will be protected. Numerous domestic violence cases result in serious injury or murder.

The Rape, Abuse and Incest National Network (RAINN) is a nonprofit organization founded by singer/songwriter Tori Amos, who is herself a rape survivor. Based in Washington, DC, RAINN operates a national toll-free hotline (800-656-HOPE) and maintains an Internet Web site (http://feminist.com/rainn.htm) for victims of sexual assault. The organization also provides information about rape crisis centers across the United States.

One group of women is often ignored when the issue of rape and sexual assault arises: female prisoners. According to Amnesty International–USA,

Incarcerated women in U.S. prisons often suffer punishment far in excess of their state imposed sentence. At the hands of correctional officers they face widespread sexual abuse ranging from unauthorized body frisks to rape.

Although most state and federal laws criminalize sexual assaults of inmates in correctional institutions, enforcement of those laws "is often sporadic or non-existent. Nationwide, rape and sexual abuse of incarcerated women is so widespread that inmates often consider it a customary aspect of the prison experience. The recent explosion in the number of women incarcerated exacerbates the problem, increasing instances of physical and emotional violation." (Amnesty International) *See also* Adolescent Girls' Health; Domestic Violence

Further Reading

Amnesty International, USA. "The State of Laws and Lawlessness: A Survey of Statutes on Custodial Sexual Contact." Fact Sheet (1999).

Hall, Rob. *Rape in America.* Santa Barbara, CA: ABC-CLIO, 1995.

Muehlenhard, Charlene L. "What Sexual Scientists Know about Rape." Brochure. Mt. Vernon, IA: The Society for the Scientific Study of Sexuality, 1995.

Kaplan, Deborah. "Clinical Management of Rape in Adolescent Girls." *Patient Care* (April 30, 1999).

Senate Judiciary Committee. "Violence against Women, The Response to Rape: Detours on the Road to Equal Justice."(May 1993).

United States Department of Justice, Bureau of Justice Statistics. "Violence against Women." Report. (1994).

RESOLVE

RESOLVE, the National Infertility Association, is a volunteer organization founded in 1974 by Barbara Eck Menning, a nurse, to assist individuals experiencing infertility, a health problem affecting as many men as women. Today RESOLVE has more than 50 chapters across the United States and maintains a Web site. The organization provides information and support on many aspects of infertility and family building, including treatment, medications, and adoption.

One of the important health issues RESOLVE addresses is the increasing in-cidence of multiple births that result from fertility treatments such as the implantation of several embryos. Following participation in a meeting at the National Institutes of Health (NIH) in November 1999, RESOLVE called for increased consumer education and research on this public health concern.

Another major issue RESOLVE has been addressing for years is comprehensive insurance coverage for infertility treatment and other family-building measures. Currently many insurance companies and about three-fourths of health management organizations do not cover infertility treatments, and RESOLVE has supported federal legislation for such benefits. Three federal bills were introduced in the 106th Congress to focus on increasing access to infertility insurance coverage. *See also* Artificial Insemination; Assisted Reproductive Technologies; Infertility; Surrogate Mother

Further Reading

Aronson, Diane, and RESOLVE. *Resolving Infertility: Understanding the Options and Choosing Solutions When You Want to Have a Baby.* New York: Harper, 1999.

"Resolve Joins with United States Senator to Introduce Federal Infertility Insurance Legislation." Press Release (February 17, 2000).

RESOLVE, the National Infertility Association <http://www.resolve.org>.

Roe v. Wade

A 1973 U.S. Supreme Court decision in a case known as *Roe v. Wade* protects a woman's fundamental right to privacy under the U.S. Constitution and encompasses a woman's right to decide whether to continue her pregnancy. The case was named for a pregnant single woman, Jane Roe (a pseudonym), who sought an abortion in Texas, where state law criminalized abortion except when a woman's life was in danger. A class action suit against the state attorney (Wade) challenged the constitutionality of the Texas criminal abortion law. Justice Harry A. Blackmun, who wrote the Court's decision, pointed out that the justices acknowledged "the sensitive and emotional nature of the abortion controversy" and "the deep and seemingly absolute convictions that the subject inspires." Blackmun wrote:

> One's philosophy, one's experiences, one's exposure to the raw edges of human existence, one's religious training, one's attitudes toward life and family and their values, and the moral standards one establishes and seeks to observe, are all likely to influence and to color one's thinking and conclusions about abortion.

However, the Court noted as well that the restrictive criminal abortion laws in effect in a majority of states at that time were "of relatively recent vintage. Those laws...are not of ancient or even of common law origin. Instead, they derive from statutory changes effected, for the most part, in the latter half of the 19th century." Many laws restricting abortion except to save the life of the mother were passed due to the efforts of the American Medical Association, citing the need to prevent injuries and deaths from botched abortions performed by unlicensed practitioners. With the *Roe v. Wade* decision, state laws could not interfere with a woman's choice to have an abortion during the first trimester, or first third of her pregnancy, except to require that the abortion be performed by a licensed physician. After fetal viability (when the fetus could live outside the uterus), the state was free to ban or restrict abortion to promote its interest in the fetus as long as it made exceptions to protect a woman's life or health. The Court ruled that, at the beginning of the third trimester, government can regulate or prohibit abortion in order to protect fetal life unless the abortion is necessary to preserve the life of the woman.

One of the important aspects of *Roe v. Wade* was the recognition of a woman's right to privacy. This right, Blackmun wrote,

> whether it be founded in the Fourteenth Amendment's concept of personal liberty and restrictions upon state action, as we feel it is, or, as the District Court determined, in the Ninth Amendment's reservation of rights to the people, is broad enough to encompass a woman's decision whether or not to terminate her pregnancy. The detriment that the State would impose upon the pregnant woman by denying this choice altogether is apparent. Specific and direct harm medically diagnosable even in early pregnancy may be involved. Maternity, or additional offspring, may force upon the woman a distressful life and future. Psychological harm may be imminent. Mental and physical health may be taxed by child care. There is also the distress, for all concerned, associated with the unwanted child, and there is the problem of bringing a child into a family already unable, psychologically and otherwise, to care for it. In other cases, as in this one, the additional difficulties and continuing stigma of unwed motherhood may be involved. All these are factors the woman and her responsible physician necessarily will consider in consultation.

Since the *Roe v. Wade* ruling, numerous antiabortion groups have challenged the decision, and some have advocated and taken part in violence against abortion providers. Those who oppose women's reproductive choices also have lobbied against the use of RU-486, or mifepristone, a drug that can be used to induce abortion. In addition antiabortion forces have promoted state and federal laws to restrict reproductive choices. Some of these laws were challenged and appealed to the U.S. Supreme Court. One such case in Missouri (*Webster v. Reproductive Health Services*) reached the High Court in 1989; another case,

Planned Parenthood of Southeastern Pennsylvania v. Casey, was decided by the Court in 1992. In 2000, the High Court ruled on so-called "partial-birth abortion" laws, striking down these bans as unconstitutional. *See also* Abortion; Abortion Providers; Mifepristone; *Planned Parenthood of Southeastern Pennsylvania v. Casey; Webster v. Reproductive Health Services*

Further Reading

Bender, David L., and Bruno Leone, eds. *Abortion: Opposing Viewpoints.* San Diego, CA: Greenhaven Press, 1991.

Harrison, Beverly Wildung. *Our Right to Choose: Toward a New Ethic of Abortion.* Boston: Beacon Press, 1983.

Hitt, Jack. "Who Will Do Abortions Here?" *New York Times* (January 18, 1998).

Supreme Court of the United States, 410 U.S. 113, December 13, 1971. Reargued October 11, 1972, January 22, 1973, Appeal from the United States District Court for The Northern District of Texas.

Roulet, Sister Elaine (1930–)

See **Women in Prison**

RU-486

See **Mifepristone**

S

Sanger, Margaret Louise (Higgins) (1879–1966)

Margaret Louise Higgins Sanger is known for her efforts to disseminate birth control information and for advocating the use of contraceptives so that working women could free themselves from the financial burden of unwanted pregnancies. She founded the first birth control clinic in the United States and throughout her life fought the strenuous opposition of the Catholic Church and legislators who passed laws banning contraceptives. She adamantly opposed the Comstock Law named for Anthony Comstock, an overly zealous moralist. Passed by the federal government in 1873, the law banned distribution through the mail of any "obscene, lewd, or lascivious book, pamphlet, picture, paper, print, or other publication of an indecent character." Birth control information was considered obscene.

Born into a poor family in Corning, New York, Margaret Louise was the sixth of 11 children of Michael and Anne Purcell Higgins. Michael Higgins' activism in labor and social reform movements did not endear him to townspeople, but because of his activities Margaret developed a rebellious spirit of her own.

Margaret Sanger. Courtesy of Barbara Flaxman.

Anne Higgins died before she was 50 years old, and Margaret blamed her mother's early death on frequent pregnancies as well as the family's poverty. Determined to escape a similar fate, Margaret set out to become a nurse. While in a New York nursing program, she met her future husband, William Sanger, an architect. The couple was married in 1902 and eventually had two sons and a daughter.

The Sangers lived for awhile in a New York City suburb, but in 1910 they moved to the city and became activists in radical political and labor groups. Members included the well-known Russian anarchist, Emma Goldman, who, as one of the earliest birth control advocates, consistently spoke out on the right of women to choose the number of children they would bear. Goldman was Sanger's mentor for a time, but the two women began to differ in their approaches to the birth control movement and eventually severed their relationship.

Sanger's interest in birth control stemmed not only from witnessing her mother's poor health but also from her work as a visiting nurse in New York City's slums. There she helped deliver babies and cared for mothers who were in poor health due to frequent childbearing or botched abortions. Women begged Sanger to tell them how to prevent pregnancy, but she was forbidden by law from distributing such information. When one of her patients died in childbirth, Sanger determined to try to help women obtain effective birth control. In 1914, Sanger began publishing a monthly magazine called *The Woman Rebel*, which discussed women's rights issues and advocated for birth control information. Even though Sanger did not distribute information on contraception in her magazine, the federal government banned it and indicted Sanger for violating the Comstock Law. Rather than stand trial, she fled the United States, leaving her husband and children behind and went to England under the alias Bertha Watson. After she was gone, her friends distributed 100,000 copies of her pamphlet, *Family Limitation*, "which, in straightforward language and with the aid of diagrams, explained the common forms of birth preventives employed furtively but often without confidence by millions of American women,

and still unknown to many more." (Chesler, 102–3)

While she was in Europe, Sanger decided to end her marriage, which had been strained for several years. She began to live as she believed—as a sexually liberated woman. As she stated in a manifesto for her first issue of *The Woman Rebel,* "I believe that woman is enslaved by the world machine, by sex conventions, by motherhood and its present necessary childbearing, by wage-slavery, by middle-class morality, by customs, laws and superstitions." (Quoted in Chesler, 98)

Defying convention, Sanger had a series of affairs. Among her lovers were prominent British liberals, psychologist Havelock Ellis and writer H.G. Wells. In late 1915, Sanger returned to the United States to face obscenity charges for distributing birth control information. She believed the law under which she was charged was unconstitutional and hoped to defend herself and birth control at her trial. She also had gathered much more information on birth control and had developed a philosophy that justified contraception on the basis of theories of John Stuart Mills and Thomas Robert Malthus, who declared that world stability and peace depended on population control.

While Sanger was preparing for her trial, her son died suddenly of pneumonia and Sanger became deeply depressed. She began to consider pleading guilty to the charges against her, not only because of her emotional state but also because her lawyer and some friends in the birth control movement were urging her to do so. However, Sanger entered a plea of not guilty "in order to separate the idea of prevention of conception and birth control from the sphere of pornography, from the gutter of slime and filth where the lily-livered legislators have placed it, under the direction of...Anthony Comstock." (Quoted in Falk, 144)

Sanger did not achieve the forum she expected, because the government dropped charges against her, primarily because of media attention and sympathetic public support for Sanger. The Comstock Law was not changed, and women still did not have access to the information they needed to prevent conception. So Sanger and her sister, who was also a nurse, set up a birth control clinic in Brooklyn, New York. Such a clinic was prohibited by state law, which prevented doctors from providing birth control information to their patients and from treating venereal diseases unless the patient was male. Authorities quickly closed the clinic, and Sanger and her sister served 39 days in jail for the offense. But they appealed their case, and in 1918 the state Court of Appeals ruled that doctors were exempt from New York's obscenity law and could advise on matters of birth control as well as treat venereal disease.

Sanger continued to fight legislation blocking contraceptive use and to increase awareness of birth control by publishing *The Birth Control Review,* established in 1917, and by creating the American Birth Control League (ABCL) in 1921, which was the forerunner of Planned Parenthood Federation of America. During the 1920s, she also formed the National Committee on Federal Legislation for Birth Control, who lobbied for laws that would allow physicians the right to provide contraceptives, although many opposed birth control. In 1922, Sanger married wealthy James Noah Slee, who generously supported the birth control movement. Biographer Chesler described the relationship as "at once foolishly romantic and eminently practical." (Chesler, 245) Slee not only provided funds for Sanger's work but also accompanied her on trips to Asia, where Sanger lectured on overpopulation and birth control. Throughout the 1930s, Sanger consistently lobbied for the legalization of birth control. While bans continued in states, the U.S. Court of Appeals ruled in 1936 that physicians could prescribe or distribute contraceptives. Margaret Sanger retired from the birth control movement in the 1940s, but after World War II she became involved in international birth control efforts. She also helped find funding for contraceptive research, which led to the development of the birth control pill. Not until the 1965 High Court decision in *Griswold v. Connecticut* was birth control legalized for married couples. Margaret Sanger died a few months later in September 1966. *See also* Birth Control; Comstock Law; *Griswold v. Connecticut*; Planned Parenthood Federation of America

Further Reading

Chesler, Ellen. *Woman of Valor: Margaret Sanger and the Birth Control Movement in America.* New York: Simon & Schuster, 1992.

Falk, Candace Serena. *Love, Anarchy, and Emma Goldman,* Chapter 9. New Brunswick, NJ: Rutgers University Press, 1990.

Gay, Kathlyn, and Martin K. Gay. *Heroes of Conscience: A Biographical Dictionary.* Santa Barbara, CA: ABC-CLIO, 1996.

Margaret Sanger Papers Project, Department of History, New York University. "Biographical Sketch." <http://www.nyu.edu/projects/sanger/ms.bio.htm>.

Sanger, Margaret. *Margaret Sanger: An Autobiography.* New York: Norton, 1938.

Scientific Advisory Meeting

Each year the Society for the Advancement of Women's Health Research (SAWHR) holds a Scientific Advisory Meeting (SAM) to present findings in gender-based biology, the study of gender differences in health and illness. "These differences extend beyond the obvious areas like reproductive differences to areas such as reactions to specific drugs, and how men and women respond to the same disease or treatment," noted Phyllis Greenberger, executive director of the Society, at the 1998 SAM. "The more scientists look for such differences, the more they find, and the more they recognize how important those differences are." (Society for the Advancement of Women's Health Research)

During the tenth annual SAM in 2000, new research and data were presented on sexually transmitted diseases, pain control, and substance abuse. In previous meetings, the society discussed gender differences in such fields as autoimmune disease, immunology, neurology, pharmacology, and psychiatry. Neuroscientists, for example, presented research showing the effects of estrogen on the brain and the neurotransmitter serotonin, which could help explain why women have a higher incidence of depression than men. Findings also showed that hormones likely play a role in the fact that 70 percent of people with multiple sclerosis are female. *See also* Gender-Based Biology; Gender-Biased Research and Treatment; Society for the Advancement of Women's Health Research

Further Reading

Society for the Advancement of Women's Health Research, Tenth Annual Scientific Advisory Meeting. "Annual Update on Women's Health Research: Discoveries and Implications." (October 26–27, 2000). Report. <http://www.womens-health.org/gbb.html>

Sexual Abuse

See **Child Sexual Abuse; Rape and Sexual Assault; Sexual Harassment**

Sexual Harassment

Sexual harassment is unwanted and unwelcome sexual behavior that in most cases involves male abuse of power and frequently consists of demands for sex in exchange for getting and keeping a job. Other types of sexual harassment of women and girls include unwanted touching and grabbing of breasts or other parts of the body, objectionable sexual comments, and sexual jokes. While male harassers may consider sexual advances as harmless and part of the "mating game," sexual harassment often adversely affects women, causing extreme stress, loss of self-esteem, anxiety and feelings of humiliation, degradation, and anger. If harassment continues over a long term, women who are victims may suffer psychological and physical health problems that interfere with their work or school life.

Women in the workplace have long been subjected to sexual harassment but they seldom discussed the issue openly or took action to stop it because they feared reprisals from harassers, who are usually in positions of authority or older than their victims. Female workers who complain about harassment have risked losing their jobs and being labeled as "loose" women or as women deluded by sexual fantasies. Thus the victims are victimized twice.

During the 1970s, women's rights groups began to demand that sexual harassment be defined as sexual discrimination, which is prohibited by the Civil Rights Act of 1964. Women hoped to call attention to lax enforcement of provisions in the Act dealing with sexual discrimination. By the 1980s, the Equal Employment Opportunity Commission (EEOC), which was established to administer the Civil Rights Act, had explicitly defined sexual harassment as a form of illegal sex discrimination and issued guidelines on what constituted sexual harassment in the workplace:

> Unwelcome sexual advances, requests for sexual favors, and other verbal or physical conduct of a sexual nature constitute sexual harassment when
>
> 1. submission to such conduct is made either explicitly or implicitly a term or condition of an individual's employment,
>
> 2. submission to or rejection of such conduct by an individual is used as the

basis for employment decisions affecting such individual, or

3. such conduct has the purpose or effect of unreasonably interfering with an individual's work performance or creating an intimidating, hostile, or offensive working environment.

These guidelines also apply to school situations in which unwanted sexual behavior interferes with a person's education or ability to participate in school activities. A 1991 amendment to the Civil Rights Act contains provisions for victims of sexual harassment to file lawsuits against their harassers.

From the late 1970s through the 1990s, numerous books, articles, and television documentaries dealt with sexual harassment of women in the workplace. However, the issue did not gain widespread public attention until the fall of 1991 when the U.S. Senate Judiciary Committee held televised hearings on whether to confirm Clarence Thomas as a Supreme Court judge. Rumors had been circulating that Thomas had sexually harassed a co-worker, Anita Hill, when they were both employed by the EEOC during the 1980s. The committee called Hill (by then a law professor in Oklahoma) to testify. Senators who supported Thomas clearly demonstrated that they did not believe Hill's account of sexual harassment and tried to belittle her. Millions of women across the United States were enraged and, after the confirmation of Judge Thomas, numerous victims of sexual harassment began to file complaints and lawsuits. In addition, some states passed legislation to combat the problem and companies and school systems began conducting seminars to educate employees about sexual harassment and how it intimidates, frightens, humiliates, embarrasses, and financially damages women. *See also* Sexuality; *Women: Work and Health*

Further Reading

Eskenazi, Martin, and David Gallen. *Sexual Harassment: Know Your Rights!* New York: Carroll & Graf Publishers, 1992.

Faludi, Susan. *Backlash: The Undeclared War against American Women.* New York: Crown, 1991.

Gay, Kathlyn. *Rights and Respect: What You Need to Know About Gender Bias and Sexual Harassment.* Brookfield, CT: Millbrook Press, 1995.

Petrocelli, William, and Barbara Kate Repa. *Sexual Harassment on the Job.* Berkeley, CA: Nolo Press, 1992.

Siegel, Deborah L. for The National Council for Research on Women. *Sexual Harassment: Research & Resources.* New York: The National Council for Research on Women, 1992.

Strauss, Susan, with Pamela Espeland. *Sexual Harassment and Teens.* Minneapolis, MN: Free Spirit Publishing, 1992.

Sexuality

Sexual feelings and desires comprise a person's sexuality, which can be expressed in a great variety of ways throughout the life span. A more detailed definition of sexuality comes from the Sex Information and Education Council of the United States (SIECUS), a nonprofit organization established in 1964 to affirm that sexuality is a natural and healthy part of life:

Human sexuality encompasses the sexual knowledge, beliefs, attitudes, values, and behaviors of individuals. Its dimensions include the anatomy, physiology, and biochemistry of the sexual response system; identity, orientation, roles and personality; and thoughts, feelings, and relationships. The expression of sexuality is influenced by ethical, spiritual, cultural, and moral concerns.

Sexuality was seldom discussed with candor in the United States until the 1960s, when the so-called sexual revolution resulted in fewer restrictions on sexual relations. Yet, sexual freedom usually applied to men who expected women to be sexually available to them and submissive. Today female sexuality has become an issue for an increasing number of American women who do not accept the male standard for sex and understand that women experience sexuality differently than men.

"Every norm that has ever been established for female sexuality has been based on male patterns, perceptions, and distortions," writes Eileen Hoffman, M.D. Dr. Hoffman explains:

Men and women are viewed as different sides of the same coin, with essentially similar physiological responses. The goal of sex is viewed as a genitally-based physical gratification, a perspective that ignores women's drive toward intimacy and emotional communion, as well as their more complex physiological response... the focus is centered on the male erection and the physiology of the erection. There has been a great deal of attention given to finding mechanical and pharmacological solutions to men's performance problems, while labeling women's sexual dysfunctions according to their inability to comply with men.... Many studies have shown that women rate affection and emotional communication as more important than orgasm in a sexual relationship. This is not to say that women don't care about orgasm as long as they have intimacy. Rather, it says that the intimacy of a sexual act with another person, in which orgasm plays a part, is a full mind-body event for women. (Hoffman, 304)

Another female sexuality issue focuses on the double standards of morality for males and females in regard to sexual relations. While many adolescent girls are sexually active today, social mores still expect females to abstain from sex until marriage. On the other hand, boys are expected to have numerous premarital sexual experiences. Females also are expected to take the major responsibility for birth control and in many instances they are blamed if they become pregnant out of wedlock.

Sexuality issues are of special concern to such groups of women as lesbians, women with disabilities, and older women. Lesbians, who desire other women rather than men as sex partners, frequently face irrational fear and hatred and physical assaults or harassment from people who believe that heterosexual relationships are the only acceptable way to express sexuality. The sexuality of disabled women is often discounted or denigrated, and some women with disabilities lose confidence in their ability to enjoy their sexuality or to satisfy their sexual needs. Older women have long been viewed as less "sexy" than younger women in society, but surveys in recent years show that sexuality—sexual feelings and desires—do not necessarily disappear as women age. Chronic health problems, medications, or lack of a partner are more likely factors in diminished sexual activity. *See also* Adolescent Girls' Health; Lesbian Health; Teenage Pregnancy and Childbearing; Women with Disabilities

Further Reading

Hite, Shere. *The Hite Report on Female Sexuality.* New York: Macmillan and Bertelsmann, 1976.

Hubbard, Ruth. *The Politics of Women's Biology.* New Brunswick, NJ: Rutgers University Press, 1990.

Jacoby, Susan. "Great Sex What's Age Got to Do with It?" *Modern Maturity* (September–October 1999).

Planned Parenthood Federation of America. *The Planned Parenthood Women's Health Encyclopedia.* New York: Crown Trade Paperbacks, 1996.

SIECUS. "Making the Connection: Definitions of Sexually Related Health Terminology" (1999). <http://www.siecus.org/pubs/cnct/cnct0002.html>.

Sexually Transmitted Diseases (STDs)

Sexually transmitted diseases (STDs), or sexually transmitted infections (STIs) as they are often called, are infections passed from person to person through intimate sexual contact. These STDs have created major health, social, and economic concerns in the United States. The diseases include gonorrhea and syphilis, ancient scourges that have declined in the United States, though new cases still occur in alarming numbers, health officials say. Other, more common STDs are genital herpes, which is caused by a virus; a bacterial infection known as chlamydia; a viral infection called human papillomavirus (HPV) that causes genital warts; a common vaginal infection called trichomoniasis; and infections caused by the hepatitis B virus (HBV). The most devastating STD is HIV, the human immune deficiency that causes AIDS, which is passed on not only through sexual contact but also through intravenous drug use.

A disproportionate number of women and teenage girls are affected by STDs. Because of the female biological structure, infections thrive in internal, moist cavities. Another problematic issue for women is that infections frequently are asymptomatic, resulting in delayed diagnosis and treatment. This often puts women at risk for serious complications, such as cervical cancer, infertility, miscarriages, stillborn babies, and having babies with major health problems. Chlamydia, for example, is one of the most common and rapidly spreading STDs among women, four million of whom contract the disease each year. Unlike men with chlamydia who have symptoms and seek treatment, up to 80 percent of women with chlamydia show no signs, and the infection may be active for a long time before being diagnosed. Untreated chlamydia can cause pelvic inflammatory disease (PID), which leads to infertility. Chlamydia has also been linked to heart disease, according to a study reported in the February 1999 issue of *Science*.

In 1996, the Institute of Medicine (IOM) set off alarms with its report, *The*

Hidden Epidemic: Confronting Sexually Transmitted Diseases. The IOM reported that more than 12 million new cases of STDs occur each year, although a study released in 1998 estimated new cases to be more than 15.3 million annually. Teenagers who are sexually active account for at least three million of these cases.

The title of the IOM report underscores a significant political and social concern—how to alert Americans to the fact that an epidemic of STDs exists. Many people are reluctant to openly discuss STDs because of the social stigma attached, and relatively few doctors routinely test for or inquire about possible STDs, often assuming that their patients are not the "type" who would have such infections. Yet people of all backgrounds and economic levels contract STDs.

Approximately $10 billion is spent annually for treatment of major STDs and their complications, excluding costs for HIV/AIDS, which adds another $7 billion. One issue the IOM raised focused on preventive measures, such as distributing condoms in schools, a highly controversial approach that many Americans believe encourages teenage sex. However, no scientific evidence shows that this is the case, the IOM contends.

In 1998, the U.S. Centers for Disease Control and Prevention began an extensive campaign to encourage better detection and treatment of STDs. Various health information sites have been launched on the Internet to provide data and explain some of the symptoms of infections. MEDLINEplus is one example <http://www.nlm.nih.gov/medlineplus/ sexuallytransmitteddiseases.html>. Another is the Women's Health STD Information Center sponsored by the *Journal of the American Medical Association* <http://www.ama-assn.org/special/std/std. htm>. The Centers for Disease Control and Prevention also has an online site focusing on STDs <http://www.cdc.gov/od/ owh/whstd.htm>. *See also* AIDS

Further Reading

DiClemente, Ralph J. "Preventing Sexually Transmitted Infections among Adolescents." *Journal of the American Medical Association* (May 20, 1998).

Howard, Beth. *Mind Your Body: A Sexual Health and Wellness Guide for Women.* New York: St. Martin's Press, 1998.

Institute of Medicine. Committee on Prevention and Control of Sexually Transmitted Diseases. *The Hidden Epidemic: Confronting Sexually Transmitted Diseases.* Eng, T.R. and W.T. Butler, eds. Washington, DC: National Academy Press, 1997.

Stolberg, Sheryl Gay. "U.S. Awakes to Epidemic of Sexual Diseases." *New York Times* (March 9, 1998).

Villarosa, Linda. "Two Lesser Known Sexually Transmitted Diseases Account for Most New Cases." *New York Times* (December 8, 1998).

Watanabe, Myrna. "Scientists Using New Tactics to Curb STD Rates in U.S." *The Scientist* (September 15, 1997).

Silent Spring Institute

Based in Massachusetts, the Silent Spring Institute (SSI) is a coalition of scientists and citizens concerned about the possible links between environmental toxins and breast cancer, a major women's health issue. Named for Rachel Carson's book, *Silent Spring,* which alerted the public to the adverse effects of pesticides on wildlife, the SSI began in the early 1990s when women's health activists from the Massachusetts Breast Cancer Coalition demanded a scientific investigation of the suspected link between environmental hazards and the significantly higher rates of breast cancer among the women in Cape

Rachel Carson, speaking before Senate Government Operations subcommittee studying pesticide spraying. Library of Congress/LC-USZ62-111207.

Cod than among women elsewhere in Massachusetts. Because of SSI advocacy, the Massachusetts legislature funded the Cape Cod Breast Cancer and Environment Study, administered by the state's Department of Public Health. During the initial three-year phase (1995–1998) of the study, SSI's "research team developed a sophisticated geographic information system to analyze associations between breast cancer and environmental features, studied historical records on pesticide use and drinking water quality, and developed new methods for field study of environmental estrogens." The team found that even after known risk factors (a family history of breast cancer, for example) were taken into account,

- Breast cancer is about 20 percent higher on Cape Cod than in the rest of the state.
- Breast cancer incidence is at least 15 percent higher than in the rest of the state in 11 of the 15 towns on the Cape. In eight of these towns, the elevation is statistically significant.
- Cape Cod women 55 to 64 years old are at 29 percent greater risk of breast cancer than women of their age in the rest of Massachusetts.

In a brochure describing the results of its study, SSI states that its "research has clearly shown that higher breast cancer incidence is a long-standing problem that extends to all regions of the Cape. The results also show that sustained study of breast cancer and the Cape environment should continue to be a public health priority." The research team continues its efforts, collecting and analyzing data to "determine how women are exposed to pesticides, compounds that mimic estrogen, and other hormones in the environment." The group hopes to answer questions about the environment and women's health, and to identify preventable causes of disease, which would benefit women

nationwide. *See also* Breast Cancer; Environmental Health Hazards

Further Reading

Silent Spring Institute. "The Cape Cod Breast Cancer and Environment Study: Results of the First Three Years of Study." Brochure. Newton, MA: Silent Spring Institute, 1998.

Skin Cancer

See Melanoma

Smoking

Since the 1960s, the health problems associated with smoking and nicotine addiction have been well publicized by such organizations as the American Cancer Society, the American Lung Association, and the Centers for Disease Control and Prevention. Smoking became a legal issue in the United States during the 1990s when states sued tobacco companies for reimbursement of health costs paid out for smoking-related illnesses. In November 1998, 46 states won a total settlement of $206 billion from tobacco companies, which will make restitution over a 25-year period. The settlement also bans or restricts various types of cigarette advertising and merchandising.

Teenagers smoking behind school. ©Will and Deni McIntyre/Photo Researchers, Inc.

Several individuals also sued tobacco companies for smoking-related health problems. One woman, Patricia Henley, who began smoking at the age of 15, was diagnosed more than 30 years later with inoperable lung cancer. She won a lawsuit against Philip Morris, claiming the tobacco company had deliberately misled her and millions of other smokers about the health risks of smoking.

Between 23 and 25 percent of U.S. women 18 years of age and older smoke cigarettes, and most of these women began smoking in their preadolescent or early teenage years. As an increasing number of young women begin smoking, some health experts contend that female smokers may equal or outnumber male smokers in the near future.

Young girls and women take up smoking for a variety of reasons, not the least of which is the influence of advertising and television and movie images depicting female smokers as desirable, exciting, and independent. Women also "seem to be more strongly influenced than men by growing up in households with parents who smoke." (Hoffman, 362) In addition, female smokers frequently express the belief that smoking helps them control their weight and reduce stress. However, smoking over the long term is a risk factor in most of the major health problems that afflict women, including various types of cancer and lung diseases. Studies conducted at Tulane Medical School in New Orleans and at the Centers for Disease Control and Prevention found that "smoking causes more lung damage in women than in men," primarily because women's lungs are smaller than men's. "From 1979–1992, women's deaths from obstructive lung disease rose 108 percent." (Friend)

In 1996 the United States and Canada proposed joint initiatives to prevent tobacco use among girls and young women, such as educating girls and women about the dangers of smoking and promoting physical activity as an alternative to smoking. A recent study conducted by researchers at The Miriam Hospital in Providence, Rhode Island, found that women who exercise regularly while they try to quit smoking are twice as successful in kicking the habit as sedentary women.

Smoking Rates Among Women 18–44 Years Old, by Educational Attainment (1991)

Educational Group	Current Smokers
Some high school education	40%
Graduated from high school	32%
Some college education	24%
Graduated from college	12%

Source of Data: U.S. Centers for Disease Control and Prevention.

Smoking (All figures are for 1995)

Percent of Men Ages 18 and Over Who Smoke Cigarettes	27%
Percent of Women Ages 18 and Over Who Smoke Cigarettes	23%
Percent of High School Dropouts Age 25 and Over Who Smoke	35.7%
Percent of people with 16 or More Years of Education Who Smoke	13.6%

Source: U.S. Centers for Disease Control and Prevention.

Although smoking among both women and men in the United States has declined significantly since the 1960s, each day 3,000 teenagers begin smoking, putting themselves at risk for long-term health problems. Nearly 9 of every 10 adult smokers start smoking in childhood or adolescence. A report in the *Journal of the*

National Cancer Institute "suggests early smoking [in preadolescent years] may trigger changes in DNA that put young smokers at higher risk for cancer, even if they later quit." Early smoking could permanently damage the "normal processes of cell renewal," an epidemiologist explained. (Quoted in Golden, 48)

Among young smokers are pregnant teenagers, ages 15 to 19 whose numbers have increased since the mid-1990s. The young women are endangering not only themselves but also their children, who are likely to be born prematurely and later may suffer respiratory problems from passive smoking—being exposed to smoke in the household. *See also* Adolescent Girls' Health; Drug-Dependent Mothers; Lung Cancer; Teenage Pregnancy and Childbearing

Further Reading

Associated Press. "Exercise Helps Women Quit Smoking." *New York Times* (June 14, 1999).

Born, Dorothy. "More Warnings Given to Teenage Smokers." *The Lancet* (April 1999).

Friend, Tim. "Smoking Damages Women's Smaller Lungs." *USA TODAY* (May 13, 1996).

Golden, Frederic. "Smoking Gun for the Young." *Time* (April 19, 1999).

Hoffman, Eileen, M.D. *Our Health, Our Lives: A Revolutionary Approach to Total Health Care for Women.* New York: Simon & Schuster, 1995.

Kelley, Timothy. "A $51 Million Habit?" *Scholastic Update* (April 12, 1999).

U.S. Department of Health and Human Services, Centers for Disease Control, National Center for Health Statistics. "Fewer Pregnant Women Smoke; Teen Rate Rises." News Release (November 19, 1998).

Worth, Robert. "Making It Uncool." *Washington Monthly* (March 1999).

Society for Women's Health Research

A nonprofit advocacy organization, the Society for Women's Health Research (SWHR), formerly the Society for the Advancement of Women's Health Research, promotes the health of women through research. The Society was founded in 1990 because of the growing "concern that the health of all American women was at risk due to biases in biomedical research." Thus the organization advocates for more funding to research what are often called "women's diseases," such as breast cancer, osteoporosis, and cancer of reproductive organs, as well as heart disease and lung cancer. The Society's "aim is to highlight several of the alarming gaps in knowledge which make effective preventive methods, treatments, and cures impossible" among American women.

Since its founding the SWHR has successfully lobbied for federal legislation that requires the inclusion of women in federally funded medical research and the establishment of the Office of Research on Women's Health at the National Institutes of Health. At the urging of SWHR, the United States Food and Drug Administration set up new guidelines to include women in all stages of drug testing.

To keep Congress informed about women's health issues, the SWHR provides members with briefings and conducts educational meetings. The Society also publishes reports, produces educational videotapes for the public, and sponsors the *Journal of Women's Health*. Its Web site includes a list describing the major differences between men and women that impact on women's health:

1. After consuming the same amount of alcohol, women have higher blood alcohol content than men, even when you allow for size differences.

2. Women who smoke are 20 to 70 percent more likely to develop lung cancer than men who smoke the same amount of cigarettes.

3. Women tend to wake up from anesthesia more quickly than men—an average of 7 minutes for women and 11 minutes for men.

4. Some pain medications (known as kappa-opiates) are far more effective in relieving pain in women than in men.

5. Women are more likely than men to have a second heart attack within a year of the first one.

6. The same drug can cause different reactions and different side effects in women and men; even common drugs like antihistamines and antibiotics.

7. Just as women's stronger immune systems protect them from disease, women are more likely to get autoimmune diseases (diseases where the body attacks its own tissues) such as rheumatoid arthritis, lupus, scleroderma, and multiple sclerosis.

8. During unprotected intercourse with an infected partner, women are 2 times more likely than men to contract a sexually transmitted disease and 10 times more likely to contract HIV.

9. Depression is 2 to 3 times more common in women than in men, in part because women's brains make less of the hormone serotonin.

10. After menopause, women lose more bone than men, which is why 80% of people with osteoporosis are women.

The SWHR Web site also provides links to fact sheets, Society publications, information about gender-based biology, and other health issues of concern to women. *See also* Breast Cancer; Gender-Based Biology; Heart Disease; Osteoporosis

Further Reading
Society for the Advancement of Women's Health Research. "10 Differences between Men and Women That Make a Difference in Women's Health." <http://www.womens-health.org/insertB.htm>.

Sports Injuries and Ailments

Since the 1980s, the number of women and girls participating in competitive and recreational sports has increased at a fairly rapid pace. Along with their participation has come a marked increase in female sports injuries and ailments. Female athletes are more vulnerable to certain types of sports injuries and health ailments than are men, according to experts in sports medicine. While medical practitioners laud the many benefits of sports and physical activity, they also express concern about the paucity of information on how to help women prevent sports injuries and ailments.

One of the most common sports injuries among female athletes is to the anterior cruciate ligament (ACL), the primary ligament that provides stability to the knee. Female soccer, basketball, and volleyball players are two to four times more likely than their male counterparts to suffer such injuries. "The greater incidence of ACL injuries in women probably stems from complex, interrelated factors, possibly including hamstring-quadriceps strength imbalances, joint laxity, and the use of ankle braces. Successful treatment often includes surgery," according to a report in a 1997 issue of *The Physician and Sportsmedicine.* (Moeller and Lamb) Researchers are still investigating specific causes of gender differences in ACL injuries.

Another health problem among female athletes that has gained attention in recent years is the female athlete triad, a syndrome named in 1992 by a group of women physicians and experts in sports science. The triad is comprised of three distinct problems that are closely related: amenorrhea (cessation of the menstrual period); disordered eating; and loss of bone density. Eating disorders (anorexia and bulimia) among some well-known female athletes, especially gymnasts, have been widely publicized, but women who suffer the triad syndrome do not necessarily fit the psychiatric criteria for anorexia and bulimia. Rather the female athletes become preoccupied with weight loss and restrict their eating in order to stay thin and competitive. In fact, the female athlete who maintains low body fat often receives praise for her self-control and denial of appetite. Eventually she believes incorrectly that continued dieting (or disordered eating) will make her quicker, faster, and stronger. A dangerous side effect of the restricted eating and intense physical training, such as performed by runners and gymnasts, is amenorrhea; the disruption of the menstrual cycle can lead to loss of bone tissue and osteoporosis.

In 1999, the National Institutes of Health and the American Academy of Orthopaedic Surgeons held a joint seminar to discuss the triad problem and what to do about it. The U.S. Olympic Committee and the American College of Sports Medicine also conferred on the subject. In addition, the annual Women's Health Congress in 1999 spotlighted sports injuries and ailments among female athletes as an emerging women's health issue. *See also* Eating Disorders; Menstruation; Osteoporosis

Further Reading

American Academy of Orthopaedic Surgeons. "Female's Running Posture Can Cause ACL Injuries." Press Release (February 5, 1999).

Moeller, James L., M.D., and Mary M. Lamb, M.D. "Anterior Cruciate Ligament Injuries in Female Athletes: Why Are Women More Susceptible?" *The Physician and Sportsmedicine* (April 1997).

Villarosa, Linda. "Tri-Fold Ailment Stalks Female Athletes." *New York Times* (June 22, 1999).

Substance Abuse

See **Alcohol Abuse and Alcoholism; Drug Abuse and Addiction**

Super Moms

The term "super moms" became popular in the 1980s to describe mothers who attempted to do everything for their families: prepare meals; wash clothes; shop; work outside the home; take their children to ball games, music and art lessons, soccer and hockey practice, the circus, and countless other activities. Many were single mothers who took full responsibility for their households and childcare duties. As super moms become more and more overburdened with tasks, some report health problems related to stress, guilt, and fatigue, often failing to realize that they cannot reach the unattainable goal of being super human beings, "perfect" moms. Depression is frequently the result.

In the 1990s, "perfect" moms were labeled "soccer moms." The term usually refers to suburban women who left the workplace to care for their children and not only transport them to soccer games but also create well-rounded and enriched lives for their families. As in the 1980s, soccer moms attempt to help their children excel as athletes, students, and citizens.

Some family experts believe that the super-hyper mothers and their children of the 1980s, 1990s, and into the twenty-first century have become so stressed out trying to "have it all" that they risk physical and mental health problems. Mothers who work outside the home are especially vulnerable because, in general, they are the primary homemakers and caregivers. Although many more men today than in the past help out with household chores and childcare duties, working women constantly juggle household and job duties, and these super moms experience frustration and exhaustion. They often turn to self-help books and articles and Internet Web sites for information on how to find time for themselves and protect their own mental and physical health. *See also* Depression; Family Caregiving; Mental Illness

Surrogate Mother

A surrogate mother is a woman who agrees to allow her womb to be used to develop an embryo, which may be created from her egg or another woman's egg that is artificially inseminated in a laboratory. A surrogate mother carries a baby to birth and turns over the infant to the couple or single person who has contracted for her services. In some cases, women volunteer to be unpaid surrogates for relatives or friends who are unable to have children. In most situations, however, surrogacy is a paid service that agents, clinics, or surrogacy centers provide. These paid surrogacy arrangements as well as some volunteer services have prompted numerous legal, ethical, and religious questions.

Opponents of commercial surrogacy argue that the practice is degrading and is not much different from the time when it was common to buy and sell children. Another concern is whether women who become surrogates are being exploited, particularly when they are paid more than they earn annually from their jobs. One of the harshest criticisms of surrogacy is that the practice is like prostitution, paying for the use of a woman's body.

The rights of a surrogate mother have been widely debated since the well-publicized case of Mary Beth Whitehead in the late 1980s. Whitehead had signed an agreement with William and Elizabeth Stern of New Jersey to be artificially inseminated with Stern's sperm. After Whitehead gave birth to a girl, she did not want to give up the child. Although she turned the baby girl over to the Sterns, Whitehead asked to have the baby for a visit, then fled to Florida with the child, her husband, and their two children. The FBI found Whitehead and returned the child to the Sterns. In a court case that followed, the judge ruled that Whitehead had no parental rights to the child she had borne.

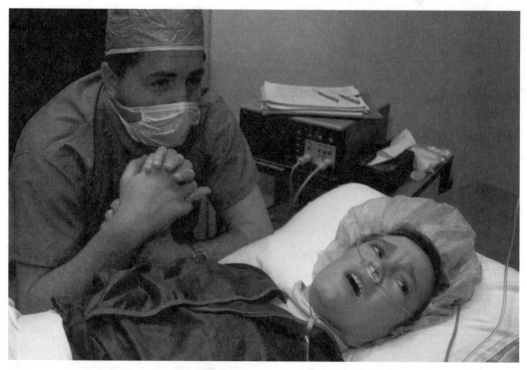

Woman having eggs retrieved in an attempt to have children with the help of a surrogate mother. ©Annie Griffiths Belt/CORBIS

Only a few states have laws regarding surrogacy, and debates over parental rights of surrogate mothers have continued. Some argue that laws should recognize the rights of women who are "gestational mothers," or women who carry to term an embryo developed from genetic material (the egg and sperm) of the intended parents. Usually, the surrogate relinquishes any rights to the child. But such a surrogate, some contend, is actually the birth mother since her womb provides the nourishment and protection needed for a growing fetus. According to this view, the birth mother should have a grace period in which to change her mind if she determines she cannot give up the child she brought to term.

Other issues regarding surrogacy focus on how children of such arrangements will fare. Some psychologists contend that young people may be traumatized by the notion that they have been produced and bought and sold like commodities. Others argue that children born through surrogacy arrangements will thrive in healthy families, just as adopted children do. Several surrogacy centers, such as Surrogate Mothers, Inc. (SMI) and The American Surrogacy Center (TASC) have created Internet Web sites designed to assist couples worldwide in building families through surrogacy. *See also* Artificial Insemination; Egg Donors

Further Reading

Gay, Kathlyn. *Pregnancy: Private Decisions, Public Debates.* New York: Franklin Watts, 1994.

Surrogate Mothers, Inc. home page. <http://www.surrogatemothers.com>.

The American Surrogacy Center home page <http://www.surrogacy.com>.

Sweatshops

The U.S. Department of Labor defines a sweatshop as a workplace that violates two or more of the most basic U.S. labor laws, including those prohibiting child labor or forced labor and those providing for the right to a safe and healthy workplace. Women make up 90 percent of sweatshop laborers, and companies that use sweatshop labor to increase their own profits exploit predominantly young women (ages 15 to 22). Many of these women are immigrants, who may not know their rights or do not have the power to bring about enforcement. In a global economy, American-based firms also contract with sweatshop owners or managers in countries where cheap labor is readily available to produce clothing, shoes, sports equipment, and other goods. Whether in the United States or other countries, sweatshops expose women to significant health hazards.

In the 1800s and early 1900s, sweatshops were cramped, New York tenements where immigrant women worked as seamstresses, usually with the help of their children. The word "sweatshop" referred to a subcontracting system in which the middlemen earned their profits from the margin between the amount they received for a contract and the amount they paid workers with whom they subcontracted. The margin was said to be "sweated" from the workers because they received minimal wages for excessive hours worked under unsanitary conditions.

Today sweatshops are common in the apparel industry and still exist in New York and other large cities like Los Angeles; but in various parts of the nation, sweatshops also include large, brightly lit factories along with hidden sites where people are forced to work in slave-like conditions. Female workers frequently are subjected to not only low wages or nonpayment of their wages, but also sexual harassment, verbal abuse, and physical punishment. In some reported cases, workers are only allowed two glasses of water and one bathroom break during a shift. Sweatshop operators are known for firing pregnant women in order to avoid paying maternity leave, or for forcing female workers to use birth control or to abort their pregnancies. Many workers also suffer from carpal tunnel syndrome or other hand and wrist injuries caused by repeated motions, such as hammering straps onto leather handbags or working in garment factories, poultry industries, or food-processing plants. In the electronics industry, women are subjected to toxic chemicals as well as repetitive motion injuries.

Media coverage of sweatshop conditions during the 1990s outraged the public. In 1995, for example, local and federal law enforcement agents conducted a raid on a sweatshop in El Monte, California, just east of Los Angeles, where immigrants were locked in an apartment complex surrounded by razor wire and worked for 69 cents an hour. Workers were threatened with rape and murder if they stopped working. After the raid, then-Labor Secretary Robert Reich launched a crusade against sweatshops, promoting a "No Sweat" label for goods produced without sweatshop labor.

A Stop Sweatshop campaign of UNITE (Union of Needletrades, Industrial and Textile Employees) has a six-point agenda, which includes working with members of Congress to pass the Stop Sweatshops Act. The law would hold manufacturers and retailers responsible for violations of labor standards in the contracting shops that produce their work. UNITE is also lobbying at the state and federal level for sufficient funds to enforce U.S. labor laws and protect workers' safety and job security.

Another effort to curtail the unhealthy and unsafe conditions of sweatshops is United Students Against Sweatshops (USAS), which began with a handful of students on university campuses in 1998. More than 100 chapters of USAS are now organized across the United States and Canada. Students are fighting for sweatshop-free labor conditions, women's rights, adequate safety and health standards, and workers' right to bargain collectively. They also are demanding that their school logos appear only on hats, T-shirts, sweatshirts, and other goods manufactured under good working conditions.

Other groups fighting for the elimination of sweatshops include the Feminist Majority Foundation and its Feminists Against Sweatshops campaign. Co-op America has established an Internet site called Sweatshops.org in its efforts to inform the public about sweatshop labor and also products made without extreme exploitation of workers. *See also* Abortion; Birth Control; Carpal Tunnel Syndrome; Sexual Harassment; *Women: Work and Health*

Further Reading

Blackman, Ann, Nichole Christian, and Alison Jones. "Campus Awakening: The Sweatshop Issue Has Galvanized College Activists." *Time* (April 12, 1999).

Capellaro, Jennie, "Students for Sweat-Free Sweatshirts." *The Progressive* (April 1999).

Hemphill, Thomas A. "The White House Apparel Industry Partnership Agreement: Will Self-Regulation Be Successful?" *Business and Society Review* (Summer 1999).

Ivins, Molly, and Fred Smith. "Do Consumer Boycotts Help the World's Poor?" (symposium) *Insight on the News* (November 29, 1999).

"Slaves of New York," *Time* (November 2, 1998).

T

Teenage Pregnancy and Childbearing

Teenage pregnancy and childbearing have been major social, religious, political, and economic issues in the United States for decades. Countless Americans have condemned "children having children," pointing to the fact that teenage childbearing frequently begets or perpetuates a cycle of poverty. Nevertheless, the United States leads all other industrialized nations in the rate of teenage pregnancies, 95 percent of which are unintended. Each year about one million teenage girls between ages 15 and 19 become pregnant; about half that number become mothers, while the rest obtain abortions or have miscarriages.

Teenage pregnancy can present significant physical and psychological health risks as well as economic concerns for the young women involved. Societal costs are high, too. Families started by adolescents account for the majority receiving public assistance—estimated at $15 to $20 billion annually. The average initial cost for a low birth weight infant is $20,000—about three times the cost for a normal birth, and total lifetime medical costs for a low birth weight infant average $400,000, according to the National Women's Health Informa-

tion Center of the U.S. Department of Health and Human Services.

One contributing factor to the high teenage pregnancy rate is the paucity of birth control information for teenagers and

Birth Rates for Teenagers by Age: United States, 1950–96

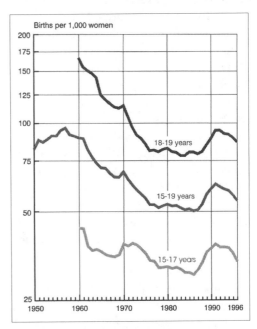

NOTE: Rates are plotted on a log scale.

Source: U.S. Centers for Disease Control and Prevention.

poor understanding of contraceptive devices. The Institute of Medicine's *Guide to Women's Health Issues* points out that

> Compared to Sweden, Canada, England and Wales, France, and the Netherlands, American teens make the least use of contraceptives, and when they do use them, they use the least effective kinds.... Countries that accept both the existence of teen sexuality and the need to provide effective protection against its likely outcome succeed much better than [the United States] in reducing teenage conception. (Benderly, 67)

Many religious groups, however, oppose efforts to educate teenagers about birth control. They view sexual activity outside of marriage as "sinful" and teenage pregnancy as morally repugnant. Therefore, religious leaders argue, encouraging the use of contraceptives among teenagers would be tantamount to condoning premarital sex.

In spite of resistance to sex education, health and social service agencies encourage distribution of information about the use of condoms as protection against the threat of sexually transmitted diseases (STDs), particularly the threat of human immunodeficiency virus (HIV) that causes AIDS. Some schools in major cities have set up school-based programs to distribute condoms, and many birth control experts are convinced that schools should also conduct sex education programs or classes that promote personal responsibility as a means to prevent teenage pregnancies. However, some researchers are pessimistic about changes in sexual behavior among teenagers, especially when media images frequently depict couples having sex and myriad advertising promotes sexual attractiveness.

Teenagers who become pregnant and give birth are faced with serious health problems. Generally pregnant teenagers are unable or unwilling (because of financial concerns or lack of knowledge) to seek prenatal care. Thus they are more likely than adult pregnant women to face such risks as anemia and complications stemming from poor nutrition.

> Because nutrition directly affects the health of mother and child, babies born to teenagers, particularly poor teenagers, may be in greater danger of long-term health and developmental problems. Adolescents often have poor eating habits and these are magnified among low-income teens...[and] their newborns suffer disproportionately from prematurity, low birth weight, and other conditions that require extensive—and expensive—hospital care. (Wymelenberg, 79)

Teenage mothers, especially those who are unmarried, also face the distinct possibility of being unable to provide for themselves and their families. Most will not finish high school, although as their children get older many return to school to complete their education and go on for advanced schooling or training. Because job opportunities are usually linked to a prospective employee's educational level, a limited education in most cases means limited income. As a result, many teenage mothers seek financial assistance from tax-funded federal and state welfare programs.

Since the 1980s, a variety of community groups, government agencies, health-care professionals, and youth organizations have been involved in efforts to encourage teenagers to delay childbearing until they have the maturity and financial means to rear their own children. Federal legislation has been part of this effort. The Personal Responsibility and Work Opportunity Reconciliation Act (PRWORA) of 1996 (the so-called welfare reform act), for example, includes special requirements for pregnant teenagers and mothers. To be eligible for financial assistance, unmarried mothers who are minors must live at home or in a setting with adult supervision and participate in educational and training activities. The law also requires the secretary of the U.S. Department of Health and Human Services to assure that pregnancy prevention programs are set up in communities across the United States.

In 1999, the Centers for Disease Control and Prevention (CDC) announced that teenage pregnancies and birth rates had dropped dramatically over a six-year period from 1991 to 1997, although the rates are not as low as in the mid-1980s. The birth rate among teenage girls between 15 and 17 years old fell 16 percent. "Particularly noteworthy has been the 21-percent decline in the rate of second births for teenagers who have had one child," states the CDC's report compiled by the National Center for Health Statistics of the National Vital Statistics System. Two major factors in the declining pregnancy and birth rates among teenagers are a decline in sexual activity and an increase in the use of birth control devices, especially condoms. Nevertheless, repeat pregnancies among teenagers are still a significant problem. Repeat births represent more than one in five births to teenagers, or approximately 110,000 births in 1998. These births are often closely spaced. "Almost one in three women whose first birth occurred before age 17 has a second birth within 24 months. The large majority of repeat births to teenagers—7 in 10—occur to those who are unmarried," noted the Alan Guttmacher Institute (AGI) in its June 2000 issue of *The Guttmacher Report on Public Policy.* The AGI recommends more federally supported programs that emphasize family planning for pregnant and parenting teenagers. *See also* Abortion; AIDS; Birth Control; National Women's Health Information Center; Sexually Transmitted Diseases; United States Department of Health and Human Services

Further Reading
Benderly, Beryl Lieff for the Institute of Medicine. *In Her Own Right: The Institute of Medicine's Guide to Women's Health Issues.* Washington, DC: National Academy Press, 1997.
Dailard, Cynthia. "Reviving Interest in Policies and Programs to Help Teens Prevent Repeat Births." *The Guttmacher Report on Public Policy* (June 2000). <http://www.agi-usa.org/pubs/journals/gr030301.html>.
Geronimus, Arline T. "Teenage Childbearing and Personal Responsibility: An Alternative View." *Political Science Quarterly* (Fall 1997).
Stolberg, Sheryl Gay. "U.S. Birth Rate at New Low as Teenage Pregnancy Falls." *New York Times* (April 29, 1999).
United States Department of Health and Human Services. "The Personal Responsibility and Work Opportunity Reconciliation Act of 1996." Fact Sheet (May 27, 1998).
Ventura, Stephanie J., T.J. Mathews, and Sally C. Curtin. *Declines in Teenage Birth Rates, 1991–97: National and State Patterns.* National Vital Statistics Reports. Hyattsville, MD: National Center for Health Statistics, 1998.
Wymelenberg, Suzanne for the Institute of Medicine. *Science and Babies Private Decisions, Public Dilemmas* Washington, DC: National Academy Press, 1990.

Tobacco Use

See Smoking

Toxic Shock Syndrome

Toxic Shock Syndrome (TSS) is a disease that is primarily associated with menstruating women who use highly absorbent tampons. Although TSS can affect anyone and may be caused by infections stemming from wounds, burns, or surgery, the syndrome was identified in the late 1970s when hundreds of American women between the ages of 15 and 19 began to exhibit a combination of flu-like symptoms, including sudden high fever, high blood pressure, rash, diarrhea, and vomiting. If not treated quickly with antibiotics, many of the women went into shock, suffered kidney failure, and died.

During the early 1980s several dozen women died from TSS, and the Institute of Medicine (IOM) formed a committee to study the problem and try to determine the cause. By the fall of 1980, writes Beryl Benderly for the IOM,

> Investigators had found a strong association between TSS, the bacterium Staphylococcus aureus (an organism already well-known as the culprit in a number of human diseases), and the use of tampons during menstruation, especially a superabsorbent brand known as Rely. The scientific evidence then available did not permit an IOM committee studying the outbreak to identify either the exact mechanism connecting these sanitary products to the disease or the reasons that the condition preferentially targeted young whites. It did conclude, however, that "a marked reduction in the number of cases would be expected in the absence of tampon use." (Benderly, 42)

The use of rolled material inserted into the vagina to absorb menstrual flow is a practice stemming from ancient Greek and Roman times when women wore wool devices internally. Manufactured cotton tampons appeared in the United States during the 1930s, primarily because of women's fashions. Body-hugging clothing of the time sometimes revealed the outlines of bulky sanitary napkins or folded cloth pads. Thus manufacturers responded to women's demand for an internal device to use as protection during menstrual periods.

Because of the low absorbency of cotton tampons, they do not pose the health risks of the high-absorbency synthetic materials fabricated during the 1970s. The high-absorbent tampons, specifically those made by Rely with polyester foam and carboxymethylcellulose, created conditions for the TSS bacteria to thrive and lead to staph infections. These materials are now banned, although some synthetic materials such as rayon are used in combination with cotton for the manufacture of some brands of tampons. Medical experts recommend all cotton tampons that do not produce the TSS bacteria, while "most major brands that contain synthetic materials increase the production of the bacteria—at least under laboratory conditions," according to a 1994 New York University Medical Center study. (Howard, 47)

Widespread publicity about TSS waned during the 1980s after the U.S. Food and Drug Administration (FDA) banned Rely products, and the U.S. Centers for Disease Control and Prevention stopped gathering information about the disease. As a result there are no exact statistics on the number of women today who are affected by TSS. However, the FDA estimates that, out of 100,000 menstruating women, 17 contract the disease annually. *See also* Menstruation

Further Reading

Benderly, Beryl Lieff. *In Her Own Right: The Institute of Medicine's Guide to Women's Health Issues.* Washington, DC: National Academy Press, 1997.

Hoffman, Eileen, M.D. *Our Health, Our Lives: A Revolutionary Approach to Total Health Care for Women.* New York: Simon & Schuster, 1995.

Howard, Beth. *Mind Your Body: A Sexual Health and Wellness Guide for Women.* New York: St. Martin's Press, 1998.

Planned Parenthood Federation of America. *The Planned Parenthood Women's Health Encyclopedia.* New York: Crown Trade Paperbacks, 1996.

U

United States Department of Health and Human Services

The United States Department of Health and Human Services (DHHS) is the federal government's principal agency for protecting the health of all Americans and providing essential human services. In January 2000, the DHHS launched *Healthy People 2010*, a guide for ways diverse groups and organizations can work to improve the nation's health.

Improving the health of all American women is a top priority at DHHS; a department statement declares that it "is committed to a comprehensive, science-based approach that will help address longstanding inequities in women's health." To meet this commitment, the department has increased funding for women's health research, services, and education. The DHHS requires that women be included in clinical research trials and that differences between men and women in cause, treatment, and prevention of disease be examined. Other actions include a major focus on women's health through the life cycle—adolescence, reproductive and middle years, and older women; efforts to eliminate barriers to health-care services for underserved American women; and endeavors to assure that women have equal access to senior positions in health and science careers.

In 1998, the Public Health Service Office on Women's Health established the National Women's Health Information Center, a combination Internet Web site and toll-free hotline that serves as a "one-stop shopping" resource for women's health information. The center can be reached at <http://www.4woman.gov> or (800) 994-WOMAN. Among other offices within the department is the Administration for Children and Families, Administration on Aging, Centers for Disease Control and Prevention, Food and Drug Administration, National Institutes of Health, and Substance Abuse and Mental Health Services Administration.

Because of the DHHS focus on women's health, Medicare coverage has been expanded for the more than 22 million elderly and disabled women who make up about 57 percent of the program's 39 million beneficiaries and more than 72 percent of those ages 85 and older. Medicare provides insurance benefits for mammograms, pap smears, colorectal cancer screening, bone mass measurement for women at risk for osteoporosis and other bone abnormalities, and diabetes self-management.

The DHHS also is attempting to correct the misperceptions about the need for mammography among older women. Even though breast cancer risk increases with age, more than one-third of women ages 65 and older are not as concerned about getting breast cancer as they were when they were younger, according to a study conducted by the National Cancer Institute (NCI) and the Health Care Financing Administration (HCFA). Additionally, only 57 percent of the nationally representative sample of 814 women ages 65 and older know they should have screening mammograms every one or two years. The DHHS has sponsored television public service announcements to encourage older women to get mammography screening and use Medicare coverage for mammography.

Besides serving older women, the DHHS also provides screening services for low-income and medically underserved women in all 50 states, six U.S. territories, the District of Columbia, and 12 American Indian/Alaska Native organizations through the Centers for Disease Control and Prevention's National Breast and Cervical Cancer Early Detection Program. The program has provided more than 2.2 million screenings since 1991, including over one million mammograms, with minority women making up nearly half of those screened.

Another major effort of the DHHS is to focus on six major areas of racial and ethnic disparities in health access: infant mortality; cancer screening and management; cardiovascular disease; diabetes; HIV infection/AIDS; and immunizations. These health issues affect a disproportionate number of African-American, Latina, Asian-American, and American Indian women compared to Anglo women.

Under the Violence Against Women Act of 1994, the DHHS administers various programs to protect women who have been or are in danger of being physically abused. In the late 1990s, the agency established a national toll-free domestic violence hotline (800-799-SAFE), more than tripled resources for battered women's shelters, and worked to raise awareness of domestic violence in the workplace and among health-care providers, along with other initiatives. *See also* African-American Women's Health; Asian-American Women's Health; Domestic Elderly Abuse; Domestic Violence; *Healthy People 2000* and *Healthy People 2010*; Latina Women's Health; Mammogram; Native American Women's Health; Osteoporosis; Pap Smear; Poor Women's Health Care; Violence Against Women Act of 1994

Further Reading

United States Department of Health and Human Services. "Medicare: Protecting Women's Health." Press Release (March 19, 1999).

United States Department of Health and Human Services. "Despite Increases in Mammography among Older Women, Misperceptions Persist." Press Release (October 20, 1999).

United States Department of Health and Human Services. "Preventing Violence Against Women." Fact Sheet (February 26, 1999).

United States Department of Health and Human Services, "Improving Women's Health." Fact Sheet (March 12, 1999).

United States Health Resources and Services Administration

The United States Health Resources and Services Administration (HRSA) is part of the U.S. Department of Health and Human Services. Its major responsibility is to provide national leadership to increase access to primary and preventive health care for those who are medically underserved. In fulfilling this role, HRSA attempts to ensure that its policies and programs reflect the health needs of women and girls, especially minorities and those who are most vulnerable.

HRSA's education and training activities, community-based health services, and research incorporate the unique needs of women and girls with a view that health is a life-span issue, and that race, ethnicity, culture, and socioeconomic factors along with other life experiences must be considered throughout policy and program development. HRSA supports a wide array of health education and training projects, a number of which help strengthen provider knowledge and skill in delivering high-quality, culturally competent health services to women. It increases access to prenatal care, immunizations, physical exams, and other preventive health care through its Health Centers Program, which includes Community and Migrant Health Centers, Health Care for the Homeless, and Health Care for Residents of Public Housing.

Community-based health services for women and girls are also provided by states with the assistance of Maternal and Child Health Services Block Grants. Girl Neighborhood Power! promotes messages about disease prevention and health promotion, and helps girls ages nine to 14 improve their family and community relationships. Health and dental care, treatment, and related support services are provided to women living with HIV/AIDS. In addition, more than half of HRSA-supported, nurse-managed clinics are focusing on domestic violence prevention and interventions. *See also* Adolescent Girls' Health; AIDS; Domestic Violence; Female Migrant/Seasonal Workers; Homeless Women; United States Department of Health and Human Services

Further Reading
Health Resources and Services Administration. <http://www.hrsa.gov>.

Urinary Incontinence

The involuntary loss or leakage of urine is called urinary incontinence. This condition, which has no cure but can be controlled, has social, psychological, and economic consequences for many Americans. Urinary incontinence affects all age groups and is particularly common in the elderly, although the normal aging process is not the cause of this condition. More than 13 million American adults, 85 percent of them women, suffer from urinary incontinence, creating a major health problem because it can lead to disability and dependency.

Urinary incontinence is related to numerous factors, such as chronic illness, urinary infections, and various medications. Women are likely to develop incontinence because of weakened pelvic muscles brought about by pregnancy and childbirth, or after the hormonal changes of menopause. The issue is exacerbated by the fact that only about half the people who suffer from the condition seek medical help. Many women will wait an average of eight years before seeking medical care for their incontinence symptoms, using menstrual and incontinence pads in the interim. These women cite embarrassment and an assumption that incontinence is a normal part of aging as the two primary reasons for the delay.

The National Institutes of Health developed a consensus statement about urinary incontinence in 1988, which declares:

Studies of women show that the condition is associated with depressive symptoms and leads to embarrassment about appearance and odor, although such reactions may be related more to illness than to incontinence. Excursions outside the home, social interactions with friends and family, and sexual activity may be restricted or avoided entirely in the presence of incontinence. Spouses and other intimates also may share the burden of this condition. A highly conservative estimate of the direct costs of caring for persons with incontinence of all ages in the community is $7 billion annually in the United States.

During the 1990s, the monetary costs of managing urinary incontinence were conservatively estimated at $10.3 billion annually. Added to this are the psychological and social burdens of urinary inconti-

nence that have not been adequately measured. *See also* Aging; Menopause; Pregnancy

Further Reading

Newman, Diane Kaschak, Mary K. Dzurinko (Contributor), and Ananias C. Diokno. *The Urinary Incontinence Sourcebook*. Lincolnwood, IL: NTC/ Contemporary Books, 1997.

"Overview: Urinary Incontinence in Adults, Clinical Practice Guideline Update." Agency for Health Care Policy and Research (March 1996). <http://www.ahcpr.gov/clinic/uiovervw.htm>.

V

Violence Against Women Act of 1994

The comprehensive federal law known as the Violence Against Women Act (VAWA) is included in the Violent Crime Control and Law Enforcement Act of 1994. Passage of the law was prompted by the fact that women were six times more likely than men to experience violence committed against them by an intimate, with devastating health, economic, and social consequences for women and their families. Under the law, which is administered by the Department of Health and Human Services (DHHS) and the Department of Justice, the federal government works in close coordination with state, tribal, and local law enforcement to combat domestic violence and violence against women, "combining tough new penalties with programs to prosecute offenders and assist women victims of violence." (HHS Fact Sheet) However, even though violence against women is a national problem, some legal scholars argued that the U.S. Congress exceeded its constitutional authority in passing the law.

The law provides funds to train prosecutors, police officers, and health and social services professionals in how to deal with and combat domestic violence. Federal appropriations (about $89 million in fiscal year 1999) also provide for a National Domestic Violence hotline, a nationwide, 24-hour, toll-free number (800-799-SAFE) for crisis intervention, counseling, and referral to emergency services and shelters if needed.

Battered women shelters and counseling services are supported with federal funding as is research into causes and effective community campaigns to reduce violence against women. "In addition, VAWA set new federal penalties for those who cross state lines to continue abuse of a spouse or partner, making interstate domestic abuse and harassment a federal offense. VAWA also made it unlawful for any person who is subject to a restraining order to possess ammunition or a firearm, requires states to honor protective orders issued in other states, and has given victims the right to mandatory restitution and the right to address the court at the time of sentencing." (HHS Fact Sheet)

In 1999, the U.S. Court of Appeals for the Fourth Circuit ruled in *Brzonkala v. Virginia Polytechnic Institute and State University* that the civil suit provisions (Section 13981) of the VAWA were unconstitutional. The case involved Christy

Brzonkala who brought suit against two fellow students at Virginia Polytechnic, alleging rape and charging that the men had violated her rights under the VAWA to be free of gender-based crimes of violence.

The purpose of Section 13981 of the VAWA is "to protect the civil rights of victims of gender motivated violence and to promote public safety, health, and activities affecting interstate commerce by establishing a Federal civil rights cause of action for victims of crimes of violence motivated by gender." Section 13981 enables victims to obtain compensation for the lost earnings, medical expenses, and other losses associated with gender-moti-

vated violence. But the court determined that Congress's power "to regulate commerce among the several states" and its power under the 14th Amendment to enforce the Equal Protection Clause are not applicable in VAWA. The case was appealed to the U.S. Supreme Court (*United States v. Morrison*), and in 2000 the High Court ruled that Section 13981 of the VAWA was unconstitutional. *See also* Domestic Violence

Further Reading
United States Department of Health and Human Services. "Preventing Violence Against Women." Fact Sheet (February 26, 1999).

W

Wald, Florence (1916–)

See **Hospice Care**

Weight Discrimination

Countless medical practitioners, drug makers, dieting and reducing industries, and advertisers insist that Americans, especially women, must be thin to be accepted in society and to be healthy; therefore, big women face prejudicial attitudes that result in what is called weight or size discrimination. Although obesity (excess body fat that damages health) has been linked to increased risk of diabetes, heart disease, some cancers, osteoarthritis, and other diseases, the health issue is used in many cases to justify discrimination against large women. They face social stigmas in employment, human relationships, health care, recreation, travel, and a host of other situations.

When seen only in terms of their weight, many large women pay physical, emotional, and financial costs. They may, for example, have been constantly urged since childhood to diet and lose weight (spending large sums of money in the process) when in fact research suggests that the human body has a genetically determined "set point" weight. If a person tries to lose weight, the body fights that effort by adjusting the rate at which calories are burned. When dieting does not bring the

Actress Camryn Manheim at Angel Awards in 1999, Project Angel Food, in Los Angeles. ©Lisa Rose/Globe Photos.

desired results, a young girl or woman may suffer from poor self-esteem, guilt, and other stress-related problems.

U.S. culture is so permeated with the notion that the "ideal" female body should be thin that many girls and women worry constantly about being fat, fearing their weight will bar them from good jobs or careers and prevent them from establishing or maintaining romantic relationships. Concern about "being fat" sometimes leads to eating disorders such as anorexia and bulimia among teenage and young adult women.

Weight discrimination and its accompanying physical and emotional health problems often stem from myths about fat people and society's prejudicial attitudes about what is or is not attractive. One common assumption that leads to weight discrimination is the belief that an overweight person could be thin if she had self-control: ate less and maintained a low-calorie diet. However, as Eileen Hoffman, M.D. states:

> Fat people diet more than thin people, and dieting itself can result in health risks. People who have dieted and then regained their weight have higher mortality rates than those who have never dieted and stayed at the same high weight.... Our society has medicalized obesity and unconditionally equated it with illness. This image is so deeply ingrained that it is hard for us to conceive of fat, healthy women. (Hoffman, 332–333)

Studies on whether weight loss is truly beneficial to a person's health have been ongoing for decades, but findings are contradictory. Some research shows that fat people who exercise regularly live as long as thin people, while other studies conclude that a person who is just 20 pounds over the accepted standard for her age and height risks deadly health problems.

Since the late 1960s, various advocacy groups and organizations have formed to combat weight discrimination and to educate the public about weight control issues, particularly the national obsession with being thin. Among these groups are the National Association to Advance Fat Acceptance (NAAFA), which publishes *Radiance Magazine* for large women and sponsors an annual No Diet Day; and Largesse, an international network that promotes "size esteem" and provides various resources including legal references on weight and size discrimination cases. Numerous Web sites and published references also cover weight discrimination issues and the problem of fruitlessly trying to obtain a "perfect" body image versus maintaining a healthy weight. *See also* Dieting and Diet Drugs; Eating Disorders; Obesity

Further Reading

Boston Women's Health Book Collective. *The New Our Bodies, Ourselves.* New York: Simon & Schuster, 1992.

Freedman, Rita. *Body Love: Learning to Like Our Looks and Ourselves.* New York, NY: Perennial Library/Harper Row, 1988.

Goodman, Charisse. *The Invisible Woman: Confronting Weight Prejudice in America.* Carlsbad, CA: Gürze Books, 1995.

Hoffman, Eileen, M.D. *Our Health, Our Lives: A Revolutionary Approach to Total Health Care for Women.* New York: Simon & Schuster, 1995.

Johnston, Joni E. *Appearance Obsession: Learning to Love the Way You Look.* Deerfield Beach, FL: Health Communications, 1994.

Wolf, Naomi. *The Beauty Myth: How Images of Beauty Are Used against Women.* New York, NY: William Morrow Company, 1991.

Zerbe, Katheryn. *The Body Betrayed.* Washington, DC: American Psychiatric Press, 1993.

Widowhood

Widowhood is a time of lifestyle changes and economic and social concerns for millions of American women. Many more American women than men have lost their spouses and are widowed—11 million women compared to 2.6 million men. According to U.S. government statistics, 1.3

A widow and her daughter-in-law place Easter flowers on the gravesite of the older woman's deceased husband. ©The Terry Wild Studio, Inc.

million African-American women are widows, and more than half—54 percent—ages 65 and older are widows.

Many women who have been part of traditional marriages for decades are not prepared to cope with the immediate adjustments needed in widowhood, which include possible changes in housing, family relations, finances, legal requirements, and social demands. Some women experience fear, apprehension, anxiety, and resentment; midlife and younger women especially may be overwhelmed by their loss and isolation.

In widowhood, women frequently find that they are not welcome in groups that are made up predominately of couples. Caroline Bird, the well-known author of books on women's issues, explained:

Widows have to contend with the embarrassment of becoming an object of pity. They report that people they've known for years cross the street to avoid them and the effort of the insincere sympathy they are expected to express. Acquaintances nervously tell them how well they look, and for the first time, the clergy may come to call. (Bird, 157–158)

The health of some women declines noticeably after the deaths of their spouses. Some research shows, for instance, that disorders and malnourishment may be linked to changes in eating habits. Food selection and mealtime enjoyment no longer seem important. Alcohol consumption, smoking, and the use of antidepressants and other medications may increase.

Because women typically live longer than men and tend to outlive their husbands, they are more likely than men to be living alone and in need of assistance for daily living. Thus many must face the issue of long-term care.

Numerous groups and countless books and articles address the issues of women and aging and those who are widowed. Organizations include AARP, the Older Women's League, and the National Center on Women and Aging at Brandeis University. Countless individual women have taken charge of their lives and in widowhood become political activists, women's health advocates, Peace Corps volunteers, writers, and painters. Others have pursued new careers and avocations. *See also* African-American Women's Health; Aging; Life Expectancy; National Center on Women and Aging; Older Women's League

Further Reading

Bird, Caroline. *Lives of Our Own: Secrets of Salty Old Women.* Boston and New York: Houghton Mifflin, 1995.

Brothers, Joyce. *Widowed.* New York: Ballantine, 1992.

Lief, Louise. "Alone Too Soon: Young Widows and Widowers Learn to Cope on Their Own." *U.S. News & World Report* (January 20, 1997).

Women's Institute for a Secure Retirement. "Widowhood: Why Women Need To Talk About This Issue." *WISERwoman Newsletter* (Fall 1999).

Women as Patients

Beginning in the early 1990s, dozens of books and numerous magazine and newspaper articles began to appear on the issue of women as patients. These books and articles described the kinds of sexist attitudes physicians have toward female patients and how doctors treat women who come to them for medical advice. The books and articles as well as a number of studies and surveys show that many American women are dissatisfied with their health care. This dissatisfaction is frequently related to the fact that many male doctors do not treat women's complaints as seriously as they do men's. Doctors, for instance, may misdiagnose serious health problems like heart disease and cancer as psychosomatic or imagined, as articles in the *Journal of the American Medical Association* have documented. In other instances, women are looked upon as if they are "a disease just waiting to be treated." (Hick, 11)

Normal events from childbirth to menopause to the aging process are "medicalized" as if they were disorders or ailments. As a result, women are frequently advised to undergo unnecessary surgeries ranging from cesarean sections to hysterectomies to plastic surgery. In addition, advocates for women's health accuse male practitioners of inadvertently or deliberately using women over the past few decades as guinea pigs for various medications and devices later found to be health hazards, such as diethylstilbestrol (DES) and other estrogen drugs, and devices like silicone breast implants and the intrauterine Dalkon Shield. The authors of *Outrageous Practices* noted

So fragmented and inconsistent is women's health care that some advocates are suggesting that women specifically seek out female physicians. Some women have gone even further. Tired of being ignored or humiliated by their male doctors, they are abandoning physicians altogether and seeking health services from nurse practitioners, who teach them how to be caretakers of their own bodies and who view patients as partners, not chattel. (Laurence and Weinhouse, 6)

Until about the beginning of the twentieth century, medical science believed that most if not all of women's health problems were related to ailments or diseases of the reproductive system. While that concept has slowly changed, an obstetrician-gynecologist is the primary care physician for up to two-thirds of American women. Yet these specialists are not particularly informed about diseases that affect women differently than men; if gynecologists are male, they are likely to exhibit gender bias and discrimination in regard to their patients. One physician, in his exposé of women's medical treatment and mistreatment, wrote:

It is common and acceptable among practicing [male] gynecologists to speak about their patients and their patients' bodies, sexual behavior, or medical problems indiscriminately, in terms that are demeaning and reflect a lack of simple kindness and respect. Some of this is learned in those years of specialty training, where exposure to higher-level residents and staff sets the standards of behavior...empathy, compassion, and sensitivity are seldom exhibited or taught along with...technical and intellectual skills. All the old male stereotypical thinking about women is reinforced in these males, who are supposed to be unique in their ability to relate to, understand, and care for women. (Smith, 27)

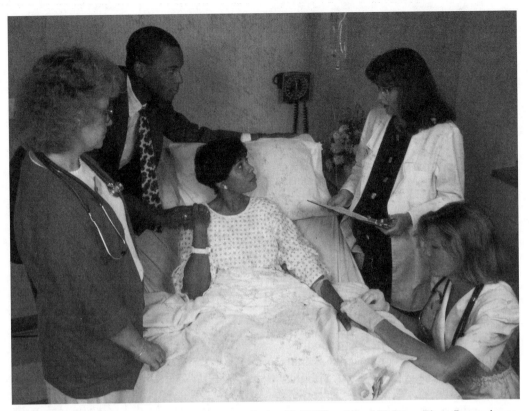

Hospital patient and her husband are visited by medical staff. ©Will and Deni McIntyre/Photo Researchers, Inc.

Women as patients and as the major consumers of health care in the United States are concerned about other issues that affect their well-being. These concerns include sexual offenses by male doctors against female patients, which are underreported and seldom penalized; the lack of affordable health care for poor women, especially for women of color and rural women; inadequate or no health insurance coverage for many low-income women; the increasing tendency among many doctors to be more concerned about the health of a woman's fetus than the pregnant woman's health and safety; and the growing number of elderly women who are being ignored, patronized, or undertreated for their health problems.

Nevertheless, steps have been taken since the early 1990s and are under way today to empower more and more women within the health-care system. They are being aided by an increasing number of women entering medical practice and biomedical research. "Women, both as physicians and as patients, are primed to transform the way medicine is practiced" in the United States and to make the health-care system more responsive to women. (Laurence and Weinhouse, 354) *See also* Breast Implants; Cesarean Section; Diethylstilbestrol; Gender-Biased Research and Treatment; Women in Medicine; Women in Science

Further Reading

Benderly, Beryl Lieff. *In Her Own Right: The Institute of Medicine's Guide to Women's Health Issues.* Washington, DC: National Academy Press, 1997.

Hicks, Karen M., ed. *Misdiagnosis: Woman as a Disease.* Allentown, PA: People's Medical Society, 1994.

Laurence, Leslie, and Beth Weinhouse. *Outrageous Practices: The Alarming Truth about How Medicine Mistreats Women.* New York: Fawcett Columbine/Ballantine, 1994.

Nechas, Eileen, and Denise Foley. *Unequal Treatment: What You Don't Know about How Women Are Mistreated by the Medical Community.* New York: Simon & Schuster, 1994.

Smith, John M. *Women and Doctors: A Physician's Explosive Account of Women's Medical Treatment—and Mistreatment—in America Today and What You Can Do about It.* New York: The Atlantic Press, 1992.

Women for Sobriety

Women for Sobriety (WFS) was founded in 1976 by Jean Kirkpatrick, who learned to overcome her own alcoholism through a self-help program that she developed. Although Kirkpatrick is convinced that many alcoholics have been helped by Alcoholics Anonymous (AA), her attempts to recover from her disease through their methods did not work. Because recovery rates for male alcoholics are higher than for female alcoholics in most programs, Kirkpatrick became convinced that women require a program different from the recovery programs that help men. She points out: "Although the physiological recovery from alcoholism is the same for both sexes, the psychological (emotional) needs for women are very different in recovery from those of the male alcoholic." Women have to deal with not only the disease of alcoholism but also lack of self-esteem, which can have such negative effects as guilt feelings, a sense of powerlessness, dependencies, depression, shame, and sometimes sexual dysfunction.

WFS is based on a self-help program called New Life, which includes 13 positive statements encouraging emotional and spiritual growth. These are:

1. I have a life-threatening problem that once had me.
   I now take charge of my life. I accept the responsibility.

2. Negative thoughts destroy only myself.
   My first conscious act must be to remove negativity from my life.

3. Happiness is a habit I will develop.
   Happiness is created, not waited for.

4. Problems bother me only to the degree I permit them to.
   I now better understand my problems and do not permit problems to overwhelm me.

5. I am what I think.
   I am a capable, competent, caring, compassionate woman.

6. Life can be ordinary or it can be great.
   Greatness is mine by a conscious effort.

7. Love can change the course of my world.
   Caring becomes all important.

8. The fundamental object of life is emotional and spiritual growth.
   Daily I put my life into a proper order, knowing which are the priorities.

9. The past is gone forever.
   No longer will I be victimized by the past, I am a new person.

10. All love given returns.
    I will learn to know that others love me.

11. Enthusiasm is my daily exercise.
    I treasure all moments of my new life.

12. I am a competent woman and have much to give life.
    This is what I am and I shall know it always.

13. I am responsible for myself and for my actions.
    I am in charge of my mind, my thoughts, and my life. (Women for Sobriety)

Women learn how to cope on their own with life's stresses without depending on alcohol. According to WFS, their program "is being used not only by women alcoholics in small self-help groups but also in hospitals, clinics, treatment facilities, women centers, and wherever alcoholics are being treated." (Women For Sobriety) *See also* Alcohol Abuse and Alcoholism

Further Reading

Kirkpatrick, Jean. *Turnabout: New Help For The Woman Alcoholic* New York: Doubleday, 1978.

Women for Sobriety. "Introducing Women for Sobriety." <http://www.womenforsobriety.org>.

Women in Medicine

The number of American women in medicine has been growing steadily over the past few decades; by 2010, women will account for 30 percent of the practicing physicians in the United States. Yet women in medicine and in medical schools still face discrimination in this male-dominated profession, an issue that can affect not only the health of women practicing medicine but also the health of women and men who prefer their advice.

Women have made great strides since 1849 when Elizabeth Blackwell overcame numerous obstacles and discrimination to become the first woman to earn her medical degree. Later, Blackwell founded a Women's Medical College. She was followed by hundreds of pioneer women in medicine and dentistry during the late 1800s and early 1900s. Mary E. Walker, for example, was a physician in the Civil War. She earned the Congressional Medal of Honor in 1865, but it was rescinded in 1917, perhaps because of her activism in the woman's suffrage movement. The U.S. Congress reinstated the medal posthumously in 1977.

Mary E. Britton was the first African-American woman to practice as a physician, in Lexington, Kentucky, during the late 1870s. Georgia Dwelle Rooks, who received a medical degree from Meharry Medical College in 1904, founded the first obstetric hospital for black women in Atlanta, Georgia. Emeline Roberts Jones (1836–1916) was the first female dentist in America, learning her profession while working with her dentist husband and carrying on the practice after his death in 1864 until 1915.

Elizabeth Blackwell. Courtesy of the National Library of Medicine

Well-known women in medicine today include Bernadine Healy, the first female director of the National Institutes of Health (now head of the American Red Cross); Susan M. Love, breast-cancer specialist; Helen Caldicott, a pediatrician who interrupted her practice to educate the public about the medical dangers of the nuclear age; Antonia Novello, former surgeon general of the United States; and many more.

Women physicians are in great demand, primarily because an increasing number of patients (women in particular) prefer them and consider them to be more caring and less autocratic than male doctors. Nevertheless, even as women make an impact on the practice of medicine, they frequently have to deal with the same issues that confront other career women. For instance, in a study published in a 1998 issue of *Archives of Internal Medicine,* nearly half of the 4,501 women physicians surveyed reported that they were subjected to gender-based harassment, "generally interpreted as related to being female in a traditionally male environment, without having a sexual or physical component." More than one-third suffered sexual harassment, unwanted physical or verbal sexual attention. Most of the reported instances of harassment occurred while the women were medical students, interns, or residents. The study concluded that

> Despite strong statements against harassment and gender discrimination in the medical literature, harassment experiences are still common in the training sites where the medical community's values are instilled. As physicians must update their understanding of appropriate practice for patient care, they must also update appropriate practice for professional interactions. Our data suggest that there has been and remains a substantial divide between what many women and some men consider acceptable professional interactions, and this could have considerable professional and human consequences. (Frank, Brogan, and Schiffman)

Women in medicine also earn less than men—an average of about $155,590 annually compared to more than $273,690 per year for male doctors. One reason for the disparity is that women are still the primary family caregivers and household managers, and many female physicians, like other career women, try to balance their home lives with their professions. They may opt to work part time rather than full time by forming practices with other female physicians. Or they may choose to work for medical practices operated by managed-care firms, giving up higher salaries for "an office life that is closer to 9 to 5," which, as the *New York Times* reported, was "virtually unheard of in medicine" until recently. The *Times* report pointed to a Commonwealth Fund study, which

found that 25 percent of female doctors who were surveyed said that they worked

fewer than 40 hours a week, compared with 12 percent of male doctors. And 17 percent of female doctors said they worked 30 hours a week or fewer, compared with only 8 percent of males... while this kind of work has become a welcome option for some doctors looking for more balanced lives, experts say that it has created a "pink-collar" level of medicine—in which more women are concentrated in the lowest-paying, least prestigious specialties. (Steinhauer)

Yet women also are taking positions in medicine that do not necessarily involve caring for patients. Some are working as both lawyers and doctors in medical examiner's offices. They are financial advisors to health-care companies, medical ethicists, medical writers, or professors of medicine, or they have successful careers in other aspects of medicine. A small percentage are involved in dual careers. An example is Nancy Snyderman, M.D., who not only practices medicine in San Francisco, California, but also is ABC-TV's medical correspondent and writes monthly medical columns for several major magazines. *See also* Family Caregiving; Novello, Antonia; Sexual Harassment; Women in Science

Further Reading

Eisenberg, Anne. "Female M.D.'s More Open with Options, Patients Say." *New York Times* (August 17, 1999).

Frank, Erica, Donna Brogan, and Melissa Schiffman. "Prevalence and Correlates of Harassment among U.S. Women Physicians." *Archives of Internal Medicine* (February 23, 1998).

Snyder, Charles M. *Dr. Mary Walker—"The Little Lady in Pants."* New York: Arno Press, 1974.

Steinhauer, Jennifer. "For Women in Medicine, a Road to Compromise, Not Perks." *New York Times* (March 1, 1999).

Women in Prison

Women make up the fastest-growing prison population in the United States. Approximately 90,000 women, most of them mothers, are incarcerated in the United States on any given day, primarily for drug violations and economic crimes such as credit card fraud. Many women in prison are victims of domestic violence; about 4,000 women are serving sentences for killing husbands, ex-husbands, or boyfriends, often because of physical abuse.

Women in prison must cope with major health problems, ranging from AIDS to physical and sexual abuse by guards or other correctional facility employees. In 1996 Human Rights Watch conducted a prison study and reported that

> being a woman prisoner in U.S. state prisons can be a terrifying experience. If you are sexually abused, you cannot escape from your abuser. Grievance or investigatory procedures, where they exist, are often ineffectual, and correctional employees continue to engage in abuse

because they believe they will rarely be held accountable, administratively or criminally. Few people outside the prison walls know what is going on or care if they do know. Fewer still do anything to address the problem.

Another major issue for women in prison is child custody. Many incarcerated mothers lose custody of their children, sometimes forever. Pregnant women, who comprise six percent of female prisoners, are usually separated from their children right after giving birth.

Most states have no provisions for keeping babies and their imprisoned mothers united; after a woman gives birth, she sees her baby for only a day and then the infant is turned over to a relative for care, placed in a foster home, or released for adoption. Some states "are experimenting with alternatives to prison, such as halfway houses where female offenders can serve

A prison guard observes inmates moving from one area to another at the Broward County Correctional Institute for Women. ©Bill Gentile/CORBIS.

their time while raising their babies." (Tomaso)

One program in New York to help women in prison and their children is under the direction of Sister Elaine Roulet, founder and executive director of Providence House, which is affiliated with Catholic Charities. Providence House is a temporary home and shelter for women just released from prison, homeless women, and battered women. Sister Elaine is also in charge of the Children's Center at Bedford Hills Correctional Center in Bedford Hills, New York. The facility includes a parenting program, children's playroom, and nursery, where babies born in prison are allowed to stay for up to one year and mothers are able to be with their children.

Health care for women in prison is, like all prison medical care, inadequate. Prison health-care systems were created for men; thus routine gynecological care, such as pap smears, breast exams, and mammograms, is extremely rare in prisons. As a research brief for the U.S. Department of Justice notes:

> Women offenders have needs different from those of men, stemming in part from their disproportionate victimization from sexual or physical abuse and their responsibility for children. They are also more likely to be addicted to drugs and to have mental illnesses. Many states and jail jurisdictions, particularly those with small female offender populations, have little special provision, either in management or programming, for meeting the needs of women.

Economic discrimination and racism are other issues affecting female prisoners, who are overwhelmingly poor and disproportionately African-Americans. African-American women, for example, are twice as likely to be convicted of killing their abusive husbands than are white women. They also receive longer sentences and higher fines than do white women for the same crimes. *See also* AIDS; African-American Women's Health; Domestic Violence; Poor Women's Health Care; Rape and Sexual Assault

Further Reading

Morash, Merry, Timothy S. Bynum, and Barbara A. Koons. "Women Offenders: Programming Needs and Promising Approaches." Research Brief, U.S. Department of Justice Office of Justice Programs, National Institute of Justice (August 1998).
"Sexual Abuse of Women in U.S. State Prisons." *Human Rights Watch* (December 1996).
Tomaso, Bruce. "Birth behind Bars." *Dallas Morning News* (February 21, 1999).

Women in Science

Across the United States in recent years there has been a major thrust to increase the number of women in science. This focus on women in science is because through the centuries they have often been overlooked or dismissed as insignificant. Yet from the time of ancient Greece to the present day, women have had an impact on many science fields, ranging from agronomy to women's health, from biology to zoology. American women in science include diverse individuals such as anthropologist Margaret Mead; environmentalist Rachel Carson; and medical researcher and physicist Rosalyn Sussman Yalow, who shared a Nobel Prize with Solomon A. Berson for together developing radioimmunoassay, a technique to detect minute substances in plasma and other bodily tissues.

Other examples of women in science include Mary Whiton Calkins, Nettie Stevens, and Alice Hamilton. Calkins was a pioneer during the late 1800s and early 1900s in psychology, founder of the psychology department at Wellesley College, and the first female president of both the American Psychological Association, in 1905, and the American Philosophical Association, in 1918. Also a nineteenth century pioneer, biologist Nettie Stevens

Rosalyn Sussman Yalow. AIP Emilio Segrè Visual Archives, Physics Today Collection.

found that the X and Y chromosomes determine gender. During the early 1900s, Alice Hamilton founded occupational medicine and was the first woman professor at Harvard Medical School.

Czechoslovakian-born Gerty Cori and her husband, Carl, were biochemists who studied malignant diseases at the New York State Institute and became known for the "Cori Ester," or the isolation of the glucose compound; they won the Nobel Prize in Chemistry in 1947. A 1983 Nobel Prize winner, geneticist Barbara McClintock showed that genes could transpose within chromosomes. In recent years, microbiologist Dorothy McClendon coordinated microbial research for the U.S. Army Tank Automotive Command in Warren, Michigan, developing methods to prevent contamination of fuel supplies and materiel.

During the late 1980s and throughout the 1990s and early 21st century, the lack of information about women in science prompted the publication of numerous biographies and encyclopedias with biographical sketches of hundreds of women in various scientific fields. Internet Web sites also began to appear with biographies on women in science. These Web sites are continually being modified with additional postings. *See also* Hamilton, Alice; Women in Medicine

Further Reading

Arnold, Lois Barber. *Four Lives in Science: Women's Education in the Nineteenth Century.* New York: Schocken Books, 1984.

Bailey, Martha J. *American Women in Science: A Biographical Dictionary.* Santa Barbara, CA: ABC-CLIO, 1994.

Four Thousand Years of Women in Science. <http://crux.astr.ua.edu/4000WS/4000WS.html>.

Hamilton, Alice. *Exploring the Dangerous Trades: The Autobiography of Alice Hamilton, M.D.* Boston: Little, Brown and Company, 1943.

Humphreys, Sheila M., ed. *Women and Minorities in Science: Strategies for Increasing Participation.* Boulder, CO: Westview Press for the American Association for the Advancement of Science, 1982.

Keller, E. E. *A Feeling for the Organism. The Life and Work of Barbara McClintock.* San Francisco: Freeman, 1983.

McGrayne, Sharon Bertsch. *Nobel Prize Women in Science: Their Lives, Struggles, and Momentous Discoveries.* Secaucus, NJ: Carol Publishing Group, 1993.

Shearer, Benjamin F., and Barbara S. Shearer, eds. *Notable Women in the Life Sciences: A Biographical Dictionary.* Westport, CT: Greenwood Press, 1996.

The Faces of Science: African-Americans in the Sciences. Louisiana State University Libraries, Baton Rouge, Louisiana. <http://www.lib.lsu.edu/lib/chem/display/faces.html>.

"Women Living Long, Living Well"

"Women Living Long, Living Well" (WLLLW) is the theme of a framework proposed in January 1999 by the U.S. Department of Health and Human Services (DHHS) and the U.S. Public Health Service's Coordinating Committee on Women's Health. The framework provides guidelines for articulating, developing, and implementing women's health research, services, and education throughout DHHS; its goals, which derive from the national objectives established by the U.S. Public Health Service's *Healthy People 2000* and *Healthy People 2010,* address the major causes of death and disability among American women of all racial, ethnic, and socioeconomic backgrounds. They focus in particular on the behavioral elements of risk while acknowledging the complexity introduced by genetic or environmental risks, which individuals often cannot control. Explaining behavioral elements, the DHHS notes:

Overall, an individual's behavior may surpass family history or genetic risks in their importance to living a long and healthy life. Strong evidence suggests that critical elements of a healthy lifestyle are physical activity, adequate nutrition, personal safety, mental health, and the avoidance of tobacco use. Evolving research on the relationship between, and influences on, behavior and health outcomes suggests a need for innovative health-enhancing efforts that engage children, youth, and adults often in gender-specific ways. At the same time, as knowledge about the human genome develops over the next decade, a clearer picture of genetic risks for morbidity will emerge. For their own health and because they are likely to remain the primary care givers of their families, women will need a better understanding of what these risks mean, when it is appropriate to be tested, and how to treat or mitigate the effects of a genetic risk factor. Behavioral and lifestyle factors are likely to remain significant targets of intervention in modulating some genetic risks.

As women live longer, they should be able to delay if not entirely avoid the onset of chronic conditions once thought to be the inevitable consequences of aging. These conditions include osteoporosis, arthritis, urinary incontinence, heart failure, hypertension, and diabetes. These conditions significantly affect individuals' ability to participate in activities of daily living. Among women ages 65 to 85, at least 27 percent suffer from two chronic diseases, and 24 percent suffer from three or more. Persons at any age with more than one chronic condition report the highest number of days of activity limitation, suggesting potential economic consequences as assistance is required to accomplish household or personal tasks, and time is diverted from either employment or leisure activities.

DHHS representatives convened sessions around the United States and in Puerto Rico in early 1999 to discuss the framework of "Women Living Long, Living Well" and to gather input on women's health needs and priorities. These major concerns developed from the sessions:

- Women's health must be addressed holistically and throughout the life span.
- Women's health does not begin and end with childbearing. Lifelong good health begins with early education on healthy behaviors, nutrition, exercise, and self-esteem development.
- Lack of universal and affordable health insurance is a major barrier to preventive and comprehensive health care for women.

Information on WLLLW and *Healthy People 2000* and *Healthy People 2010* is available by telephone from the National Women's Health Information Center (800-994-WOMAN) or on the Internet <http://www.4woman. gov>. *See also* Aging; Cardiovascular Diseases; *Healthy People 2000* and *Healthy People 2010*; Nutritional Factors; Osteoporosis; United States Department of Health and Human Services

Women with Disabilities

Women with disabilities are defined in a variety of ways but generally include women with physical, neurological, hearing, speech, and visual impairments as well as women with psychiatric, learning, and developmental disabilities. One issue that women with disabilities face is that they are seldom seen in traditional women's roles as nurturers, mothers, wives, homemakers, and lovers. Although many American women do not view marriage or traditional female roles as desirable for themselves, "non-disabled women are more likely than women with disabilities to have...[choices] between traditional and nontraditional life-styles. Women with disabilities rarely have the same options and their access to even the most traditional female roles is very restricted." (Traustadottir)

Approximately 26 percent of the more than 28 million women with disabilities live in rural areas in the United States. This population group faces many barriers to independent living and improved health, such as poverty, limited employment opportunities, lack of access to health care (including major physical obstacles to breast cancer screening), secondary health problems (in addition to their disabilities), and physical and emotional abuse. These deterrents may be more pronounced in ru-

Disability Status, All Ages, by Race/Ethnicity and Sex, 1991–92 (Numbers in thousands)

| Race/Gender | Total | | With a Disability | | | | | |
| | | | Number | | Percent | | With a Severe Disability | |
							Number	Percent
All	251,796	---	48,936	---	19.4	---	24,117	---	9.6	---
Male	122,692	---	22,916	---	18.7	---	9,929	---	8.1	---
Female	129,104	---	26,020	---	20.2	---	14,187	---	11.0	---
White	210,873	---	41,521	---	19.7	---	19,736	---	9.4	---
Male	103,287	---	19,731	---	19.1	---	8,123	---	7.9	---
Female	107,586	---	21,791	---	20.3	---	11,613	---	10.8	---
Black	31,420	---	6,277	---	20.0	---	3,836	---	12.2	---
Male	14,764	---	2,655	---	18.0	---	1,582	---	10.7	---
Female	16,656	---	3,622	---	21.7	---	2,253	---	13.5	---
Native American	1,649	---	361	---	21.9	---	162	---	9.8	---
Male	852	---	187	---	21.9	---	76	---	9.0	---
Female	797	---	174	---	21.8	---	85	---	10.7	---
Asian/Pacific Islander	7,855	---	777	---	9.9	---	384	---	4.9	---
Male	3,789	---	343	---	9.1	---	148	---	3.9	---
Female	4,066	---	434	---	10.7	---	236	---	5.8	---
Hispanic Origin*	21,905	---	3,343	---	15.3	---	1,838	---	8.4	---
Male	10,957	---	1,568	---	14.3	---	756	---	6.9	---
Female	10,948	---	1,775	---	16.2	---	1,082	---	9.9	---
ALL LISTINGS	---	---	---	---	---	---	---	---	---	---

* Hispanic Origin may include people of any race.

Source: McNeil, John M., Americans With Disabilities: 1991–92, U.S. Bureau of the Census, Current Population P79-33.

ral areas because of isolation and lower levels of education.

In the general population, women have a higher rate of disability than men, and except for Native Americans this difference prevails within each racial or ethnic group. The National Women's Health Information Center points out that

> Minority women with disabilities often face "triple jeopardy:" discrimination on the basis of race, gender, and disability.... As minorities, economic, social, and cultural factors can negatively affect their health. Disparities in educational resources, disproportionately low-wage jobs, and higher unemployment rates typically found in some minority groups are also barriers to high-quality, affordable, and accessible health care. In addition to all these challenges, these minority women must also cope with the difficulties presented by their disabilities.

Most women with disabilities in the United States face health concerns that are not well understood by the general public or the medical community. For example, symptoms of a disease may be disguised by a disability, and standard treatments for various health problems may not be appropriate for women with disabilities. In addition, women with disabilities find it difficult to obtain good information about health care when they are homebound or face financial constraints. Even those who are able to search for information often cannot find resources that address their special needs.

While research over the past decade has been conducted on numerous health issues affecting women in general and women in minority groups, women with disabilities have not been included in most studies. This is particularly true of studies conducted on violence against women. According to the Center for Research on Women with Disabilities (CROWD) at Baylor University,

> The literature in the disability arena has focused mostly on abuse of developmentally disabled children. A few studies have looked at the situation of women with disabilities; however, concepts are not well defined and the samples mix children and adults, and include the full spectrum of mental, sensory, and physical disabilities. Further, we found that the system of programs for battered women was only beginning to incorporate the need for accessibility for women with disabilities, and the system of disability-related services was almost totally unprepared to deal with issues of abuse. (Nosek, et al., National Study)

For women both with and without disabilities, the most common perpetrators of abuse are husbands and parents. Abuse may include withholding needed equipment like wheelchairs and braces, and refusing to provide medications, transportation, or essential assistance with personal tasks, such as dressing or getting out of bed. In cases of emotional and sexual abuse of women with disabilities, the perpetrator is likely to be an attendant or health-care worker.

Women with disabilities frequently are unable to escape abusive situations because programs to help abused and battered women are not accessible. Buildings and other facilities may not comply with the Americans with Disabilities Act, which requires that physical barriers to public accommodations, transportation, and communication be removed. Battered women shelters often lack interpreter services for deaf women and are unable to help women who need assistance with medications and daily self-care. In 1998 the U.S. Congress passed the Crime Victims with Disabilities Awareness Act, "To increase public awareness of the plight of victims of crime with developmental disabilities, to collect data to measure the magnitude of the problem, and to develop strategies to address the safety and justice needs of victims of crime with developmental disabilities."

Efforts to focus attention on the many health issues facing women with disabilities include conferences such as the one held in San Antonio, Texas: "Promoting the Health and Wellness of Women with Disabilities." The four-day event in the summer of 1999 was sponsored by a variety of organizations, including the Centers for Disease Control and Prevention's Office of Women's Health, the World Institute on Disability, and the Ohio Women with Disabilities Network. Such topics as pregnancy, parenting, menopause, domestic violence, HIV/AIDS, aging with disability, and managed care were discussed.

Other institutions working to improve the lives of women with disabilities include the Rural Institute on Disabilities at the University of Montana; the Center on Human Policy at Syracuse (New York) University; Breast Health Access for Women with Disabilities in Berkeley, California; Breast Health for Women with Physical Disabilities at the Albert Einstein Medical Center's Marion-Louise Saltzman Women's Center in Philadelphia, Pennsylvania; and the National Institute on Disability and Rehabilitation Research. *See also* Aging; AIDS; Breast Cancer; Domestic Violence; National Women's Health Information Center; Menopause; Pregnancy

Further Reading

Bradsher, Julia E. "Disability among Racial and Ethnic Groups." Disability Statistics Abstract, Number 10. University of California, San Francisco: Disability Statistics Center, January 1996. <http://128.218.183.95/UCSF/pdf/ABSTRACT10.pdf>

Nosek, Margaret A., Diana H. Rintala, Mary Ellen Young, Catherine Clubb Foley, Carol Howland, Gail F. Chanpong, Don Rossi, Jama Bennett, and Kathy Meroney. *National Study of Women with Physical Disabilities*. Houston: Center for Research on Women with Disabilities, 1997.

Szalda-Petree, Ann, Tom Seekins, and Bill Innes. "Women with Disabilities: Employment, Income, and Health." Research and Training Center on Rural Rehabilitation Services. RURALfacts (June 1999). <http://ruralinstitute.umt.edu/rtcrural/RuDis/DisWomenFact.htm>.

Traustadottir, Rannveig. *Women with Disabilities: Issues, Resources, Connections*. Rev. and updated by Perri Harris. Syracuse, NY: Research and Training Center on Community Integration, Center on Human Policy, Division of Special Education and Rehabilitation, Syracuse University, 1997.

Women: Work and Health

Working women's health and well-being were the focus of *Women: Work and Health*, a report issued in 1997 by the U.S. Department of Health and Human Services (DHHS). The report compiles data on the more than 60 million women who are part of the American labor force. It also describes the socio-demographics, household characteristics, and health of women according to workforce status and job conditions, with comparative data for men.

Basic statistics in the report help assess the health needs of working women. The report includes chapters on workplace characteristics; health effects attributed to work—such as work injuries, illnesses, and fatalities; health status as it affects work; knowledge of health risks and behaviors; and worksite health-promotion programs and health-related employee benefits.

Although women do not have as high a rate of injuries on the job as men do, they equal men in job-related injuries affecting the back. Several million women suffer from this pain. More than half of the women employed in service or blue-collar occupations and almost half of the working black women attributed their back pain to activities on the job.

Yet some employers are attempting to provide programs geared toward improving workers' health. Analysts found that at worksites with 750 or more employees, 40 percent of the employers offered female workers prenatal education and weight control information. Cancer education was offered by some employers. DHSS noted that "The employer is an important source of private health insurance; 73 percent of working women and 71 percent of working men cited the employer as the source of insurance.... Three-quarters of the working women had the private insurance paid in full or in part by the employer or union." *See also* Working Women

Further Reading
Wagener, D.K., J. Walstedt, L. Jenkins, et al. *Women: Work and Health.* Hyattsville, MD: U.S. Department of Health and Human Services, Centers for Disease Control and Prevention, National Center for Health Statistics, December 1997. <http://www.cdc.gov/nchswww>.

Women-Only Health Clubs

Although health and fitness clubs catering to females only have existed for decades, controversy over women-only health clubs in the United States gained public attention during the late 1990s when the legality of these facilities was challenged in several states. Men have charged that such health clubs are discriminatory. But in 1998, a Massachusetts law protecting single-gender health clubs was passed.

Women have long fought for the right to equal access to voting, higher education, the military, and employment opportunities, but the issue of excluding men from female health and fitness clubs has been supported by women participants who charge that they will be subjected to sexual harassment and will be extremely uncomfortable if men are around. The International Health, Racquet & Sportsclub Association (IHRSA), which supports women-only health clubs, issued a position statement that begins with an emphasis on privacy concerns:

Women-only clubs should be allowed to exclude men from membership and employment because there is a legitimate gender-based privacy interest that needs to be protected and there is no overriding public policy that necessitates the inclusion of men in these types of clubs.

Courts and legislatures have recognized certain settings, including rest rooms, shower rooms and changing rooms, in which gender-based discrimination in public places is acceptable because there is a compelling and overriding privacy issue involved. This same privacy issue is involved in women-only health clubs. Court cases involving the privacy interest of women-only club members have affirmed this privacy right.

The privacy issue stems from the unique setting of a health club. In the course of normal business, members expose parts of their body about which they are very sensitive, focus on parts of their body which need improvement, wear revealing attire, assume awkward and compromising positions, move themselves in a manner which would be embarrassing to them if men were present, and are measured and touched by instructors.

The right to privacy in locker rooms, shower rooms, bathrooms and changing rooms is well established in the courts. However, the privacy interest is not limited to those situations where there is nudity or touching of "intimate areas." The privacy interest is also protected in situations involving a person's body, whether they are dressed or undressed.

In addition, there is no public policy interest that would make admitting men necessary. In this setting, members' privacy interests are entitled to protection under the law and override laws meant to eliminate discrimination based on gender.

The IHRSA contends that most members prefer all-female environments and would discontinue their memberships if the clubs became coed. In addition, IHRSA's policy states:

Health clubs, unlike country clubs, are purely health, recreation and sports clubs. They are not social in nature and are not places where business networking takes place. Therefore, there is no economic harm in excluding men from women-only health clubs.

Yet traditional women's rights organizations such as the National Organization of Women (NOW) oppose women-only health clubs, even though in the short run they benefit women. NOW and other groups insist that laws passed to protect women-only health clubs essentially legalize discrimination based on gender. Some women's rights activists contend that all public facilities need to work harder to prevent sexual harassment and other assaults against women. *See also* Sexual Harassment; Women's Fitness

Further Reading

Associated Press. "Women-Only Health Clubs Protected under New Massachusetts Law" (February 6, 1998).
International Health, Racquet & Sportsclub Association. "Issues Affecting IHRSA Clubs" <http://www.ihrsa.org/i_wonly.html>.
McLaughlin, Abe. "Women's Rights Take New Twist." *The Christian Science Monitor* (February 6, 1998).

Women's Fitness

The emphasis on women's fitness in the United States is part of a nationwide movement that began about the 1980s, and has increased since then as numerous medical experts and federal agencies such as the U.S. Department of Health and Human Services (DHHS) have emphasized that staying physically fit is as significant a health issue as being free of ailments and chronic disease. Women in sports and the military have always taken part in fitness programs, but today countless other women also are taking responsibility for their own health through exercise programs and changes in dietary patterns.

Woman working out in weight room. ©Marc Romanelli/The Image Bank.

Physical fitness is also a health issue in the workplace, where employers, insurance companies, and others offer physical fitness programs for both women and men to lower health-care costs. A Canadian study found that

Enthusiastic participation in work-site wellness programs can yield a variety of health benefits: decreases in body fat; increases in aerobic power, muscle strength, and flexibility; enhanced mood state; and reduced medical insurance claims, with associated decreases in absenteeism and increases in productivity. However, only a minority of employees participate in work-site wellness programs, and even fewer have the enthusiasm needed to realize health benefits. Neither program participation nor wellness response rises in direct proportion to the capital invested in wellness personnel, programs, facilities, and equipment.

It seems that the most effective—and certainly most cost-effective—tactic is to provide a moderately well-equipped facility coupled with an active outreach to nonparticipating employees, one-to-one counseling, and a corporate environment that encourages a healthy lifestyle. The optimal approach probably is to supplement a simple exercise facility with optional program modules addressing such issues as diet, weight loss, cholesterol reduction, smoking withdrawal, substance abuse, and stress reduction. Nevertheless, the development of wellness programs that will sustain the involvement of the majority of employees is a continuing research challenge. (Shephard)

Women's fitness programs abound in the United States and include centers and health clubs with treadmills, stationary bicycles, stairclimbers, weight-lifting and other exercise equipment, and nutritional programs. One aspect of female physical fitness that has created some concern is bodybuilding. A small study by Massachusetts researchers found that "Women who spend 5 days or more per week at the gym lifting weights often have eating disorders and a distorted perception of their own body...[and] also may abuse steroids, an action more commonly associated with male bodybuilders." (Reuters)

Nevertheless, the President's Council on Physical Fitness and Sports stresses the importance of female participation in physical activity and sports to stay fit. People of all ages and both genders can improve the quality of their lives through a lifelong practice of regular moderate physical activity, the council notes. A 1997 report prepared under the direction of the Center for Research on Girls & Women in Sport, University of Minnesota, stresses that

participation in physical activity and sport can help girls weather the storms of adolescence and lay the foundation for a healthier adult life. The report looks at "the complete girl" through an interdisciplinary approach to investigate the impact of physical activity and sport participation.

The conclusions are striking: regular physical activity can reduce girls' risk of many of the chronic diseases of adulthood; female athletes do better academically and have lower school drop-out rates than their nonathletic counterparts; and, regular physical activity can enhance girls' mental health, reducing symptoms of stress and depression and improving self-esteem.

The council warns that further vigilance and research are needed to ensure that females as well as males are encouraged to participate in physical activity and sports in order to enhance their fitness. *See also* Adolescent Girls' Health; Nutritional Factors

Further Reading

President's Council on Physical Fitness and Sports. "Physical and Mental Health Dimensions from an Interdisciplinary Approach, President's Council on Physical Fitness & Sports Report, Physical Activity and Sport in the Lives of Girls." (Spring 1997). <http://www.kls.coled.umn.edu/crgws/pcpfs/default.html>

Reuters Health News Service. "Female Bodybuilders at Risk for Body Image Disorder." (February 21, 2000).

Shephard, Roy J. "Do Work-Site Exercise and Health Programs Work?" *The Physician and Sports Medicine Online* (February 1999). <http://www.physsportsmed.com/issues/1999/02_99/shephard.htm>.

Women's Health and Cancer Rights Act of 1998

An important piece of federal legislation for women who undergo mastectomy due to breast cancer is the Women's Health and Cancer Rights Act of 1998. It amends the

Employee Retirement Income Security Act and the Public Health Service Act. The amendment requires that if an insurance plan provides medical and surgical benefits for a mastectomy and a woman elects reconstruction, the plan must cover (1) all stages of reconstruction of the breast on which the mastectomy has been performed; (2) surgery and reconstruction of the other breast to produce a symmetrical appearance; and (3) prostheses and physical complications of mastectomy, including lymphedemas. An annual written notice of the availability of such benefits must also be provided. *See also* Breast Cancer; Health Insurance; Mastectomy

Women's Health Conferences

Since the 1990s, women's health conferences and symposia have become commonplace in the United States and other countries. The gatherings focus on general and specific health issues affecting women and are sponsored by various health organizations, medical institutions, medical schools, and federal agencies. A few examples during 2000 include the Annual Congress on Women's Health and Gender Based Medicine sponsored by the Ohio State University Medical Center/Center for Continuing Medical Education and the *Journal of Women's Health*; the Annual Congress on Women's Health co-sponsored by the *Journal of Women's Health* and the Society for Women's Health Research; the Centers for Disease Control and Prevention conference on prevention of sexually transmitted diseases; and the "2000 Women in Medicine Conference" sponsored by the Gay and Lesbian Medical Association in San Francisco, California. Other conferences focus on such diseases as breast cancer, heart disease, and osteoporosis.

Women's health research is another topic discussed at conferences and seminars. Even though such research has improved tremendously in recent years, the number of researchers in women's health is small within traditional academic departments. To create more visibility and encourage dialogue on women's health research, Harvard Medical School's Center of Excellence in Women's Health sponsored a Celebrate Women's Health Research Day conference in 2000. Discussions centered on present and future opportunities in women's health research and what is under way in the field at Harvard Medical School.

Along with Harvard Medical School, most major medical schools in the United States and health organizations such as the American Heart Association and the American Cancer Society maintain Internet Web sites to disseminate information about women's health conferences under their auspices. The Department of Health and Human Services' National Women's Health Information Center publishes a calendar of women's health conferences and other events on its Web site. *See also* Breast Cancer; National Women's Health Information Center; Osteoporosis; Sexually Transmitted Diseases

Further Reading
National Women's Health Information Center. "Calendar of Federal Women's Health Events." <http://www.4woman.gov/nwhic/current/Calendar/Assoc_Events.htm>.

Women's Health Education

Women's health education was seldom a topic of widespread public concern until about the early 1990s when women's health issues began to gain increasing attention. Women's health education is now a featured part of the curriculum at most major medical schools in the United States, and in many cases is included in a university's broader commitment to women's health. For example, women's health centers have been established on numerous university campuses, offering an array of preventive, diagnostic, and therapeutic health services. Some of these health centers have been named National Centers of Excellence in Women's Health by the U.S. Office of Public Health in the Department of Health and Human Services.

Scores of resource organizations, federal and state government agencies, and hundreds of published books and articles and Internet Web sites focus on women's health education. Examples of important sources for women's health education are the National Women's Health Information Center, the National Women's Health Resource Center, and the National Institutes of Health's Office of Research on Women's Health. Dozens of organizations focus on the health education of specific women's groups—adolescents, minorities, the aging, the poor, and others. The health issues covered range from alcohol and substance abuse to women's fitness programs. A bibliography at the back of this book lists many references that include information on women's health education.

One important book that helped set the trend for women's health education (and the women's health movement) is *Our Bodies, Ourselves,* first published commercially in 1973 by the Boston Women's Health Book Collective. Other printed works that have helped readers understand the varied and sometimes controversial issues surrounding many women's health issues include *In Her Own Right: The Institute of Medicine's Guide to Women's Health Issues* by Beryl Lieff Benderly and *A New Perspective for Women's Health* by Bernadine Healy. *See also* Adolescent Girls' Health; Aging; Alcohol Abuse and Alcoholism; Boston Women's Health Book Collective; National Centers of Ex-

cellence in Women's Health; National Women's Health Information Center; National Women's Health Resource Center

Further Reading

Benderly, Beryl Lieff for the Institute of Medicine. *In Her Own Right: The Institute of Medicine's Guide to Women's Health Issues.* Washington, DC: National Academy Press, 1997.

Boston Women's Health Book Collective. *The New Our Bodies, Ourselves.* New York: Simon & Schuster, 1992.

Healy, Bernadine. *A New Prescription for Women's Health.* New York: Viking, 1995.

Women's Health Hot Line

Women's Health Hot Line is a quarterly, commercial-free newsletter created by Charlotte Libov, medical author and founder of the National Women's Heart Health Day. The *Hot Line* fosters awareness of important women's health issues. Articles published in the newsletter focus on such issues as migraine, skin cancer, heart attack, dieting fads, breast and colon cancer, women's sports, and exercise. An electronic version of the newsletter can be found at <http://www.libov.com/>. *See also* Cardiovascular Diseases; National Women's Heart Health Day; Women's Health-Care Advocates

Women's Health Initiative

The Women's Health Initiative (WHI) is a long-term national health study that attempts to address the inequities in women's health research. A 15-year multimillion dollar program, WHI was established by the National Institutes of Health and its National Heart, Lung, and Blood Institute in 1991. The program focuses on strategies for preventing cardiovascular (heart) disease, breast and colorectal cancer, and osteoporosis in post-menopausal women. These chronic diseases are the major causes of death, disability, and frailty in older women of all races and socioeconomic backgrounds.

The crucial need to involve women in medical studies was recognized by the NIH in 1990 when the institute established the Office of Research on Women's Health (ORWH). One of ORWH's earliest efforts included the development of a research agenda to identify and address gaps in the biomedical community's knowledge of women's health. The office also began strengthening and revitalizing existing NIH guidelines and policies for the inclusion of women and minorities in clinical studies.

The WHI study has three components: a randomized clinical trial, an observational study, and a community prevention study. The randomized controlled clinical trial (CT) enrolled over 68,000 post-menopausal women between the ages of 50 and 79. Eligible women could enroll in one, two, or all three of the following trial components: (1) hormone replacement therapy (HRT), which examines the effect of HRT on the prevention of heart disease and osteoporosis, and any associated risk for breast cancer; (2) Dietary Modification, which evaluates the effect of a low-fat, high-fruit, -vegetable and -grain diet on the prevention of breast and colorectal cancer and heart disease; (3) a Calcium/Vitamin D component, which evaluates the effect of calcium and vitamin D supplements on the prevention of osteoporosis-related fractures and colorectal cancer.

The observational study (OS) examines the relationship between lifestyle, health and risk factors, and specific disease outcomes by tracking the medical history and health habits of approximately 100,000 women. Recruitment for the observational study was completed in 1998 and participants will be followed for 8 to 12 years.

The community prevention study (CPS) is a collaborative effort between the Centers for Disease Control and Prevention (CDC) and the National Institutes of Health. The CDC has funded eight university-based prevention centers, which are conducting and evaluating health programs that encourage women of all races and socioeconomic backgrounds to adopt healthful behaviors, such as diet improvement, nutritional supplementation, smoking cessation, exercise, and early detection of treatable health problems. The goal of the community prevention study is to develop carefully evaluated, model programs that can be implemented in a wide range of communities throughout the United States. *See also* Breast Cancer; Cardiovascular Diseases; Menopause; National Institutes of Health Office of Research on Women's Health; Nutrition; Osteoporosis

Further Reading

Healy, Bernadine. *A New Prescription for Women's Health.* New York: Viking, 1995.

The National Institutes of Health, the National Heart, Lung, and Blood Institute, Women's Health Initiative home page. <http://www.nhlbi.nih.gov/whi/index.html>.

Women's Health Interactive

In 1996 a health information company called Women's Health Interactive (WHI) was launched on the Internet. The site provides information, education, and instruction on women's health issues. The company states that it is "dedicated to delivering a wide range of health-related services specifically tailored to women. Through the use of the digital interactive technologies, women can access pertinent information about important health issues, simply by switching on their computers." In announcing its Web site, WHI proclaimed that its mission is to

provide an innovative environment for learning—where multidisciplinary health education resources are made accessible to women—consumers as well as healthcare professionals.... WHI offers women a comfortable and proactive network where they are empowered to learn holistically—about their physical health, as well as their personal and "job-related" health.

By creating a forum where women can communicate directly with healthcare professionals, join a discussion group, or assess their own situation through the use of health profiles, *Women's Health Interactive* furnishes a holistic view of women's health ... completely from the perspective of women.

WHI is just one of hundreds of Internet Web sites on women's health issues that have appeared in recent years. Searches on the Web reveal sites that focus not only on general women's health issues but also on specific diseases or health conditions of concern primarily to women. *See also* Online Medicine

Further Reading

Women's Health Interactive home page. <http://www.womens-health.com>.

Women's Health Issues in the U.S. Congress

Until a U.S. Public Health Service task force investigated women's health issues in the late 1980s and found that knowledge about health care specific to women was inadequate or completely lacking, the U.S. Congress hardly addressed women's health issues. After the Government Accounting Office (GAO) issued a report in 1990 showing that for years women had been systematically excluded from medical studies, congressional members and the public began to call for discussion and debate on women's health issues in the U.S. Congress. Since 1990, due to the efforts of women in Congress as well as those of many male allies, numerous bills and resolutions have been proposed regarding women's health concerns. Although these efforts do not necessarily result in passage

of federal laws, congressional actions frequently call attention to women's health needs.

During the 106th Congress (1999–2000), for example, a resolution was introduced proclaiming the month of January as "National Cervical Health Month." Another resolution, called "Women and Heart Disease Awareness Resolution," declares that the House of Representatives recognizes (1) the severity of the issue of women and heart disease; (2) the importance of federally funded programs that provide research and collect data on the rate of heart disease among women, according to age, ethnicity, and socioeconomic status; and (3) the importance of the National Heart, Lung, and Blood Institute at the National Institutes of Health, and the need for adequate funding to continue research and data collection about women and heart disease, particularly with respect to minority populations. The resolution also calls on the people of the United States to learn about heart disease, its symptoms, and the steps women can take to lower their risk.

The Breast Cancer Patient Protection Act of 1999 was introduced in the 106th Congress; the proposed legislation, if passed, would amend the Public Health Service Act to require that group health plans and insurers offering group health insurance cover no less than a 48-hour hospital stay after mastectomies or less than 24 hours after lymph node dissections. The law would also prevent insurers from denying eligibility, enrollment, or renewal to avoid these requirements.

Another bill would provide funds for research to determine the extent of environmental hazards to women's health. The research would determine whether the presence of dioxin, synthetic fibers, and other additives in tampons and similar products used by women with respect to menstruation pose any risks to the health of women, including risks relating to cervical cancer, endometriosis, infertility, ovarian cancer, breast cancer, immune system deficiencies, pelvic inflammatory disease, and toxic shock syndrome.

Congressional efforts have been made to amend the Social Security Act to increase the amount of payment under the Medicare Program for pap smear laboratory tests, and to provide medical assistance for certain women screened and found to have breast or cervical cancer under a federally funded screening program. Goals of other bills would be to:

- promote research to identify and evaluate the health effects of silicone breast implants, and to ensure that women and their doctors receive accurate information about such implants

- restore freedom of reproductive choice to women in the uniformed services serving outside the United States

- protect women's reproductive health and constitutional right to choice

- require group health plans to provide coverage for reconstructive surgery following mastectomy, consistent with the Women's Health and Cancer Rights Act of 1998

- ensure that a woman can designate an obstetrician or gynecologist as her primary care provider

- provide economic security and safety for battered women

- prevent violence against women.

In addition to the hundreds of bills and resolutions on women's health introduced in the 106th Congress, women's health issues were the subject of dozens of articles in the *Congressional Record.* Some articles were "extensions of remarks" on bills introduced or reintroduced, or were articles in support of particular legislation. *See also* Breast Cancer; Breast Implants; Cervical Cancer; Domestic Violence; Environmental Health Hazards; Health Insurance

Further Reading

"Women's Health" Thomas Legislative Information. <http://thomas.loc.gov>.

Women's Health Movement

The women's health movement, a form of social protest and activism, has been ongoing since the 1800s, although many people assume it was spawned with the women's rights movement of the 1960s. Actually the women's health movement has occurred in waves, according to Carol Weisman, University of Michigan professor who addressed a 1998 seminar on "The History and Future of Women's Health" sponsored by the Public Health Service (PHS) Office on Women's Health and the PHS Coordinating Committee on Women's Health.

During the first wave of the 1830s and 1840s, women organized self-help groups to promote health education and healthy lifestyles, "emphasizing such things as proper diet, exercise, dress reform to eliminate corsets, and the use of sexual abstinence in marriage to promote family size limitation." There was also "a reaction against the role of elitist, formally trained physicians who promoted heroic treatments. Lay practitioners, including midwives, were promoted as a way of returning some degree of control to women as domestic healers." (Weisman)

As female physicians became more prominent, they began to challenge the accepted idea that women's reproductive organs could be damaged if they physically exerted themselves or became too excited. It was believed that fragile women's health had to be protected, although that belief usually excluded women of color and poor women who frequently labored long hours at difficult jobs just to survive.

Since female physicians generally were excluded from training and working in mainstream hospitals, they founded new women's hospitals, where both female physicians and nurses could be trained and employed. These hospitals—some of which became showcases for obstetrical and gynecological care—represented a clear example of an institution created by women for women's health care. (Weisman)

During the early 1900s the women's health movement coincided with efforts to achieve women's rights—from birth control to suffrage. At the same time, some women's groups were attempting to improve prenatal and child health care, eventually gaining government support for such services. By the 1960s and 1970s women at the grassroots level were challenging male authorities in many walks of life and particularly in the health-care system. Not only were abortion rights an issue, but also questioned were childbirth practices and procedures, the safety of such products as birth control pills and devices, and whether the increase in such surgeries as hysterectomy, mastectomy, and cesarean section was justified. Women also began to establish health-care organizations, women's health centers, self-help groups focusing on women's health, clinics offering family planning and abortion services, and birth centers with midwives in charge. In short, women began to take care of themselves, which was the basis for the Boston Women's Health Book Collective and its immensely popular self-help book, *Our Bodies, Ourselves,* first published in 1970 with numerous editions released since then.

The concept of women caring for their own health and demanding informed consent for surgeries was the "shocking" thesis of a 1974 film, produced by Cambridge Documentary Films. Titled *Taking Our Bodies Back: The Women's Health Movement*, the film documents the growing women's health movement in the 1970s and shows how women began to assert their rights in dealing with the medical community. It is still widely used to introduce the subject of women's health and present historical material about the women's health movement.

As the women's health movement expanded and became more influential during the 1980s, women gained leadership roles in numerous health-care agencies, organizations, and institutions. Women also established advocacy organizations to address health issues related to disabilities, environmental hazards, poverty, aging, and lesbian relationships. Organizations formed to call attention to health problems and diseases that disproportionately affect women of color. These include the National Black Women's Health Project, National Latina Women's Health Organization, the Native American Women's Health Education and Resource Center, and the National Asian Women's Health Organization. "These groups particularly focused on conditions related to racism and poverty that were not always understood or seen as priorities by largely white and middle-class movement groups." (Ruzek)

By the early 1990s, women's health issues were being addressed throughout the U.S. Government. The U.S. Congress passed the Women's Health Equity Act, and offices on women's health were established in federal agencies and bureaus, including the Department of Health and Human Services and its National Institutes of Health, the Public Health Service, and the Centers for Disease Control and Prevention.

Women's health issues were discussed at numerous national and international conferences during the 1990s, and university and college courses on women's health began to proliferate. The University of Michigan describes its study of women's health as an interdisciplinary field "especially concerned with those environmental, psychological, and physiological characteristics that are unique to, or more prevalent among, women." The university's

Michigan Initiative for Women's Health "has three main objectives: to identify ongoing research efforts related to women's health, to facilitate and stimulate such research at the University of Michigan, and, finally, to educate the University and general community by disseminating information pertaining to women's health." (University of Michigan course description)

Ongoing concerns for the women's health movement are access to health insurance, which is not affordable for many low-income women, and the type of coverage available for women. Legislative efforts are under way, for example, to require that insurance companies provide coverage for contraceptives like other prescription drug benefits. *See also* African-American Women's Health; Asian-American Women's Health; Birth Control; Boston Women's Health Book Collective; Cesarean Section; Conferences on Women and Health; Environmental Health Hazards; Health Insurance; Hysterectomy; Latina Women's Health; Mammogram; Native American Women's Health; Poor Women's Health Care

Further Reading
Boston Women's Health Book Collective. *Our Bodies, Ourselves for the New Century: A Book by and for Women.* New York: Touchstone/Simon & Schuster, 1998.
Howes, Joanne, and Marie Bass. "A Review of Gender-Specific Legislation, 1999." *Journal of Gender-Specific Medicine* (November–December 1999).
Ruzek, Sheryl Burt, and Julie Becker. "The Women's Health Movement in the United States: From Grass-Roots Activism to Professional Agendas." *Journal of the American Medical Women's Association* (Winter 1999).
Weisman, Carol S. "Two Centuries of Women's Health Activism." Paper presented at *The History and Future of Women's Health* seminar. Sponsored by the Office on Women's Health and Public Health Service Coordinating Committee on Women's Health, June 11, 1998. <www.4woman.gov/x/owh/pub/History/2century.htm>.

Women's Health Weekly

The weekly magazine *Women's Health Weekly* is both a print and an electronic publication providing news stories, research abstracts from medical conferences worldwide, summaries of medical journal articles, and information about grants from the National Institutes of Health. Established in 1994, the magazine's purpose is "to inform and educate women about diseases, disorders, and conditions that are unique to, more prevalent among, or more serious in women or for which there are different risk factors or interventions for women than men." The weekly also maintains an online database on women's health for subscribers. (Women's Health Weekly)

Further Reading
Women's Health Weekly. "About Women's Health Weekly." <http://www.newsfile.com/facts.htm>.

Women's Health-Care Advocates

Since ancient times, "wise women" in communities have been health-care advocates, educating other women about how to maintain good health and freely sharing their cures and healing methods. According to two long-time health-care advocates, during the fourteenth to sixteenth centuries in Europe,

> The art of healing was linked to the tasks and spirit of motherhood; it combined wisdom and nurturance, tenderness and skill. All but the most privileged women were expected to be at least literate in the language of herbs and healing techniques; the most learned women traveled widely to share their skills. The women who distinguished themselves as healers were not only midwives caring for other women, but "general practitioners," herbalists, and counselors serving men and women alike. (Ehrenreich and English, 36)

During the past few decades, American women who have become known for their health-care advocacy have been medical practitioners, midwives, or counselors, and they also have been in a variety of other professions. Some have served in government. Numerous women elected to the U.S. Congress during the 1990s, for example, have sponsored bills or helped pass laws that support health-care programs for women, such as the Violence Against Women Act of 1994 and its later amendments, and the Women's Health Equity Act of 1991.

One high-profile health-care advocate in government was Donna Shalala, the longest-serving Secretary of Health and Human Services (DHHS) in U.S. history. The department oversees numerous programs and offices, among them the "Women Living Long, Living Well" project, the National Women's Health Information Clearinghouse, and the Office of Minority Health Resource Center, which deals with specific health concerns of African-Americans, Asian-Americans, Hispanics/Latinos, Native Americans, and Native Hawaiians/Pacific Islanders. During the administration of President Bill Clinton, Shalala devoted much effort to the problems of young women and their families, helping to establish the Children's Health Insurance Plan to cover health care for those not eligible for Medicaid or other government-funded programs. She also launched a public education campaign to prevent alcohol and other drug use among girls ages 9 to 14.

Another well-known government official advocating for woman's health care is Bernadine Healy, M.D., physician, cardiologist, and professor of medicine, who in 1990 became the first woman to head the National Institutes of Health (NIH). At NIH she established the Office of Women's Health "in response to concerns expressed by the Congressional Women's Caucus" regarding clinical studies that excluded women. As NIH director she "was able to institute a nationwide research effort called the Women's Health Initiative," which is "the largest clinical research study of women and their health ever undertaken in the United States." The NIH itself also began "to enforce its long-ignored policy that a study or trial inappropriately excluding women would not be funded." (Healy, 10) Even before her appointment to NIH, Healy headed the American Heart Association; in 1988 she initiated a nationwide campaign alerting the public to heart disease in women. In 1999 she became director of the American Red Cross.

Other women who are prominent women's health-care advocates include authors and lecturers, such as Charlotte Libov, an award-winning medical writer who founded the National Women's Heart Health Day. She is editor of *Women's Health Hot Line*, an electronic newsletter. She is also on the advisory board for a public awareness campaign, "The Difference in a Woman's Heart," which is supported by the American Heart Association and the American Medical Women's Association.

One of the most well-known women's health-care advocates is Susan M. Love, surgeon and medical school professor, who has lectured and written extensively on breast cancer and menopause. Two of her books, *Dr. Love's Breast Book* and *Dr. Susan Love's Hormone Book: Making Informed Choices about Menopause,* are widely read and quoted. In recent years, she has developed an independent think tank on women's health issues focusing on ways that women's health care can be improved through managed care insurance programs.

Women's activists groups have long advocated for women's health care, particularly the Boston Women's Health Book Collective, a group who published the revolutionary health book for women, *Our*

Bodies, Ourselves, in 1970 and sparked a modern-day women's health movement. Many activist organizations focus on specific health issues of concern to women, such as the Planned Parenthood Federation of America's effective advocacy for reproductive health and the right to reproductive choice. Other groups advocate for women with diseases such as AIDS, alcoholism, breast cancer, endometriosis, and mental health disorders. Health problems of aging are addressed by such groups as the Older Women's League, which has an ongoing project called "Women and Heart Disease: A Neglected Epidemic."

Women are maintaining numerous Internet Web sites devoted to women's health care. However, many health experts caution that these online medical sites should be viewed critically with an eye for the source and reliability of the information presented. *See also* American Medical Women's Association; Boston Women's Health Book Collective; Breast Cancer; Emma Goldman Clinic; Health Insurance; Menopause; Midwifery; Older Women's League; Online Medicine; Planned Parenthood Federation; Violence Against Women Act of 1994; "Women Living Long, Living Well"; Women's Health Initiative; Women's Health Movement

Further Reading

Ehrenreich, Barbara, and Deirdre English. *For Her Own Good: 150 Years of the Experts' Advice to Women.* New York: Doubleday/Anchor Books, 1978.

Healy, Bernadine. *A New Prescription for Women's Health: Getting the Best Medical Care in a Man's World.* New York: Viking, 1995.

Hubbard, Ruth. *The Politics of Women's Biology.* New Brunswick: Rutgers University Press, 1990.

Working Women

More than half of American adult women are in the labor force, and these working women face numerous health concerns, ranging from risks to health and safety at worksites to emotional stress from trying to juggle home life and family relationships with job responsibilities. Since the beginning of the industrial revolution in the mid-nineteenth century, women have been part of the paid labor force, working outside the home because of necessity or choice, but it was not until the women's rights movement got under way during the latter part of the twentieth century that widespread public attention began to focus on the physical and mental health of working women, particularly those with children at home. In recent years, there has been an

explosion in the number and percentage of women who perform a substantial number of hours of paid work while they raise young children. Whereas poor, minority, and working-class women have long contributed economically to their families in whatever way they could, now most women, not just those with the greatest economic need, expect to work for pay outside the home. (Bianchi)

Equality for women in the workplace is an important aspect of women's health issues. In spite of the gains women have made toward equal status in society and in the workplace, women in the United States still have less physical, social, and economic power than men. While some women have gone beyond the "glass ceiling" to find success in high-paying careers and can afford whatever health care they need, the majority still work at entry-level or low-paying clerical or service jobs. Most women are "mired in the 'sticky floor' of the workplace [and] often deal with sweatshop conditions, low pay, unpaid overtime and other forms of economic oppression." (Malveaux)

Conditions for many working women today are similar to those described by a psychology professor in a 1991 article for *Second Opinion,* a publication exploring various perspectives on health and ethics:

In this culture women have seen their bodies defined as objects of desire, reproductive intent, or aggression. There has been much social pressure and coercion to get women to fulfill male needs at the expense of their own. Both in medicine and in the world of work the male body has been the operating norm; women's health needs and necessary social supports for women workers in their childbearing years have been ignored. Worse still, women have been socially penalized for having children. In education, in the professions, and in the workplace, arrangements have been structured for men who either are single or have a wife for domestic support. Women rearing children have been socially and economically devalued in our society, despite lip service to the importance of family life. Women at work have had to overcome overt and hidden barriers to success, and they are subject to increasing pressures to fill several diverse and competing roles at once. Today women suffer the stress of working at a job and then taking on the second shift at home. (Callahan, 74)

In some workplaces, flextime and family leave have helped ease some of the stresses working women face. Some corporations also provide child-care programs and lactation rooms for breastfeeding working moms, offer health-care insurance, and make other efforts to improve the working environment so that women's health is not jeopardized. State and federal legislation passed during the 1990s, such as laws against sexual harassment and violence against women, have diminished some of the threats to working women's health and safety.

In December 1997, the U.S. Department of Health and Human Services issued the first comprehensive report on the health and well-being of America's working women. Titled *Women: Work and Health*, the report compiles national data that are the most critical for assessing the complex relationship between employment and women's health in the United States. The statistics provide an important baseline for various government agencies and private organizations to learn more about the needs of working women and opportunities to improve their health. *See also* Occupational Safety and Health Administration; Sweatshops; *Women: Work and Health*

Further Reading

Apter, Terri. *Working Women Don't Have Wives.* New York: St. Martin's Griffin, 1993.

Bianchi, Suzanne M., and Daphne Spain. "Women, Work, and Family in America." *Population Bulletin* (December 1996).

Callahan, Sidney. "Does Gender Make a Difference in Moral Decision Making?" *Second Opinion* (October 1991).

Collins, Gail. "A Social Glacier Roars" in Special Issue: "The Shadow Story of the Millennium: Women." *New York Times Magazine* (May 16, 1999).

Malveaux, Julianne. "Women at Work." *In These Times* (November 28, 1999).

Wagener, D.K., J. Walstedt, L. Jenkins, et al. *Women: Work and Health.* Hyattsville, MD: United States Department of Health and Human Services, Centers for Disease Control and Prevention, National Center for Health Statistics, 1997.

"Women: The Road Ahead." Special Issue. *Time* (Fall 1990).

Bibliography

Aburdene, Patricia, and John Naisbitt. *Megatrends for Women.* New York: Villard Books, 1992.

Adams, Diane L. *Health Issues for Women of Color: A Cultural Diversity Health Perspective.* Thousand Oaks, CA: Sage, 1995.

Administration on Aging. "Grandparents as Caregivers." May 1997. <http://www.aoa.dhhs.gov/May97/grandparents.html>.

Administration on Aging. "Older Women: A Diverse and Growing Population." Fact Sheet. Washington, DC: Administration on Aging, U.S. Department of Health and Human Services.

"Advocacy for Women." Emma Goldman Clinic home page <http://www.emmagoldman.com>.

Alan Guttmacher Institute. "Induced Abortion." February 2000. <http://www.agi-usa.org/pubs/fb_induced_abortion.html>.

Alan Guttmacher Institute. "Teen Sex and Pregnancy." September 1999. <http://www.agi-usa.org/pubs/fb_teen_sex.html>.

Allison, Kathleen Cahill, and Ramona I. Slupik, M.D., medical editor. *American Medical Association Complete Guide to Women's Health.* New York: Random House, 1996.

Altman, Lawrence K. "Rates of Gonorrhea Rise After a Long Decline." *New York Times* (December 6, 2000).

Alzheimer's Association. "Alzheimer's Disease: A Major Health Issue for Women," September 24, 1999. <http://www.alz.org/media/news/1998/cwomens_health.htm >.

American Academy of Pediatrics Committee on Bioethics. "Policy Statement, Female Genital Mutilation." *Pediatrics* (July 1998).

American Cancer Society. The Cervical Cancer Resource Center. "Cervical Cancer Overview," March 16, 2000. <http://www3.cancer.org/cancerinfo/load_cont.asp?ct=8&doc=25&Language=English>.

American College of Obstetricians and Gynecologists. "ACOG Works to Improve Health among Native American Women." *ACOG Today* (March 1999).

———. "American College of Obstetricians and Gynecologists Release Ethical Guidelines on Nonselective Embryo Reduction." News Release, April 5, 1999.

———. "Statement on the Death of Dr. Barnett Slepian." News Release, October 26, 1998.

———. "The American College of Obstetricians and Gynecologists Launch National Calcium Campaign." News Release, May 11, 1998.

American Heart Association. "Cardiovascular Disease in Women: A Scientific Statement from the American Heart Association." *Clinician Reviews.* (April 1998). <http://cardiology.Medscape.com/CPG/ClinReviews/public/archive/1998/toc-0804.html>.

American Medical Association Council on Scientific Affairs, "The Reduction of Medical and Public Health Consequences of Drug Abuse." Report 8, June 1997.

American Obesity Association. "The Facts about Women and Obesity." <http://www.obesity.org/Obesity_Women.htm>.

American Society for Reproductive Medicine. "Fact Sheet: Infertility." <http://www.asrm.org/fact/infertility.htm>.

American Society of Plastic Surgeons, Plastic Surgery Information Service. "Most Popular Cosmetic Surgery Procedures Just Became More Popular." Press Release, July 20, 2000. <http://www.plasticsurgery.org/mediactr/stats.htm>.

American Society of Plastic and Reconstructive Surgeons. "Cosmetic Surgery Jumps 50 Percent: Liposuction and Breast Augmentation Top Procedures." Press Release, April 28, 1999.

Amnesty International, USA. "The State of Laws and Lawlessness: A Survey of Statutes on Custodial Sexual Contact." Fact Sheet, 1999. <http://www.amnestyusa.org/rightsforall/women/factsheets/laws.html>.

Angier, Natalie. *Woman: An Intimate Geography.* New York: Houghton Mifflin, 1999.

Apter, Terri. *Working Women Don't Have Wives*, New York: St. Martin's Griffin, 1993.

Arnold, Lois Barber. *Four Lives in Science: Women's Education in the Nineteenth Century.* New York: Schocken Books, 1984.

Aron, Laudan Y., and Janet M. Fitchen. "Rural Homelessness: A Synopsis." In *Homelessness in America.* Edited by Jim Baumohl for the National Coalition for the Homeless. Phoenix, AZ: Oryx Press, 1996.

Aronson, Diane, and RESOLVE. *Resolving Infertility: Understanding the Options and Choosing Solutions When You Want to Have a Baby.* New York: Harper, 1999.

Ashford, Nicholas A., and Claudia S. Miller. *Chemical Exposures; Low Levels and High Stakes.* 2nd Ed. New York: Van Nostrand Reinhold, 1998.

"Assisted Reproductive Technology Success Rate Report." Press Release (February 2, 1999).

Associated Press. "Blacks More Likely to Die during Pregnancy." *USA Today* (June 18, 1999).

Associated Press. "Exercise Helps Women Quit Smoking." *New York Times* (June 14, 1999).

Bailey, Martha J. *American Women in Science: A Biographical Dictionary.* Santa Barbara, CA: ABC-CLIO, 1994.

Baird, Karen L. "The New NIH and FDA Medical Research Policies: Targeting Gender, Promoting Justice." *Journal of Health Politics, Policy and Law.* (June 1999).

Ballweg, Mary Lou, and the Endometriosis Association. *The Endometriosis Sourcebook.* Lincolnwood, IL: Contemporary Books, 1995.

Barrett, Stephen, and Ronald E. Gots. *Chemical Sensitivity: The Truth about Environmental Illness.* Amherst, NY: Prometheus Books, 1998.

Barrett, Stephen, MD. "Multiple Chemical Sensitivity: A Spurious Diagnosis." Quackwatch home page, July 24, 1999. <http://www.quackwatch.com/01QuackeryRelated Topics/mcs.html>.

"Barriers to Health Care for HIV-Positive Women: Deadly Denial." <http://hivinsite.ucsf.edu/social/misc._documents/2098.3e45.html>.

Barth, Richard P. "Revisiting the Issues: Adoption of Drug-Exposed Children." *The Future of Children* (Spring 1993).

Bartha, Liliane, et al. "Multiple Chemical Sensitivity: A 1999 Consensus." *Archives of Environmental Health* (May–June 1999).

Baumgardner, Jennifer. "Immaculate Contraception." *The Nation* (January 25, 1999).

Begley, Sharon. "The Mammogram War." *Newsweek* (February 24, 1997).

Bell, Ruth, with members of the Teen Book Project. *Changing Bodies, Changing Lives.* New York: Times Books, 1998.

Beller, Tanya, Michelle Pinker, Sheila Snapka, and Denise Van Dusen. "Korean-American Health Care Beliefs and Practices." <http://www.baylor.edu/~Charles_Kemp/korean_health.htm>.

Bender, David L., and Bruno Leone, eds. *Abortion: Opposing Viewpoints.* San Diego, CA: Greenhaven Press, 1991.

Benderly, Beryl Lieff for the Institute of Medicine. *In Her Own Right: The Institute of Medicine's Guide to Women's Health Issues.* Washington, DC: National Academy Press, 1997.

Berger, Joseph. "Doctor's Slaying Leaves Buffalo Clinic Struggling." *New York Times* (January 24, 1999).

Berkow, Robert, editor-in-chief. *Merck Manual of Medical Information—Home Edition*, Chapter 248. Whitehouse Station, NY: Merck & Co., 1997. <http://www.merck.com/pubs/mmanual_home>.

Bianchi, Suzanne M. and Daphne Spain. "Women, Work, and Family in America." *Population Bulletin* (December 1996).

Bird, Caroline. *Lives of Our Own: Secrets of Salty Old Women.* Boston and New York: Houghton Mifflin, 1995.

Blackman, Ann, Nichole Christian, and Alison Jones, "Campus Awakening: The Sweatshop Issue Has Galvanized College Activists." *Time* (April 12 1999).

Blumenthal, Susan J., U.S. Department of Health and Human Services. "Introduction and Opening Remarks." *Healthy Women 2000* conference (June 1996). <http://www.4women.gov/owh/autoimm/opening.htm>.

Blythe, Bruce. "Eye on Workplace Violence." *Risk Management* (April 1999).

Bonavoglia, Angela, ed. *The Choices We Made: Twenty-Five Women and Men Speak Out about Abortion.* New York: Random House, 1991.

Booksh, Alicia Clemens. "Getting off the Back Room Team." *New Beginnings* (March–April 1994).

Booth, William. "Doctor Killed During Abortion Protest." *Washington Post* (March 11, 1993).

Born, Dorothy. "More Warnings Given to Teenage Smokers." *The Lancet* (April 1999).

Boston Women's Health Book Collective. *Our Bodies, Ourselves for the New Century: A Book by and for Women.* New York: Touchstone/Simon & Schuster, 1998.

The Boston Women's Health Book Collective. *The New Our Bodies, Ourselves.* New York: Simon & Schuster, 1992.

Bradsher, Julia E. "Disability among Racial and Ethnic Groups." University of California, San Francisco: Disability Statistics Center. Abstract (January 1996). http://128.218.183.95/UCSF/pdf/ABSTRACT10.pdf.

Brewerton, Derrick. *All about Arthritis.* Cambridge, MA.: Harvard University Press, 1992.

Brody, Jane E. "Alternative Medicine Makes Inroads, but Watch Out for Curves." *New York Times* (April 28, 1998).

———. "Point-and-Click Medicine: A Hazard to Your Health." *New York Times* (August 11, 1999).

———. "A Fatal Shift in Cancer's Gender Gap." *New York Times* (May 12, 1998).

———. "Coping with Fear: Keeping Breast Cancer in Perspective." *New York Times* (October 12, 1999).

Brothers, Joyce. *Widowed.* New York: Ballantine, 1992.

Brotman, Barbara. "(The) Change Is Good." *Chicago Tribune* (July 21, 1999).

Brown, Ellen. "Waging War on Lung Cancer." *FDA Consumer* (May–June 1999).

Browne, Angela, Amy Salomon, and Shari S. Bassuk. "The Impact of Recent Partner Violence on Poor Women's Capacity to Maintain Work." *Violence against Women* (April 1999).

Bureau of Justice Statistics Special Report: National Crime Victimization Survey, Violence against Women. Washington, DC: U.S. Department of Justice (January 1994).

Burt, Martha. *Practical Methods for Counting Homeless People: A Manual for States and Local Jurisdictions*, 2d ed. Washington, DC: The Urban Institute, 1996.

Califano, Joseph A. "The Least among Us." *America* (April 24, 1999).

Callahan, Sidney. "Does Gender Make a Difference in Moral Decision Making?" *Second Opinion* (October 1991).

Calle, Eugenia E., Michael J. Thun, Jennifer M. Petrelli, Carmen Rodriguez, and Clark W. Heath, Jr. "Body-Mass Index and Mortality in a Prospective Cohort of U.S. Adults." *The New England Journal of Medicine* (October 7, 1999).

Capellaro, Jennie, "Students for Sweat-Free Sweatshirts." *The Progressive* (April 1999).

Carlson, Karen J, Stephanie A. Eisenstat, and Terra Ziporyn. *The Harvard Guide to Women's Health.* Cambridge, MA: Harvard University Press, 1996.

Carson, Rachel. *Silent Spring.* Greenwich, CT: Fawcett Crest, 1962.

Carson, Sandra, and Peter Casson, eds. *Complete Guide to Fertility.* Chicago, IL: Contemporary Books, 1999.

Casey, Terri. *Pride and Joy: The Lives and Passions of Women without Children.* Hillsboro, OR: Beyond Words, 1998.

Cassileth, Barrie R. *The Alternative Medicine Handbook: The Complete Reference Guide to Alternative and Complementary Therapies.* New York: W.W. Norton, 1998.

Center for Reproductive Health. "Assisted Reproductive Technologies." <http://www.fertilitext/org/art.htm>.

Centers for Disease Control and Prevention, National Institute of Occupational Safety and Health. "Carpal Tunnel Syndrome." Fact Sheet (June 1997).

Centers for Disease Control and Prevention. "Alice Hamilton, M.D." *Morbidity and Mortality Weekly Report* (June 11, 1999).

———. "HIV/AIDS among US Women: Minority and Young Women at Continuing Risk." Fact Sheet, August 1999. <http://www.cdc.gov/nchstp/hiv_aids/pubs/facts/women.htm>.

———. "Pregnancy-Related Behaviors among Migrant Farm Workers—Four States, 1989–1993." *Journal of the American Medical Association* (May 21, 1997).

Centers for Disease Control and Prevention, Office of Women's Health. "Breast and Cervical Cancer." <http://www.cdc.gov/od/owh/whbc.htm>.

Chasnoff, Ira J., D.R. Griffith, et al. "Cocaine/Polydrug Use in Pregnancy: Two Year Follow Up." *Pediatrics* (February 1992).

Chen, Constance M. *"The Sex Side of Life": Mary Ware Dennett's Pioneering Battle for Birth Control and Sex Education.* New York: The New Press, 1996.

Chesler, Ellen. *Woman of Valor: Margaret Sanger and the Birth Control Movement in America.* New York: Simon & Schuster, 1992.

Children's Defense Fund. "The Waiting Game." Focus Group Report on the Children's Health Insurance Program and Medicaid (March 1998).

Chivers, C.J. "The Great Childbirth Debate: Drug-Assisted, or Natural?" *New York Times* (October 18, 1999).

Chrvala, Carole A., and Roger J. Bulger, eds. *Leading Health Indicators for Healthy People 2010: Final Report.* Washington, DC: National Academy Press, 1999.

Claiborne, William. "Study Links Abortion Laws, Aid to Children." *Washington Post* (October 9, 1999).

Coburn, Susan. "Turning a Medical Mountain into a Manageable Molehill," *New York Times* (June 25, 2000).

Cohen, Elizabeth. "Moms At Last: How 8 Friends Faced Infertility." *Family Circle* (September 15, 1998).

Cole, Helene M. "Women's Health on the Web." *Journal of the American Medical Association* (October 6, 1999).

Collins, Catherine F. *African-American Women's Health and Social Issues.* Westport, CT: Greenwood, 1996.

Collins, Gail. "A Social Glacier Roars." In "The Shadow Story of the Millennium: Women." *New York Times Magazine*, Special Issue (May 16, 1999).

The Commonwealth Fund. "Facts on Access to Health Care," September 1997. <http://www.cmwf.org/programs/women/acesfact.asp>.

The Commonwealth Fund. "Health Care Hazards for Midlife Americans." Press Release, January 27, 2000.

The Commonwealth Fund. "Health Insurance Coverage and Access to Care for Working-Age Women." Fact Sheet from The Commonwealth Fund 1998 Survey of Women's Health, May 1999.

The Commonwealth Fund. "Losing Ground: Working-Age Women Increasingly Likely to Lack Health Insurance." Press Release, September 16, 1999.

Conklin, Melanie. "Blocking Women's Health Care: Your Hospital May Have a Policy You Don't Know about." *The Progressive* (January 1998).

Cowley, Geoffrey, and Karen Springen. "Lowdown on Liposuction." *Newsweek* (May 24, 1999).

Cowley, Geoffrey. "Multiplying the Risks: More Group Births Mean More Preemies and, Often, More Problems." *Newsweek* (December 1, 1997).

Dailard, Cynthia. "Reviving Interest in Policies and Programs to Help Teens Prevent Repeat Births." *The Guttmacher Report on Public Policy* (June 2000). <http://www.agi-usa.org/pubs/journals/gr030301.html>.

Delaney, Janice, Mary Jane Lupton, and Emily Toth. *The Curse: A Cultural History of Menstruation.* Rev. ed. Urbana and Chicago, IL: University of Illinois Press, 1988.

Dennis, Leslie K. "Increasing Risk of Melanoma with Increasing Age." *The Journal of the American Medical Association* (September 15, 1999).

Department of Health and Human Services, National Institutes of Health, National Institute of Diabetes and Digestive and Kidney Diseases. "Understanding Adult Obesity" (November 1993).

"DES: The Controversy about Hormone Replacement." *The DES Action Voice* (Spring 1994).

"Detecting Melanoma." *Harvard Health Letter* (May 1999).

Deutchman, Mark. "Cesarean Section in Family Medicine." Position paper prepared for the American Association of Family Physicians' Commission on Quality and Scope of Practice, 1997.

deYoung, Mary. "Another Look at Moral Panics: The Case of Satanic Day Care Centers." *Deviant Behavior: An Interdisciplinary Journal* (July–September, 1998).

DiClemente, Ralph J. "Preventing Sexually Transmitted Infections among Adolescents." *Journal of the American Medical Association* (May 20, 1998).

"Disappearing Act." *Time* (November 2, 1998).

Dolan, Bridget. *Why Women? Gender Issues and Eating Disorders.* Atlantic Highlands, NY: Humanities Press International, 1994.

"Domestic Violence and Women's Health." *Journal of the American Medical Women's Association* (May–July 1996).

Doress-Worters, Paula, and Diana Laskin Siegal, in cooperation with the Boston Women's Health Book Collective. *The New Ourselves, Growing Older.* New York: Simon & Schuster, 1994.

Dower, C.M., J.E. Miller, and E.H. O'Neil and the Taskforce on Midwifery. *Charting a Course for the 21st Century: The Future of Midwifery.* San Francisco, CA: Pew Health Professions Commission and the UCSF Center for the Health Professions, April 1999.

Doyal, Lesley. *What Makes Women Sick: Gender and the Political Economy of Health.* New Brunswick, NY: Rutgers University Press, 1995.

Doyle, Margaret. *Woman's Body: An Owner's Manual.* Lincolnwood, IL: Contemporary Books, 1999.

"Dr. Bernadine Healy Named Red Cross President." *U.S. Newswire* (July 8, 1999).

Druss, Benjamin G., and Robert A. Rosenheck. "Association between Use of Unconventional Therapies and Conventional Medical Services." *Journal of the American Medical Association* (August 18, 1999).

Dugger, Celia M. "Tug of Taboos: African Genital Rite vs. American Law." *New York Times* (December 28, 1996).

Editors of the Johns Hopkins Medical Letter, Health After 50. The *Johns Hopkins Medical Handbook: The 100 Major Medical Disorders of People over the Age of 50.* New York: Rebus, 1992.

Ehrenreich, Barbara, and Deirdre English. *For Her Own Good: 150 Years of the Experts' Advice to Women.* New York: Doubleday/Anchor Books, 1978.

Eisenberg, Anne. "Female M.D.s More Open with Options, Patients Say." *New York Times* (August 17, 1999).

Elders, M. Joycelyn. "Adolescent Pregnancy and Sexual Abuse." *Journal of the American Medical Association* (August 19, 1998).

Emanuel, Ezekiel J., Diane L. Fairclough, Julia Slutsman, Hillel Alpert, DeWitt Baldwin, Linda L. Emanuel. "Assistance from Family Members, Friends, Paid Care Givers, and Volunteers in the Care of Terminally Ill Patients." *The New England Journal of Medicine* (September 23, 1999).

"Emma and University of Iowa Launch New Era of Collaboration." *Emma's Journal: Newsletter of the Emma Goldman Clinic*, Special Edition (November 1998).

Epstein, Harriet. "The Grande Dame of Sex Education." *The Humanist* (January 1999).

"Explorations: Treating Eating Disorders." *Scientific American* (March 2, 1998).

Faces of Science: African Americans in the Sciences. Baton Rouge, Louisiana: <http://www.lib.lsu.edu/lib/chem/display/faces.html>.

Falk, Candace Serena. *Love, Anarchy, and Emma Goldman.* New Brunswick, NY: Rutgers University Press, 1990.

Faludi, Susan. *Backlash: The Undeclared War against American Women.* New York: Crown, 1991.

Feinberg, Madaline. "The Boston Women's Health Book Collective Celebrates Its 25th Anniversary!" *The Network News* (May–June 1996).

Feminist Majority Foundation. "Feminist Majority Foundation Reports on Mifepristone." <http://www.feminist.org/gateway/ru486one.html>.

———. "National Feminist Leader Eleanor Smeal Calls for Use of Criminal RICO to End Violence." Press Release, April 20, 1998.

Field, Susan, and Ros Bramwell. "An Investigation Into the Relationship between Caregiver Responsibilities and the Levels of Perceived Pressure Reported by Female Employees." *Journal of Occupational and Organizational Psychology* (June 1998).

Finger, Anne L. "How Would You Handle These Ethical Dilemmas?" *Medical Economics* (October 27, 1997).

Fink, Leslie, and Francis S. Collins, M.D. "The Human Genome Project: View from the National Institutes of Health." *Journal of the American Medical Women's Association* (Winter 1997).

Fleischhauer, Carl, and Beverly Brannan, eds. *Documenting America, 1935–1943.* Berkeley: University of California Press, 1988.

Foley, Denise, Eileen Nechas, and the Editors of *Prevention Magazine. Women's Encyclopedia of Health & Emotional Healing.* Emmaus, PA: Rodale Press, 1993.

Folkart, Burt A. Obituary. *Los Angeles Times* (April 23, 1995).

Ford, Betty. *A Glad Awakening.* Garden City, NY: Doubleday, 1987.

Ford, Betty, with Chris Chase. *The Times of My Life.* New York: Harper & Row, 1978.

Foreman, Judy. "The Midwives' Time Has Come—Again." *Boston Globe* (November 2, 1998).

Four Thousand Years of Women in Science <http://crux.astr.ua.edu/4000WS/4000WS.html>.

Franck, Ellen J. "Prenatally Drug-Exposed Children in Out-of-Home Care: Are We Looking at the Whole Picture?" *Child Welfare* (January–February 1996).

Frank, Erica, Donna Brogan, and Melissa Schiffman. "Prevalence and Correlates of Harassment among U.S. Women Physicians." *Archives of Internal Medicine* (February 23, 1998).

Freitag, Frederick G. "Manage Your Migraines." *The DO* (June 1999).

Friend, Tim. "Smoking Damages Women's Smaller Lungs." *USA TODAY* (May 13, 1996).

Fritsch, Jane. "95% Regain Lost Weight. Or Do They?" *New York Times* (May 25, 1999).

———. "The Secret Loss That Women Try to Keep under Their Hats." *New York Times* (June 21, 1998).

Futrelle, David. "Making Ourselves Sick." *Salon* (August 6, 1997).

Gale Group: Women's History. "Healy, Bernadine." <http://www.gale.com/library/resrcs/womenhst/healyb.htm>.

Gallagher, Susan, "Tailoring Care for Obese Patients." *RN* (May 1999).

Garrett, Carol B. "The Majority of Family Caregivers of the Elderly Are Women." *Womansword* (November 1997).

Gay, Kathlyn. *Breast Implants: Making Safe Choices.* New York: New Discovery Books/Macmillan, 1993.

———. *Pollution and the Powerless.* New York: Franklin Watts, 1994.

———. *Pregnancy: Private Decisions, Public Debates.* New York: Franklin Watts, 1994.

———. *Rights and Respect: What You Need to Know about Gender Bias and Sexual Harassment.* Brookfield, CT: Millbrook Press, 1995.

Gay, Kathlyn, and Martin K. Gay. *Heroes of Conscience: A Biographical Dictionary.* Santa Barbara, CA: ABC-CLIO, 1996.

Geronimus, Arline T. "Teenage Childbearing and Personal Responsibility: An Alternative View." *Political Science Quarterly* (Fall 1997).

Gilbert, Susan. "Benefits of Assistant for Childbirth Go Far Beyond the Birthing." *New York Times* (May 19, 1998).

———. "Gauging the Risk Factors in the Search for a Perfect Face." *New York Times* (June 21, 1998).

Gill, Derek. *Quest: The Life of Elisabeth Kübler-Ross.* New York: Harper & Row, 1980.

Goff, Karen Goldberg. "A Safe Place in the Sun." *Insight on the News* (August 30, 1999).

Goldberg, Burton, and *Alternative Medicine Digest* eds. *Alternative Medicine Guide to Chronic Fatigue, Fibromyalgia and Environmental Illness.* Tiburon, CA: Future Medicine Publishers, 1998.

Goldberg, Carey. "Getting to the Truth in Child Abuse Cases: New Methods." *New York Times* (September 8, 1998).

Goldberg, Joan E. "A Short Term Approach to Intervention with Homeless Mothers: A Role for Clinicians in Homeless Shelters." *Families in Society: The Journal of Contemporary Human Services* (March/April 1999).

Golden, Frederic. "Smoking Gun for the Young." *Time* (April 19, 1999).

Goodman, Charisse. *The Invisible Woman: Confronting Weight Prejudice in America.* Carlsbad, CA: Gürze Books, 1995.

Gotsch, Gwen. *Breastfeeding Pure and Simple.* Franklin Park, IL: La Leche League International, 1994.

Grady, Denise. "Breast Cancer Data, Hope, Fear and Confusion." *New York Times* (January 26, 1999).

———. "In Birth Study, No Less a Risk in a Caesarean." *New York Times* (December 2, 1999).

———. "New Test for Cancer Surpasses the Pap One, Studies Show." *New York Times* (January 5, 2000).

———. "Something's Often Missing in Childbirth Today: The Pain." *New York Times* (October 13, 1999).

"Gray Power." Editorial. *The Nation* (May 28, 1990).

Greenhouse, Linda. "Justices Uphold Abortion Clinic Buffer Zone." *New York Times* (February 20, 1997).

Grelsamer, Ronald P. *The Columbia Presbyterian Osteoarthritis Handbook.* New York: Simon & Schuster, 1996.

Gross, Amy, and Dee Ito. *Women Talk about Breast Surgery.* New York: HarperPerennial, 1990.

Haack, Mary R., ed. *Drug-Dependent Mothers and Their Children.* New York: Springer Publishing Company, 1997.

Hall, Rob. *Rape in America.* Santa Barbara, CA: ABC-CLIO, 1995.

Halmi, Katherine A. "A 24-Year-Old Woman with Anorexia Nervosa." The *Journal of the American Medical Association* (June 24, 1998).

Hamilton, Alice. *Exploring the Dangerous Trades: The Autobiography of Alice Hamilton, M.D.* Boston: Little, Brown and Company, 1943.

Hardy, Lammers. *Issues in Women's Health.* New York: Churchill Livingstone, 1989.

Harrison, Beverly Wildung. *Our Right to Choose: Toward a New Ethic of Abortion.* Boston: Beacon Press, 1983.

Hazelton, Richard A. "The Breast Implant Controversy." *Vital Speeches* (December 1, 1998).

Health Care Financing Administration. "Problem Nursing Homes to Face Immediate Sanctions." Press Release, December 14, 1999.

"Health for Life: What Every Woman Needs to Know." *Newsweek*, Special Edition (Spring/Summer 1999).

Healy, Bernadine. *A New Prescription for Women's Health.* New York: Viking, 1995.

Heaton, Tim B., Cardell K. Jacobson, and Kimberlee Holland. "Persistence and Change in Decisions to Remain Childless." *Journal of Marriage and the Family* (May 1999).

Heavner, Jay. "Broken Treaties, Empty Promises." <http://www.rcrc.org/wocp/native.html>.

Hemphill, Thomas A. "The White House Apparel Industry Partnership Agreement: Will Self-Regulation Be Successful?" *Business and Society Review* (Summer 1999).

Henry, Ed. "Covering the Cost of Fighting Infertility." *Kiplinger's Personal Finance Magazine* (August 1999).

Hickins, Michael. "Docs Yawn at Women's Work." *Management Review* (April 1998).

Hicks, Karen M., ed. *Misdiagnosis: Woman as a Disease.* Allentown, PA: People's Medical Society, 1994.

Hill, Susan. "On the Racketeer Influenced Corrupt Organization Act." Testimony before the U.S. House of Representatives Committee on Judiciary, July 17, 1998.

Hite, Shere. *The Hite Report on Female Sexuality.* New York: MacMillan and Bertelsmann, 1976.

Hitt, Jack. "Who Will Do Abortions Here?" *New York Times.* (January 18, 1998).

Hoffman, Eileen, M.D. *Our Health, Our Lives: A Revolutionary Approach to Total Health Care for Women.* New York: Simon & Schuster, 1995.

Holmes, Helen Bequaert, and Laura M. Purdy, eds. *Feminist Perspectives in Medical Ethics.* Bloomington and Indianapolis, IN: Indiana University Press, 1992.

Hope, Toni Gerber. "The Ultimate Fertility Guide." *Redbook* (November 1998).

Hopkins, Anthony, and Richard Appleton. *Epilepsy: The Facts*, 2d ed. Oxford: Oxford University Press, 1996.

Hopkins, Mary Alden. "Birth Control and Public Morals: An Interview with Anthony Comstock." *Harper's Weekly* (May 22, 1915).

Horiuchi, Vince. "Eating Disorders Are Not Going Away." *Salt Lake Tribune* (April 2, 1998).

Howard, Beth. *Mind Your Body A Sexual Health and Wellness Guide for Women.* New York: St. Martin's Press, 1998.

Howes, Joanne, and Marie Bass. "A Review of Gender-Specific Legislation, 1999." *Journal of Gender-Specific Medicine* (November–December 1999).

Hu, X. Henry, Leona E. Markson, Richard B. Lipton, Walter F. Stewart, and Marc L. Berger. "Burden of Migraine in the United States." *Archives of Internal Medicine* (April 26, 1999).

Huckle, Patricia. *Tish Sommers, Activist: and the Founding of the Older Women's League.* Knoxville, TN: University of Tennessee Press, 1991.

Humphreys, Sheila M., ed. *Women and Minorities in Science: Strategies for Increasing Participation.* Boulder, CO: Westview Press for the American Association for the Advancement of Science, 1982.

Hwang, Mi Young. "Are You Obese?" *Journal of the American Medical Association* (October 27, 1999).

Institute of Medicine. Committee on Prevention and Control of Sexually Transmitted Diseases. *The Hidden Epidemic: Confronting Sexually Trans-mitted Diseases.* Edited by T.R. Eng and W.T. Butler. Washington, DC: National Academy Press, 1997.

Interagency Workgroup on Multiple Chemical Sensitivity. *A Report on Multiple Chemical Sensitivity.* Atlanta: Agency for Toxic Substances and Disease Registry, August 24, 1998.

International Health, Racquet & Sportsclub Association. "Single-Sex Health Clubs." <http://www.ihrsa.org/publicpolicy/industryissues/womenonly.html>

International The Planned Parenthood Federation. "Statement by the International Medical Advisory Panel" (November 1991).

Ireland, Mardy S. *Reconceiving Women: Separating Motherhood from Female Identity.* New York: Guilford Publications, 1993.

Ivins, Molly, and Fred Smith. "Do Consumer Boycotts Help the World's Poor?" *Insight on the News* (November 29, 1999).

Jacobson, Joan Mathews. *Midlife Women Contemporary Issues.* Boston: Jones and Bartlett Publishers, 1995.

Jacobson, Joseph L. "Drinking Moderately and Pregnancy." *Alcohol Research & Health*, Winter 1999.

Jacobson, Sandra W. "Assessing the Impact of Maternal Drinking During and After Pregnancy." *Alcohol Health & Research World* (Summer 1997).

Jacoby, Susan. "Great Sex—What's Age Got to Do with It?" *Modern Maturity,* Special Report (September–October 1999).

———. "I Liked the Way I Looked, Until I Talked to a Plastic Surgeon." *New York Times* (June 21, 1998).

Jang, Kerry L., Murray B. Stein, Steven Taylor, and W. John Livesley. "Gender Differences in the Etiology of Anxiety Sensitivity: A Twin Study." *Journal of Gender-Specific Medicine* (April 1999).

Jenkins, Christopher, Stephen J. McPhee, Joyce Adair Bird, Giao Qui Pham, Bang H. Nguyen, Thoa Nguyen, Ky Quoc Lai, Ching Wong, and Thomas B. Davis, "Effect of a Media-Led Educational Campaign on Breast and Cervical Cancer Screening among Vietnamese-American Women." *Preventive Medicine* (April 28, 1999).

Joe, Jennie R. "The Health of American Indian and Alaska Native Women." *Journal of the American Medical Women's Association* (August–October 1996).

Kang, David S., Lucinda R. Kahler, and Catherine M. Tesar. "Medicine and Society: Cultural Aspects of Caring for Refugees." *American Academy of Family Physicians* (March 15, 1998).

Kaplan, Deborah. "Clinical Management of Rape in Adolescent Girls." *Patient Care* (April 30, 1999).

Keller, E. E. *A Feeling for the Organism. The Life and Work of Barbara McClintock.* San Francisco: Freeman, 1983.

Kelley, Timothy. "A $51 Million Habit?" *Scholastic Update* (April 12, 1999).

Kemp, Charles. "Loatian Health Care Beliefs and Practices: A Summary." <http://www.baylor.edu/~Charles_Kemp/laotian_summary.html>.

Kenen, Regina. *Reproductive Hazards in the Workplace: Mending Jobs, Managing Pregnancies.* Binghamton, NY: Haworth Press, 1992.

Kirby, Michael. "Genetic Testing and Discrimination: The Development of Genetic Testing Confronts Humanity with Urgent Challenges." *UNESCO Courier* (May 1998).

Kling, Cynthia. "Childless by Choice." *Harper's Bazaar* (June 1996).

Kohn, Anna. "Mothering the Mothers: Meet the Doulas." *Chatelaine* (October 1997).

Kolata, Gina. "$50,000 Offered to Tall, Smart Egg Donor." *New York Times* (March 3, 1999).

———. "Panel Confirms No Major Illness Tied to Breast Implants." *New York Times* (June 21, 1999).

———. "Soaring Price of Donor Eggs Sets off Debate." *New York Times* (February 25, 1998).

Komesaroff, Paul A., Philipa Rothfield, and Jeanne Daly. *Reinterpreting Menopause: Cultural and Philosophical Issues.* New York: Routledge, 1997.

Koonin, Lisa M., Lilo T. Strauss, Camaryn E. Chrisman, Myra A. Montalbano, Linda A. Bartlett, and Jack C. Smith, Division of Reproductive Health, National Center for Chronic Disease Prevention and Health Promotion, CDC. *Abortion Surveillance—United States, 1996* (July 30, 1999). <http://www.cdc.gov/epo/mmwr/preview/mmwrhtml/ss4804a1.htm>

Kopstein, Andrea N. *Drug Abuse among Racial/Ethnic Groups.* Upland, PA: DIANE Publishers, 1996.

Krieger, Lisa M. "U.S. Drug Makers in No Hurry to Make Abortion Pill RU486." *Detroit News* (February 1, 1998).

Krueger, Curtis. "Rosalynn Carter Attacks Stigma of Mental Illness." *St. Petersburg Times* (May 26, 1999).

Kübler-Ross, Elisabeth. *On Death and Dying.* New York: Macmillan Publishing, 1969.

———. *The Wheel of Life: A Memoir of Living and Dying.* New York: Scribner, 1997.

La Leche League International. *The Womanly Art of Breastfeeding,* 35th Anniversary ed. Franklin Park, IL: La Leche League International, 1991.

Lamberg, Lynne. "Putting a New Face on Women's Health. *The Journal of the American Medical Association* (April 14, 1999).

Lanzillo, Anthony. "Men and Depression: It's Not Just a Woman's Problem." *WebMed* (1999). <http://my.webmd.com/content/article/1685.50047>.

LaRosa, Judith H., and Vivian W. Pinn. "Gender Bias in Biomedical Research." *Journal of the American Medical Women's Association* (September/October 1993).

Laurence, Leslie, and Beth Weinhouse. *Outrageous Practices: The Alarming Truth about How Medicine Mistreats Women.* New York: Fawcett Columbine/Ballantine, 1994.

Leary, Warren E. "Contraceptive Sponge Returns to Market." *New York Times* (March 30, 1999).

Leopold, Ellen. *A Darker Ribbon: Breast Cancer, Women and Their Doctors in the Twentieth Century.* Boston: Beacon Press, 1999.

Lewis, Paul. "Increased Breast Feeding Could Save Lives, Study Finds." *New York Times* (March 4, 1999).

Lewis, Ricki. "Gender-Based Biology Courses Take Diverse Forms." *The Scientist* (November 9, 1998).

Libov, Charlotte. *Beat Your Risk Factors: A Woman's Guide to Reducing Her Risk for Cancer, Heart Disease, Stroke, Diabetes, and Osteoporosis.* New York: Plume, 1999.

Lief, Louise. "Alone Too Soon: Young Widows and Widowers Learn to Cope on Their Own." *U.S. News & World Report* (January 20, 1997).

Lipton, Eric. "In Houses of Healing, an Uneasy Alliance; Worried by Church Rules, Hospital May End Union with Catholic Facility." *Washington Post* (April 3, 1998).

Lisle, Laurie. *Without Child: Challenging the Stigma of Childlessness.* New York: Ballantine, 1995.

Love, Susan M. *Dr. Susan Love's Breast Book.* 2d rev ed. Reading, MA: Addison-Wesley, 1995.

Lowry, Vicky. "Researchers Fix Their Sights on an Elusive Silent Killer." *New York Times* (June 25, 2000).

Magill, Michael K. and Anthony Suruda. "Multiple Chemical Sensitivity Syndrome." *American Family Physician* (September 1, 1998).

Malveaux, Julianne. "Women at Work." *In These Times* (November 28, 1999).

Manly, Libby, Alejandra Okie, and Melinda Wiggins, eds. *Fields without Borders/Campos*

Sin Fronteras: An Anthology of Documentary Writing. Durham, NC: Student Action with Farmworkers, 1998.

Maranto, Gina. "Embryo Overpopulation." *Scientific American* (April 1996).

Margaret Sanger Papers Project, Department of History, New York University, "Biographical Sketch." <http://www.nyu.edu/projects/sanger/ms-bio.htm>.

Margen, Sheldon, and the editors of the University of California at Berkeley *Wellness Letter. The Wellness Encyclopedia of Food and Nutrition,* New York: Rebus, 1992.

Mark, Saralyn, and Carol Krause. "Federal Role in Nutrition Education, Research, and Food for Women and Their Families." *Journal of the American Dietetic Association* (June 1, 1999).

Marron, Kevin. "Net Boon and Bane to Patients: Site Prescriptions." *Globe and Mail* (July 30, 1999).

Mayo Health Clinic. "Hair Loss in Women." *Mayo Clinic Health Letter* (February 1997).

McCollum, Monica J. "Spirited Controversy: Reproductive Services Force Executives to Weigh Church Teaching vs. Community Good." *Hospitals and Health Networks* (June 20, 1998).

McGrath, Ellen H. *Women and Depression: Risk Factors and Treatment Issues.* Washington, DC: American Psychological Association, 1990.

McGrayne, Sharon Bertsch. *Nobel Prize Women in Science: Their Lives, Struggles, and Momentous Discoveries.* Secaucus, NJ: Carol Publishing Group, 1993.

McIlwain, Harris D., and Debra Fulghum Bruce. *The Fibromyalgia Handbook.* New York: Henry Holt, 1996.

McKeegan, Michele. *Abortion Politics.* New York: The Free Press, 1992.

McLaughlin, Abe. "Women's Rights Take New Twist." *The Christian Science Monitor* (February 6, 1998).

McNeil, Caroline, Public Information Office, National Institute on Aging. *Alzheimer's Disease: Unraveling the Mystery.* Washington, DC: U.S. Department of Health and Human Services, Public Health Service, National Institutes of Health, National Institute on Aging, October 1995.

MCS Referral & Resources. "What Is MCS Referral & Resources?" <http://www.mcsrr.org/whoweare.html>.

"Medicine & Health Perspectives: The Long Winding Road to Integration of." *Medicine & Health* (May 24, 1999).

Meilaender, Gilbert. "Biotech Babies." *Christianity Today* (December 7, 1998).

Miller, Annetta, and Joan Raymond. "The Infertility Challenge." *Newsweek,* Special Issue (Spring/Summer 1999).

Miller, Robert, M.D. "Bayfront Sought Greatest Good for the Community." *St. Petersburg Times* (August 31, 1999).

Mintz, Suzanne. "Family Caregivers Want Real Help from Real People," 1999. <http://www.nfcacares.org>.

Momeni, Jamshid A. *Homelessness in the United States.* New York: Greenwood Press, 1990.

Mooney, Linda. "The Cancer Your Doctor May Miss." *Prevention* (May 1999).

Morash, Merry, Timothy S. Bynum, and Barbara A. Koons. "Women Offenders: Programming Needs and Promising Approaches." Research Brief, U.S. Department of Justice Office of Justice Programs, National Institute of Justice (August 1998).

Muehlenhard, Charlene L. *What Sexual Scientists Know about Rape.* Brochure. Mt. Vernon, IA: The Society for the Scientific Study of Sexuality, 1995.

Murray, Kathleen. "The Childless Feel Left Out When Parents Get a Lift." *New York Times* (December 1, 1996).

Must, Aviva. "The Disease Burden Associated with Overweight and Obesity." *Journal of the American Medical Association* (October 27, 1999).

National Abortion Federation. "1999 Year-End Analysis of Trends of Violence and Disruption against Reproductive Health Care Clinic." (January 19, 2000). <http://www.prochoice.org/violence/vdanaly99.htm>.

National Cancer Institute. "Misconceptions Persist among Older Women in Spite of Rising Mammography Rates." Press Release, October 20, 1999.

———. "Questions and Answers about the Pap Test." Fact Sheet, 1997.

———. "What You Need to Know about Cancer of the Cervix." Booklet, 1998.

———. "What You Need to Know about Ovarian Cancer." Booklet, 1998. <http://cancernet.nci.nih.gov/wyntk_pubs/ovarian.htm>.

———. "Breast Cancer Prevention Study Seeks Volunteers: Study of Tamoxifen and Raloxifene (STAR) Under Way across North America." Press Release, May 25, 1999.

———. "Despite Increases in Mammography among Older Women, Misperceptions Persist." Press Release, October 20, 1999. <http://search.nci.nih.gov/search97cgi/s97_cgi>.

———. "Estimating Breast Cancer Risk." Press Release, October 6, 1998.

National Center for Environmental Health, Centers for Disease Control and Prevention. "Fetal Alcohol Syndrome." Fact Sheet, August 1999.

National Center for Farmworker Health. "Farmworker Health—about America's Farmworkers." <http://www.ncfh.org/aboutfws.htm>.

National Center for Health Statistics, Centers for Disease Control and Prevention. "New Study Shows Lower Mortality Rates for Infants Delivered by Certified Nurse Midwives." Press Release, May 19, 1998.

National Center on Addiction and Substance Abuse at Columbia University. "CASA Study Reveals Dangerous Connection Between Teen Substance Use and Sex." Press Release, December 7, 1999.

National Center on Addiction and Substance Abuse. *Under the Rug: Substance Abuse and the Mature Woman*. New York: Columbia University, 1998.

National Center on Elder Abuse. *The National Elder Abuse Incidence Study*. Washington, DC: U.S. Department of Health and Human Services, the Administration on Aging, September 1998.

National Center on Women and Aging. "Challenges to Women in the 21st Century." *Women and Aging Letter* (December 1998).

———. "National Study Shows Doctors Neglecting Emotional Health of Older Women." Press Release, October 8, 1998.

National Clearinghouse for Alcohol and Drug Information, Substance Abuse and Mental Health Services Administration. *1999 National Household Survey on Drug Abuse*. Washington, DC: U.S. Department of Health and Human Services, August 31, 2000.

National Family Caregivers Association. "A Profile of Caregivers." <http://www.nfcacares.org/>.

National Institute of Allergy and Infectious Diseases, National Institutes of Health. "Chronic Fatigue Syndrome." Fact Sheet, 1995.

———. "Overview of the NIAID Chronic Fatigue Syndrome Research Program." Fact Sheet, 1999.

National Institute on Alcohol Abuse and Alcoholism. *Alcohol: What You Don't Know Can Harm You*. Pamphlet. Bethesda, MD: NIAAA, National Institutes of Health, 1999.

National Institutes of Health. "Economic Costs of Alcohol and Drug Abuse Estimated at $246 Billion in the United States." Press Release, May 13, 1998.

National Institutes of Health, National Center for Complementary and Alternative Medicine, "What Is Complementary and Alternative Medicine?" <http://nccam.nih.gov/nccam/fcp/faq/index.html#what-is>.

National Law Center on Homelessness and Poverty. *Out of Sight—Out of Mind? A Report on Anti-Homeless Laws, Litigation, and Alternatives in 50 United States Cities*. Washington, DC: National Law Center on Homelessness and Poverty, 1999.

National Library of Medicine. "Cesarean Section—A Brief History." Brochure issued to accompany an exhibit at the National Library of Medicine in Bethesda, MD (April 30–August 31, 1993). <http://www.nlm.nih.gov/exhibition/cesarean/cesarean_1.html >.

National Mental Health Association. "Mental Illness and the Family-Stigma: Building Awareness and Understanding about Mental Illness." Fact Sheet, 1996.

National Organization on Fetal Alcohol Syndrome. "What Is FAS?" 2000. <http://www.nofas.org/what.htm>.

National Women's Health Information Center, "Asian American & Pacific Islander Women's Health." <http:// www.4woman.org/faq/Asian_Pacific.htm>.

———. "Critical Health Issues: Reproductive Health Issues." <http://www.4woman.gov/owh/pub/adolescent/adcritical.htm>

———. "Factors Affecting the Health of Women of Color, Adolescent Females of Color." *Women of Color Health Data Book* <http://www.4woman.gov/x/owh/pub/woc/adolesc.htm>.

———. "Minority Women." <http://www.4women.gov/faq/minority.htm>.

———. "Priority Women's Health Issues." <http://www.4woman.org/owh/pub/womhealthissues/whipriority.htm>.

———. "University of Illinois at Chicago, Center of Excellence in Women's Health." <http://www.4woman.gov/x/owh/coe/UI_C.htm>.

Ncayiyana, Daniel J. "Millennial Landmarks in Obstetrics and Gynecology." *Medscape General Medicine* (February 28, 2000). <http://womenshealth.medscape.com/Medscape/GeneralMedicine/journal/2000/v02.n01/mgm0228.ncay/mgm0228.ncay.html>.

Nechas, Eileen, and Denise Foley. *Unequal Treatment: What You Don't Know about How Women Are Mistreated by the Medical Community*. New York: Simon & Schuster, 1994.

Nelson, Lin, Regina Kenen, and Susan Klitzman. *Turning Things Around: A Woman's Occupational and Environmental Health Resource Guide*. Washington, DC: National Women's Health Network, 1990.

"New Treatments for Panic Disorder: An Interview with Mark H. Pollack, MD." *Therapeutic Spot-*

light: Psychiatric Illness in Primary Care, Supplement to *Clinician Reviews* (March 1999).

New York Online Access to Health (NOAH), New York Hospital Cornell Medical Center. "Fact Sheet: Panic Disorder (and Agoraphobia)." <http://www.noah.cuny.edu/illness/mentalhealth/cornell/conditions/panicago.html>.

Newman, Diane Kaschak, Mary K. Dzurinko (contributor), and Ananias C. Diokno. *The Urinary Incontinence Sourcebook*. Lincolnwood, IL: NTC/Contemporary Books, 1997.

Nichols, Mark. "Women's Health: New Attitudes and Solutions." *Maclean's* (January 12, 1998).

Nordenberg, Tamar. "Heading off Migraine Pain." *FDA Consumer Magazine* (May–June 1998).

———. "Overcoming Infertility." *FDA Consumer* (January–February 1997).

Noren, Jay. "Challenges to Native American Health Care." *Public Health Reports* (January-February 1998).

Nosek, Margaret A., Diana H. Rintala, Mary Ellen Young, Catherine Clubb Foley, Carol Howland, Gail F. Chanpong, Don Rossi, Jama Bennett, and Kathy Meroney. *National Study of Women with Physical Disabilities*. Houston: Center for Research on Women with Disabilities, 1997.

Notelovitz, Morris, M.D., and Diana Tonnessen. *Menopause and Midlife Health*. New York: St. Martin's Press, 1993.

———. *The Essential Heart Book for Women*. New York: St. Martin's Griffin, 1996.

Nurse Practitioners, Physician Assistants, and Certified Nurse-Midwives: A Policy Analysis. Washington, DC: Office of Technology Assessment, U.S. Congress, 1986.

O'Donnell, Jayne. "Antitrust Health Fight Catholic Hospital Deals Limit Access, Activists Say." *USA Today* (April 8, 1999).

Office of Minority Health Resource Center. "Eliminating Racial and Ethnic Disparities in Health." <http://www.omhrc.gov/>.

Office on Women's Health, "National Centers of Excellence in Women's Health." Flyer. <http://www.4woman.gov/owh/coe/flyer.htm>.

Office on Women's Health, Department of Health and Human Services. "The Health of Adolescent Girls." Information Sheet, January 1998.

Orney, V. Michailevskaya, and I. Lukashov. "The Developmental Outcome of Children Born to Heroin Dependent Mothers Raised at Home or Adopted." *Child Abuse & Neglect* (1996).

"Our Commitment to Women" <http://www.Emmagoldman.com/journal/98_nov/committment.html>.

"Out of Control: Weight-Obsessed, Stressed-Out Coeds Are Increasingly Falling Prey to Eating Disorders." *People Weekly* (April 12, 1999).

"Overview: Urinary Incontinence in Adults, Clinical Practice Guideline Update." Rockville, MD: Agency for Health Care Policy and Research, March 1996. <http://www.ahcpr.gov/clinic/uiovervw.htm>.

Pear, Robert. "Research Neglects Women, Studies Find." *New York Times* (April 30, 2000).

Petrocelli, William, and Barbara Kate Repa. *Sexual Harassment on the Job*. Berkeley, CA: Nolo Press, 1992.

Phillips, Pat. "Migraine as a Woman's Issue—Will Research and New Treatments Help?" *Journal of the American Medical Association* (December 16, 1998).

"PHS Offers One-Stop Shopping for Women's Health." *Public Health Reports* (March 1999).

The Planned Parenthood Federation of America. "Fact Sheet—A Short History of Emergency Hormonal Contraception," September 1998. <http://www.plannedparenthood.org/library/BIRTHCONTROL/EmergContra.htm>.

The Planned Parenthood Federation of America. *The Planned Parenthood Women's Health Encyclopedia*. New York: Crown Trade Paperbacks, 1996.

Poole, Catherine M., and DuPont Guerry. *Melanoma: Prevention, Detection, and Treatment*. New Haven, CT: Yale University Press, 1998.

"Protecting Our Children: Sexual Abuse of Children Is Common, and Too Often Undetected." *The Journal of the American Medical Association* (December 2, 1998).

Public Justice Center. *Disposable Workforce: A Worker's Perspective. A Documentation Study Conducted by The Public Justice Center of Working Conditions in Delmarva Poultry Processing Plants*. Baltimore, MD: Public Justice Center, January 1998. <http://www.publicjustice.org/reports/poultry.pdf>.

Radetsky, Peter. *Allergic to the Twentieth Century: The Explosion in Environmental Allergies—From Sick Buildings to Multiple Chemical Sensitivity*. Boston: Little Brown, 1997.

Rao, Rama B., Susan F. Ely, and Robert S. Hoffman. "Deaths Related to Liposuction." *New England Journal of Medicine* (May 13, 1999).

Ratner, Elaine. *The Feisty Woman's Breast Cancer Book*. New York: Hunter House, 1999.

Read, Phyllis J., and Bernard L. Witlieb. *The Book of Women's Firsts: Breakthrough Achievements of Almost 1,000 American Women*. New York: Random House, 1992.

Reagan, Leslie J. *When Abortion Was a Crime: Medicine and Law in the United States, 1867–1973.* Berkeley: University of California Press, 1998.

Reif, Wanda J. "Women's Health: From Puberty to the Grave." *The Lancet* (May 1, 1999).

"Resolve Joins with United States Senator to Introduce Federal Infertility Insurance Legislation." Press Release, February 17, 2000.

Rogan, Mary. "Judgment Call." *Chatelaine* (October 1998).

Rogers, Albert R., ed. *Battered Women and Their Families.* New York: Springer Publishing Company, 1998.

Romero, Gloria J., Gaile E. Wyatt, Tamra Burns Loeb, Jennifer Vargas Carmona, and Beatriz M. Solis. "The Prevalence and Circumstances of Child Sexual Abuse among Latina Women." *Hispanic Journal of Behavioral Sciences* (August 1, 1999).

Rooks, Judith. *Midwifery and Childbirth in America.* Philadelphia, PA: Temple University Press, 1997.

Ruzek, Sheryl Burt. "The Women's Health Movement from the 1960s to the Present and Beyond." Paper presented at *The History and Future of Women's Health* seminar. Sponsored by the Office on Women's Health and Public Health Service Coordinating Committee on Women's Health, June 11, 1998. <http://www.4woman.org/owh/pub/History/healthmvmt.htm>.

Ruzek, Sheryl Burt, and Julie Becker. "The Women's Health Movement in the United States: From Grass-Roots Activism to Professional Agendas." *Journal of the American Medical Women's Association* (Winter 1999).

Sachs, Benjamin P., Cindy Kobelin, Mary Ames Castro, and Fredric Frigoletto. "The Risks of Lowering the Cesarean-Delivery Rate." *The New England Journal of Medicine* (January 7, 1999).

Sanger, Margaret. *Margaret Sanger: An Autobiography.* New York: Norton, 1938.

Sargent, Marilyn for the National Institute of Mental Health, National Institutes of Health. "Plain Talk about Depression." Pamphlet, 1994.

Satcher, David. Letter to colleagues as part of Alcohol Awareness Month kit. New York: National Council on Alcoholism and Drug Dependence, 1999.

Scanlon, Colleen. "The Legal Implications of Genetic Testing." *RN Magazine* (March 1998).

Schieve, Laura A., Herbert B. Peterson, Susan F. Meikle, Gary Jeng, Isabella Danel, Nancy M. Burnett, and Lynne S. Wilcox. "Live Birth Rates and Multiple-Birth Risk Using in Vitro Fertilization." *Journal of the American Medical Association* (November 17, 1999).

Schnabel, Freya R. "Breast Cancer: What the History Can Tell You about Risk—and What You Can Tell Your Patient." *Consultant* (September 1998).

Schroedel, Jean. *Is the Fetus a Person: A Comparison of Fetal Policies across the 50 States.* Ithaca, NY: Cornell University Press, 2000.

Schroeder, Patricia. "Female Genital Mutilation—A Form of Child Abuse." *The New England Journal of Medicine* (September 15, 1994).

Sechzer, Jeri A. *Forging A Women's Health Research Agenda: Policy Issues for the 1990s.* New York: Academy of Sciences, 1995.

"Sexual Abuse of Women in U.S. State Prisons." *Human Rights Watch* (December 1996).

Shearer, Benjamin F., and Barbara S. Shearer, eds. *Notable Women in the Life Sciences: A Biographical Dictionary.* Westport, CT: Greenwood Press, 1996.

Shields, Laurie. *Displaced Homemakers: Organizing for a New Life.* New York: McGraw-Hill, 1981.

"Should I Buy Long Term Care Insurance?" *Women and Aging Letter* (November 1996).

Sidel, Ruth. *Keeping Women and Children Last: America's War on the Poor.* Rev. ed. New York: Penguin, 1998.

SIECUS. "Making the Connection: Definitions of Sexually Related Health Terminology," 1999. <http://www.siecus.org/pubs/cnct/cnct0002.html>.

Siegel, Deborah L. for The National Council for Research on Women. *Sexual Harassment: Research & Resource.* New York: The National Council for Research on Women, 1992.

Sissell, Kara. "Panel Finds No Link to Disease." *Chemical Week* (December 9, 1998).

"Slaves of New York." *Time* (November 2, 1998).

Slupik, Ramona I., ed. *American Medical Association Complete Guide to Women's Health.* New York: Random House, 1996.

Smith, John M. *Women and Doctors: A Physician's Explosive Account of Women's Medical Treatment—and Mistreatment—in America Today and What You Can Do about It.* New York: The Atlantic Press, 1992.

Smith, Mark Eddy. "Nursing the World Back to Health." *New Beginnings* (May–June 1995).

Snyder, Charles M. *Dr. Mary Walker—The Little Lady in Pants.* New York: Arno Press, 1974.

Society for Women's Health Research. "10 Differences between Men and Women That Make a

Difference in Women's Health." <http://www.womens-health.org/insertB.htm>.

Society for Women's Health Research. "Just the Facts: Gender-Based Biology." <http://www.womens-health.org/gbb.html>

Sommer, Elizabeth. *Nutrition for Women: The Complete Guide.* New York: Henry Holt, 1993.

Sommers, Tish, and Laurie Shields. *Women Take Care: The Consequences of Caregiving in Today's Society.* Gainesville, FL: Triad Publishing Co., 1987.

Spake, Amanda. "A Pain in the Neck, and Then Some." *U.S. News & World Report* (March 20, 2000).

Spano, Susan. "Hotels Get a Lot Wiser about Women Traveling on Business." *Los Angeles Times* (August 9, 1998).

Spencer, John W., and Joseph J. Jacobs, eds. *Complementary/Alternative Medicine: An Evidence-Based Approach.* St. Louis, MO: Mosby, 1999.

Springen, Karen. "A State of the Art: Pregnancy." *Newsweek,* Special Issue (Spring–Summer 1999).

Stabiner, Karen. "With Alternative Medicine, Profits Are Big, Rules Are Few." *New York Times* (June 21, 1998).

"State-Specific Maternal Mortality among Black and White Women—United States, 1987–1996." *Journal of the American Medical Association.* Newsline. <http://www.ama-assn.org/special/womh/newsline/special/mmwr99/mm4823.htm>

Staudenmayer, Herman. *Environmental Illness: Myth and Reality.* Boca Raton, FL: Lewis, 1999.

Steinhauer, Jennifer. "For Women in Medicine, a Road to Compromise, Not Perks." *New York Times* (March 1, 1999).

Stern, Phyllis N., ed. *Lesbian Health: What Are the Issues?* Washington, DC: Taylor & Francis, 1993.

Sternberg, Steve. "Toxins Not Linked to Breast Cancer." *USA Today* (February 2, 1999).

Stolberg, Sheryl Gay. "Black Mothers' Mortality Rate Is under Scrutiny." *New York Times* (August 8, 1999).

———. "F.D.A. Adds Hurdles in Approval of Abortion Pill," *New York Times* (June 8, 2000).

———. "Folk Cures on Trial, Alternative Care Gains a Foothold." *New York Times* (January 31, 2000).

———. "Study Finds Shortcomings in Care for Chronically Ill." *New York Times* (September 23, 1999).

———. "U.S. Awakes to Epidemic of Sexual Diseases." *New York Times* (March 9, 1998).

———. "U.S. Birth Rate at New Low as Teen-Age Pregnancy Falls." *New York Times* (April 29, 1999).

Stratton, Kathleen, Cynthia Howe, and Frederick Battaglia, eds. for the Institute of Medicine. *Fetal Alcohol Syndrome: Diagnosis, Epidemiology, Prevention and Treatment.* Washington, DC: National Academy Press, 1996.

Strauss, Susan, with Pamela Espeland. *Sexual Harassment and Teens.* Minneapolis, MN: Free Spirit Publishing, 1992.

Substance Abuse and Mental Health Services Administration, Office of Applied Studies. *Substance Use among Women in the United States.* Rockville, MD: National Institute on Drug Abuse (September 1997).

Szalda-Petree, Ann, Tom Seekins, and Bill Innes, Research and Training Center on Rural Rehabilitation Services, RuralFacts. "Women with Disabilities: Employment, Income, and Health." June 1999. <http://ruralinstitute. Umt.edu/rtcrural/general_disability/women_with_disabilities. htm>.

"Teaching Alternative Treatments in Medical School." *Los Angeles Times* (May 31, 1999).

Thornton, Yvonne S. *Woman to Woman.* New York: Dutton, 1997.

Tielemans, E. "Pesticide Exposure and Decreased Fertilisation Rates in Vitro." *The Lancet* (August 7, 1999).

Tomaso, Bruce. "Birth behind Bars." *Dallas Morning News* (February 21, 1999).

Traustadottir, Rannveig. *Women with Disabilities: Issues, Resources, Connections*, Rev., updated by Perri Harris. Syracuse, NY: Research and Training Center on Community Integration, Center on Human Policy, Division of Special Education and Rehabilitation, Syracuse University, 1997.

Treichler, Paula, "Feminism, Medicine, and the Meaning of Childbirth." In *Body/Politics: Women and the Discourses of Science.* Mary Jacobus, Evelyn Fox Keller, and Sally Shuttleworth, eds. New York: Routledge, 1990.

United States Conference of Mayors. *A Status Report on Hunger and Homelessness in America's Cities: 1998.* Washington, DC: U.S. Conference of Mayors, 1998.

United States Department of Agriculture. "Dietary Guidelines for Consumers," 1995. <http://www.nal.usda.gov/fnic/dga/dguide95.html>.

United States Department of Health and Human Services. "Despite Increases in Mammography among Older Women, Misperceptions Persist." Press Release, October 20, 1999.

———. "Mammogram Law Takes Effect." Press Release, April 27, 1999.

———. "Medicare: Protecting Women's Health." Press Release, March 19, 1999.

———. "Preventing Violence against Women." Fact Sheet, February 26, 1999.

———. "The Personal Responsibility and Work Opportunity Reconciliation Act of 1996." Fact Sheet, May 27, 1998.

———. *Tenth Special Report on Alcohol and Health* (to the U.S. Congress, June 2000). <http://silk.nih.gov/silk/niaaa1/publication/10report/10-order.htm>.

United States Department of Health and Human Services, Centers for Disease Control and Prevention, National Center for Health Statistics. "Fewer Pregnant Women Smoke; Teen Rate Rises." News Release, November 19, 1998.

United States Department of Health and Human Services, Children's Bureau. *Child Maltreatment 1996: Reports from the States to the National Child Abuse and Neglect Data System.* Washington, DC: U.S. Government Printing Office, 1998.

United States Department of Health and Human Services, Public Health Service, National Institutes of Health, National Institute on Aging. "Alzheimer's Disease Fact Sheet," August 1995.

United States Department of Justice. *Violence against Women.* U.S. Department of Justice, Bureau of Justice Statistics, 1994.

United States Housing and Urban Development. *Priority Home!: The Federal Plan to Break the Cycle of Homelessness.* Washington, DC: Interagency Council on the Homeless, March 1994.

Unsworth, Edwin. "Telecommuting Brings Ergonomics Risks." *Business Insurance* (May 11, 1998).

Ventura, Stephanie J., T.J. Mathews, and Sally C. Curtin. *Declines in Teenage Birth Rates, 1991–97: National and State Patterns.* National Vital Statistics Reports. Hyattsville, MD: National Center for Health Statistics, 1998.

Verhovek, Sam Howe. "Creators of Anti-Abortion Web Site Told to Pay Millions." *New York Times* (February 3, 1999).

Villarosa, Linda. "Two Lesser Known Sexually Transmitted Diseases Account for Most New Cases." *New York Times* (December 8, 1998).

Villarosa, Linda. "Tri-Fold Ailment Stalks Female Athletes." *New York Times* (June 22, 1999).

Wagener, D.K, J. Walstedt, L. Jenkins, et al. *Women: Work and Health.* Hyattsville, MD: United States Department of Health and Human Services, Cen-

ters for Disease Control and Prevention, National Center for Health Statistics, 1997.

Watanabe, Myrna. "Scientists Using New Tactics to Curb STD Rates in U.S." *The Scientist* (September 15, 1997).

"Weight Control: What Works and Why." Medical Essay, Supplement to *Mayo Clinic Health Letter.* Rochester, MN: Mayo Foundation for Medical Education and Research, 1997.

Weisberger, Bernard A. "Chasing Smut in Every Medium." *American Heritage* (December 1997).

Weisman, Carol S. "Two Centuries of Women's Health Activism." Paper presented at *The History and Future of Women's Health* seminar. Sponsored by the Office on Women's Health and Public Health Service Coordinating Committee on Women's Health, June 11, 1998. <www.4woman.gov/x/owh/pub/History/2century.htm>.

Wertz, Sidney M., and Dorothy C. Wertz. *Lying-in: A History of Childbirth in America.* New Haven, CT: Yale University Press, 1989.

Wetherington, Cora Lee, and Adele B. Roman, eds. U.S. Department of Health and Human Services, National Institutes of Health, National Institute on Drug Abuse. *Drug Addiction Research and the Health of Women, Executive Summary.* Rockville, MD: National Institute on Drug Abuse, 1998.

Wetzel, Miriam S., David M. Eisenberg, and Ted J. Kaptchuk. "Courses Involving Complementary and Alternative Medicine at US Medical Schools." *Journal of the American Medical Association* (September 2, 1998).

White, Evelyn C., ed. *The Black Women's Health Book: Speaking for Ourselves.* Seattle, WA: Seal Press, 1990.

Wingo, Phyllis A., Lynn A. G. Ries, Gary A. Giovino, Daniel S. Miller, Harry M. Rosenberg, Donald R. Shopland, Michael J. Thun, and Brenda K. Edwards. "Annual Report to the Nation on the Status of Cancer, 1973–1996, with a Special Section on Lung Cancer and Tobacco Smoking." *Journal of the National Cancer Institute,* Special Issue (April 21, 1999).

Wolf, Naomi. *The Beauty Myth: How Images of Beauty Are Used against Women.* New York: Morrow, 1991.

Wolfe, Sidney M. *Women's Health Alert.* Reading, MA: Addison-Wesley, 1991.

Wolfe, Suzanne. "The Great Mammogram Debate." *RN* Magazine (August 1997).

"Women Offenders: Programming Needs and Promising Approaches." Research Brief, U.S. Department of Justice Office of Justice Programs, National Institute of Justice, August 1998.

"Women: The Road Ahead." *Time*, Special Issue (Fall 1990).

"Women's Health Exhibit to Tour US." *Public Health Reports* (May 1999).

Women's Institute for a Secure Retirement. "Widowhood: Why Women Need to Talk about This Issue." *WISERwoman Newsletter* (Fall 1999).

Worcester, Nancy, and Miriamne Whatley, eds. *Women's Health: Readings on Social, Economic and Political Issues.* Dubuque, IA: Kendall/Hunt, 1994.

Worth, Robert. "Making It Uncool." *Washington Monthly* (March 1999).

Wren, Christopher S. "Many Women 60 and Older Abuse Alcohol and Prescribed Drugs, Study Says." *New York Times* (June 5, 1998).

Wymelenberg, Suzanne for the Institute of Medicine. *Science and Babies Private Decisions, Public Dilemmas.* Washington, DC: National Academy Press, 1990.

Yardley, Jim. "After Embryo Mix-Up, Couple Say They Will Give Up a Baby." *New York Times* (March 30, 1999).

Zhan, Lin, ed. *Asian Voices: Asian and Asian American Health Educators Speak Out.* Sudbury, MA: Jones and Bartlett Publishers, 1999.

Zimmerman, Joy, and the Rural Information Center Health Service. "Nurse Practitioners, Physician Assistants and Certified Nurse-Midwives: Primary Care Providers in Rural Areas," Beltsville, MD: National Agricultural Library, Rural Information Center, Office of Rural Health Policy, July 1994.

Zouves, Christo and Julie Sullivan. *Expecting Miracles: on the Path of Hope from Infertility to Parenthood.* New York: Holt, 1999.

Zuckerman, Barry. "Effects on Parents and Children." In *When Drug Addicts Have Children.* Douglas Besharov, ed. Washington, DC: Child Welfare League of America/American Enterprise Institute, 1994.

Selected World Wide Web Sites

(Note: Most of these sites include a search engine and e-mail contact forms.)

Alan Guttmacher Institute
http://www.agi-usa.org/
This web site is part of the Institute's mission to provide information individuals need "to achieve their full human rights, safeguard their health and exercise their individual responsibilities in regard to sexual behavior, reproduction and family formation."

American Surrogacy Center
http://www.surrogacy.com
This site provides legal, medical, psychological, and personal information about surrogacy along with agencies and directories of surrogacy providers. Messages from surrogate mothers, intended parents, egg donors, and leading experts in the field are also posted on the site.

Ann Rose's Ultimate Birth Control Links Page
http://gynpages.com/ultimate/
This page provides extensive links to information for individuals of all ages to make informed decisions about sexual activity and potential childbearing.

Black Women's Health
http://www.blackwomenshealth.com/
This site, founded in 1999, aims to improve the African-American woman's economic health and wellness. It covers health topics ranging from alcohol addiction to self-esteem and presents financial information.

Canadian Women's Health Network
http://www.cwhn.ca/about.html
This informal network of organizations is involved in various information-sharing and advocacy efforts relating to women's health.

Childbirth Organization
http://www.childbirth.org/
This site is aimed at educating pregnant women to be good consumers, and to know their options in providing themselves with the care needed for healthy pregnancies. It includes many links to educational and informational sites.

Community Breast Health Project
http://www-med.stanford.edu/CBHP/
The Community Breast Health Project is a clearinghouse for information and support for breast cancer survivors and friends. It offers volunteer opportunities to help others with the disease. The site is an educational resource and a community center for all who are concerned about breast cancer and breast health. The project is committed to providing services free of charge.

DisAbled Women's Network Ontario
http://dawn.thot.net/
The DisAbled Women's Network (DAWN), based in Ontario, Canada, is a province-wide feminist organization controlled by and for

women with all types of disabilities. Its goal is to support women in their struggles to control their own lives.

Eating Disorders Shared Awareness
http://www.mirror-mirror.org/eatdis.htm
This site began in 1996 as a way for two women recovering from eating disorders to reach out and help others through awareness, education, support (both online and off) and friendship.

Epilepsy Foundation
http://www.efa.org/
This is the site of the national organization that works, through research, education, advocacy and service, for people affected by seizures. Organization volunteers are committed to the prevention and cure of epilepsy and a positive quality of life for everyone who lives with seizure disorders.

Family Health International
http://www.fhi.org/
Family Health International's site includes information about ways to improve reproductive and family health worldwide through biomedical and social science research, innovative health-service delivery interventions, and training programs. The organization works in partnership with universities, ministries of health, and non-governmental organizations, conducting ongoing projects in the United States and more than 40 developing countries.

FDA Milestones in Women's Health
http://www.fda.gov/womens/milesbro.html
This site includes a timeline of women's health milestones and charts that show Food and Drug Administration actions regarding medications, medical devices, clinical trials, and data comparing U.S. women in 1900 and the 1990s.

Feminist Women's Health Center
http://www.fwhc.org/
This is the site of the Feminist Women's Health Center, a non-profit organization in Yakima, Washington, founded in 1980 to promote and protect a woman's right to choose and receive reproductive health care and to bring reproductive choice to women in the large rural area known as Central Washington.

Go Girl Magazine: Sports and Fitness for Women
http://www.gogirlmag.com/
This is the site of the Go Girl! Magazine which includes numerous online articles for beginning and accomplished athletes regarding fitness programs and ideas about training, motivation, nutrition, and taking care of themselves. Articles also cover what is happening in professional and amateur women's sports.

Healthfinder
http://www.healthfinder.gov/
The U.S. Department of Health and Human Services founded this site in 1997 to provide a centralized place to search for online information from many different federal agencies, including the Centers for Disease Control and Prevention, the National Institutes of Health, and the Food and Drug Administration.

InteliHealth
http://www.intelihealth.com/IH/ihtIH/
WSIHW000/408/408.html
This site contains a page with news and features on many aspects of women's health and related areas such as fitness and sports, caregivers, and questions and answers from doctors.

International Women's Health Coalition
http://www.intelihealth.com/IH/ihtIH/
WSIHW000/408/408.html
This is the site of a nonprofit organization that works with individuals and groups to promote the reproductive and sexual health and rights of women in Africa, Asia, and Latin America.

Medlineplus
http://medlineplus.adam.com
This site contains information from the world's largest medical library, the National Library of Medicine at the National Institutes of Health. Medlineplus is for anyone with a medical question—health professionals and consumers. This service provides access to extensive information about specific diseases and conditions and also has links to consumer health information from the National Institutes of Health, dictionaries, lists of hospitals and physicians, health information in Spanish and other languages, and clinical trials.

MedNets
http://www.mednets.com/
An international research site, MedNets provides search engines that allow medical professionals, the health industry, and patients to access medical databases covering topics from AIDS to Urology.

Medscape Women's Health
http://www.medscape.com/Home/Topics/
WomensHealth/WomensHealth.html
This site requires a one-time free registration and includes a collection of news features, journal articles, and medline abstracts with a special focus on women.

Merck Manual Home Edition: Women's
Health Issues
http://www.merck.com/pubs/mmanual_home/
The *Merck Manual Home Edition*, like all the Merck manuals, is published by Merck & Co., Inc., on a not-for-profit basis. This Web version is only a small part of the *Home Edition*, but it includes entire sections on the heart, infections, the eye, gynecology and obstetrics, along with the complete Table of Contents and list of contributors.

Midlife Mommies
http://www.midlifemommies.com/
As its title suggests, this site focuses on midlife pregnancy. It includes information on staying in shape and eating in a healthy manner, resources for midlife women, and personal stories from midlife moms.

Mother's Voices United to End AIDS
http://www.mvoices.org/
This site is designed to mobilize mothers to become educators and increase advocacy to help prevent HIV and eliminate AIDS.

Museum of Menstruation and Women's
Health
http://www.mum.org/
A tour of this online museum is available on this site, which includes the history and graphic portrayals of advertising of menstrual products, views about menstruation, lists of books and articles about menstruation, and many other interesting and informative materials on menstruation.

National Center for Policy Research for
Women and Families
http://www.cpr4womenandfamilies.org/
This site, developed by the nonprofit organization of the same name, is "dedicated to improving the lives of women and families" by disseminating information on women's health, breast implants, breast cancer, poverty and welfare, and other topics.

National Women's Health Information Center
http://www.4woman.org/
The Office of Women's Health of the U.S. Department of Health and Human Services developed this site to provide a great wealth of information, statistics, and reports on women's health issues and links to numerous agencies focusing on women's health concerns.

NOAH: New York Online Access to Health
http://www.noah.cuny.edu/
A collaborative project of four New York organizations, including the City University of New York and the New York Public Library, this site is committed to providing relevant, unbiased, and accurate consumer health information to an underserved population. It is currently available in both Spanish and English and has information on topics ranging from aging to diabetes to patient rights.

RESOLVE, the National Infertility Association
http://www.resolve.org
RESOLVE's site provides support and information for people who are experiencing infertility. The site is also a means for the organization to increase awareness of infertility issues.

Sexual Assault Information Page
http://www.cs.utk.edu/~bartley/saInfoPage.html
On this page is a list of links to a large number of sites covering such sexual assault issues as acquaintance rape, crime victims compensation, domestic violence, incest, post-traumatic stress disorder, rape, self-defense, sexual harassment, and women's resources.

Surrogate Mothers, Inc.
http://www.surrogatemothers.com
This site provides questions and answers about surrogacy, information on artificial insemina-

tion, egg donor programs, and current trends in surrogacy.

Take Wellness to Heart
http://women.americanheart.org/
The American Heart Association sponsors this site, which posts facts on women's heart disease and stroke, describes risks women face for heart disease and stroke, and explains how lifestyle changes can lower those risks.

Tucker Center for Girls & Women in Sports
http://www.kls.coled.umn.edu/crgws/
The Tucker Center for Research on Girls & Women in Sport is dedicated to exploring how sport, recreation, and physical activity affect the lives of girls and women. The first of its kind in the country, it is an interdisciplinary center leading a pioneering effort on significant research, education, community outreach, and public service.

Web by Women for Women
http://www.io.com/~wwwomen/
This protest site encourages political, legal, and social action to prevent censorship of information about women's health issues and the social taboos and governmental laws that have made it difficult for knowledgeable women and mothers to talk to young girls about their growing bodies and their lives.

WebMedLit: Women's Health
http://webmedlit.silverplatter.com/topics/womens.html
This site provides access to articles in medical journals on the Web, such as the *Archives of Family Medicine, Archives of Internal Medicine, British Medical Journal, Journal of the American Medical Association,* and *Journal of Clinical Oncology.*

Women and Disability Resources
http://members.tripod.com/~Barbara_Robertson/Women.html
This site lists and provides links to a great variety of resources on women with disabilities.

Women of Color Health Data Book
http://www.4women.gov/owh/pub/woc/index.htm

The National Women's Health Information Center provides this data book in its entirety on this site. It also allows searches by health topics, information on special groups, online medical dictionaries and journals related to women's health, links to the U.S. Office on Women's Health, and answers to frequently asked questions about women's health.

Women of Color Web
http://www.hsph.harvard.edu/grhf/WoC/
This site provides writings by and about women of color in the United States. The writings provide perspectives and experiences often lacking in other women's health materials. The site focuses on gender, sexuality, and reproductive health, and provides links to organizations, discussion lists, and academic tools concerned specifically with women of color.

Women with DisAbilities
http://www.4women.gov/wwd/index.htm
The National Women's Health Information Center provides this site to address the numerous issues of particular interest to women with disabilities, such as abuse, parenting, and sexuality. It offers general resources about critical health issues for a variety of disabilities, including physical, neurological, hearing, speech, and visual impairment. It also provides information on psychiatric, learning, and developmental disabilities; information on federal laws and regulations that protect disabled citizens; services and support resources; news about medical research; statistical information on disabled women; and information for health-care professionals on improving health-care access for women with physical limitations.

Women's Cancer Network
http://www.wcn.org/
The Gynecological Cancer Foundation sponsors this site, which provides information about cancer risks, how to find a doctor, and links to other cancer groups.

Women's Health (AMA)
http://www.ama-assn.org/insight/h_focus/wom_hlth/wom_hlth.htm
This site, sponsored by the American Medical Association, provides health and fitness information for women.

Women's Health (New York Times)
http://www.nytimes.com/specials/women/
whome/index.html
This site offers online articles from a special
section on women's health published in the
New York Times.

Women's Health (WebMD)
http://my.webmd.com/condition_center/whp
Health problems and conditions of concern to
women are the focus of this site, which includes information on topics ranging from abnormal uterine bleeding to weight control.

Women's Health Information Center (JAMA)
http://www.ama-assn.org/special/womh/
womh.htm
Peer-reviewed resources on women's health
are available on this site, which is designed "for
physicians and other health professionals" and
"is produced and maintained by *JAMA* editors
and staff."

Women's Health Initiative Exhibit
http://nihlibrary.nih.gov/about/exhibits/
WHIExhibit/wmhlthexwebpage.htm

The National Institutes of Health Library has
created an online exhibit on the Women's
Health Initiative (WHI) to highlight information resources that pertain to women's health
issues. The site presents images of Women's
Health Initiative posters, bibliographies on areas of study in the WHI, and a collection of
links to Internet sites related to Women's
Health.

Women's Health Interactive
http://www.womens-health.com/
This site provides women with information on
gynecology, natural health, menopause, infertility, heart disease, mental health, migraine
and other headaches, nutrition, and personal
development.

Women's Place
http://www.geocities.com/HotSprings/Villa/
2998/
This site provides links to information on
women with HIV and their families, friends,
and others who care for them.

Organization Addresses

Abortion Clinics OnLine
PO Box 500788
Atlanta, GA 31150
770.552.6591
http://www.gynpages.com/

Administration on Aging
U.S. Department of Health and Human Services
330 Independence Avenue, SW
Washington, DC 20201
202.619.0724
http://www.aoa.dhhs.gov/

AIDS Legal Referral Panel
582 Market Street, Suite 912
San Francisco, CA 94104
415.291.5454
http://www.alrp.org/

Alan Guttmacher Institute
120 Wall Street
New York, NY 10005
212.248.1111
http://www.agi-usa.org/

Alzheimer's Disease Education and Referral
Center
PO Box 8250
Silver Spring, MD 20907-8250
800.438.4380
http://www.alzheimers.org/

American Anorexia/Bulimia Association
165 West 46th Street #1108
New York, NY 10036
212.575.6200
http://www.aabainc.org/

American Association of Colleges of Nursing
One Dupont Circle, Suite 530
Washington, DC 20036
202.463.6930
http://www.aacn.nche.edu/

American Association of Health Plans
1129 20th Street, Suite 600
Washington, DC 20036-3421
202.778.3200
http://www.aahp.org

American Autoimmune Related Disease
Association, Inc.
Michigan National Bank Building
15475 Gratiot Avenue
Detroit, MI 48205
313.371.8600
http://www.aarda.org/

American College of Nurse-Midwives
818 Connecticut Avenue, NW, Suite 900
Washington, DC 20006
202.728.9860
http://www.acnm.org/

American College of Obstetricians and
Gynecologists
409 12th Street, SW
PO Box 96920
Washington, DC 20090-6920
202.638.5577
http://www.acog.org/

American Council for Headache Education
19 Mantua Road
Mount Royal, NJ 08061
800.255.ACHE (800.255.2243)
http://www.achenet.org/

American Headache Society
19 Mantua Road
Mount Royal, NJ 08061
856.423.0043
http://www.ahsnet.org/

American Hospice Foundation
1130 Connecticut Avenue, NW, Suite 700
Washington, DC 20036-4101
202.223.0204
http://www.americanhospice.org/

American Life League
PO Box 1350
Stafford, VA 22554
540.649.4171
http://www.all.org

American Medical Association
Office of Women's and Minority Health
515 North State Street
Chicago, IL 60610
312.464.4523
http://www.ama-assn.org/

American Medical Women's Association
801 N. Fairfax Street, Suite 400
Alexandria, VA 22314
703.838.0500
http://www.amwa-doc.org/

American Obesity Association
1250 24th Street, NW, Suite 300
Washington, DC 20037
800.98.OBESE
800.986.2373
http://www.obesity.org/

American Psychological Association
750 First Street, NE
Washington, DC 20002-4242
202.336.6050
http://www.apa.org/

American Social Health Association
PO Box 13827
Research Triangle Park, NC 27709
919.361.8425
http://www.ashastd.org/

American Society for Reproductive Medicine
1209 Montgomery Highway
Birmingham, AL 35216-2809
205.978.5000
http://www.asrm.com/

Anxiety Disorders Association of America
11900 Parklawn Drive, Suite 100
Rockville, MD 20852-2624
301.231.9350
http://www.adaa.org/

Arthritis Foundation
1330 West Peachtree Street
Atlanta GA 30309
800.283.7800
http://www.arthritis.org/

Asian & Pacific Islander American Health
Forum
942 Market Street, Suite 200
San Francisco, CA 94102
415.954.9988
http://www.apiahf.org/

Association of American Medical Colleges
2450 N Street, NW
Washington, DC 20037
202.828.0400
http://www.aamc.org/

Association of Asian Pacific Community
Health Organizations
1440 Broadway, Suite 510
Oakland, CA 94612
510.272.9536
http://www.aapcho.org/

Association of Professors of Gynecology and
Obstetrics
Women's Healthcare Education Office
409 12th Street, SW
Washington, DC 20024
202.314.2303
http://www.apgo.org/

Association of Reproductive Health
Professionals (ARHP)
2401 Pennsylvania Avenue, NW, Suite 350
Washington, DC 20037-1718
202.466.3825
http://www.arhp.org

Association of Women's Health, Obstetric and
Neonatal Nurses
2000 L Street, NW, Suite 740
Washington, DC 20036
800.673.8499 (U.S.)
800.245.0231 (Canada)
http://www.awhonn.org/

Breast Health Access for Women with
Disabilities
2001 Dwight Way
Berkeley, CA 94704
510.204.4866
http://www.bhawd.org/

Canadian Women's Health Network
419 Graham Avenue, Suite 203
Winnipeg, Manitoba
Canada R3C 0M3
204.942.5500
Clearinghouse: 888.818.9172
http://www.cwhn.ca/

Center for Health, Environment and Justice
PO Box 6806
Falls Church, VA 22040
703.237.224
http://www.chej.org/

Center for Research on Women with
Disabilities
Department of Physical Medicine and Reha-
bilitation
Baylor College of Medicine
3440 Richmond Avenue, Suite B
Houston, TX 77046
713.960.0505

800.44.CROWD (800.442.7693)
http://www.bcm.tmc.edu/crowd/crowd3.html

Center for Research on Women and Gender
1640 W. Roosevelt Road, 5th Floor
Chicago, IL 60608
312.413.1924
http://www.uic.edu/depts/crwg/outline.htm

Center for Women Policy Studies
1211 Connecticut Avenue, NW, Suite 312
Washington, DC 20036
202.872.1770
http://www.centerwomenpolicy.org/

Centers for Disease Control and Prevention
Office of Women's Health
1600 Clifton Road, MS: D-51
Atlanta, GA 30033
404.639.7230
http://www.cdc.gov/od/owh/whhome.htm

CFIDS Association of America, Inc.
(Chronic Fatigue and Immune Dysfunction
Syndrome)
3941 Legacy Drive, #204-135B
Plano, TX 75023
800.442.3437
http://www.cfids.org/

Children's Defense Fund
25 E Street, NW
Washington, DC 20001
202.628.8787
http://www.childrensdefense.org/

The Commonwealth Fund, The
Commission on Women's Health
Columbia University
College of Physicians and Surgeons
630 West 168th Street, P and S, 2-463
NY, NY 10032
212.305.8118
http://www.cmwf.org/programs/women/
index.asp

Eating Disorders Awareness and Prevention,
Inc. (EDAP)
603 Stewart Street, Suite 803
Seattle, WA 98101
206.382.3587

800.931.EDAP
http://edap.org

Emma Goldman Clinic
227 North Dubuque Street
Iowa City, IA 52245
319.337.2112
http://www.emmagoldman.com/

Endometriosis Association
8585 N. 76th Place
Milwaukee, WI 53223
800.992.3636
http://www.endometriosisassn.org/

Environmental Defense Fund
444 Park Avenue South
New York, NY 10016
http://www.edf.org

Epilepsy Foundation
4351 Garden City Drive
Landover, MD 20785
800.EFA.1000
http://www.efa.org

Fetal Alcohol Syndrome Branch
Division of Birth Defects, Child
Development, and Disability and Health
National Center for Environmental Health,
MS:F-49
Centers for Disease Control and Prevention
4770 Buford Highway, NE
Atlanta, GA 30341-3724
770.488.7696
http://www.cdc.gov/nceh/cddh/fashome.htm

Health Resources and Services
Administration
5600 Fishers Lane, Room 14-45
Rockville, MD 20857
301.443.3376
http://www.hrsa.dhhs.gov/

Hospice Foundation of America
2001 S Street, NW, Suite 300
Washington, DC 20009
800.854.3402
http://www.hospicefoundation.org/

Jacobs Institute of Women's Health
409 12th Street, SW

Washington, DC 20024-2188
202.863.4990
http://www.jiwh.org/

La Leche League International
PO Box 4079
Schaumburg, IL 60168
847.519.7730
http://www.lalecheleague.org/

Lamaze International
1200 19th Street, NW, Suite 300
Washington, DC 20036-2422
800.368.4404
202.857.1128
http://www.lamaze-childbirth.com/index1.htm

Lilly Centre for Women's Health
Eli Lilly and Company
Lilly Corporate Center
Indianapolis, IN 46285
317.276.1078
http://www.lilly.com/health/women/
index.html

MAGNUM (Migraine Awareness Group: A
National Understanding for Migraineurs)
113 South Saint Asaph Street, Suite 300
Alexandria, VA 22314
703.739.9384
http://www.migraines.org/home/migraine.htm

Mothers against Sexual Abuse
503 1/2 S. Myrtle Avenue, #9
Monrovia, CA 91016
626.305.1986
http://208.236.140.168/index.html

National Abortion Federation
1436 U Street, NW, Suite 103
Washington, DC 20009
202.667.5881
http://www.prochoice.org/

National Abortion and Reproductive Rights
Action League
1156 15th Street, NW, Suite 700
Washington, DC 20005
202.973.3000
http://www.naral.org/

National Academy on Women's Health
Medical Education
Allegheny University of the Health Sciences
MCP Hahnemann University
Broad and Vine, MS 490
Philadelphia, PA 19102
215.762.4260
http://www.auhs.edu/institutes/iwh/nawhme/
academy.html

National Alliance of Breast Cancer
Organizations
9 E. 37th Street, 10th Floor
New York, NY 10016
800.719.9154
http://www.nabco.org/

National Asian Women's Health Organization
250 Montgomery Street, Suite 410
San Francisco, CA 94104
415.989.9747
http://www.nawho.org/

National Association of Anorexia Nervosa
and Associated Disorders
PO Box 7
Highland Park, IL 60035
847.831.3438
847.432.8000
http://www.anad.org/

National Association for Continence
PO Box 8310
Spartanburg, SC 29305-8310
803.579.7900
800.252.3337
http://www.nafc.org/

National Black Women's Health Project
1211 Connecticut Avenue, NW, Suite 310
Washington, DC 20036
202.835.0117
http://www.blackfamilies.com/community/
groups/WomensHealth/

National Cancer Institute
NCI Public Inquiries Office
Building, 31, Room 10A03
31 Center Drive, MSC 2580
Bethesda, MD 20892-2580
800.4.CANCER

800.422.6237
http://www.nci.nih.gov/

National Center for Farmworker Health, Inc.
PO Box 150009
Austin, TX 78715
512.312.2700
http://www.ncfh.org/

National Center on Women & Aging
Heller Graduate School, MS 035
Brandeis University
Waltham, MA 02454-9110
800.929.1995
781.736.3866
http://heller.brandeis.edu/national/ind.html

National Cervical Cancer Coalition
16501 Sherman Way, Suite 110
Van Nuys, CA 94106
818.909.3849
http://www.nccc-online.org/

National Clearinghouse on
Child Abuse and Neglect Information
330 C Street, SW
Washington, DC 20447
800.FYI.3366
703.385.7565
http://www.calib.com/nccanch/

National Coalition for the Homeless
1012 Fourteenth Street, NW, Suite 600
Washington, DC 20005-3410
202.737.6444
http://nch.ari.net/

National Council for Research on Women
11 Hanover Square
New York, NY 10005
212.785.7335
http://www.ncrw.org/

National Council of Negro Women
633 Pennsylvania Avenue
Washington, DC 20004
202.737.0120
http://www.ncnw.com/

National Council on Women's Health
1300 York Avenue
PO Box 52

New York, NY 10021
212.746.6967
http://www.ncoa.org/

National Headache Foundation
428 West Saint James Place, 2nd Floor
Chicago, IL 60614
800.843.2256
http://www.headaches.org/

National Hemophilia Foundation
116 West 32nd Street, 11th Floor
New York, NY 10001
212.328.3700
800.42.HANDI
http://www.hemophilia.org/

National Hispanic Council on Aging
2713 Ontario Road, NW
Washington, DC 20009
202.265.1288
http://www.hispanichealth.org/

National Institute of Mental Health
NIMH Clinical Center, Building 10 3N234
Bethesda, MD 20892
800.647.2642
http://www.nimh.nih.gov/

National Institutes of Health
Office of Research on Women's Health
9000 Rockville Pike, Building 1, Room 201
Bethesda, MD 20892
301.402.1770
http://www4.od.nih.gov/orwh/

National Latina Health Organization
PO Box 7567
Oakland, CA 94601
510.534.1362
http://clnet.ucr.edu/women/nlho

National Law Center on Homelessness and
Poverty
918 F Street, NW, Suite 412
Washington, DC 20004-1406
202.638.2535
http://www.nlchp.org/

National Hospice and Palliative Care
Organization
1700 Diagonal Road, Suite 300

Alexandria, VA 22314
703.243.5900
http://www.nho.org/

National Institute of Arthritis and
Musculoskeletal and Skin Diseases
One AMS Circle
Bethesda, MD 20892-3675
301.495.4484
http://www.nih.gov/niams/

National Institute of Neurological Disorders
and Stroke
National Institutes of Health
PO Box 5801
Bethesda, MD 20824
301.496.5751
http://www.ninds.nih.gov/index.htm

National Organization on Fetal Alcohol
Syndrome
216 G Street, NE
Washington, DC 20002
202.785.4585
http://www.nofas.org/index2.htm

National Osteoporosis Foundation
1150 17th Street, Suite 500
Washington, DC 20036-4603
202.223.2226
http://www.nof.org/

National Ovarian Cancer Coalition
PO Box 4472
Boca Raton, FL 33429
954.351.9555
888.OVARIAN
http://www.ovarian.org/

National Right to Life Committee
419 Seventh Street, NW, Suite 500
Washington, DC 20005
http://www.nrlc.org/

National Women's Health Organization, Inc.
3613 Haworth Drive
Raleigh, NC 27609
800.532.5383
http://gynpages.com/nwho/

National Women's Health Network
514 10th Street, NW, Suite 400

Washington, DC 20004
202.347.1140
http://www.womenshealthnetwork.org/

National Women's Health Resource Center
2425 L Street, NW, 3rd Floor
Washington, DC 20037
202.293.6045
http://www.healthywomen.org/

Native American Women's Health Education
Resource Center
PO Box 572
Lake Andes, SD 57356
605.487.7072
gopher://gopher.igc.apc.org/00/orgs/nawherc/
about

North American Menopause Society, The
PO Box 94527
Cleveland, Ohio 44101-4527
440.442.7550
http://www.menopause.org/

Office of Disease Prevention and Health
Promotion
Hubert H. Humphrey Building, Room 738G
200 Independence Avenue, SW
Washington, DC 20201
202.205.8583
800.367.4725
http://odphp.osophs.dhhs.gov/

Office of Minority Health Resource Center
Office of Minority Health
U.S. Department of Health and Human Services
200 Independence Avenue, SW
Washington, DC 20201
800.444.6472
http://www.omhrc.gov/omhrc/index.htm

Office on Women's Health
200 Independence Avenue, SW, Room 712 E
Washington, DC 20201
800.994.WOMAN
http://www.4woman.gov/owh

Older Women's League
666 11th St., NW, Suite 700
Washington, DC 20001
202.783.6686
http://www.owl-national.org/

Ovarian Cancer National Alliance
1627 K Street, NW, 12th floor
Washington, DC 20006
202.331.1332
http://www.ovariancancer.org/

The Planned Parenthood Federation of
America
810 Seventh Avenue
New York, NY 10019
212.541.7800
800.230.7526
800.829.7732
http://www.plannedparenthood.org/

President's Council on Physical Fitness and
Sports
Department of Health and Human Services
Hubert H. Humphrey Building
200 Independence Avenue, SW, Room 738H
Washington, DC 20201
202.690.9000
http://www.surgeongeneral.gov/ophs/pcpfs.htm

Pro-Life America
1840 S. Elena Avenue, 103
Redondo Beach, CA 90277
310.373.0743
http://www.prolife.com/

Rape, Abuse & Incest National Network
252 Tenth Street, NE
Washington, DC 20002
202.544.1034
800.656.HOPE
http://www.rainn.org/

RESOLVE, Inc.
1310 Broadway
Somerville, MA 02144-1731
617.623.1156
http://www.resolve.org/

Rural Institute on Disabilities
The University of Montana
32 Campus Dr., #7056
Missoula, MT 59812-7056
800.932.4647
406.243.4860
http://ruralinstitute.umt.edu/

Sexuality Information and Education Council
of the United States
130 West 42d Street, Suite 350
New York, NY 10036-7802
212.819.9770
http://www.siecus.org/

Society for Occupational and Environmental
Health
6278 Old McLean Village Drive
McLean, VA 22101
703.556.9222
http://www.soeh.org/

Society for Women's Health Research
1828 L Street, NN, Suite 625
Washington, DC 20036
202.223.8224
http://www.womens-health.org/

Student Action with Farmworkers
1317 West Pettigrew Street
Durham, NC 27705
919.660.3652
http://www-cds.aas.duke.edu/saf/

Tucker Center for Research on Girls &
Women in Sport
203 Cooke Hall
1900 University Avenue SE
University of Minnesota
Minneapolis, MN 55455
612.625.7327
http://www.kls.umn.edu/crgws/

U.S. Conference of Mayors
1620 Eye Street, NW, 4th Floor
Washington, DC 20006-4005
202.293.7330
http://www.usmayors.org/

U.S. Department of Health and Human
Services
200 Independence Avenue, SW
Washington, DC 20201
202.619.0257
http://www.os.dhhs.gov/

Women For Sobriety, Inc.
PO Box 618
Quakertown, PA 18951-0618
215.536.8026
http://www.womenforsobriety.org/

Women's Cancer Network
401 N. Michigan Avenue
Chicago, IL 60611
800.444.4441
http://www.wcn.org/

Women's Health America Group
429 Gammon Place
PO Box 259690
Madison, WI 53725
800.222.4767
http://www.womenshealth.com/

Women's Health Initiative Program Office
1 Rockledge Centre, Suite 300, MS 7966
6705 Rockledge Drive
Bethesda, MD 20892-7966
301.402.2900
http://rover.nhlbi.nih.gov/whi/overback.html

Women's Health Interactive
PO Box 271276
Fort Collins, CO 80527-1276
970.282.9437
http://www.womens-health.com/index.phtml

Women's Policy, Inc.
409 12th Street, SW, Suite 705
Washington, DC 20024
202.554.2323
http://www.womenspolicy.org/

Women's Sports Foundation
Eisenhower Park
East Meadow, NY 11554
800.227.3988
http://www.womenssportsfoundation.org/

Y-ME National Breast Cancer Organization
212 West Van Buren, 5th Floor
Chicago, IL 60607
800.221.2141
http://www.y-me.org/

DHHS Agencies/Offices with Women's Health Initiatives

A number of agencies and offices within the U.S. Department of Health and Human Services have initiated programs to address women's health issues. The Office on Women's Health coordinates these efforts and maintains an Internet Web site: http://www.4woman.gov.owh/. Other offices and agencies are listed below and some are also listed in Selected World Wide Web Sites and Organization Addresses.

Administration on Aging
www.aoa.dhhs.gov

Administration on Children and Families
www.acf.dhhs.gov

Agency for Healthcare Research and Quality
www.ahcpr.gov

Centers for Disease Control and Prevention
www.cdc.gov

Food and Drug Administration's Office of Women's Health
www.fda.gov/womens/

Health Care Financing Administration
www.hcfa.gov

Health Resources and Services Administration
www.hrsa.dhhs.gov

Indian Health Service
http://www.ihs.gov/

National Institutes of Health
www.nih.gov

Office of Disease Prevention and Health Promotion
odphp.osophs.dhhs.gov

Office of Minority Health
www.omhrc.gov

Substance Abuse and Mental Health Services Administration
www.samhsa.gov

Index

Page numbers in **boldface type** refer to main entries in the encyclopedia.

AAPI. *See* Asian-American and Pacific Islander women's health

Abankwah, Adelaide, 95–96

Abortion, **1–4**, 191; and AIDS, 15; and Alan Guttmacher Institute, 17; and American College of Obstetricians and Gynecologists, 21; and Comstock Law, 65, 66; and Emma Goldman Clinic, 85; and Freedom of Access to Clinic Entrances Act, 99–100; and hospital mergers, 121, 122; and law, 1–3, 4, 6–7, 65, 66, 99–100, 201; and mifepristone, 150–51; and National Abortion and Reproductive Rights Action League, 158; and National Abortion Federation, 158, 159; and National Women's Health Organization, 163, 164; and Novello, 169; partial-birth, 4, 52, 203; and *Planned Parenthood of Southeastern Pennsylvania v. Casey,* 185; and poverty, 189; and prenatal testing, 193; and prolife movement, 194; providers of, 5–7; rate of, 35; and risk, 194; and *Roe v. Wade,* 200–202; and Sanger, 33, 204; and sweatshop, 218; and violence, 21. *See also* Pregnancy; Prochoice movement; Prolife movement

Abortion clinics. *See* Abortion; Freedom of Access to Clinic Entrances Act of 1994

Abortion providers, **5–7**

Abuse: and adolescent, 8; and Asian-Americans and Pacific Islanders, 24–25; and children, 56–57, 78, 79; and disability, 242–43; and domestic violence, 74; and elders, 73–74; and factitious disorder, 91; and lesbians, 135; and life expectancy, 136; and prison, 237; sexual, 56, 57, 78, 237. *See also* Violence

Acacia, 33

Access, 99–100, 111–12; and abortion, 6–7; and disability, 241–42; and health clubs, 244; and Health Resources and Services Administration, 224, 225; and hospital mergers, 121, 122; and Latinas, 134; and lesbians, 135; and life expectancy, 136; and mental illness, 146–47; and National Center on Women and Aging, 159; and National Centers of Excellence in Women's Health, 160; and National Institutes of Health, 162; and Native Americans, 167; and Planned Parenthood Federa-

tion of America, 185; and poverty, 112, 189; and race, 233; and women patients, 233

Access Initiative Project, 6

Accident, 7, 18

Acquired Immunodeficiency Syndrome. *See* AIDS

Acupuncture, 63

Addiction, 18, 32, 44–45, 77. *See also* Alcohol abuse and alcoholism; Drug abuse and addiction

Adenocarcinoma, clear-cell, 72

Administration on Aging, 12, 13

Adolescent girls' health, **7–9**; and access, 112; and American College of Obstetricians and Gynecologists, 21; and cervical cancer, 53; and drug abuse, 78; and fitness, 246; and Girl Neighborhood Power!, 225; and healthy habits, 153; and lung cancer, 138; and pregnancy, 56; and rape, 199; and sexual abuse, 56. *See also* Child; Teenager

Advertising, 138, 143, 145–46, 174, 212. *See also* Commercialization

Advocacy, 29, 163, 253, 254–55

African-American women's health, **9–11**; and AIDS, 15; and cardiovascular disease, 10, 49, 165; and drug abuse, 80; and life expectancy, 136;

About the Author

KATHLYN GAY is the author of more than 100 books, including young adult books, encyclopedias, teacher manuals and portions of textbooks. Most of her work focuses on social and environmental issues, culture, history, and communication. In 1983, her book *Acid Rain* was selected as an "Outstanding Book" by the National Council for Social Studies and National Science Teachers' Association. *Silent Killers* received the same award in 1988. *Global Garbage: International Trade in Toxic Waste* was chosen as a Notable Book for Young People in 1993. In recent years, Kathlyn Gay has collaborated with family members, sons Martin and Douglas Gay and daughter Karen Hamilton, on various books.